New Imaginaries

**Dilip Parameshwar Gaonkar
and Benjamin Lee
Guest Editors**

PUBLIC CULTURE

Society for Transnational Cultural Studies

PUBLIC CULTURE

Volume 14   Number 1   Winter 2002

New Imaginaries

PUBLIC CULTURE

Society for Transnational Cultural Studies

Coming Attractions

In 2002

Vol. 14, no. 2:

Includes the following: John Borneman on ethnic cleansing and reconciliation; Li Zhang on urban citizenship in China; Brian Keith Axel on violence and diaspora; Sheila Miyoshi Jager on commemorating the Korean War; Joseph Massad on the Gay International and the Arab world; and more . . .

Editor's Note

This special issue of *Public Culture* is the product of a working group at the Center for Transcultural Studies that has been supported by a grant from the Rockefeller Foundation. The Rockefeller Foundation has funded a variety of Center projects, starting in 1989 with a postdoctoral residency program on civil society and the public sphere that brought in academics, intellectuals, journalists, and cultural practitioners from Russia, China, Hong Kong, Turkey, and India at the moment when those societies were undergoing global transformations that have continued to affect them to this day. From the days of those initial collaborations, the Center has expanded into an international network of individuals and institutions whose goal is to support the development of the multiple perspectives needed to understand the global processes affecting all of us.

The ideas for this special issue arose out of discussions over the last several years that built on the earlier work on civil society and the public sphere with a fresh emphasis on the cultural forces shaping contemporary issues, such as globalization and the politics of recognition. International developments following the attacks on the Pentagon and World Trade Center highlight the need for new ways of looking at contemporary global transformations, and the Rockefeller Foundation's support for the present project on new imaginaries has been as timely as its sponsorhip of our earlier work on civil society in the wake of 1989.

We would like to thank Elizabeth Povinelli for inviting us to publish the Center's current work in *Public Culture*. Like all special issues, *New Imaginaries* placed extra demands on the staff of *Public Culture*'s editorial office, including Kaylin

Goldstein, William Elison, and Kathleen Lowrey, who rose to the occasion, as always, with verve, humor, and imagination. We thank them for their consideration and support.

This issue is dedicated to Dr. Harold M. Visotsky, Owen Coon Professor Emeritus at Northwestern University Medical School, current chairperson of the board of the Center for Transcultural Studies and a board member since the Center's founding thirty years ago. He and Bernard Weissbourd, the founder of the Center, provided the crucial inspirational guidance and creative imagination during its early years as the Center for Psychosocial Studies. The successful transformation of the Center into a decentered transnational network is due to its adoption of some of the attributes of its chairperson—a heightened sensitivity to intercultural relations, an expansiveness of vision, and a flexibility in dealing with both people and ideas—if not yet his wit and sense of humor.

—Dilip Parameshwar Gaonkar and Benjamin Lee
Evanston, Illinois, and Houston, Texas
October 2001

In Honor of

Harold M. Visotsky, M.D.
Mentor, Benefactor, Scholar

Call for Contributions

mis·cel·la·ny, *n.*: a collection of various kinds, especially news clippings, literary extracts, postcards, and other images. Includes media accounts of items relevant to public discourse and debate throughout the world. The section seeks to highlight not only the reported phenomena as such but also the mediated nature of media coverage. *Public Culture* especially seeks pieces that are witty or (unintentionally) ironic. Submissions should include all relevant facts of publication and should be no longer than three pages.

et·y·mol·o·gies, *n., pl.*: true sense or form of the network of keywords: *public*, *publicity*, *public opinion*, *public sphere*. Investigates the contemporary uses and meanings of the terms *public*, *publicity*, and *public opinion*. Short essays (of approximately six to eight pages) that consider the semantics and pragmatics of one or more of these interrelated terms in the context of a particular language and a particular people are welcome. How do these terms compare across cultures and languages? Do their meanings "translate," and what do their "mistranslations" bode for comparative social theory grounded in what may be hidden ontological statements about civil society?

art·works, *n., pl.*: brief reports (up to 750 words) on innovative critical cultural work within and outside established institutions. Includes new kinds of museums; alternative or oral history projects; the expansion of musical performance and recording into forgotten musical histories or the dissemination of a broader range of musics; alternative publishing ventures or exhibition practices in film, theater, and dance; innovative cultural work with children; public art and art in public such as murals and graffiti; innovative uses of television, radio, or other mass media; and reports on past cultural work—the modernist, socialist, and avant-garde counterinstitutions of the early twentieth century. Send material and proposals to artworks editor Katie Trumpener.

from the field, *n., sing.*: briefly annotated single photographs for inclusion as a photo feature at the end of the issue. Submissions are not limited by style or content but should be glossy prints of at least 5" × 7".

CyberSalon: To join *Public Culture*'s on-line discussion group, send an e-mail message, "Add me to on-line discussion," to public-culture-journal@uchicago.edu.

Public Culture, University of Chicago, 1010 E. 59th Street, Chicago, IL 60637; tel. 773-702-0814; fax: 773-702-9861; e-mail: public-culture-journal@uchicago.edu; World Wide Web: http://www.uchicago.edu/research/jnl-pub-cult/

 **New Imaginaries**

Toward New Imaginaries:
An Introduction

Dilip Parameshwar Gaonkar

The idea of a social imaginary as an enabling but not fully explicable symbolic matrix within which a people imagine and act as world-making collective agents has received its fullest contemporary elaboration in the work of Cornelius Castoriadis, especially in his influential book *The Imaginary Institution of Society* (1987).[1] Castoriadis was drawn to the idea of the social imaginary in the late 1960s as he became progressively disillusioned with Marxism. Reacting against the deterministic strands within Marxism, which he regarded as both dominant and unavoidable, Castoriadis sought to identify the creative force in the making of social-historical worlds.

The authors of essays in this issue, while familiar with the work of Castoriadis, are drawn to the idea of the social imaginary for a different set of reasons. Writing more than a quarter century after the publication of *The Imaginary Institution of Society*, they are responding to a radically different intellectual and political milieu signaled by the cataclysmic events of 1989 and their aftermath. A majority of these authors were brought together in a working group nearly two decades ago by the Center for Transcultural Studies (CTS), a Chicago-based not-for-profit research network with close links to the *Public Culture* editorial collec-

For conversations and comments that were useful in writing this introductory essay, I am grateful to Kaylin Goldstein, Jayson Harsin, Benjamin Lee, Thomas McCarthy, Elizabeth Povinelli, and Charles Taylor.

1. See also Castoriadis 1997a, 1997b. For relevant secondary material, see Habermas 1990, Howard 1988, Kalyvas 2001, and Thompson 1984.

Public Culture 14(1): 1–19

tive, to investigate how globalization of culture and communication is transforming contemporary societies.

The intellectual mood at that time was optimistic. There was a renewed interest in the concept of civil society and its political counterpart, the public sphere, precipitated by political developments as well as intellectual interventions. In the Soviet Union and its satellite states in Eastern Europe, the Leninist model of governance (i.e., the state-directed total mobilization of society to achieve revolutionary ends) was collapsing under its own weight. Here the idea of civil society seemed to offer an alternative that was neither confrontational nor partook of the usual Cold War anticommunist rhetoric. Minimally, civil society refers to the existence of free associations that are not under the control of state power. But in a stronger sense, as Charles Taylor (1995: 208) notes, civil society is said to exist "where society as a whole can structure itself and coordinate its actions through such free associations" and, further, whenever those "associations can significantly determine or inflect the direction of state policy." It was hoped that the Soviet bloc countries could gradually reform themselves structurally by nurturing and expanding the institutions of civil society and thereby paving the way for democratization.

At the same time, democratic movements were also resurgent in much of Asia and Latin America and authoritarian regimes seemed to be on the defensive everywhere. New social movements with demands that ranged from human rights and cultural recognition of minorities to gender equity, public health, and ecological protection were spreading across the globe. Here the idea of the public sphere became highly relevant. It seemed to capture something that was missing in earlier discussions of civil society by pointing to institutions such as coffeehouses, salons, publishing houses, journals, and newspapers that could nurture public discussion on issues of common concern that would ideally have an effect on public policy. The idea of the public sphere, as elaborated by Jürgen Habermas, also drew attention to the fact that new forms of subjectivity necessary for the development of democratic public criticism arise in and through circulation of discourses in multiple genres, such as epistolary novels, literary magazines, and newspapers. If civil society was made up of nongovernmental institutions that create a buffer between the market and the state, the idea of the public sphere seemed to identify and promote those institutions that were crucial for the development of democratic debate and will formation. The CTS working group's discussions of these issues drew upon advance copies of the English translation of Habermas's *The Structural Transformation of the Public Sphere* (1989).

The tumultuous events of the late eighties and early nineties—the downfall of the Soviet Union, the liberation of Eastern Europe, democracy movements in Asia, Tiananmen, and the Rushdie affair—not only confirmed the centrality of these two concepts but also gave them a global inflection. The initial impulse was simply to extend the terms analogically and to imagine an international version of civil society that would grow out of transnational institutions, such as the United Nations, the World Bank, the International Monetary Fund, and newly emergent NGOs, with their global reach and affiliations. It was assumed that those institutions in conjunction with the increasingly powerful global media would provide the forum and framework for discussing issues of global concern and thereby influencing the policies of individual nations and of the world community. The result would be the emergence of a transnational public sphere dedicated to promoting democratic values, human rights, and ecological justice through a potential "dialogue of cultures."

In retrospect, that scenario looks optimistic and naïve. The events of the last decade have shown that these early hopes are being undercut by the realities of contemporary globalization. The arrival of the new millennium is accompanied by the rise of new and destructive nationalisms and fundamentalisms and the growing social inequalities created by a predatory economic globalization. Far from the hopes for an international civil society and a new, more equitable world economic order, we now face the realities of "ethnic cleansing" in the former Yugoslavia, the Asian economic crisis, and the anti-American rage in the Muslim world. And the ongoing spectacle of political demonstrations, ethnic warfare, terrorist acts, police actions, aerial bombings, and peacekeeping missions ricocheting across television sets around the world raises grave doubts about the prospects of a transnational public sphere. For Americans especially, the spectacle has new meaning after the events of 11 September 2001. The reality of global terror, long known and experienced in other parts of the world, has touched the shores of the United States.

The members of the working group at the Center were always somewhat skeptical about conceiving the international versions of civil society and the public sphere as simple extensions of their respective national models. They saw how the very transnational processes (especially those connected with the transfer of capital, information, and populations) invoked as the facilitators of an international civil society and a transnational public sphere were already undermining the ideology, power, and sovereignty of nation-states so that they could not be the building blocks of such an order. They also recognized that the concepts of civil society and the public sphere and their possible transnational variants had to be understood in the larger historical and cultural context of the development of modernity.

In their recent writings, several of the Center's most active participants—Arjun Appadurai (1996), Craig Calhoun (1997), Charles Taylor (1995), and Michael Warner (1990)—have argued that civil society and the public sphere, along with nationalism, are the key components in the advent and spread of modernity. Moreover, they subscribe to what might be called the "multiple modernities" thesis that holds that each nation or region produces its own distinctive modernity in its encounter with the allegedly culture-neutral forms and processes (science and technology, industrialization, secularization, bureaucratization, and so on) characteristic of societal modernization. Under the impact of modernity, all societies will undergo certain changes in both outlook and institutional arrangements. But different starting points ensure that new variances will emerge in response to relatively similar changes. The dialectic of convergence and divergence, played out at different national/cultural sites under the contingencies of history and politics, produces multiple modernities. Equally important is the fact that the encounter with modernity does not take place in isolation but is invariably mediated by colonialism and imperialism in the past and today by the implacable forces of global media, migration, and capital. In fact, this aspect of contemporary globalization might be characterized as the struggle over the means of production of multiple modernities. It is through exploring the productive tension between globalization and multiple modernities that the working group at the Center has turned to the idea of the social imaginary.

This conceptual turn toward the social imaginary crystallized in the summer of 1999 when a small group—Benjamin Lee, Charles Taylor, Michael Warner, and myself—met at a farm near Montreal to draft a statement on *new imaginaries*. This statement, the basis of a project subsequently funded by the Rockefeller Foundation, consisted of five key ideas.

First, social imaginaries are ways of understanding the social that become social entities themselves, mediating collective life. Often, social scientists and historians have tried to understand these entities in terms of ideas, theories, philosophies—what might be called "third-person" or "objective" points of view. But some crucial self-understandings are not formulated in explicit or theoretical molds. They are first-person subjectivities that build upon implicit understandings that underlie and make possible common practices. They are embedded in the habitus of a population or are carried in modes of address, stories, symbols, and the like. They are imaginary in a double sense: they exist by virtue of representation or implicit understandings, even when they acquire immense institutional force; and they are the means by which individuals understand their identities and their place in the world (see Taylor's essay in this issue for elaboration).

Second, modernity in its multiple forms seems to rely on a special form of social imaginary that is based on relations among strangers. The stranger sociability is made possible through mass mediation, yet it also creates and organizes spaces of circulation for mass media (see Warner's essay in this issue for elaboration).

Third, the national people is a paradigmatic case of modern social imaginary. Its distinctive features include its representation as a "we"; its transparency between individual and collectivity; its agential subjectivity, in which a people acts in time; its unfolding in progressive history; and its posited environment of mutuality with other national peoples.

Fourth, a national people lives amid many other social imaginaries, penumbral to them. Other modern social imaginaries—such as the ethnos, the mainstream, the public, and humanity—differ from the national model in important ways. Some are not articulated as a *we* but are third-person objectifications of society; these include the market, the mainstream, and ethnic and census categories. Some are experienced vicariously or through indirect mediation. Some are not collective agents like the people but are experienced through affects, such as mass sentiment or grief, rather than through will formation. For example, Princess Diana's death inspired intense collective emotions but did not result in any kind of movements for social reform or change. Under some conditions, social imaginaries that are third-person objectifications can suddenly acquire agency; this is the case with at least some of the new social movements. And those movements, once agentialized, can under other conditions gravitate back to modes of passive belonging or vicarious agency.

Fifth, the agency of modern social imaginaries comes into being in a number of secular temporalities rather than existing eternally in cosmos or higher time. The moment of revolution or violence, of spectacular mutual display, or the quasi-sacred moment of redemptive breakthrough are modes of sociality that rival the progressive history of national peoples. It is perhaps in order to contain the violent potential of these temporalities that postfascist modern society has developed so many organized dramas of social temporality, such as sports and the quadrennial international competition for that badge of national pride, the Olympics.

These ideas were discussed and developed in considerable detail by larger groups that met at different venues—Chicago, Montreal, Hong Kong, and Istanbul—during the last two years. This issue is a product of the initial statement on new imaginaries and the meetings that were arranged around it. The ideas about the social imaginary that emerge in this collection of essays are significantly different from those enunciated by Castoriadis. Since Castoriadis's name is so closely associated with the very idea of social imaginary, it seems appropriate to provide a brief account of his formulation so as to distinguish it from the ones submitted here.

✦ ✦ ✦

Castoriadis's orientation is decidedly ontological and is triggered by the basic question: How are a multiplicity of social-historical worlds, in all their novelty and alterity, possible? According to Castoriadis, the dominant strain within the Western intellectual tradition, which he calls an ontology of determinacy, has consistently failed to recognize the true nature of society and history. In that view, *to be* is *to be determined*. Hence, the genesis and development of social-historical worlds are seen as an unfolding of an immanent logic or law that governs the universe and the human endeavors within it. The new and emergent forms of social life, despite their specificity and multiplicity, are explained away as adaptive surface variations of an underlying essential order that reason deciphers as biology, or economy, or the mind.

Against that view, Castoriadis elaborates an ontology of creation. For Castoriadis, society is a self-creating, self-instituting enterprise. Each society in instituting itself inaugurates a new ontological form, or *eidos*, that could not be deduced from or produced by the preexisting conditions. The invention of philosophy and democracy in the ancient Greek city-states, a favorite example of Castoriadis, cannot be explained in terms of the antecedent conditions. It was a rupture, a break in historical time. "For what is given in and through history," according to Castoriadis (1987: 184), "is not the determined sequence of the determined but the emergence of radical otherness, immanent creation, non-trivial novelty." A social-historical world is created ex nihilo in a burst of imaginative praxis carried out not by conscious individuals or groups but by anonymous masses who constitute themselves as a people in that very act of founding. This world-forming and meaning-bestowing creative force is the social imaginary of the instituting society. Like Hannah Arendt, Castoriadis treats as paradigmatic those moments when something absolutely new comes into being, when the instituting society supplants the instituted society, to illuminate the ceaseless creativity of the imaginary dimension that informs and motivates everything that transpires in a social domain.

Within the traditional ontology of determinacy, the imaginary dimension is seen as derivative, the mere reflection of what is already there, of the real; often it is held in suspicion as a medium of distortion and displacement. For Castoriadis, on the other hand, the imaginary is the constitutive magma of meaning, the structuring matrix without which chaos would reign. It is only through the mediation of the imaginary that we are able to conceive of the real in the first place and to make the elementary distinctions between form and content, object and image, the original and the copy. According to Castoriadis (1987: 145):

> This element—which gives a specific orientation to every institutional system, which overdetermines the choice and the connections of symbolic networks, which is the creation of each historical period, its singular manner of living, of seeing and of conducting its own existence, its world, and its relations with this world, this originary structuring component, this central signifying-signified, the source of that which presents itself in every instance as an indisputable and undisputed meaning, the basis for articulating what does matter and what does not, the origin of the surplus of being of the objects of practical, affective, and intellectual investment, whether individual or collective—is nothing other than the *imaginary* of the society or of the period considered.

Thus it is through the collective agency of the social imaginary that a society is created, given coherence and identity, and also subjected to auto-alterations, both mundane and radical, within historical time. Each society is created differently, subsists differently, and transforms itself differently.

To be sure, Castoriadis qualifies the ex nihilo rhetoric by acknowledging that a social imaginary has to recognize and contend with different orders of constraints: the external (those imposed by the natural strata, especially biology), the internal (the task of transforming "psychic monads" into socialized individuals), the historical (the reproductive inertia within the instituted society), and the intrinsic (the need for coherence and closure within the symbolic order). But none of those constraints warrants a deterministic reading. What is crucial here is not that human beings always eat, raise children, tinker with the established ways, and tell stories but that they do so in such a variety of ways. Therein lies the hold of the social imaginary. Our response to material needs, however technically impoverished, is always semiotically excessive. We lean on nature but are steered by the social imaginary.

Each society derives its unity and identity by representing itself in symbols, myths, legends, and other collectively shared significations. Language is the medium par excellence in which these social imaginary significations become manifest and do their constitutive work. Like all social institutions, language too has what Castoriadis calls its ensemblistic-identitary dimension, the equivalent of the structuralist *code*. But *code* cannot capture the open, inventive, and unruly

7

character of signifying practices. Language is essentially tropic, prone to generate surplus meaning. Creation of new meaning in language, say through meta-phorization, can serve as a heuristic model for understanding how social imaginary significations arise and rupture the existing social code to disclose a new horizon of meaning, a new order of things, a new world.[2]

Castoriadis's account of the social imaginary as the matrix of innovation and change is linked to his central political project of promoting autonomy. According to Castoriadis, one cannot strive for autonomy without striving simultaneously for the autonomy of others. This requires rethinking the concept of human action along Aristotelian lines as praxis. Unlike instrumental action, the dominant and dehumanizing mode under capitalism, praxis unfolds in public space where one freely engages with others in activities that have no predetermined purpose. In praxis, unlike *poiesis* (making), the agent is neither detached from nor in control of what he or she is doing. Emotion as well as intellect, character as well as interests, indeed, being itself, are caught up in praxis. Occurring as it does under conditions of plurality and contingency, praxis is fragile and frustrating. Yet the agent is drawn to praxis because only in praxis can one grasp and experience what it is to be autonomous. Castoriadis radicalizes Aristotle's notion of praxis by deemphasizing its connection to *phronesis*, or practical knowledge, while rearticulating it as a future-oriented emancipatory endeavor that generates novelty and alterity in its wake. Thus, praxis is rendered indistinguishable from a transformative revolutionary politics.

Autonomy at the societal level requires a collective capacity to question the institutional order and the social imaginary significations embedded in it. Castoriadis distinguishes between two types of social-historical formations: heteronomous and autonomous. In heteronomous societies—often glossed as "primitive"—the laws, norms, values, myths, and meanings are posited as given once and for all, and their indisputable status is derived from an extra-social or action-transcendent source. In contrast, the autonomous societies habitually call into question their own institutions and representations and the social imaginary that underwrites them. Here the people as collective agents recognize the contingency and constructedness of their world and how that world is made possible through the workings of the social imaginary. Hence, one need not think of the social imaginary as a demiurge that sets itself to work behind the backs of the people. It can be reflexively interrogated and hermeneutically reappropriated.

2. Castoriadis's views on social creativity in language are similar to those of M. M. Bakhtin (1981), Paul Ricoeur (1977), and Richard Rorty (1989).

For Castoriadis, the reflexive turn that shatters the closure of meaning characteristic of heteronomous social imaginaries is made possible through the simultaneous invention and institution of philosophy and democracy. While philosophical reflection interrogates the givenness of the social imaginary's significations, democratic praxis challenges the legitimacy of institutions that embody those significations. Autonomy can be attained through making explicit society's process of self-instituting and self-understanding and becoming willing to take responsibility for it. According to Castoriadis, this has happened only twice in human history, first in the ancient Greek city-states and later in Western Europe at the end of the Middle Ages, when autonomy was experienced and understood as radical openness to novelty and alterity. The contemporary West and those who participate in its globally mediated imaginary are the heirs to the incomplete project of autonomy initiated by those two epochal ruptures.

Aside from its staggering Eurocentrism (which hardly requires elaboration) and its idealization of ancient Greece, Castoridias's account is notable for rarely departing from the highly abstract level of ontological reflection where it begins. To be sure, Castoriadis displays a remarkable command of comparative cultural and historical data in his polemics against the deterministic theories. He does not carefully work through that data, however, and instead deploys it opportunistically, albeit with considerable rhetorical brilliance, to reduce the opponent's grand narratives, especially those of Marxism and structuralism, to seeming absurdity. When it comes to positive formulations, he reverts to a grand narrative of his own in a distinctly philosophical idiom. As grand narratives go, it has considerable plausibility; it is internally coherent and comprehensive in scope and offers a compelling perspective on the human condition. But Castoriadis rarely engages the question of how change and difference are produced locally through the workings of the social imaginary's significations at specific social-historical conjunctures.

A philosophical theory of social-historical multiplicity, cogently argued but historically anecdotal, leaves the idea of multiplicity relatively abstract and empty. It leads Castoriadis to dichotomize societies as if they could be subsumed under the ideal types of *heteronomous* and *autonomous* instead of recognizing that all social formations, at least the modern ones, differentially incorporate aspects of both. One can understand why Castoriadis might have elected this mode of theorizing, given his avowed and lifelong mission to deconstruct the hegemonic hold of the ontology of determinacy. In such a context, multiplicity becomes the axiomatic starting point in a new ontology of creation and not a vexatious social-historical fact that poses a hermeneutic challenge. For Castoriadis, multiplicity is the answer to a philosophical riddle but not a riddle itself—as it is for the authors of essays in this issue.

✦ ✦ ✦

Charles Taylor, whose essay serves as a conceptual frame for this issue, invokes the idea of the social imaginary in his continuing engagement with the theme of "multiple modernities." In a series of previously published essays (Taylor 2000, 2001) as well as in the present one, Taylor attempts to get at the specificities of Western modernity by differentiating it both from its predecessor cultures and from cultures of other modernities.

To account for the differences among modernities, Taylor deploys the idea of *social imaginary* to refer broadly to the way a given people imagine their collective social life. Within the folds of a social imaginary, we see ourselves as agents who traverse a social space and inhabit a temporal horizon, entertain certain beliefs and norms, engage in and make sense of our practices in terms of purpose, timing, and appropriateness, and exist among other agents. The social imaginary is something more than an immediate practical understanding of how to do particular things—such as how to buy a newspaper, ride a subway, order a drink, wire money, make small talk, or submit a petition. It involves a form of understanding that has a wider grasp of our history and social existence. It is closer to Pierre Bourdieu's notion of *habitus* or what some contemporary philosophers, following Martin Heidegger and Ludwig Wittgenstein, call the *background*. It is a complex, unstructured, and not fully articulated "understanding of our whole situation, within which particular features of our world become evident" (Taylor, in this issue). It gives us a sense of who we are, how we fit together, how we got where we are, and what we might expect from each other in carrying out collective practices that are constitutive of our way of life.

Although Taylor shares Castoriadis's view of the social imaginary as a generative matrix, he emphasizes its role in the hermeneutics of everyday life. This is evident in his attempt to further distinguish the social imaginary from both explicit doctrine and habitus-based embodied understanding. Unlike theory, which only a small minority entertain and comprehend, the social imaginary "is shared by large groups of people, if not the whole society" (Taylor, in this issue). Given such widespread adherence, the social imaginary can confer legitimacy on our common practices and pursuits and embed them in a normative scheme. Moreover, the idiom of social imaginary is distinct. It is expressed and carried in images, stories, legends, and modes of address that constitute a symbolic matrix that cannot be reduced to theoretical terms. That idiom also distinguishes it from habitus. In a manner similar to Castoriadis, Taylor (2001: 189) claims that the social imaginary, "while nourished in embodied habitus, is given expression on the symbolic level." The social imaginary therefore occupies a fluid middle ground between embodied practices and explicit doctrines. The relation between the three is dynamic. The line of influence is not causative but circular. A social imaginary carries within it an image of moral order, which imbues embodied practices and the accompanying cultural forms with meaning and legitimacy. That image of the moral order might have, in turn, originated in an explicit doctrine or theory, but the process through which it penetrates and takes hold of a social imaginary is slow and complex.

What is distinctive about Taylor's approach to the social imaginary—and of considerable methodological significance—is that he deploys it as a key concept in the hermeneutics of history and culture. In the essay included in this issue, he gives an account of the interplay among theory, social imaginary, and embodied practices in the making of Western modernity. According to Taylor, the modern Western imaginary is animated by an image of moral order based on the mutual benefit of equal participants. This moral order is radically different from the premodern version, which was based either on the law of the people (a people bound by law that has existed since time immemorial) or on the principle of hierarchical complementarity (a people organized into different orders that are functionally interdependent but unequal in rank and worth). The new image of unmediated mutuality and equality, first elaborated in theories of natural law and contract by seventeenth-century thinkers such as Hugo Grotius and John Locke, gradually penetrated and took hold of the social imaginary of Western people. As the older images faded and became marginalized, they continued to have some residual hold in cultural spaces such as family and gender relations. But the "long march," to use Taylor's phrase, was already underway. The new image, incubated in the Grotian-Lockean theory, steadily permeates and saturates a social imaginary as new cultural forms and social practices emerge, or old ones are modified and acquire new meanings. One cannot map that long march in the manner of a history of an idea because it is at once a march and a mutation of an image into a fertile cluster of cultural forms, symbolic expressions, and institutional practices. Hence, Taylor does not trace the career of the image from one theoretical text to the next. Instead, he gives a brief but highly suggestive account of the emergence of three key cultural forms and the accompanying institutional arrangements—the economy, the public sphere, and the self-governing people—in the womb of the modern social imaginary.

Taylor's account of these three cultural formations provides a fresh perspective on how to read the specificities of Western modernity: how we came to imagine society primarily as an economy for exchanging goods and services to promote mutual prosperity; how we began to imagine the public sphere as a metatopical place for deliberation and discussion among strangers on issues of mutual concern; how we invented the idea of a self-governing people capable of "founding" acts in a purely secular time without recourse to action-transcendent principles. The style and substance of these forms cannot be understood apart from the social imaginary within which they have evolved and are embedded. More importantly, Taylor's account provides a new frame for the "multiple modernities" thesis. Some versions of these three pivotal forms of collective life and agency are visible (installed and fought over) in almost any non-Western cultural/national formation that is undergoing the passage to modernity. But those versions — entrepreneurial culture in Singapore, the Islamic public sphere in Turkey, democratic self-rule in India — differ from their counterparts in the West in important ways. That difference should be understood not as a deviation from an idealized model but as an expression of a location in an alternative social imaginary. Taylor's key insight here is that these cultural forms — notwithstanding their seeming portability and replicability — are refigured both in meaning and function when placed within a social imaginary calibrated by an image of a moral order different from that of the West. And that refiguration is not a corruption but a creative adaptation. Thus, Taylor invites us to explore the cultural face of "multiple modernities" by attending to its refractions within the symbolic matrix of alternative social imaginaries.

In her essay, Mary Poovey draws on Taylor's formulation of the modern social imaginary to show that the idea of *the social* was deployed in justifying a new form of liberal governmentality in early-eighteenth-century British moral philosophy. According to Poovey, the social is a secondary abstraction derived from a more fundamental abstraction, human nature, which occupies a mediating hermeneutic position between observable human practices and institutions and the invisible underlying providential order that allegedly animates them. The eighteenth-century British theories of human nature stress that human beings have a natural tendency to benefit one another in the course of pursuing their individual interests. Thus, the social order of mutual benefit is seen as rooted in human nature itself rather than as a product of political imagination and intervention. Poovey tracks the secularization of human nature as it sheds its "providential framework" and takes on secondary properties, especially that of the social, which in turn becomes an objectifying abstraction in its own right.

For Poovey, the rise and proliferation of objectifying abstractions like human nature and the social are an integral part of the modern Western social imaginary and its constitutive force. Through her innovative explication of the rhetorical structure of those key abstractions, Poovey is able to disclose what she calls the "self-authenticating" and "recursive" structure of the modern social imaginaries.

Like Taylor, Arjun Appadurai has been preoccupied for more than a decade with tracking the career of modernity but from a decidedly global perspective. In his earlier work, especially *Modernity at Large*, Appadurai (1996: 5) writes about imagination as a "collective, social fact" that is at "work" in the multiple ways that people find their lot, make a dwelling, and build a world in and through modernity. According to Appadurai, "imagination has broken out of the special expressive space of art, myth, and ritual and has now become a part of the quotidian mental work of ordinary people in many societies." The entry of imagination into the logic of everyday life is given a global inflection by the twin forces of modernity: mass migration and mass mediation. Whether moving voluntarily in search of better lives or moving involuntarily as refugees and persecuted peoples, the migrants have lost the worlds into which they were born and are therefore forced to construct new imagined worlds that rarely coincide with geopolitical space or the ideologies of nation-states. These imagined worlds, which combine memory and desire in unexpected ways, can create loyalties and affiliations that are sometimes violently hostile to the modernizing projects of nation-states and sometimes to modernity itself. But there are also other imagined worlds that, while operating within the nation-state system, are animated by postnational projects that attest to the ongoing struggle over the production of multiple, translocal modernities. In the opening essay of this issue, Appadurai presents a brilliant case study of the latter type.

Appadurai's case study examines the political vision and organizational practices of the Alliance, a partnership among three grassroots organizations, which is involved in a struggle to secure adequate and durable housing and access to urban infrastructure (e.g., water, electricity, transport, and sanitation) for slum-dwellers in Mumbai. The three partners are SPARC (an NGO formed by social work professionals), NSDF (the National Slum Dwellers' Federation), and Mahila Milan (an organization of poor women). According to Appadurai, the Alliance is involved in a new form of urban governmentality that combines local activism with horizontal global networking. The work of the Alliance is predicated on reimagining politics in terms of partnership, patience, self-empowerment through visibility, and performative competence.

The Alliance has cultivated close global links with not only donor institutions in the West but also activist organizations of the urban poor in fourteen other countries, notably South Africa and Thailand. Among other things, it brings together in small groups the urban poor from different countries to share practical knowledge gleaned from local struggles and thus decenters the developmental model of an expert/client relationship where knowledge flows unidirectionally and asymmetrically. Aside from such innovations in the politics of globalization from below, the work of the Alliance also challenges many of the pieties of Western modernity. Paradoxical as it might seem, its commitment to a politics of patience in the face of the daily "tyranny of emergency" is radically different from what Martin Luther King Jr. once denounced as the "tranquilizing drug of gradualism" from the normative perspective of Western liberalism. Appadurai's account of that politics of patience and its allied practices of "savings," "federating," "precedent-setting," "self-enumeration," and "toilet festivals" brilliantly captures a new form of politics of recognition from below and a new imaginary —neither fully global nor national nor local—that underwrites it.

If Appadurai explores optimistically how new translocal solidarities can be forged in the folds of new imaginaries, Achille Mbembe darkly dissects a continental imaginary of Africanity that has become profoundly corrupt and dysfunctional. According to Mbembe, the two dominant discursive modes of imagining the African self and its relation to the world have reached a dead end. Neither of these modes—the Marxist-nationalist and the nativist—has been able to break away from a canonical set of "closed" meanings and interpretations attributed to the three key historical events: slavery, colonization, and apartheid.

The Marxist-nationalist reading of those events leads to a conception of the African subject as a wounded victim and of African history as externally and conspiratorially determined. Such a reading in turn gives birth to a politics of self-knowledge, sovereignty, and autonomy galvanized by a radical utopic vision that holds that Africa can attain full selfhood and be made "whole" again only by disconnecting itself from the world. This is, says Mbembe, "the mad dream of a world without Others." On the other hand, the nativist reading, which is not dissimilar from its Marxist-nationalist counterpart, posits an emancipatory politics based on Africa's cultural uniqueness. Here African subjecthood is so deeply grounded in race and geography that the distinctions between "racial body," "spatial body," and "civic body" are erased, and the idea of an Africanity that is not black becomes unimaginable.

Out of such an impasse, Mbembe desperately wants to be able to imagine a politics of Africanity not rooted exclusively in victimhood and blackness. He searches for the intimations of newly emergent imaginaries that would, among other things, reflect on the status of suffering in history (as in Jewish thought and experience), recuperate the collective memory of the African collaboration in the crime of slavery and break the silence over that secret guilt, and recognize that the involuntary diaspora has produced different temporalities and affiliations on the opposite shore of the Atlantic. What Mbembe finds is disturbing: an imaginary of *states of war* where the African self seeks to transcend and reinvent itself through excessive, sacrificial violence; an imaginary of religion where the self awaits the gifts of tongues and of divine healing; and an imaginary of scarcity where the self longs for goods to which it has no material access.

Elizabeth Povinelli, like Mbembe, engages an aspect of modern imaginaries that has deadlocked if not reached a dead end. In her essay, she explores how the politics of recognition within the modern liberal imaginary is beset with contradictory pulls and pressures from two different grids of social bondage—the genealogical and the intimate. A characteristic feature of liberal modernity is that one's unmarked membership in an abstract social order, rather than one's marked placement in the genealogical grid of kinship, descent, and rank, increasingly defines one's rights and obligations. As the old regime of genealogy is replaced with the new regime of citizenship, the rhetoric of intimacy ("love makes true families and just nations") begins to permeate the ideologies of nationalism and the public sphere. But intimacy is not easily institutionalized; its rhythm and duration are multiple and unpredictable. Besides, the genealogical grid does not disappear but is reconfigured. Citizenship itself continues to have a strong genealogical component, as do other state-mediated dispensations such as inheritance, child welfare, and taxation. Povinelli gives a provocative parallel reading of two archives—the Australian indigenous people's claim to land tenure and lesbian, gay, and queer struggles for recognition—to show how the genealogical grid, while diminished at the cosmopolitan/heteronormative center, continues to hold sway in the postcolony and in regimenting same-sex desires and world-making.

The essays by Michael Warner, Craig Calhoun, and Nilüfer Göle further extend our understanding of the public sphere and its shifting status in the spread of global modernity. Warner, whose previous work on the public sphere has been highly influential, offers a conceptualization of the public sphere in terms of its seven quasi-formal features: (1) a public is self-organized; (2) a public is a relation among strangers; (3) the address of public speech is both personal and impersonal; (4) a public is constituted through mere attention; (5) a public is the social space created by the reflexive circulation of discourse; (6) publics act historically according to the temporality of their circulation; and (7) a public is poetic world-making. Starting with the simple propositions that "a public is a space of discourse organized by nothing other than discourse itself," and that "it exists *by virtue of being addressed*," Warner draws out a series of conceptual implications with such rigor and insight that it significantly extends and modifies our modernist Habermasian understanding of the public sphere. Aside from the formal rigor, which is impressive, the essay is richly historicizing as it draws on readings of some key textual moments (e.g., the eighteenth-century English journal the *Spectator* and the making of the public sphere in the West). Although Warner's analysis is based on the Euro-American experience, his conceptual extensions and innovations, most notably regarding "stranger sociability" and the "multiple temporalities of circulation," provide tools for mapping the unfolding logic of multiple publics and counterpublics across the terrain of global modernity.

In his essay, Calhoun calls for a reconceptualization of the public sphere "not simply as a setting for rational debate and decision-making—thus largely disregarding or transcending issues of identity—but as a setting for the development of social solidarity as a matter of choice, rather than necessity." According to Calhoun, it is a mistake to view identities and solidarities, especially those linked to the idea of nationality, as preconstituted in a cultural matrix of language, tradition, and ethnicity before they appear as collective agents within the discursive arena of the public sphere. This leads to a host of errors, such as equating nationalism with ethnic nationalism, drawing false distinctions between the *irrational* sources of cultural integration and the *rational* sources of political legitimization, and saddling the inclusionary cosmopolitan democratic projects with thin identities while allocating thick identities to the exclusionary projects of cultural nationalisms and religious fundamentalisms. For Calhoun, this is not only a conceptual error but also a politically dangerous one because a democratic imaginary depends on a notion of solidarity richer than one based merely on juridical equality. Drawing on the work of Hannah Arendt, he argues that the public sphere is a form of social solidarity, a unique one in the sense that it exists "in, through, and for talk." What transpires in the public sphere is not limited to rational-critical discourse about affairs of common concern. Here more than anywhere else reflexive choice and solidarity are joined together in an imaginative act of worldmaking.

Calhoun's call for an enlarged notion of the public sphere gets a strong endorsement from Göle's case study of the semiotic struggle over "performing" Islam and making it visible in the political public sphere in Turkey, a self-styled secular republic with a complex history of voluntary but authoritarian modernization. The case involves the election of Merve Kavakçı, a headscarf-wearing

Muslim woman from the pro-Islamic party who was unable to take the oath on the opening day of the parliamentary session due to the vehement opposition from the members of secular parties. At the heart of controversy is the white headscarf, an overdetermined sign of the Islamization of a woman's body, worn by Kavakçı. But Kavakçı was not a transparent vehicle for transmitting Islamist political symbology. A divorced, United States–trained computer engineer, Kavakçı dressed fashionably in modern business suits, spoke fluent English, and remained calm and composed in the face of political heckling. She had at her command all the idioms and accoutrements of modernity. According to Göle, it is precisely the ambivalent quality of a figure simultaneously so modern and yet Muslim that terrified the secularists. In Göle's account, what is at stake here is the struggle between two imaginaries, the secular and the Islamic, to define the contours of the public sphere. The "excess" of modernity of the secularists, easily overwrought by "small differences" as exemplified by Kavakçı's headscarf, is what leads to the frightful narrowing of the public sphere and to the exclusion of cultural performances and counterperformances out of which solidarities are formed.

In a far-ranging essay that swiftly moves from structural linguistics through speech-act theory to Marxism, Benjamin Lee and Edward LiPuma provocatively argue that the modern Western imaginaries of the public sphere, the citizen-state, and the market—the three singled out by Taylor—are based on a social contract model of society. In that model, as elaborated by Thomas Hobbes and others, out of an imagined state of nature, "individuals exchange promises and create a transcendent power to govern the social totality they create" (Lee and LiPuma, in this issue). Thus, the sovereign becomes the third-person authority that transcends the "I-You" exchanges of promises that constitute it. According to Lee and LiPuma, this complex interplay of first- and third-person perspectives is the structuring form out of which surplus—both transcendent and tangible—is produced and circulated in different realms. Surplus emerges as surplus value in the market economy, sovereign power in the citizen-state, and general will in the public sphere.

For Lee and LiPuma, the reflexive structures and cultures of circulation through which those surpluses move and encompass social life are of greater importance than the matrix within which they are produced. They argue that circulation is something more than mere movement of people, ideas, and commodities from one place or culture to another. Rather, it is "a cultural process with its own process of abstraction, evaluation, and constraint" that facilitates the performative constitution of collective agency and subsequent visions of social totality.

17

Lee and LiPuma unpack the construction of capital as a self-reflexive temporal agency in its "two objectified forms—historically as abstract labor time and surplus value, nowadays as risk and finance. . . ." Further, they argue that the collective agencies such as the market, the public sphere, and the sovereign people so central to the modern imaginary are "fetishized figurations" of the underlying performativity of capital. Lee and LiPuma's highly suggestive argument is based on an analysis of the circulation—in terms of both its structure and culture—of the equity-based derivatives and currency swaps in the contemporary global financial markets.

Thus, from Taylor to Lee and LiPuma, we have come full circle in our exploration of new imaginaries. The key institutional sites of modern imaginary identified by Taylor are seen by Lee and LiPuma as "fetishized figurations" of capital that circulate at a dizzying speed across the globe. The essays in this issue offer a rich array of approaches to new imaginaries that disclose new possibilities and challenges at the crossings of globalization and multiple modernities. Many of the essays are provisional statements of work and thought still in progress but are sufficiently developed for public offering and discussion. These essays are written by a group of scholars with varied academic, political, and cultural backgrounds who came together by chance, contingency, and good fortune but have stayed together through will, sagacity, and emergent solidarity to work on common projects such as this one. This is a collective work with multiple voices and multiple trajectories groping toward new imaginaries.

Dilip Parameshwar Gaonkar is co-director of the Center for Transcultural Studies and teaches rhetoric and cultural studies at Northwestern University. He is the editor of *Alternative Modernities* (2001).

References

Appadurai, Arjun. 1996. *Modernity at large: Cultural dimensions of globalization*. Minneapolis: University of Minnesota Press.
Bahktin, M. M. 1981. *The dialogic imagination: Four essays*, edited by Michael Holquist and translated by Caryl Emerson and Michael Holquist. Austin: University of Texas Press.
Calhoun, Craig. 1997. *Nationalism*. Minneapolis: University of Minnesota Press.
Castoriadis, Cornelius. 1987. *The imaginary institution of society*, translated by Kathleen Blamey. Cambridge: MIT Press.

————. 1997a. Radical imagination and the social instituting imaginary. In *The Castoriadis reader*, edited by David A. Curtis. Oxford: Blackwell.

————. 1997b. *World in fragments: Writings on politics, society, psychoanalysis and the imagination*, translated by David A. Curtis. Palo Alto, Calif.: Stanford University Press.

Habermas, Jürgen. 1989. *The structural transformation of the public sphere*, translated by Thomas Burger with Frederick Lawrence. Cambridge: MIT Press.

————. 1990. *The philosophical discourse of modernity: Twelve lectures*, translated by Frederick Lawrence. Cambridge: MIT Press.

Howard, Dick. 1988. *The Marxian legacy*. 2d ed. Minneapolis: University of Minnesota Press.

Kalyvas, Andreas. 2001. The politics of autonomy and the challenge of deliberation: Castoriadis contra Habermas. *Thesis Eleven* 64: 1–19.

Ricoeur, Paul. 1977. *The rule of metaphor: Multi-disciplinary studies of the creation of meaning in language*. Toronto: University of Toronto Press.

Rorty, Richard. 1989. *Contingency, irony, and solidarity*. Cambridge: Cambridge University Press.

Taylor, Charles. 1995. *Philosophical arguments*. Cambridge: Harvard University Press.

————. 2000. Modernity and difference. In *Without guarantees: In honour of Stuart Hall*, edited by Paul Gilroy, Lawrence Grossberg, and Angela McRobbie. New York: Verso.

————. 2001. Two theories of modernity. In *Alternative modernities*, edited by Dilip Parameshwar Gaonkar. Durham, N.C.: Duke University Press.

Thompson, John B. 1984. *Studies in the theory of ideology*. Berkeley: University of California Press.

Warner, Michael. 1990. *The letters of the republic: Publication and the public sphere in eighteenth-century America*. Cambridge: Harvard University Press.

Deep Democracy:
Urban Governmentality and
the Horizon of Politics

Arjun Appadurai

Globalization from Below

Post-1989, the world seems marked by the global victory of some version of neoliberalism, backed by the ubiquitous presence of the United States and sustained by the common openness to market processes of regimes otherwise varied in their political, religious, and historical traditions. At the same time, more than a decade after the fall of the Soviet order, it is clearer than ever that global inequality has widened, intranational warfare has vastly outpaced international

This essay is based on research funded by the Ford Foundation. I owe special thanks to Carol A. Breckenridge, who first suggested to me that the work of the Mumbai Alliance could be characterized in the image of "deep democracy." The first draft of this essay was written in June 2000 at the University of Amsterdam's School of Social Science Research, where I was honored to serve as a Distinguished Visiting Professor. Since then, it has been debated by audiences in Chicago, Buenos Aires, Montevideo, and Paris. For their useful criticism and help in organizing these discussions, I must thank Marc Abélès, Hugo Achugar, Irene Belier, Partha Chatterjee, Dilip Parameshwar Gaonkar, Christophe Jaffrelot, Elizabeth Jelin, Benjamin Lee, Achille Mbembe, Mariella Pandolfi, Charles Taylor, and Peter van der Veer. In a separate vein, I owe thanks to various members and supporters of the Alliance in India and the Shack/Slum Dwellers International network for their critical support and encouragement of the research process and the direction of the first draft: to Arputham Jockin, Srilatha Batliwala, Somsook Boonyabancha, William Cobbett, Celine D'Cruz, Ellen Schaengold, Marjolijn Wilmink, and Patrick Wakely, in addition to Joel Bolnick, Sundar Burra, Diana Mitlin, Ruth McLeod, and Sheela Patel, whose own draft papers have helped me to get a more balanced picture of the Alliance's activities. This essay also appears in *Environment and Urbanization* 13 (2002).

Public Culture 14(1): 21–47

warfare (thus leading some observers to suggest the image of a Cold Peace), and various forms of violent ethnicization seem to erode the possibilities of sustainable pluralism. All this in a period that has also witnessed increased flows of financial capital across national boundaries and innovations in electronic communications and information storage technologies—the paradoxes abound, and have led to the proliferation of new theories of civilizational clash and of global gaps between safe and unsafe physical zones and geographical spheres. Fears of cyberapartheid mix with hopes for new opportunities for inclusion and participation.

In this confusion, now exacerbated by the knowledge that neither the most recent innovations in communications nor the defeat of the Soviet Union has created the conditions for global peace or equity, two great paradigms for enlightenment and equity seem to have become exhausted. One is the Marxist vision, in all its global variants, which promised some sort of politics of class-based internationalism premised on class struggle and the transformation of bourgeois politics by proletarian will. This is an internationalist vision that nevertheless requires the architecture of the nation-state as the site of effective struggle against capital and its agents. In this sense Marxism was, politically speaking, realist. The other grand vision, salient after 1945, was that of modernization and development, with its associated machinery of Western lending, technical expertise, and universalist discourses of education and technology transfer, and its target polity of the nationally based electoral democracy. This vision, born in such experiments as the Marshall Plan, has been subjected to intense criticism on numerous scores, but the starkest challenge to it is presented by the fact that today, over half a century after the Bretton Woods accords, more than half of the world's population lives in severe poverty.

In this context, a variety of other visions of emancipation and equity now circulate globally, often at odds with the nationalist imagination. Some are culturalist and religious, some diasporic and nonterritorial, some bureaucratic and managerial. Almost all of these recognize that nongovernmental actors are here to stay and somehow need to be made part of new models of global governance and local democracy.

The alliances and divisions in this new global political economy are not always easy to predict or understand. But among the many varieties of grassroots political movements, at least one broad distinction can be made. On the one hand are groups that have opted for armed, militarized solutions to their problems of inclusion, recognition, and participation. On the other are those that have opted for a politics of partnership—partnership, that is, between traditionally opposed groups, such as states, corporations, and workers. The alliance of housing activists whose story occupies the bulk of this essay belongs to the latter group and is part of the emergent process through which the physics of globalization is being creatively redeployed.

The Story

What follows is a preliminary analysis of an urban activist movement with global links. The setting is the city of Mumbai, in the state of Maharashtra, in western India. The movement consists of three partners and its history as an alliance goes back to 1987. The three partners have different histories. The Society for the Protection of Area Resource Centres, or SPARC, is an NGO formed by social work professionals in 1984 to work with problems of urban poverty in Mumbai. NSDF, the National Slum Dwellers' Federation, is a powerful grassroots organization established in 1974 and is a CBO, or community-based organization, that also has its historical base in Mumbai. Finally, Mahila Milan is an organization of poor women, set up in 1986, with its base in Mumbai and a network throughout India, which is focused on women's issues in relation to urban poverty and concerned especially with local and self-organized savings schemes among the very poor. All three organizations, which refer to themselves collectively as the Alliance, are united in their concern with gaining secure tenure of land, adequate and durable housing, and access to elements of urban infrastructure, notably to electricity, transport, sanitation, and allied services. The Alliance also has strong links to Mumbai's pavement dwellers and to its street children, whom it has organized into an organization called Sadak Chaap (Street Imprint), which has its own social and political agenda. Of the six or seven nonstate organizations working directly with the urban poor in Mumbai, the Alliance has by far the largest constituency, the highest visibility in the eyes of the state, and the most extensive networks in India and elsewhere in the world.

This essay is an effort to understand how this came to be by looking at the horizon of politics created by the Alliance and by seeing how it has articulated new relations to urban governmentality. It is part of a larger ongoing study of how grassroots movements are finding new ways to combine local activism with horizontal, global networking. It is also, methodologically speaking, a partial effort to show how the anthropological study of globalization can move from an ethnography of locations to one of circulations. In my conclusion, I use the story of this particular network to discuss why it is useful to speak of "deep democracy" as a concept of wider potential use in the study of globalization.

Theoretical Points of Entry

Three theoretical propositions underlie this presentation of the story of the Alliance in Mumbai.

First I assume, on the basis of my own previous work (Appadurai 1996, 2000, 2001) and that of several others from a variety of disciplinary perspectives (Castells 1996; Giddens 2000; Held 1995; Rosenau 1997), that globalization is producing new geographies of governmentality. Specifically, we are witnessing new forms of globally organized power and expertise within the "skin" or "casing" of existing nation-states (Sassen 2000). One expression of these new geographies can be seen in the relationship of "cities and citizenship" (Appadurai and Holston 1999), in which wealthier "world-cities" increasingly operate like city-states in a networked global economy, increasingly independent of regional and national mediation, and where poorer cities—and the poorer populations within them—seek new ways to claim space and voice. Many large cities like Mumbai display the contradictions between these ideal types and combine high concentrations of wealth (tied to the growth of producer services) and even higher concentrations of poverty and disenfranchisement. Movements among the urban poor, such as the one I document here, mobilize and mediate these contradictions. They represent efforts to reconstitute citizenship in cities. Such efforts take the form, in part, of what I refer to as *deep democracy*.

Second, I assume that the nation-state system is undergoing a profound and transformative crisis. Avoiding here the sterile terms of the debate about whether or not the nation-state is ending (a debate to which I myself earlier contributed), I nevertheless wish to affirm resolutely that the changes in the system are deep, if not graspable, as yet, in a simple theory. I suggest that we see the current crisis as a crisis of redundancy rather than, for example, as one of legitimation (Habermas 1975). By using the term *redundancy*, I mean to connect several processes that others have identified with different states and regions and in different dimensions of governance. Thus, in many parts of the world, there has been undoubted growth in a "privatization" of the state in various forms, sometimes produced by the appropriation of the means of violence by nonstate groups. In other cases, we can see the growing power in some national economies of multilateral agencies such as the World Bank and International Monetary Fund, sometimes indexed by the voluntary outsourcing of state functions as part of the neoliberal strategies that have become popular worldwide since 1989. In yet other cases, activist NGOs and citizens' movements have appropriated significant parts of the means of governance.

Third, I assume that we are witnessing a notable transformation in the nature of global governance in the explosive growth of nongovernment organizations of all scales and varieties in the period since 1945, a growth fueled by the linked development of the United Nations system, the Bretton Woods institutional order, and especially the global circulation and legitimation of the discourses and politics of "human rights." Together, these developments have provided a powerful impetus to democratic claims by nonstate actors throughout the world. There is some reason to worry about whether the current framework of human rights is serving mainly as the legal and normative conscience—or the legal-bureaucratic lubricant—of a neoliberal, marketized political order. But there is no doubt that the global spread of the discourse of human rights has provided a huge boost to local democratic formations. In addition, the combination of this global efflorescence of nongovernmental politics with the multiple technological revolutions of the last fifty years has provided much energy to what has been called "cross-border activism" through "transnational advocacy networks" (Keck and Sikkink 1998). These networks provide new horizontal modes for articulating the deep democratic politics of the locality, creating hitherto unpredicted groupings: examples may be "issue-based"—focused on the environment, child labor, or AIDS —or "identity-based"—feminist, indigenous, gay, diasporic. The Mumbai-based movement discussed here is also a site of such cross-border activism.

Together, these three points of entry allow me to describe the Mumbai Alliance of urban activists as part of an emergent political horizon, global in its scope, that presents a post-Marxist and postdevelopmentalist vision of how the global and the local can become reciprocal instruments in the deepening of democracy.

The Setting: Mumbai in the 1990s

I have recently completed a lengthy examination of the transformation of Mumbai's cultural economy since the 1970s, with an emphasis on the brutal ethnic violence of December 1992–January 1993 (Appadurai 2001). That essay contains a relatively detailed analysis of the relationships between the politics of right-wing Hindu nationalism—seen mostly in the activities of India's major urban xenophobic party, the Shiva Sena—the political economy of deindustrialization, and the spectral politics of housing in Mumbai. I analyze the steady expansion of anti-Muslim politics by the Shiva Sena, the radical inequality in access to living space in the city, and the transformation of its industrial economy into a service economy. I argue that Mumbai became a perfect site for the violent rewriting of national geography as urban geography through a paroxysmal effort to eliminate Muslims from its public sphere and its commercial world.

I will not retell that story here, but I will review some major facts about Mumbai in the 1990s that are not widely known. Mumbai is the largest city in a country, India, whose population has just crossed the 1 billion mark (one-sixth of the world's population). The city's population is at least 12 million (more, if we include the growing edges of the city and the population of the twin city, New Mumbai, that has been built across Thane Creek). This means a population totaling 1.2 percent of one-sixth of the world's population. Not a minor case, even in itself.

Here follow some facts about housing in Mumbai on which there is a general consensus. About 40 percent of the population (about 6 million persons) live in slums or other degraded forms of housing. Another 5 to 10 percent are pavement dwellers. Yet according to one recent estimate, slum dwellers occupy only 8 percent of the city's land, which totals about 43,000 hectares. The rest of the city's land is either industrial land, middle- and high-income housing, or vacant land in the control of the city, the state (regional and federal), or private owners. The bottom line: 5 to 6 million poor people living in substandard conditions in 8 percent of the land area of a city smaller than the two New York City boroughs of Manhattan and Queens. This huge and constricted population of insecurely or poorly housed people has negligible access to essential services, such as running water, electricity, and ration cards for food staples.

Equally important, this population—which we may call *citizens without a city*—is a vital part of the urban workforce. Some of them occupy the respectable low end of white-collar organizations and others the menial low end of industrial and commercial concerns. But many are engaged in temporary, physically dangerous, and socially degrading forms of work. This latter group, which may well comprise 1 to 2 million people in Mumbai, is best described, in the striking phrase of Sandeep Pendse (1995), as Mumbai's "toilers" rather than as its proletariat, working class, or laboring classes—all designations that suggest more stable forms of employment and organization. These toilers, the poorest of the poor in the city of Mumbai, work in menial occupations (almost always on a daily or piecework basis). They are cart pullers, ragpickers, scullions, sex workers, car cleaners, mechanic's assistants, petty vendors, small-time criminals, and temporary workers in petty industrial jobs requiring dangerous physical work, such as ditch digging, metal hammering, truck loading, and the like. They often sleep in (or on) their places of work, insofar as their work is not wholly transient in character. While men form the core of this labor pool, women and children work wherever possible, frequently in ways that exploit their sexual vulnerability. To take just one example, Mumbai's gigantic restaurant and food-service economy is almost completely dependent on a vast army of child labor.

Housing is at the heart of the lives of this army of toilers. Their everyday life is dominated by ever-present forms of risk. Their temporary shacks may be demolished. Their slumlords may push them out through force or extortion. The torrential monsoons may destroy their fragile shelters and their few personal possessions. Their lack of sanitary facilities increases their need for doctors to whom they have limited access. And their inability to document their claims to housing may snowball into a general invisibility in urban life, making it impossible for them to claim any rights to such things as rationed foods, municipal health and education facilities, police protection, and voting rights. In a city where ration cards, electricity bills, and rent receipts guarantee other rights to the benefits of citizenship, the inability to secure claims to proper housing and other political handicaps reinforce each other. Housing—and its lack—set the stage for the most public drama of disenfranchisement in Mumbai. In fact, housing can be argued to be the single most critical site of this city's politics of citizenship.

This is the context in which the activists I am working with are making their interventions, mobilizing the poor and generating new forms of politics. The next three sections of this essay are about various dimensions of this politics: its vision, its vocabularies, and its practices.

The Politics of Patience

In this section, I give a sketch of the evolving vision of the Alliance of SPARC, Mahila Milan, and the National Slum Dwellers' Federation as it functions within the complex politics of space and housing in Mumbai. Here, a number of broad features of the Alliance are important.

First, given the diverse social origins of the three groups that are involved in the Alliance, their politics awards a central place to negotiation and consensus-building. SPARC is led by professionals with an anglophone background, connected to state and corporate elites in Mumbai and beyond, with strong ties to global funding sources and networking opportunities. However, SPARC was born in 1984 in the specific context of work undertaken by its founders—principally a group of women trained in social work at the Tata Institute for the Social Sciences—among poor women in the neighborhood of Nagpada. This area has a diverse ethnic population and is located between the wealthiest parts of South Mumbai and the increasingly difficult slum areas of Central and North Mumbai.

Notable among SPARC's constituencies was a group of predominantly Muslim ex–sex trade workers from Central Mumbai who later became the cadre of another partner in the Alliance, Mahila Milan. The link between the two organizations dates to around 1986, when Mahila Milan was founded, with support from SPARC.

The link with the NSDF, an older and broader-based slum dwellers' organization, was also made in the late 1980s. The leadership of the three organizations cuts across the lines between Hindus, Muslims, and Christians and is explicitly secularist in outlook. In a general way, SPARC contributed technical knowledge and elite connections to state authorities and the private sector. NSDF, through its leader, Arputham Jockin (who himself has a background in the slums), and his activist colleagues, brought a radical brand of grassroots political organization in the form of the "federation" model, to be discussed later in this essay. Mahila Milan brought the strength of poor women who had learned the hard way how to deal with police, municipal authorities, slumlords, and real estate developers on the streets of Central Mumbai but had not previously had a real incentive to organize politically.

These three partners still have distinct styles, strategies, and functional characteristics. But they are committed to a partnership based on a shared ideology of risk, trust, negotiation, and learning among their key participants. They have also agreed upon a radical approach to the politicization of the urban poor that is fundamentally populist and anti-expert in strategy and flavor. The Alliance has evolved a style of pro-poor activism that consciously departs from earlier models of social work, welfarism, and community organization (an approach akin to that pioneered by Saul Alinsky in the United States). Instead of relying on the model of an outside organizer who teaches local communities how to hold the state to its normative obligations to the poor, the Alliance is committed to methods of organization, mobilization, teaching, and learning that build on what poor persons already know and understand. The first principle of this approach is that no one knows more about how to survive poverty than the poor themselves.

A crucial and controversial feature of this approach is its vision of politics without parties. The strategy of the Alliance is that it will not deliver the poor as a vote bank to any political party or candidate. This is a tricky business in Mumbai, where most grassroots organizations, notably unions, have a long history of direct affiliation with major political parties. Moreover, in Mumbai, the Shiva Sena, with its violent, street-level control of urban politics, does not easily tolerate neutrality. The Alliance deals with these difficulties by working with whoever is in power, at the federal and state level, within the municipality of Mumbai, or even at the local level of particular wards (municipal subunits). Thus the Alliance has elicited hostility from other activist groups in Mumbai for its willingness, when deemed necessary, to work with the Shiva Sena. But it is resolute about making the Shiva Sena work for its ends, not vice versa. Indeed, because it has consistently maintained an image of nonaffiliation with all political parties, the Alliance enjoys the double advantage of appearing nonpolitical while retaining access to the potential political power of the poorer half of Mumbai's population.

Instead of finding safety in affiliation with any single party or coalition in the state government of Maharashtra or the Municipal Corporation of Mumbai, the Alliance has developed a complex political affiliation with the various levels of the state bureaucracy. This group includes civil servants who conduct policy at the highest levels in the state of Maharashtra and run the major bodies responsible for housing loans, slum rehabilitation, real estate regulation, and the like. The members of the Alliance have also developed links with quasi-autonomous arms of the federal government, such as the railways, the Port Authority, and the Bombay Electric Supply and Transport Corporation, and with the municipal authorities who control critical elements of the infrastructure, such as the regulations governing illegal structures, the water supply, and sanitation. Finally, the Alliance works to maintain a cordial relationship with the Mumbai police—and at least a hands-off relationship with the underworld, which is deeply involved in housing finance, slum landlordism, and extortion as well as in the demolition and rebuilding of temporary structures.

From this perspective, the politics of the Alliance is a politics of accommodation, negotiation, and long-term pressure rather than of confrontation or threats of political reprisal. This realpolitik makes good sense in a city like Mumbai, where the supply of scarce urban infrastructure—housing and all its associated entitlements—is entangled in an immensely complicated web of slum rehabilitation projects, financing procedures, legislative precedents, and administrative codes which are interpreted differently, enforced unevenly, and whose actual delivery is almost always attended by an element of corruption.

This pragmatic approach is grounded in a complex political vision about means, ends, and styles that is not entirely utilitarian or functional. It is based on a series of ideas about the transformation of the conditions of poverty by the poor in the long run. In this sense, the figure of a political horizon is meant to point to a logic of patience, of cumulative victories and long-term asset building, that is wired into every aspect of the activities of the Alliance. The Alliance maintains that the mobilization of the knowledge of the poor into methods driven by the poor and for the poor is a slow and risk-laden process; this premise informs the group's strong bias against "projects" and "projectization" that underlies almost all official ideas about urban change. Whether the World Bank, most Northern donors, the Indian state, or other agencies, most institutional sources of funding are strongly biased in favor of the "project" model, in which short-term logics of investment, accounting, reporting, and assessment are regarded as vital. The Alliance has steadfastly advocated the importance of slow learning and cumulative change against the temporal logics of the project. Likewise, other strategies and tactics are also geared to long-term capacity building, the gradual gaining of knowledge and trust, the sifting of more from less reliable partners, and so on. This open and long-term temporal horizon is a difficult commitment to retain in the face of the urgency, and even desperation, that characterize the needs of Mumbai's urban poor. But it is a crucial normative guarantee against the ever-present risk, in all forms of grassroots activism, that the needs of funders will gradually obliterate the needs of the poor themselves.

Patience as a long-term political strategy is especially hard to maintain in view of two major forces. One is the constant barrage of real threats to life and space that frequently assail the urban poor. The most recent such episode was the massive demolition of shacks near the railroad tracks, which, since April 2000, has produced an intense struggle for survival and political mobilization in the midst of virtually impossible circumstances that at the time of this writing had yet to be resolved. In this sense, the strategies of the Alliance, which favor long-term asset building, run against the same "tyranny of emergency," in the words of Jérôme Bindé (2000), that characterizes the everyday lives of the urban poor.

The other force that makes patience hard to maintain is the built-in tension within the Alliance about different modes and methods of partnership. Not all members of the Alliance view the state, the market, or the donor world in the same way. Thus, every new occasion for funding, every new demand for a report, every new celebration of a possible partnership, every meeting with a railway official or an urban bureaucrat can create new sources of debate and anxiety within the Alliance. In the words of one key Alliance leader, negotiating these differences, rooted in deep diversities in class, experience, and personal style, is like "riding a tiger." It would be a mistake to view the pragmatic way in which all partnerships are approached by the Alliance as a simple politics of utility. It is a politics of patience, constructed against the tyranny of emergency.

To understand how this broad strategic vision is actually played out as a strategy of urban governmentality, we need to look a little more closely at some critical practices, discursive and organizational, by which the Alliance has consolidated its standing as a pro-poor movement in Mumbai.

As with all serious movements concerned with consciousness-changing and self-mobilization, there is a conscious effort to inculcate protocols of speech, style, and organizational form within the Alliance. The coalition cultivates a highly transparent, nonhierarchical, antibureaucratic, and antitechnocratic organizational style. A small clerical staff conscientiously serves the needs of the activists, not vice versa; meetings and discussions are often held with everyone sitting on mats on the floor. Food and drink are shared during meetings, and most official business (on the phone or face-to-face) is held in the midst of a tumult of other activities in crowded offices. A constant undercurrent of bawdy humor runs through the members' discussions of problems, partners, and their own affairs. Conversation is almost always in Hindi, Marathi, or Tamil, or in English interspersed with one of these Indian languages. The leadership is at pains to make its ideas known among its members and to the residents of the actual slum communities who are, in effect, the coalition's rank and file. Almost no internal request for information about the organization, its funding, its planning, or related matters is considered out of order. Naturally, there are private conversations, hidden tensions, and real differences of personality and strategy at all levels. But these are not validated or legitimated in bureaucratic protocols or organizational charts.

This style of organization and management produces constant tensions among members of the Alliance and various outside bodies—donors, state institutions, regulators—which frequently demand more formal norms of organization, accounting, and reporting. To a very considerable extent the brunt of this stress is borne by SPARC, which has an office in Central Mumbai where the formal bureaucratic links to the world of law, accountancy, and reporting are largely centralized. This office serves partly to insulate the other two partners, NSDF and Mahila Milan, from the needs of externally mandated bookkeeping, fund management, reporting, and public legal procedures. The latter two organizations have their own headquarters in the compound of a municipal dispensary in Byculla. This office is in the heart of a slum world where many of the core members of Mahila Milan actually live, an area in which Muslims are a major presence, and the sex trades, the criminal world, and petty commerce are highly visible. The office is always filled with men and women from the communities of slum dwellers that are the backbone of the Alliance. There is constant movement among key personnel between this office, the SPARC office in Khetwadi, and the outlying new suburbs where the Alliance is building transit facilities or new houses for its members—Dharavi, Mankhurd, and Ghatkopar.

The phones are in constant use as key members of the Alliance exchange information about breaking crises, plans, and news across these various locations in Mumbai—and also across India and the world. Every few hours during an average day, a phone rings at one of these offices and turns out to be one of the members of the Alliance checking on or tracking down something—a call is as likely to come from Phnom Penh or Cape Town as from Mankhurd or Byculla. Because everyday organizational life is filled with meetings with contractors, lawyers, state officials, and politicians as well as among Alliance members, spatial fixity is not valued and the organization functions in and through mobility. In this context, the telephone and e-mail play an increasingly vital role. The key leaders of the Alliance, with a few significant exceptions, either use e-mail or have access to it through close colleagues. The phones are constantly ringing. Schedules shift at the drop of a hat as travel plans are adjusted to meet emergent opportunities or to address the presence or absence of key members. The general impression is of a fast game of ice hockey, with players constantly tumbling in and out of the most active roles in response to shifting needs and game plans.

Nevertheless, through experiences and discussions that have evolved over fifteen years (and, in some cases, more), there is a steady effort to remember and reproduce certain crucial principles and norms that offset organizational fluidity and the pressures of daily crises. These norms and practices require a much more detailed discussion than I can give in the current context, but some impression of them is vital to understanding the political horizon of this form of deep democracy.

Possibly the central norm is embodied in a common usage among the members of the Alliance and its partners around the world. It is the term *federation*, used as a noun, or *federate* and *federated*, used as verbs. This innocuous term from elementary political science textbooks has a special meaning and magic for the Alliance. At its foundation is the idea of individuals and families self-organizing as members of a political collective to pool resources, organize lobbying, provide mutual risk-management devices, and confront opponents, when necessary. Members of the Alliance often judge the effectiveness of other NGOs, in India and elsewhere, by reference to whether or not they have learned the virtues of federating. The National Slum Dwellers' Federation is clearly their own model of this norm. As an image of organization, it is significant in two ways. It emphasizes the importance of political union among already preexisting collectives (thus federating, rather than simply uniting, joining, and lobbying). And it mirrors the structure of the Indian national state, which is referred to as the Indian Union, but is in fact a federal model whose constituent states retain extensive powers.

In the usage of the Alliance, the idea of federation is a constant reminder that groups (even at the level of families) that have a claim to political agency on their own have chosen to combine their political and material power. The primacy of the principle of federation also serves to remind all members, particularly the trained professionals, that the power of the Alliance lies not in its donors, its technical expertise, or its administration, but in the will to federate among poor families and communities. At another level, the image of the federation asserts the primacy of the poor in driving their own politics, however much others may help them to do so. There is a formal property to membership in the federation, and members of the Alliance maintain ongoing debates about recruiting slum families, neighborhoods, and communities in Mumbai (and elsewhere in India) that are not yet part of the federation. For as long as the latter remain outside, they cannot participate in the active politics of savings, housing, resettlement, and rehabilitation that are the bread and butter of the Alliance.

Savings is another term that takes on a special meaning in Alliance usage. Creating informal savings groups among the poor—a process that the donor establishment has recognized under the term *microcredit*—is a current technique for improving financial citizenship for the urban and rural poor throughout the world. Often building on older models of revolving credit and loan facilities that are managed informally and locally, outside the purview of the state and the banking sector, microcredit has its advocates and visionaries in India and elsewhere. But in the life of the Alliance, savings has a profound ideological, even salvational, status. The architect of the Alliance philosophy of savings is the NSDF's Jockin, who has used savings as a principal tool for mobilization in India and as an entry point to relationship building in South Africa, Cambodia, and Thailand. He sees daily savings as the bedrock of all federation activities; indeed, it is not an exaggeration to say that in Jockin's organizational exhortations, wherever he goes, federation equals savings. When Jockin and his colleagues in the Alliance speak about savings, it becomes evident that they are describing something far deeper than a simple mechanism for meeting daily monetary needs and sharing resources among the poor. Seen by them as something akin to a spiritual practice, daily savings—and its spread—is conceived as the key to the local and global success of the federation model.

In this connection, it may be noted that Mahila Milan, the women's group within the Alliance, is focused almost entirely on organizing small savings circles. By putting savings at the core of the politics of the Alliance, its leaders are making the work of poor women fundamental to what can be achieved in every other area. It is a simple formula: Without poor women joining together, there can be no savings. Without savings, there can be no federating. Without federating, there is no way for the poor themselves to enact change in the arrangements that disempower them. What is important to recognize here is that when Alliance leaders speak about a way of life organized around the practice of saving—in Jockin's words, it is like "breathing"—they are framing saving as a moral discipline. The practice builds a certain kind of political fortitude and commitment to the collective good and creates persons who can manage their affairs in many other ways as well. Daily savings, which do not generate large resources quickly, can therefore form the moral core of a politics of patience.

A final key term that recurs in the writing and speech of the leaders of the Alliance is *precedent-setting*. I am still exploring the ramifications of this strategic locution. What I have learned so far is that underlying its bland, quasi-legal tone is a more radical idea: that the poor need to claim, refine, and define certain ways of doing things in spaces they already control and then use these practices to show donors, city officials, and other activists that their "precedents" are good ones and encourage such actors to invest further in them. This is a politics of show-and-tell, but it is also a philosophy of do first, talk later. The subversive feature of this principle is that it provides a linguistic device for negotiating between the legalities of urban government and the "illegal" arrangements to which the poor almost always have to resort, whether the illegality in question pertains to structures, living strategies, or access to water, electricity, or anything else that has been successfully siphoned out of the material resources of the city.

Precedent-setting moves practices such as these, along with new techniques for accessing food, health services, police protection, and work opportunities, into a zone of quasi-legal negotiation. By invoking the concept of precedent as enshrined in English common law, the linguistic device shifts the burden for municipal officials and other experts away from a dubious whitewashing of illegal activities to a building on "legitimate" precedents. The linguistic strategy of precedent-setting thus turns the survival tactics and experiments of the poor into sites for policy innovations by the state, the city, donor agencies, and other activist organizations. It is a strategy that moves the poor into the horizon of legality on their own terms. Most important, it invites risk-taking activities by bureaucrats within a discourse of legality, allowing the boundaries of the status quo to be pushed and stretched—it creates a border zone of trial and error, a sort of research and development space within which poor communities, activists, and bureaucrats can explore new designs for partnership.

But the world is not changed through language alone. These key words (and many other linguistic strategies not discussed here) can be positioned as the nervous system of a whole body of broader technical, institutional, and representational practices that have become signatures of the Alliance's politics. Here, I will briefly discuss three vital organizational strategies that illustrate the ways in which technical practices are harnessed to the Alliance's political horizon. They are: self-surveys and enumeration; housing exhibitions; and toilet festivals.

Contemporary scholars, led by Michel Foucault, have drawn attention to the use of censuses and other techniques of enumeration by political regimes from the seventeenth century onward; Foucault and others have indeed observed that the modern state and the idea of a countable population are historical co-productions, premised alike on distinctively modern constructions of governance, territory, and citizenship. Censuses are salient among the techniques identified by Foucault (1979) as lying at the heart of modern governmentality. Tied up by their nature with the state (note the etymological link with statistics) and its methods of classification and surveillance, censuses remain essential instruments of every modern state archive. They are highly politicized processes, whose results are usually available only in packaged form and whose procedures are always driven from above, even when many members of the population are enlisted in the actual gathering of data. Given this background, it seems all the more remarkable that, without adherence to any articulated theory of governmentality—or opposition to it—the Alliance has adopted a conscious strategy of self-enumeration and self-surveying. Alliance members are taught a variety of methods of gathering reliable and complete data about households and families in their own communities. Codifying these techniques for ease of use by its members in the form of a series of practical tips, the Alliance has created a revolutionary system that we may well call governmentality from below.

Not only has it placed self-surveying at the heart of its own archive, the Alliance is also keenly aware of the power that this kind of knowledge—and ability—gives it in its dealings with local and central state organizations (as well as with multilateral agencies and other regulatory bodies). The leverage bestowed by such information is particularly acute in places like Mumbai, where a host of local, state-level, and federal entities exist with a mandate to rehabilitate or ameliorate slum life. But none of them knows exactly who the slum dwellers are, where they live, or how they are to be identified. This fact is of central relevance to the politics of knowledge in which the Alliance is perennially engaged. All state-sponsored slum policies have an abstract slum population as their target and no knowledge of its concrete, human components. Since these populations are socially, legally, and spatially marginal—invisible citizens, as it were—they are by definition uncounted and uncountable, except in the most general terms.

By rendering them statistically visible to themselves, the Alliance comes into control of a central piece of any actual policy process—the knowledge of exactly which individuals live where, how they make their livelihood, how long they have lived there, and so forth. Given that some of the most crucial pieces of recent legislation affecting slum dwellers in Mumbai tie security of tenure to the date from which occupancy of a piece of land or a structure can be demonstrated, such information collection is vital to any official effort to relocate and rehabilitate slum populations.

At the same time, the creation and use of self-surveys are a powerful tool for the practice of democracy internally, since the principal form of evidence used by the Alliance to support slum dwellers' claims to space is the testimony of neighbors, as opposed to forms of documentation such as rent receipts, ration cards, electric meter readings, and other civic insignia of occupancy that can be used by the more securely housed classes in the city. The very absence of these amenities opens the door to radical techniques of mutual identification in the matter of location and legitimacy for slum dwellers. For, as Alliance leaders are the first to admit, the poor are not immune to greed, conflict, and jealousy, and there are always slum families who are prepared to lie or cheat to advance themselves in the context of crisis or new opportunities. Such problems are resolved by informal mechanisms in which the testimony of neighbors is utterly decisive, since the social life of slums is in fact characterized by an almost complete lack of privacy. Here, perpetual social visibility within the community (and invisibility in the eyes of the state) becomes an asset that enables the mechanisms of self-monitoring, self-enumerating, and self-regulation to operate at the nexus of family, land, and dwelling that is the central site of material negotiations in slum life.

To those familiar with Foucault's ideas, this may seem to be a worrisome form of autogovernmentality, a combination of self-surveillance and self-enumeration, truly insidious in its capillary reach. But my own view is that this sort of governmentality from below, in the world of the urban poor, is a kind of countergovernmentality, animated by the social relations of shared poverty, by the excitement of active participation in the politics of knowledge, and by its own openness to correction through other forms of intimate knowledge and spontaneous everyday politics. In short, this is governmentality turned against itself.

Housing exhibitions are the second organized technique through which the structural bias of existing knowledge processes is challenged, even reversed, in the politics of the Alliance. Since the materialities of housing—its cost, its durability, its legality, and its design—are of fundamental concern to slum life, it is no surprise that this is an area where grassroots creativity has had radical effects. As in other matters, the general philosophy of state agencies, donors, and even NGOs concerned with slums has been to assume that the design, construction, and financing of houses require the involvement of various experts and knowledge professionals, ranging from engineers and architects to contractors and surveyors. The Alliance has challenged this assumption by a steady effort to appropriate, in a cumulative manner, all the knowledge required to construct new housing for its members. This has involved some extraordinary negotiations in Mumbai, involving private developers and contractors, the formation of legal cooperatives by the poor, innovations in urban law pushed by the Alliance, new types of arrangements in housing finance between banks, donors, and the poor themselves, and direct negotiations over housing materials, costs, and building schedules. In effect, in Mumbai, the Alliance has moved into housing development, and the fruits of this remarkable move are to be seen at three major sites, in Mankhurd, Dharavi, and Ghatkopar. One of these, the Rajiv-Indira Housing Cooperative in Dharavi, is a major building exercise that stands as a decisive demonstration of the Alliance's ability to put the actual families who will occupy these dwellings at the center of a process where credit, design, budgeting, construction, and legality come together. It is difficult to exaggerate the complexity of such negotiations, which pose a challenge even for wealthy developers because of the maze of laws, agencies, and political interests (including those of the criminal underworld) that surrounds any housing enterprise in Mumbai.

Housing exhibitions are a crucial part of this reversal of the standard flows of expert knowledge. The idea of housing exhibitions by and for the poor goes back to 1986 in Mumbai and has since been replicated in many other cities in India and elsewhere in the world. The exhibitions organized by the Alliance and other like-minded groups are an example of the creative hijacking of an upper-class form—historically developed for the display of consumer goods and high-end industrial products—for the purposes of the poor.

Not only have these exhibitions enabled the poor, especially poor women, to discuss and debate designs for housing that suit their own needs, they have also allowed the poor to enter into conversations with various professionals about housing materials, construction costs, and urban services. Through this process, slum dwellers' own ideas of the good life, of adequate space, and of realistic costs were foregrounded, and they began to see that professional housing construction was only a logical extension of their own area of greatest expertise—namely, building adequate housing out of the flimsiest of materials and in the most insecure of circumstances. Poor families were enabled to see that they had always been architects and engineers and could continue to play these roles in the building of more secure housing. In this process, many technical and design innovations were made, and continue to be made. Perhaps more significantly, the exhibitions have been political events bringing together poor families and activists from different cities in order to socialize, share ideas, and simply have fun. State officials also are invited, to cut the ceremonial ribbon and give speeches in which they associate themselves with these grassroots exercises, thus simultaneously gaining points for hobnobbing with "the people" while giving poor families in the locality some legitimacy in the eyes of their neighbors, civic authorities, and themselves.

As with other key practices of the Alliance, housing exhibitions are deep exercises in subverting the existing class cultures of India. By performing their competencies in public, by addressing an audience of their peers and of representatives of the state, other NGOs, and sometimes foreign funders, the poor families involved enter a space of public sociality, official recognition, and technical legitimation. And they do so with their own creativity as the main exhibit. Thus technical and cultural capital are generated collaboratively by these events, creating leverage for further guerrilla exercises in capturing civic space and areas of the public sphere hitherto denied them. At work here is a politics of visibility that inverts the harmful default condition of civic invisibility that characterizes the urban poor.

Running through all these activities is a spirit of transgression and bawdiness expressed through body language, speech styles, and public address. The men and women of the Alliance are involved in constant banter with one another and even with the official world (although with some care for context). Nowhere is this carnivalesque spirit displayed more clearly than in the toilet festivals (*sandas mela*) organized by the Alliance, which enact what we may call the politics of shit.

Human waste management, as it is euphemistically termed in policy circles, is perhaps the key issue where every problem of the urban poor arrives at a single point of extrusion, so to speak. Given the abysmal housing, often with almost no privacy, that most urban slum dwellers endure, shitting in public is a serious humiliation for adults. Children are indifferent up to a certain age, but no adult, male or female, enjoys shitting in broad daylight in public view. In rural India, women go to the fields to defecate while it is still dark; men may go later, but nevertheless with some measure of protection from the eyes of the public (with the exception of the railway passengers, inured to the sight of the squatting bodies in the fields, whose attitude is reciprocated). But the fact is that rural shitting is managed through a completely different economy of space, water, visibility, and custom from that prevailing in cities, where the problem is much more serious.

Shitting in the absence of good sewerage systems, ventilation, and running water—all of which, by definition, slums lack—is not only humiliating, it also enables the conditions under which waterborne diseases take hold and thus is potentially life-threatening. One macabre joke among Mumbai's urban poor is that they are the only ones in the city who cannot afford to get diarrhea. Lines at the few existing public toilets are often so long that the wait is an hour or more, and of course medical facilities for stemming the condition are also hard to find. In short, shitting and its management are a central issue of slum life. Living in an ecology of fecal odors, piles, and channels, where cooking water, washing water, and shit-bearing water are not carefully segregated, adds material health risks to the symbolic risks incurred by shitting in public view.

The toilet festivals organized by the Alliance in many cities of India are a brilliant effort to resituate this private act of humiliation and suffering as the scene of technical innovation, collective celebration, and carnivalesque play with officials from the state, the World Bank, and middle-class officialdom in general. The toilet festivals feature the exhibition and inauguration not of models, but of functioning public toilets designed by and for the poor, incorporating complex systems of collective payment and maintenance with optimal conditions of safety and cleanliness. These facilities are currently small scale and have not yet been built in anything like the large numbers required for India's slum populations. But they represent another performance of competence and innovation in which the politics of shit is (to mix metaphors) turned on its head, and humiliation and victimization are transformed into exercises in technical initiative and self-dignification.

This is nothing less than a politics of recognition (Taylor 1992) from below. When a World Bank official has to examine the virtues of a public toilet and discuss the merits of this form of shit management with the shitters themselves, the condition of poverty moves from abjection to subjectivation. The politics of shit—as Gandhi showed in his own efforts to liberate the lowest castes, whom he called Harijans, from the task of hauling upper-caste ordure—presents a node at which concerns of the human body, dignity, and technology meet, a nexus the poor are now redefining with the help of movements like the Alliance. In India, where distance from one's own excrement can be seen as the virtual marker of class distinction, the poor, for too long having lived literally in their own shit, are finding ways to place some distance between their waste and themselves. The toilet exhibitions are a transgressive display of this fecal politics, itself a critical material feature of deep democracy.

In June 2001, at a major meeting held at the United Nations to mark the five years that had passed since the 1996 Conference on Human Settlements in Istanbul, the Alliance and its international partners built a model house as well as a model children's toilet in the lobby of the main UN building. The models—which were erected only after considerable internal debate within the Shack/Slum Dwellers International (SDI) and official resistance at the UN—were visited by Secretary-General Kofi Annan in a festive atmosphere that left an indelible impression on the officials of the UN and other NGOs who were present. Annan was surrounded by poor women from India and South Africa who sang and danced as he walked through the model house and toilet that had been placed in the heart of his own bureaucratic empire. It was a magical moment, full of possibilities for the Alliance, and for the secretary-general, as they engage jointly with the politics of global poverty. Housing exhibitions and toilets, too, can be built, moved, refabricated, and deployed anywhere, thus sending the message that no space is too grand—or too humble—for the spatial imagination of the poor.

These organized practices sustain one another. Self-surveys form the basis of claims to new housing and justify its exhibition; model housing built without due attention to toilets and fecal management makes no sense. Each of these methods uses the knowledge of the poor to leverage expert knowledge, redeems humiliation through a politics of recognition, and enables the deepening of democracy among the poor themselves. And each of them adds energy and purpose to the others. They enact public dramas in which the moral directives to federate, to save, and to set precedents are made material, refined, and revalidated. In this way, key words and deeds shape one another, permitting some leveling of the field of knowledge, turning sites of shame into dramas of inclusion, and allowing the poor to work their way into the public sphere and visible citizenship without resort to open confrontation or public violence.

The International Horizon

The larger study of which this essay is a part is concerned with the way in which transnational advocacy networks, associations of grassroots NGOs, are in the process of internationalizing themselves, thus creating networks of globalization from below. We have seen such networks mobilized most recently in Seattle, Prague, Göteborg, and Washington, D.C. But they have been visible for some time in global struggles over gender issues, the environment, human rights, child labor, and the rights of indigenous cultures. More recently, there has been a renewed effort to link grassroots activists in such diverse areas as violence against women, the rights of refugees and immigrants, the employment of sweat-shop labor by multinational corporations, indigenous peoples' claims to intellectual property, the production and consumption of popular media, mediation between combatants in civil conflicts, and many other issues. The underlying question for many of these movements is: How can they organize transnationally without sacrificing their local projects? When they do build transnational networks, what are their greatest assets and their greatest handicaps? At a deeper political level, can the mobility of capital and new information technologies be contained by, and made accountable to, the ethos and purpose of local democratic projects? Put another way, can there be a new design for global governance that mediates the speed of capital, the power of states, and the profoundly local nature of actually existing democracies?

These large questions go beyond the scope of this essay, and the detailed analysis of the efforts to globalize from below of this activist network, and others like it, must be left for another occasion. But a brief account of this global context is certainly in order. For more than a decade the Alliance in Mumbai has been an active part of a transnational network concerned with "horizontal learning," sharing, and exchanging. Given official form as the Shack/Slum Dwellers International, or SDI, in 1996, the network includes federations in fourteen countries on four continents. The process that led to this formalization goes back to the mid-1980s. Links among federations of the poor in South Africa, India, and Thailand appear to have been the most vital in the gradual building of these grassroots exchanges and, to a considerable extent, still are. Key to these exchanges are visits by groups of slum or shack dwellers to one another's settlements in other countries to share in ongoing local projects, give and receive advice and reactions, share in work and life experiences, and exchange tactics and plans. The mode of exchange is based on a model of seeing and hearing rather than of teaching and learning; of sharing experiences and knowledge rather than seeking to impose standard practices, key words being *exposure*, *exploration*, and *options*. By now, a large body of practical wisdom has accrued about how and when these exchanges work best, and this knowledge is constantly being refined. Visits by small groups from one city to another, either within the same or to another region, usually involve immediate immersion in the ongoing projects of the host community. These range from scavenging in the Philippines and sewer digging in Pakistan to women's savings activities in South Africa and housing exhibitions in India.

These horizontal exchanges now function at four levels. First, they provide a circulatory counterpart to the building of deep democracies locally. By visiting and hosting other activists concerned with similar problems, communities gain a comparative perspective and provide a measure of legitimation for external efforts. Thus, activist leaders struggling for recognition and space in their own localities may find themselves able to gain state and media attention for their local struggles in other countries and towns, where their presence as visitors carries a certain cachet. The fact that they are visiting as members of some sort of international federation further sharpens this image. In fact, local politicians feel less threatened by visitors than by their own activists and sometimes open themselves to new ideas because they come from outside.

Second, the horizontal visits arranged by the federations increasingly carry the imprimatur of powerful international organizations and funders such as the World Bank, state development ministries, and private charities from the Netherlands, England, the United States, and Germany, and increasingly involve political and philanthropic actors from other countries as well. These visits, designed and organized by the poor in their own communities and public spaces, become signs to local politicians that the poor themselves have cosmopolitan links—a factor that increases their prestige in local political negotiations.

Third, the occasions that these exchanges provide for face-to-face meetings between key leaders in, for example, Mumbai, Cape Town, and Bangkok actually allow them to progress rapidly in making more long-term strategic plans for funding, capacity building, and what they call *scaling up*, which is now perhaps their central aim. That is, having mastered how to do certain things on a small scale, they are eager to expand onto a broader canvas, seeking collective ways of making a dent in the vast range of problems shared by slum dwellers in different cities. In a parallel movement, they are also exploring ways of *speeding up*, by which they mean shortening the times involved in putting strategies into practice in different national and urban locations.

There is some evidence that speeding up through horizontal learning is somewhat easier than scaling up. In support of the latter goal, the core SDI leadership is working on ways to build a transnational funding mechanism that will reduce the federations' dependence on existing multilateral and private sources, putting even long-term funding in the hands of the SDI so as to free its members further from the agendas of project planners, donors, states, and other actors, whose aims can never be quite the same as those of the urban poor. Elements of such a mechanism exist among the South African and Thai members of the SDI, but the structure is yet to be realized on a fully global scale. That will require the current leadership of SDI to proceed with a demanding mixture of political cooperation, willingness to negotiate, and stubbornness of vision in their dialogues with the major funders of the battle against urban poverty worldwide. The objective of creating a worldwide fund controlled by a pro-poor activist network is the logical extension of a politics of patience combined with a politics of visibility and self-empowerment. It is directly pitched against the politics of charity, training, and projectization long recognized as the standard solution. As such, it represents a formidable wager on the capacities of the poor to create large-scale, high-speed, reliable mechanisms for the change of conditions that affect them globally. The proposal for a coordinated funding mechanism inaugurates a new vision for equalizing material resources and knowledge at one stroke. The self-organization of this network is very much in process and constitutes an ongoing experiment in globalization from below and in deep democracy.

The fourth, and most important, level at which the traffic among local and national units functions within the Shack/Slum Dwellers International is that of the circulation of internal critical debate. When members of the SDI meet in one another's localities (as well as on other occasions, such as meetings in London, New York, or the Hague), they have the occasion to raise hard questions about inclusion, power, hierarchy, and political risk or naïveté in their host's local and regional organizations. This is because their role as outsiders allows for frank questions, based on real or rhetorical ignorance—questions that would frequently be regarded as unacceptable coming from closer quarters.

Who handles the money? Why are there not more women at the meeting? Why are you being so nice to the city officials who oppress you? How do you deal with defaulters on small loans? Who is doing the real work? Who is getting the perks of foreign travel? Why are we staying in one kind of hotel and you in another? Why are some poor people in your city for you and others against you? Why did your savings group start falling apart? Are you happy with this or that leader? Is someone getting too big for his boots? Are we beginning to take up partnerships that might fail us in the long run? When we agree to a global agenda, which national partner is really setting it? How far should we go in trusting each other's intuitions about partners, strategies, and priorities?

These are some of the tough questions that are asked by friendly but skeptical visitors, and usually answered frankly by the local hosts. And when the answers are weak or unsatisfying, they continue to reverberate in the locality, long after the visitors have returned to their home communities. This critical exchange is a long-term asset, a vital part of globalization from below. The visits—and the e-mails that sustain the interims—incorporate a crucial dimension through which the challenge of facing internal criticism can be mediated: distance. The global network of poor communities turns out to be, among other things, a constant source of critical questions about theory and practice, a flow of irritating queries, doubts, and pauses. But coming from a distance, they sound less harsh than the same queries when they come from local opponents. At the same time, coming from communities equally poor, their moral urgency cannot be ignored.

It is this last consideration that now allows us to return to the relations among risk, creativity, and depth in the democratic experiments of the Alliance and its global network, the SDI. The Alliance and the transnational network of which it is a part belong to a group of nongovernmental actors that have decided to opt for various sorts of partnerships with other, more powerful actors—including the state, in its various levels and incarnations—to achieve its goals: to gain secure housing and urban infrastructure for the urban poor, in Mumbai, in other parts of India, and beyond. In opting for the politics of partnership, such movements consciously undertake certain risks. One is the risk that their partners may not hold even some moral goals in common with them. Another is that the hard-won mobilization of certain groups of the urban poor may not be best invested as political capital in partnership arrangements, as opposed to confrontation or violence.

And there is an even larger gamble involved in this strategy. This is the gamble that the official world of multilateral agencies, Northern funders, and Southern governments can be persuaded that the poor are the best drivers of shared solutions to the problems of poverty. What is at stake here is all the energy that has been invested in setting precedents for partnership at all levels, from the ward to the world. The hoped-for payoff is that, once mobilized and empowered by such partnerships, the poor themselves will prove more capable than the usual candidates—the market, the state, or the world of development funding—of scaling up and speeding up their own disappearance as a global category. In the end, this is a political wager on the relationship between the circulation of knowledge and material equalization, and about the best ways to accelerate it.

In making this wager, activist groups like the Alliance in Mumbai and its global counterparts are also striving to redefine what governance and governmentality can mean. They approach their partners on an ad hoc basis, taking advantage in particular of the dispersed nature of the state as an apparatus of local, regional, and national bodies to advance their long-term aims and form multilateral relationships. Moreover, in a country like India, where poverty reduction is a directive principle of the national constitution and the tradition of social reform and public service is woven into nationalism itself, the Alliance can play the politics of conscience to considerable effect. But even then, it hedges its bets through practices of building on, sharing, and multiplying knowledge—strategic practices that increase its hold on public resources.

Conclusion: Deep Democracy

One of the many paradoxes of democracy is that it is organized to function within the boundaries of the nation-state—through such organs as legislatures, judiciaries, and elected governments—to realize one or another image of the common good or general will. Yet its values make sense only when they are conceived and deployed universally, which is to say, when they are global in reach. Thus, the institutions of democracy and its cardinal values rest on an antinomy. In the era of globalization, this contradiction rises to the surface as the porousness of national boundaries becomes apparent and the monopoly of national governments over global governance becomes increasingly embattled.

Efforts to enact or revive democratic principles have generally taken two forms in the period since 1970, which many agree is the beginning of globalization (or of the current era of globalization, for those who wish to write globalization into the whole of human history). One form is to take advantage of the speed of communications and the sweep of global markets to force national governments to recognize universal democratic principles within their own jurisdictions. Much of the politics of human rights takes this form. The second form, more fluid and quixotic, is the sort that I have described here. It constitutes an effort to institute what we may call "democracy without borders," after the analogy of international class solidarity as conceived by the visionaries of world socialism in its heyday. This effort is what I seek to theorize in terms of deep democracy.

In terms of its semantics, *deep democracy* suggests roots, anchors, intimacy, proximity, and locality. And these are important associations. Much of this essay has been taken up with values and strategies that have just this quality. They are about such traditional democratic desiderata as inclusion, participation, transparency, and accountability, as articulated within an activist formation. But I want to suggest that the lateral reach of such movements—their efforts to build international networks or coalitions of some durability with their counterparts across national boundaries—is also a part of their "depth."

This lateral or horizontal dimension, which I have touched upon in terms of the activities of the Shack/Slum Dwellers International, seeks direct collaborations and exchanges among poor communities based on the "will to federate." But what gives this cross-national politics its depth is not just its circulatory logic of spreading ideas of savings, housing, citizenship, and participation "without borders" and outside the direct reach of state or market regimes. Depth is also to be located in the fact that, where successful, the spread of this model produces poor communities able to engage in partnerships with more powerful agencies—urban, regional, national, and multilateral—that purport to be concerned with poverty and citizenship. In this second sense, what these horizontal movements produce is a series of *stronger* community-based partners for institutional agencies charged with realizing inclusive democracy and poverty reduction. This in turn increases the capability of these communities to perform more powerfully as instruments of deep democracy in the local context. The cycles of transactions—both vertical (local/national) and horizontal (transnational/global)—are enriched by the process of criticism by members of one federated community, in the context of exchange and learning, about the internal democracy of another. Thus, internal criticism and debate, horizontal exchange and learning, and vertical collaborations and partnerships with more powerful persons and organizations together form a mutually sustaining cycle of processes. This is where depth and laterality become joint circuits along which pro-poor strategies can flow.

This form of deep democracy, the vertical fulcrum of a democracy without borders, cannot be assumed to be automatic, easy, or immune to setbacks. Like all serious exercises in democratic practice, it is not automatically reproductive. It has particular conditions of possibility and conditions under which it grows weak or corrupt. The study of these conditions—which include such contingencies as leadership, morale, flexibility, and material enablement—requires many more case studies of specific movements and organizations. For those concerned with poverty and citizenship, we can begin by recalling that one crucial condition of possibility for deep democracy is the ability to meet emergency with patience.

Arjun Appadurai is Samuel N. Harper Distinguished Service Professor of Anthropology and South Asian Languages and Civilizations at the University of Chicago. His recent publications include "Grassroots Globalization and the Research Imagination" (*Public Culture*, winter 2000) and "New Logics of Violence" (*Seminar*, July 2001).

References

Appadurai, Arjun. 1996. *Modernity at large: Cultural dimensions of globalization*. Minneapolis: University of Minnesota Press.

———. 2000. Grassroots globalization and the research imagination. *Public Culture* 12: 1–19.

———. 2001. Spectral housing and urban cleansing: Notes on millennial Mumbai. *Public Culture* 12: 627–51.

Appadurai, Arjun, and Holston, James. 1999. Introduction: Cities and citizenship. In *Cities and citizenship*, edited by Holston. Durham, N.C.: Duke University Press.

Bindé, Jérôme. 2000. Toward an ethics of the future. *Public Culture* 12: 51–72.

Castells, Manuel. 1996. *The rise of the network society*. Cambridge, Mass.: Blackwell.

Foucault, Michel. 1979. Governmentality. In *The Foucault effect: Studies in governmentality: With two lectures by and an interview with Michel Foucault*, edited by Graham Burchell, Colin Gordon, and Peter Miller. Chicago: University of Chicago Press.

Giddens, Anthony. 2000. *Runaway world: How globalization is reshaping our lives*. New York: Routledge.

Habermas, Jürgen. 1975. *Legitimation crisis*, translated by Thomas McCarthy. Boston: Beacon.

Held, David. 1995. *Democracy and the global order: From the modern state to cosmopolitan governance*. Stanford, Calif.: Stanford University Press.

Keck, Margaret E., and Kathryn Sikkink. 1998. *Activists beyond borders: Advocacy networks in international politics*. Ithaca, N.Y.: Cornell University Press.

Pendse, Sandeep. 1995. Toil, sweat and the city. In *Bombay: Metaphor for modern India*, edited by Sujata Patel and Alice Thorner. Bombay: Oxford University Press.

Rosenau, James N. 1997. *Along the domestic-foreign frontier: Exploring governance in a turbulent world*. Cambridge: Cambridge University Press.

Sassen, Saskia. 2000. Spatialities and temporalities of the global: Elements for a theorization. *Public Culture* 12: 215–32.

Taylor, Charles. 1992. The politics of recognition. In *Multiculturalism and "The politics of recognition,"* edited by Amy Gutmann and Charles Taylor. Princeton, N.J.: Princeton University Press.

Publics and Counterpublics

Michael Warner

This essay has a public. If you are reading (or hearing) this, you are part of its public. So first let me say: Welcome. Of course, you might stop reading (or leave the room), and someone else might start (or enter). Would the public of this essay therefore be different? Would it ever be possible to know anything about the public to which, I hope, you still belong?

What is a public? It is a curiously obscure question, considering that few things have been more important in the development of modernity. Publics have become an essential fact of the social landscape, and yet it would tax our understanding to say exactly what they are. Several senses of the noun *public* tend to be intermixed in usage. People do not always distinguish between *the* public and *a* public, although in some contexts this difference can matter a great deal.

The public is a kind of social totality. Its most common sense is that of the people in general. It might be the people organized as the nation, the commonwealth, the city, the state, or some other community. It might be very general, as in Christendom or humanity. But in each case the public, as a people, is thought to include everyone within the field in question. This sense of totality is brought out in speaking of the public, even though to speak of a national public implies that others exist; there must be as many publics as polities, but whenever one is addressed as *the* public, the others are assumed not to matter.

This essay has been abridged from the title essay of the volume *Publics and Counterpublics*, forthcoming from Zone Books. I thank the Center for Transcultural Studies.

Public Culture 14(1): 49–90

A public can also be a second thing: a concrete audience, a crowd witnessing itself in visible space, as with a theatrical public. Such a public also has a sense of totality, bounded by the event or by the shared physical space. A performer on stage knows where her public is, how big it is, where its boundaries are, and what the time of its common existence is. A crowd at a sports event, a concert, or a riot might be a bit blurrier around the edges, but still knows itself by knowing where and when it is assembled in common visibility and common action.

I will return to both of these senses, but what I mainly want to clarify in this essay is a third sense of *public*: the kind of public that comes into being only in relation to texts and their circulation—like the public of this essay. (Nice to have you with us, still.) The distinctions among these three senses are not always sharp and are not simply the difference between oral and written contexts. When an essay is read aloud as a lecture at a university, for example, the concrete audience of hearers understands itself as standing in for a more indefinite audience of readers. And often, when a form of discourse is not addressing an institutional or subcultural audience, such as members of a profession, its audience can understand itself not just as *a* public but as *the* public. In such cases, different senses of audience and circulation are in play at once. Examples like this suggest that it is worth understanding the distinctions better, if only because the transpositions among them can have important social effects.

The idea of *a* public, as distinct from both *the* public and any bounded audience, has become part of the common repertoire of modern culture. Everyone intuitively understands how it works. On reflection, however, its rules can seem rather odd. I would like to bring some of our intuitive understanding into the open in order to speculate about the history of the form and the role it plays in constructing our social world.

1. A public is self-organized.

A public is a space of discourse organized by nothing other than discourse itself. It is autotelic; it exists only as the end for which books are published, shows broadcast, Web sites posted, speeches delivered, opinions produced. It exists *by virtue of being addressed.*

A kind of chicken-and-egg circularity confronts us in the idea of a public. Could anyone speak publicly without addressing a public? But how can this public exist before being addressed? What would a public be if no one were addressing it? Can a public really exist apart from the rhetoric through which it is imagined? If you were to put down this essay and turn on the television, would my public be different? How can the existence of a public depend, from one point of view, on the rhetorical address—and, from another point of view, on the real context of reception?

These questions cannot be resolved on one side or the other. The circularity is essential to the phenomenon. A public might be real and efficacious, but its reality lies in just this reflexivity by which an addressable object is conjured into being in order to enable the very discourse that gives it existence.

A public in this sense is as much notional as empirical. It is also partial, since there could be an infinite number of publics within the social totality. This sense of the term is completely modern; it is the only kind of public for which there is no other term. Neither *crowd* nor *audience* nor *people* nor *group* will capture the same sense. The difference shows us that the idea of a public, unlike a concrete audience or the public of any polity, is text-based—even though publics are increasingly organized around visual or audio texts. Without the idea of texts that can be picked up at different times and in different places by otherwise unrelated people, we would not imagine a public as an entity that embraces all the users of that text, whoever they might be. Often, the texts themselves are not even recognized as texts—as for example with visual advertising or the chattering of a DJ—but the publics they bring into being are still discursive in the same way.

The strangeness of this kind of public is often hidden from view because the assumptions that enable the bourgeois public sphere allow us to think of a discourse public as a people and, therefore, as an actually existing set of potentially enumerable humans. A public, in practice, appears as *the* public. It is easy to be misled by this appearance. Even in the blurred usage of the public sphere, a public is never just a congeries of people, never just the sum of persons who happen to exist. It must first of all have some way of organizing itself as a body and of being addressed in discourse. And not just any way of defining the totality will do. It must be organized by something other than the state.

Here we see how the autotelic circularity of the discourse public is not merely a puzzle for analysis, but also the crucial factor in the social importance of the form. A public organizes itself independently of state institutions, law, formal frameworks of citizenship, or preexisting institutions such as the church. If it were not possible to think of the public as organized independently of the state or other frameworks, the public could not be sovereign with respect to the state. So the modern sense of the public as the social totality in fact derives much of its character from the way we understand the partial publics of discourse, like the public of this essay, as self-organized. The way *the* public functions in the public sphere—as *the people*—is only possible because it is really *a* public of discourse. It is self-creating and self-organized, and herein lies its power as well as its elusive strangeness.

In the kind of modern society that the idea of publics has enabled, the self-organization of discourse publics has immense resonance from the point of view of individuals. Speaking, writing, and thinking involve us—actively and immediately—in a public, and thus in the being of the sovereign. Imagine how powerless people would feel if their commonality and participation were simply defined by pre-given frameworks, by institutions and law, as in other social contexts it is through kinship. What would the world look like if all ways of being public were more like applying for a driver's license or subscribing to a professional group—if, that is, formally organized mediations replaced the self-organized public as the image of belonging and common activity? Such is the image of totalitarianism: nonkin society organized by bureaucracy and the law. Everyone's position, function, and capacity for action are specified for her by administration. The powerlessness of the person in such a world haunts modern capitalism as well. Our lives are minutely administered and recorded to a degree unprecedented in history; we navigate a world of corporate agents that do not respond or act as people do. Our personal capacities, such as credit, turn out on reflection to be expressions of corporate agency. Without a faith—justified or not—in self-organized publics, organically linked to our activity in their very existence, capable of being addressed, and capable of action, we would be nothing but the peasants of capital—which of course we might be, and some of us more than others.

In the idea of a public, political confidence is committed to a strange and uncertain destination. Sometimes it can seem too strange. Often, one cannot imagine addressing a public capable of comprehension or action. This is especially true for people in minor or marginal positions, or people distributed across political systems. The result can be a kind of political depressiveness, a blockage in activity and optimism—a disintegration of politics toward isolation, frustration, anomie, forgetfulness. This possibility, never far out of the picture, reveals by contrast how much ordinary belonging requires confidence in a public. Confidence in the possibility of a public is not simply the professional habit of the powerful, of the pundits and wonks and reaction-shot secondary celebrities who try to perform our publicness for us; the same confidence remains vital for people whose place in public media is one of consuming, witnessing, griping, or gossiping rather than one of full participation or fame. Whether faith is justified or partly ideological, a public can only produce a sense of belonging and activity if it is self-organized through discourse rather than through an external framework. This is why any distortion or blockage in access to a public can be so grave, leading people to feel powerless and frustrated. Externally organized frameworks of activity, such as voting, are perceived to be (and are) a poor substitute.

Yet perhaps just because it does seem so important to belong to a public or to be able to know something about the public to which one belongs, such substitutes have been produced in abundance. People have tried hard to find or make some external way of identifying the public, of resolving its circularity into either chicken or egg. The idea that the public might be as changeable, and as unknowable, as the public of this essay (are you still with me?) seems to weaken the very political optimism that the accessibility of the public allows.

Pollsters and some social scientists think that their method is a way to define a public as a group that could be studied empirically, independently from its own discourse about itself. Early in the history of research in communications theory and public relations, it was recognized that such research was going to be difficult, since multiple publics exist and one can belong to many different publics simultaneously. Public opinion researchers have a long history of unsatisfying debate about this problem in method. What determines whether one belongs to a public or not? Space and physical presence do not make much difference; a public is understood to be different from a crowd, an audience, or any other group that requires co-presence. Personal identity does not in itself make one part of a public. Publics differ from nations, races, professions, or any other groups that, though not requiring co-presence, saturate identity. Belonging to a public seems to require at least minimal participation, even if it is patient or notional, rather than a permanent state of being. Merely paying attention can be enough to make you a member. How, then, could a public be quantified?[1]

Some have tried to define a public in terms of a common interest, speaking for example of a foreign-policy public or a sports public. But this way of speaking only pretends to escape the conundrum of the self-creating public. It is like explaining the popularity of films or novels as a response to market demand; the claim is circular because market "demand" is entirely inferred from the popularity of the works themselves. The idea of a common interest, like that of a market demand, appears to identify the social base of public discourse, but the base is in fact projected from the public discourse itself rather than being external to it.

Of all the contrivances designed to escape this circularity, the most powerful

---

1. An instructive review of the methodological problems posed by such a project can be found in *Communications and Public Opinion: A* Public Opinion Quarterly *Reader*, ed. Robert O. Carlson (New York: Praeger, 1975); see, in particular, Floyd D. Allport, "Toward a Science of Public Opinion," and Harwood Childs, "By Public Opinion I Mean————."

by far has been the invention of polling. Polling, together with related forms of market research, tries to tell us what the interests, desires, and demands of a public are without simply inferring them from public discourse. It is an elaborate apparatus designed to characterize a public as social fact independent of any discursive address or circulation. As Pierre Bourdieu pointed out, however, this method proceeds by denying the constitutive role of polling itself as a mediating form.[2] Jürgen Habermas and others have further stressed that the device now systematically distorts the public sphere, producing something that passes as public opinion when in fact it results from a form that has none of the open-endedness, reflexive framing, or accessibility of public discourse. I would add that it lacks the embodied creativity and world-making of publicness. Publics have to be understood as mediated by cultural forms, even though some of those forms, such as polling, work by denying their own constitutive role as cultural forms. Publics do not exist apart from the discourse that addresses them. Are they therefore internal to discourse?

Literary studies has often understood a public as a rhetorical addressee, implied within texts. But the term is generally understood to name something about the text's worldliness, its actual destination—which may or may not resemble its addressee. Benjamin Franklin's autobiography, to take a famous example, remained addressed to his son even after Franklin severed relations with him and decided to publish the text; the public of the autobiography was crucially nonidentical with its addressee. Of course, one can distinguish in such a case between the nominal addressee and the implied addressee, but it is equally possible to distinguish between an implied addressee of rhetoric and a targeted public of circulation. That these are not identical is what allows people to shape the public by addressing it in a certain way. It also allows people to fail, if a rhetorical addressee is not picked up as the reflection of a public.

The sense that a public is a worldly constraint on speech, and not just a free creation of speech, gives plausibility to the opposite approach, that of the social sciences. The self-organized nature of the public does not mean that it is always spontaneous or organically expressive of individuals' wishes. In fact, although the premise of self-organizing discourse is necessary to the peculiar cultural artifact that we call a public, it is contradicted both by material limits—the means of production and distribution, the physical textual objects themselves, the social conditions of access to them—and by internal ones, including the need to pre-

2. The critique of polling appears in a number of contexts in Bourdieu's work; see "Opinion Polls: A 'Science' without a Scientist," in Pierre Bourdieu, *In Other Words: Essays toward a Reflexive Sociology*, trans. Matthew Adamson (Stanford, Calif.: Stanford University Press, 1990).

suppose forms of intelligibility already in place as well as the social closure entailed by any selection of genre, idiolect, style, address, and so forth. I will return to these constraints of circulation. For the moment I want to emphasize that they are made to seem arbitrary because of the performativity of public address and the self-organization implied by the idea of a public.

Another way of saying the same thing is that any empirical extension of the public will seem arbitrarily limited because the addressee of public discourse is always yet to be realized. In some contexts of speech and writing, both the rhetorical addressee and the public have a fairly clear empirical referent: in most paper correspondence and e-mail, in the reports and memos that are passed up and down bureaucracies, in love notes and valentines and Dear John letters, the object of address is understood to be an identifiable person or office. Even if that addressee already occupies a generalized role—for example, a personnel committee, or Congress, or a church congregation—it is definite, known, nameable, and enumerable. The interaction is framed by a social relationship. The concrete addressee in these cases is different from a public.

But for another class of writing contexts—including literary criticism, journalism, "theory," advertising, fiction, drama, most poetry—the available addressees are essentially imaginary, which is not to say unreal. The people, scholarship, the Republic of Letters, posterity, the younger generation, the nation, the Left, the movement, the world, the vanguard, the enlightened few, right-thinking people everywhere, public opinion, the brotherhood of all believers, humanity, my fellow queers: these are all publics. They are in principle open-ended. They exist by virtue of their address.

Although such publics are imaginary, writing to a public is not imaginary in the same way as writing to Pinocchio is. All public addressees have some social basis. Their imaginary character is never merely a matter of private fantasy. (By the same token, *all* addressees are to some extent imaginary—even that of a journal, especially if one writes to one's ideal self, one's posthumous biographers, etc.) They fail if they have no reception in the world, but the exact composition of their addressed publics cannot entirely be known in advance. A public is always in excess of its known social basis. It must be more than a list of one's friends. It must include strangers.

Let me call this a second defining premise of the modern idea of a public:

2. *A public is a relation among strangers.*

Other kinds of writing—writing that has a definite addressee who can be known in advance—can, of course, go astray. Writing to a public incorporates that tendency of writing or speech as a condition of possibility. It cannot go astray in the same way because reaching strangers is its primary orientation. In modernity, this understanding of the public is best illustrated by uses of print or electronic media, but it can also be extended to scenes of audible speech, if that speech is oriented to indefinite strangers, once the crucial background horizon of "public opinion" and its social imaginary has been made available. We've become capable of recognizing ourselves as strangers even when we know each other. Declaiming this essay to a group of intimates, I could still be heard as addressing a public.

The orientation to strangers is in one sense implied by a public's self-organization through discourse. A public sets its boundaries and its organization by its own discourse rather than by external frameworks only if it openly addresses people who are identified *primarily* through their participation in the discourse and who therefore cannot be known in advance. Indeed, a public might almost be said to be stranger-relationality in a pure form, because other ways of organizing strangers—nations, religions, races, guilds, and so on—have manifest positive content. They select strangers by criteria of territory or identity or belief or some other test of membership. One can address strangers in such contexts because a common identity has been established through independent means or institutions (e.g., creeds, armies, parties). A public, however, unites strangers through participation alone, at least in theory. Strangers come into relationship by its means, though the resulting social relationship might be peculiarly indirect and unspecifiable.

Once this kind of public is in place as a social imaginary, I might add, stranger-sociability inevitably takes on a different character. In modern society, a stranger is not as marvelously exotic as the wandering outsider would have been in an ancient, medieval, or early modern town. In that earlier social order, or in contemporary analogues, a stranger is mysterious, a disturbing presence requiring resolution.[3] In the context of a public, however, strangers can be treated as already belonging to our world. More: they *must* be. We are routinely oriented to them in common life. They are a normal feature of the social.

3. It is this ancient exotic that figures in Georg Simmel's much-cited 1908 essay "The Stranger." Simmel fails to distinguish between the stranger as represented by the trader or the Wandering Jew and the stranger whose presence in modernity is unremarkable, even necessary, to the nature of modern polities. One of the defining elements of modernity, in my view, is normative stranger-sociability, of a kind that seems to arise only when the social imaginary is defined not by kinship (as in nonstate societies) or by place (as in state societies until the advent of modernity), but by discourse. Simmel, "The Stranger," in *On Individuality and Social Forms: Selected Writings*, ed. Donald N. Levine (Chicago: University of Chicago Press, 1971).

Strangers in the ancient sense—foreign, alien, misplaced—might of course be located to a degree within Christendom, the *ummah*, a guild, or an army— affiliations one might share with strangers, making them a bit less strange. Strangers placed by means of these affiliations are on a path to commonality. Publics orient us to strangers in a different way. They are no longer merely people-whom-one-does-not-yet-know; rather, it can be said that an environment of strangerhood is the necessary premise of some of our most prized ways of being. Where otherwise strangers need to be placed on a path to commonality, in modern forms strangerhood is the necessary medium of commonality. The modern social imaginary does not make sense without strangers. A nation, market, or public in which everyone could be known personally would be no nation, market, or public at all. This constitutive and normative environment of strangerhood is more, too, than an objectively describable gesellschaft; it requires our constant imagining.

The expansive force of these cultural forms cannot be understood apart from the way they make stranger-relationality normative, reshaping the most intimate dimensions of subjectivity around co-membership with indefinite persons in a context of routine action. The development of forms that mediate the intimate theater of stranger-relationality must surely be one of the most significant dimensions of modern history, though the story of this transformation in the meaning of the stranger has been told only in fragments. It is hard to imagine such abstract modes of being as rights-bearing personhood, species-being, and sexuality, for example, without forms that give concrete shape to the interactivity of those who have no idea with whom they are interacting. This dependence on the co-presence of strangers in our innermost activity, when we continue to think of strangerhood and intimacy as opposites, has at least some latent contradictions—many of which come to the fore, as we shall see, in counterpublic forms that make expressive corporeality the material for the elaboration of intimate life among publics of strangers.

The oddness of this orientation to strangers in public discourse can be understood better if we consider a third defining feature of discourse that addresses publics, one that follows from the address to strangers but is very difficult to describe:

3. *The address of public speech is both personal and impersonal.*

Public speech can have great urgency and intimate import. Yet we know that it was addressed not exactly to us, but to the stranger we were until the moment we happened to be addressed by it. (I am thinking here of any genre addressed to a public, including novels and lyrics as well as criticism, other nonfictional prose, and almost all genres of radio, television, film, and Web discourse.) To inhabit public discourse is to perform this transition continually, and to some extent it remains present to consciousness. Public speech must be taken in two ways: as addressed to us and as addressed to strangers. The benefit in this practice is that it gives a general social relevance to private thought and life. Our subjectivity is understood as having resonance with others, and immediately so. But this is only true to the extent that the trace of our strangerhood remains present in our under-standing of ourselves as the addressee.

This necessary element of impersonality in public address is one of the things missed from view in the Althusserian notion of interpellation, at least as it is cur-rently understood. Louis Althusser's famous example is speech addressed to a stranger: a policeman says, "Hey, you!" In the moment of recognizing oneself as the person addressed, the moment of turning around, one is interpellated as the subject of state discourse.[4] Althusser's analysis had the virtue of showing the importance of imaginary identification — and locating it, not in the coercive or punitive force of the state, but in the subjective practice of understanding. When the model of interpellation is extracted from his example to account for public cul-ture generally, the analysis will be skewed because the case Althusser gives is not an example of public discourse. A policeman who says "Hey, you!" will be under-stood to be addressing a particular person, not a public. When one turns around, it is partly to see whether one is that person. If not, one goes on. If so, then all the others who might be standing on the street are bystanders, not addressees.

With public speech, by contrast, we might recognize ourselves as addressees, but it is equally important that we remember that the speech was addressed to indefinite others; that in singling us out, it does so not on the basis of our concrete identity, but by virtue of our participation in the discourse alone, and therefore in common with strangers. It isn't just that we are addressed in public as certain kinds of persons, or that we might not want to identify as that person (though this is also often enough the case, as when the public is addressed as heterosexual, or white, or sports-minded, or American). We haven't been misidentified, exactly. It seems more to the point to say that publics are different from persons, that the address of public rhetoric is never going to be the same as address to actual per-sons, and that our partial *nonidentity* with the object of address in public speech seems to be part of what it means to regard something as public speech.

4. Louis Althusser, "Ideology and Ideological State Apparatuses," in *Lenin and Philosophy, and Other Essays*, trans. Ben Brewster (New York: Monthly Review Press, 1971).

It might be helpful to think of public address in contrast with gossip. Gossip might seem to be a perfect instance of public discourse. It circulates widely among a social network, beyond the control of private individuals. It sets norms of membership in a diffuse way that cannot be controlled by a central authority. For these reasons, a number of scholars have celebrated its potential for popular sociability and for the weak-group politics of women, peasants, and others.[5]

But gossip is never a relation among strangers. You gossip about particular people and to particular people. What you can get away with saying depends very much on whom you are talking to and what your status is in that person's eyes. Speak ill of someone when you are not thought to have earned the privilege and you will be taken as slandering rather than gossiping. Gossip circulates without the awareness of some people, and it must be prevented from reaching them in the wrong way. Intensely personal measurements of group membership, relative standing, and trust are the constant and unavoidable pragmatic work of gossip.[6]

The appeal to strangers in the circulating forms of public address thus helps us to distinguish public discourse from forms that address particular persons in their singularity. It remains less clear how a public could be translated into an image of *the* public, a social entity. Who is the public? Does it include my neighbors? The doorman in my building? My students? The people who show up in the gay bars and clubs? The bodega owners down the street from me? Someone who calls me on the phone or sends me an e-mail? You? We encounter people in such disparate contexts that the idea of a body to which they all belong, and in which they could be addressed in speech, seems to have something wishful about it. To address a public, we don't go around saying the same thing to all these people. We say it in a venue of indefinite address and hope that people will find themselves in it. The difference can be a source of frustration, but it is also an implication of the self-organization of the public as a body of strangers united through the circulation of their discourse. Without this indefinite and impersonal address, the public would have none of its special importance to modernity.

5. See, for example, Patricia Spacks, *Gossip* (New York: Knopf, 1985), especially 121–46; and James C. Scott, *Weapons of the Weak: Everyday Forms of Peasant Resistance* (New Haven, Conn.: Yale University Press, 1985).

6. "The right to gossip about certain people," Max Gluckman writes in a classic essay, "is a privilege which is only extended to a person when he or she is accepted as a member of a group or set. It is a hallmark of membership." Moreover, this kind of membership tends to presuppose others, such as kin groups, equally distant from stranger-sociability. "To be a Makah [the Northwest Amerindian group discussed by Gluckman] you must be able to join in the gossip, and to be fully a Makah you must be able to scandalize skillfully. This entails that you know the individual family histories of your fellows; for the knowledgeable can hit at you through your ancestry" ("Gossip and Scandal," *Current Anthropology* 4 [1963]: 313, 311).

The journalist Walter Lippmann picked up on the odd nature of public address when he complained that no one could possibly be the sort of creature that is routinely addressed as the public of politics: the fully informed, universally interested and attentive, vigilant, potent, and decisive citizen. "I have not happened to meet anybody, from a President of the United States to a professor of political science, who came anywhere near to embodying the accepted ideal of the sovereign and omnicompetent citizen."[7] But it doesn't follow that politicians and journalists should be more realistic in their address. To think so is to mistake the addressee of public speech for actual persons. Lippmann thought the appropriate response was an honest assessment of the actual reception of public discourse and, therefore, a more frankly elite administration:

> We must assume as a theoretically fixed premise of popular government that normally men as members of a public will not be well informed, continuously interested, nonpartisan, creative or executive. We must assume that a public is inexpert in its curiosity, intermittent, that it discerns only gross distinctions, is slow to be aroused and quickly diverted; that, since it acts by aligning itself, it personalizes whatever it considers, and is interested only when events have been melodramatized as a conflict.[8]

Interestingly, Lippmann cannot observe his own advice. Even in writing this passage, he writes to an alert and thoughtful public ("we," he calls it) with an assumption of activity. Public discourse itself has a kind of personality different from that of the people who make up a public.

In this passage, Lippmann stumbles across another of the principal differences between a public and any already existing social group. A public is thought to be active, curious, alert. But actual people, he notices, are intermittent in their attention, only occasionally aroused, fitfully involved. He thinks this is a sad fact about the people's character, comparing unfavorably with the greater energies of concentration that elites maintain in their engagement with public questions. But between ideally alert publics and really distracted people there will always be a gap—no matter what the social class or kind of public. This is because publics are only realized through active uptake.

4. *A public is constituted through mere attention.*

Most social classes and groups are understood to encompass their members all the time, no matter what. A nation, for example, includes its members whether

7. Walter Lippmann, *The Phantom Public* (1927; reprint, New Brunswick, N.J.: Transaction, 1993), 4–5, 10–11.

8. Lippmann, *Phantom Public*, 54–55.

60

they are awake or asleep, sober or drunk, sane or deranged, alert or comatose. Because a public exists only by virtue of address, it must predicate some degree of attention, however notional, from its members.

The cognitive quality of that attention is less important than the mere fact of active uptake. Attention is the principal sorting category by which members and nonmembers are discriminated. If you are reading this, or hearing it or seeing it or present for it, you are part of this public. You might be multitasking at the computer; the television might be on while you are vacuuming the carpet; or you might have wandered into hearing range of the speaker's podium in a convention hall only because it was on your way to the bathroom. No matter: by coming into range you fulfill the only entry condition demanded by a public. It is even possible for us to understand someone sleeping through a ballet performance as a member of that ballet's public because most contemporary ballet performances are organized as voluntary events, open to anyone willing to attend or, in most cases, to pay to attend. The act of attention involved in showing up is enough to create an addressable public. But some kind of active uptake—however somnolent—is indispensable.

The existence of a public is contingent on its members' activity, however notional or compromised, and not on its members' categorical classification, objectively determined position in social structure, or material existence. In the self-understanding that makes them work, publics thus resemble the model of voluntary association that is so important to civil society. Since the early modern period, more and more institutions have come to conform to this model. The old idea of an established national church, for example, allowed the church to address itself to parish members literate or illiterate, virtuous or vicious, competent or idiotic. Increasingly, churches in a multidenominational world must think of themselves instead as contingent on their members; they welcome newcomers, keep membership rolls, and solicit attention. Some doctrinal emphases, like those on faith or conversion, make it possible for churches to orient themselves to that active uptake on which they are increasingly dependent.

Still, one can join a church and then stop going. In some cases, one can even be born into one. Publics, by contrast, lacking any institutional being, commence with the moment of attention, must continually predicate renewed attention, and cease to exist when attention is no longer predicated. They are virtual entities, not voluntary associations. Because their threshold of belonging is an active uptake, however, they can be understood within the conceptual framework of civil society—that is, as having a free, voluntary, and active membership. Wherever a liberal conception of personality obtains, the moment of uptake that constitutes a public can be seen as an expression of volition on the part of its members. And this fact has enormous consequences. It allows us to understand publics as scenes of self-activity, of historical rather than timeless belonging, and of active participation rather than ascriptive belonging. Under the right conditions, it even allows us to attribute agency to a public, even though that public has no institutional being or concrete manifestation. (More on this later.)

Public discourse craves attention like a child. Texts clamor at us. Images solicit our gaze. *Look here! Listen! Yo!* But in doing so, they by no means render us passive. Quite the contrary. The modern system of publics creates a demanding social phenomenology. Our willingness to process a passing appeal determines which publics we belong to and performs their extension. The experience of social reality at this level of modernity feels quite unlike that of contexts organized by kinship, hereditary status, local affiliation, mediated political access, parochial nativity, or ritual. In those settings, one's place in the common order is what it is regardless of one's inner thoughts, however intense their affective charge might sometimes be. The appellative energy of publics puts a different burden on us: it makes us believe our consciousness to be decisive. The direction of our glance can constitute our social world.

The themes I've discussed so far—the self-organization of publics through discourse, their orientation to strangers, the resulting ambiguity of personal and impersonal address, membership by mere attention—can be clarified if we remember their common assumption, which goes a long way toward explaining the historical development of the other four:

5. *A public is the social space created by the reflexive circulation of discourse.*

This dimension is easy to forget if we think only about a speech event involving speaker and addressee. In that localized exchange, circulation may seem irrelevant, extraneous. That is one reason why sender-receiver or author-reader models of public communication are so misleading. No single text can create a public. Nor can a single voice, a single genre, or even a single medium. All are insufficient to create the kind of reflexivity that we call a public, since a public is understood to be an ongoing space of encounter for discourse. It is not texts themselves that create publics, but the concatenation of texts through time. Only when a previously existing discourse can be supposed, and a responding discourse be postulated, can a text address a public.

Between the discourse that comes before and the discourse that comes after, one must postulate some kind of link. And the link has a social character; it is not mere consecutiveness in time, but a context of interaction. The usual way of imagining the interactive character of public discourse is through metaphors of conversation, answering, talking back, deliberating. The interactive social relation of a public, in other words, is perceived as though it were a dyadic speaker-hearer or author-reader relation. Argument and polemic, as manifestly dialogic genres, continue to have a privileged role in the self-understanding of publics; and indeed, it is remarkable how little even the most sophisticated forms of theory have been able to disentangle public discourse from its self-understanding as conversation.[9]

In addressing a public, however, even texts of the most rigorously argumentative and dialogic genres also address onlookers, not just parties to argument. They try to characterize the field of possible interplay. When appearing in a public field, genres of argument and polemic must accommodate themselves to the special conditions of public address: the agonistic interlocutor is coupled with passive interlocutors; known enemies with indifferent strangers; parties present to a dialogue situation with parties whose textual location might be in other genres or scenes of circulation entirely. The meaning of any utterance depends on what is known and anticipated from all these different quarters. In public argument or polemic, the principal act is that of projecting the field of argument itself—its genres, its range of circulation, its stakes, its idiom, its repertoire of agencies. Any position is reflexive, not only asserting itself, but also characterizing its relation to other positions up to limits that compass the imagined scene of circulation. The interactive relation postulated in public discourse, in other words, goes far beyond the scale of conversation or discussion, to encompass a multigeneric lifeworld organized not just by a relational axis of utterance and response, but by potentially infinite axes of citation and characterization.

Anything that addresses a public is meant to undergo circulation. This helps us to understand why print, and the organization of markets for print, were historically so central in the development of the public sphere. But print is neither necessary nor sufficient for publication in the modern sense; not every genre of print can organize the space of circulation. The particularly addressed genres listed earlier—correspondence, memos, valentines, bills—are not expected to circulate (indeed, circulating them can be not just strange but highly unethical), and that is why they cannot be said to be oriented to a public.

Circulation also accounts for the way a public seems both internal and external

9. For an example of a promising and rich analysis marred by this misapprehension, see Nina Eliasoph, *Avoiding Politics: How Americans Produce Apathy in Everyday Life* (Cambridge: Cambridge University Press, 1998*).* Eliasoph's stated but unexamined ideal is that of a continuity of *discussion* from small-scale interaction to the highest organizing levels of politics.

to discourse, both notional and material. From the concrete experience of a world in which available forms circulate, one projects a public. And both the known and unknown are essential to the process. The unknown element in the addressee enables a hope of transformation; the known, a scene of practical possibility. Writing to a public helps to make a world, insofar as the object of address is brought into being partly by postulating and characterizing it. This performative ability depends, however, on that object's being not entirely fictitious—not postulated merely, but recognized as a real path for the circulation of discourse. That path is then treated as a social entity.

The ability to address the world made up by the circulation of cross-referencing discourse seems to have developed over a long period in the West, at least from the late sixteenth century to the late eighteenth. In the English case, for example, many of the promotional tracts for the colonization of the New World address a world of potential investors or supporters who are understood to have been addressed by competing representations. (That is why so many are called "A True Discourse," "A True Report," etc.) Yet these same tracts tend to regard this as an unnatural and unfortunate condition that could be righted by properly authoritative and true testimony. Eventually, it became possible to thematize circulation, to regard it as an essential fact of common life, and to organize a social imaginary in which it would be regarded as normative.

It is possible to see this cultural formation emerging in England in the seventeenth century. Let me offer a curious example: a report from the reign of Charles II, in 1670, of the activities in two Whig booksellers' shops. It is an interesting example because the (presumably) royalist author of the report regards those activities with suspicion, to say the least. He describes public discourse without any of the normative self-understanding of public discourse. "Every afternoon," the report says, the shops receive from all over the city accounts of news ("all novells and occurrents so penned as to make for the disadvantage of the King and his affairs"), written reports of resolution and speeches in Parliament, and speeches on topics of public business. These reports are made available to the booksellers' regular clients, who, according to the report, include young lawyers ("who here generally receive their tincture and corruption"), "ill-affected citizens of all sorts," "ill-affected gentry," and "emissaries and agents of the severall parties and factions about town." The reports and speeches available for these readers were all registered in a central catalog and could be ordered individually from the copyists.

> Against the time of their coming the Masters of those Shops have a grand
> book or books, wherein are registred ready for them, all or most of the

forenamed particulars; which they dayly produce to those sorts of people
to be read, and then, if they please, they either carry away copies, or
bespeak them against another day.

The circulation of the scribal reports went beyond London, too.

They take care to communicate them by Letter all over the kingdome, and
by conversation throughout the City and suburbs. The like industry is
used by the masters of those shops, who together with their servants are
every afternoon and night busied in transcribing copies, with which they
drive a trade all over the kingdome.[10]

The two booksellers of the account were producing a market, in what sounds
like a very busy entrepreneurial scene. Some of the elements in the account suggest the norms of the emergent public sphere: the scribal trade promotes private
discussion of common concerns; it stands in opposition to power (although here
that is regarded as "disaffection" rather than as a normative role for criticism);
and it occupies metatopical secular space.[11] It is not clear from this account
whether the participants understood their relation to one another as a relation to
a public. (It is somewhat unlikely that they did; one scholar, claiming that "there
was as yet no 'public,'" notes that "Dryden always uses the word 'people' where
we should now say 'public.'"[12]) The genres circulated in this report are themselves mostly familiar ones of correspondence and speeches, both of which have
specific addressees. What is striking, though, is the clarity with which we can
see in this account the scene of circulation that is presupposed by the idea of a
public. And curiously, it is not simply a scene of print, but of scribal copying.
That may be one reason why the scene is so scandalous to the informer. The circulatory practices are thought to be illegitimate uses of their genres and modes
of address.

In a study that was published ten years ago, I argued that the consciousness of
the public in public address developed as a new way of understanding print, in
the context of a republican political language that served as a metalanguage for
print. (This consciousness of public address could then be extended to scenes of
speech such as political sermons.) Reading printed texts in this context, we incor-

10. Quoted in Harold Love, *Scribal Publication in Seventeenth-Century England* (Oxford: Oxford
University Press, 1993), 20–21.
11. On the necessity of any public's being metatopical, see Charles Taylor, "Modern Social Imaginaries," in this issue.
12. Alexandre Beljame, *Men of Letters and the English Public in the Eighteenth Century,
1660–1744: Dryden, Addison [and] Pope*, trans. Emily Overend Lorimer (London: K. Paul, Trench,
Trubner, 1948), 130.

porate an awareness of the indefinite others to whom it is addressed as part of the meaning of its printedness.[13] I now see that in making this argument I missed a crucial element in the perception of publicness. In order for a text to be public, we must recognize it not simply as a diffusion to strangers, but also as a temporality of circulation.

The informer's report makes this temporal dimension clear, calling attention not just to the (possibly seditious) connections forged among strangers, but also to the punctual circulation that turns those exchanges into a scene with its own expectations. Reports are said to come in "every afternoon" and are indexed regularly. Customers come or send their agents daily for copies, according to rhythms that are widely known and relied upon. We are not seeing simply a bookseller distributing copies far and wide; rather, it is a regular flow of discourse in and out, punctuated by daily rhythms and oriented to that punctuality as to news ("novells and occurrents"). Circulation organizes time. Public discourse is contemporary, and it is oriented to the future; the contemporaneity and the futurity in question are those of its own circulation.

The key development in the emergence of modern publics was the appearance of newsletters and other temporally structured forms oriented to their own circulation: not just controversial pamphlets, but regular and dated papers, magazines, almanacs, annuals, and essay serials. They developed reflexivity about their circulation through reviews, reprintings, citation, controversy. These forms single out circulation both through their sense of temporality and through the way they allow discourse to move in different directions. I don't speak just to you; I speak to the public in a way that enters a cross-citational field of many other people speaking to the public.

The temporality of circulation is not continuous or indefinite; it is punctual. There are distinct moments and rhythms, from which distance in time can be measured. Papers and magazines are dated, and when they first appear, they are news. Reviews appear with a sense of timeliness. At a further remove, there are now regular publishing seasons with their cycles of catalogs and marketing campaigns. The exception might seem to be televisual media, given the enormous significance attributed to their liveness and "flow"—formally salient features of so much broadcasting, whereby televisual forms are understood to have a greater immediacy than codex or other text formats. Yet even with television, punctual rhythms of daily and weekly emission are still observed; think of all its

13. Michael Warner, *The Letters of the Republic: Publication and the Public Sphere in Eighteenth-Century America* (Cambridge: Harvard University Press, 1990).

serial forms and marked rhythms such as prime time, the news hour, and the like.[14]

Reflexive circulation might come about in any number of ways. In the French context, as in England, it appeared first in print serial forms. *Le Mercure galant*, a newspaper edited by Donneau de Visé, seems to have pioneered many of the devices of reflexive circulation in the late 1670s, including published reader letters and a rhetoric of readerly judgment.[15] In this case, the idea that readers participated in the circulation of judgments, thought at the time by Jean de La Bruyère and others to have been a solecism,[16] gradually drew the sense of the term *public* away from the image of a passive theatrical audience. For the Abbé Du Bos in 1719, "The word *public* is used here to mean those persons who have acquired enlightenment, either through reading or through life in society [*le commerce du monde*]. They are the only ones who can determine the value of poems or paintings."[17] In France, this sense of a critical public did not easily transfer to politics since legitimate printed news was almost nonexistent under the ancien régime. Yet, as Robert Darnton has shown, eighteenth-century Paris gave rise to countless other forms of reflexive circulation. Many of them were known by names that "are unknown today and cannot be translated into English equivalents": *nouvelliste de bouche, mauvais propos, bruit public, on-dit, pasquinade, Pont Neuf, canard, feuille volante, factum, libelle, chronique scandaleuse*. More familiar genres, such as popular songs, seem to have circulated in uniquely

14. See Jane Feuer, "The Concept of Live Television: Ontology as Ideology," in *Regarding Television: Critical Approaches—An Anthology*, ed. E. Ann Kaplan (Frederick, Md.: University Publications of America, 1983), 15: "Television becomes a continuous, never-ending sequence in which it is impossible to separate out individual texts. . . . Indeed the 'central fact' of television may be that it is designed to be watched intermittently, casually, and without full concentration."

15. See Joan De Jean, *Ancients against Moderns: Culture Wars and the Making of a Fin de Siècle* (Chicago: University of Chicago Press, 1997), 31–77. De Jean (in my view mistakenly) thinks her argument contradicts Habermas's history: "In the case of *le public* . . . the terminology was not, as the Habermasian view would have it, primarily evocative of a 'medium of political confrontation' constructed 'against the public authorities themselves' for the purpose of generating 'debate over . . . the sphere of commodity exchange and social labor.' Instead, the modern vocabulary of public exchange was initially most remarkable for its connotations of a sphere in which a socially and sexually diverse audience debated for the first time the meaning and the function of public culture" (*Ancients against Moderns*, xv).

16. De Jean, *Ancients against Moderns*, 58.

17. Abbé (Jean-Baptiste) Du Bos, *Réflexions critiques sur la peinture et sur la poésie* (1719), quoted in De Jean, *Ancients against Moderns*, 64. Antoine Furetière's *Dictionnaire universel des art et des sciences* (1690) already has the sense of a public not just as an audience or theatrical public, but as a public of readers. "An author gives his works to the public when he has them printed." De Jean, *Ancients against Moderns*, 36.

Parisian ways.[18] The differences between these genres and their Anglo-American counterparts say much about the difference between the corresponding senses of public life, its legitimacy, and the conditions under which agency might be attributed to a public. Nevertheless, they were forms for giving reflexivity to a field of circulation among strangers in punctual rhythms.

6. Publics act historically according to the temporality of their circulation.

The punctual rhythm of circulation is crucial to the sense that ongoing discussion unfolds in a sphere of activity. It is not timeless, like meditation; nor is it without issue, like speculative philosophy. Not all circulation happens at the same rate, of course, and this accounts for the dramatic differences among publics in their relation to possible scenes of activity. A public can only act within the temporality of the circulation that gives it existence. The more punctual and abbreviated the circulation, and the more discourse indexes the punctuality of its own circulation, the closer a public stands to politics. At longer rhythms or more continuous flows, action becomes harder to imagine. This is the fate of academic publics, a fact very little understood when academics claim by intention or proclamation to be doing politics. In modernity, politics takes much of its character from the temporality of the headline, not the archive.

Publics have an ongoing life: one doesn't publish to them once and for all (as one does, say, to a scholarly archive). It's the way texts circulate, and become the basis for further representations, that convinces us that publics have activity and duration. A text, to have a public, must continue to circulate through time, and because this can be confirmed only through an intertextual environment of citation and implication, all publics are intertextual, even intergeneric. This is often missed from view because the activity and duration of publics are commonly stylized as conversation or decision-making. I have already suggested that these are misleading ideologizations. Now we can see why they are durable illusions: because they confer agency on publics. There is no moment at which the conversation stops and a decision ensues, outside of elections, and those are given only by legal frameworks, not by publics themselves. Yet the ideologization is crucial to the sense that publics act in secular time. To sustain this sense, public discourse indexes itself temporally with respect to moments of publication and a common calendar of circulation.

One way that the Internet and other new media may be profoundly changing the public sphere, by the way, is through the change they imply in temporality.

18. Robert Darnton, "Paris: The Early Internet," *New York Review of Books*, 29 June 2000, 43.

Highly mediated and highly capitalized forms of circulation are increasingly organized as continuous ("24/7 Instant Access") rather than punctual.[19] At the time of this writing, Web discourse has very little of the citational field that would allow us to speak of it as discourse unfolding through time. Once a Web site is up, it can be hard to tell how recently it was posted or revised, or how long it will continue to be posted. Most sites are not archived. For the most part, they are not centrally indexed. The reflexive apparatus of Web discourse consists mostly of hypertext links and search engines, and these are not punctual. So although there are exceptions—including the migration of some print serials to electronic format and the successful use of the Web by some social movements—the extent to which developments in technology will be assimilable to the temporal framework of public discourse remains unclear.[20] If the change of infrastructure continues at this pace, and if modes of apprehension change accordingly, the absence of punctual rhythms may make it very difficult to connect localized acts of reading to the modes of agency that prevail within the social imaginary of modernity. It may even be necessary to abandon "circulation" as an analytic category. But here I merely offer this topic for speculation.

Until recently, at least, public discourse has presupposed daily and weekly rhythms of circulation. It has also presupposed an ability—natural to moderns, but rather peculiar if one thinks about it at all—to address this scene of circulation as a social entity. The clearest example, or at any rate the most eloquent, is the *Spectator*, which ran from 1711 to 1714, some forty years after the report of the Whig booksellers. Like the booksellers' newsletters, the *Spectator* was a daily form, widely and industriously circulated.[21] "To be Continued every Day," announced the first number, which was designed to look like the newspapers of the day even though, as no. 262 declares, the paper "has not in it a single Word of News."[22]

19. Eyal Amiran discusses the temporality of electronic media, in a way that differs substantially from mine, in "Electronic Time and the Serials Revolution," *Yale Journal of Criticism* 10 (1997): 445–54.

20. This change is difficult to assess, not simply because the effects of change in the medium have yet to become visible, but because the infrastructure of the medium is itself changing. On this problem, the best account I know is Lawrence Lessig, *Code and Other Laws of Cyberspace* (New York: Basic Books, 1999). Lessig's book, though focused on the legal regulation of cyberspace, also raises important topics for the more general discussion of new media and their social implications.

21. Not a weekly, as Habermas mistakenly asserts. Jürgen Habermas, *The Structural Transformation of the Public Sphere: An Inquiry into a Category of Bourgeois Society*, trans. Thomas Burger with Frederick Lawrence (Cambridge: MIT Press, 1989).

22. This and all subsequent excerpts from the *Spectator* are taken from the five-volume edition by Donald F. Bond (Oxford: Clarendon, 1965). Excerpts are identified by their issue number, supplemented where necessary by their volume and page numbers in this edition.

The *Spectator* followed a model worked out by John Dunton, whose *Athenian Mercury* in 1691 was the first to print regular correspondence from readers it allowed to remain anonymous.[23] The *Spectator* developed a rhetoric that gave a new normative force to Dunton's methods. It ostentatiously avoids political polemic. Unlike the output of the Whig booksellers in the 1670 report, it could not be characterized as seditious; yet it describes its readers as an active public, a critical tribunal. Readers are called upon to pass informed and reflective judgment on fashion, taste, manners, and gender relations. The procedure of impersonal discussion gives private matters full public relevance, while allowing participants in that discussion to enjoy the kind of generality that had formerly been the privilege of the state or the church. The *Spectator* claims to be general, addressing everyone merely on the basis of humanity. It is the voice of civil society.[24]

Like Dunton's *Athenian Mercury*, but deploying a much richer formal vocabulary, the *Spectator* developed a reflexivity about its own circulation, coordinating its readers' relations to other readers. It does not merely assert the fact of public circulation, although it does frequently allude to its own popularity; it includes feedback loops, both in the letters from readers real and imagined, and in the members of the club and other devices. Essays refer to previous essays and to the reception of those essays; installments end with, and are sometimes wholly given over to, letters that are, or purport to be, the responses of readers. The fictional persona of the Spectator himself represents the embodiment of a private reader: an observant but perversely mute wanderer ("I am frequently seen in the most publick Places, tho' there are not above half a dozen of my select Friends that know me" [*Spectator*, no. 1], the essential stranger, "Mr. *what-d'ye-call-him*" [no. 4], witnessing in dumb privacy the whole social field, combining "all the Advantages of Company with all the Privileges of Solitude" [no. 131]). His club represents a model of the male reception context (constantly in need of supple-

23. Kathryn Shevelow, *Women and Print Culture: The Construction of Femininity in the Early Periodical* (London: Routledge, 1989). Shevelow treats reader correspondence and "audience production of the text" at 37–42; the development of "audience-building" at 61–66; and the importance of anonymity at 71–74.

24. For a somewhat different analysis along these lines, see Scott Black, "Eighteenth-Century Print Culture: Social and Literary Form in the *Spectator*," *Eighteenth-Century Studies* 33 (1999): 21–42. I have also found much insightful discussion in Michael G. Ketcham, *Transparent Designs: Reading, Performance, and Form in the* Spectator *Papers* (Athens: University of Georgia Press, 1985). Other pertinent treatments of the *Spectator* can be found in Edward A. Bloom and Lillian D. Bloom, eds., *Addison and Steele, the Critical Heritage* (London: Routledge and Kegan Paul, 1980); and Bloom and Bloom, *Joseph Addison's Sociable Animal: In the Market Place, on the Hustings, in the Pulpit* (Providence, R.I.: Brown University Press, 1971).

mentation by accounts of and letters from female readers). One is continually reminded of "this great City inquiring Day by Day after these my Papers" (no. 10). A repertoire of highly temporalized affects and interests—scandal, fascination, fashion, news addiction, mania, curiosity—is projected as the properties, not only of individuals, but of the scene of circulation itself, without which such affects would lack resonance. This rhetoric represents the subjective mode of being attributed to the public. It describes private and individual acts of reading, but in such a way as to make temporally indexed circulation among strangers the immanent meaning and emotional resonance of those reading acts.

Among early modern organs of print, the *Spectator* first perfected the representation of its own circulation. It marked the emergence of a standard that can now be taken for granted: that public discourse must be circulated, not just emitted in one direction. Even mass media, which because of their heavy capitalization are conspicuously asymmetrical, take care to fake a reciprocity that they must overcome in order to succeed. Contemporary mass media have even more elaborate devices of the kind that Joseph Addison and Richard Steele developed in the *Spectator*: viewer mail, call-in shows, 900-number polling, home video shows, game show contestants, town meetings, studio audiences, and man-on-the-street interviews are some examples. These genres create feedback loops to characterize their own space of consumption. As with the *Spectator*, reflexivity is managed through affect and idiom as well; the *Spectator* essays comment on slang (e.g., *jilts*) in a way that attributes to folk usage the same historical present tense as the essays' circulation.[25] Mass culture laces its speech with catchphrases that suture it to informal speech, even though those catchphrases are often common in informal speech only because they were picked up from mass texts in the first place. In the United States, sports metaphors are obvious examples, as when politicians describe their speeches or proposals as slam dunks or home runs.

Sometimes the layering of reflexive postures toward circulation can be dizzyingly complex, as happened in 2001 when Budweiser advertisements turned the black street greeting "Whassup?" into a slogan. This "signature catch phrase," as the *New York Times* called it, once broadcast, could subsequently be "joked about on talk shows, parodied on Web sites, and mimicked in other commercials." Ironically, all this repetition of "Whassup?" was understood not as new tokens of the street greeting itself, but as references to the commercial. A relation to the mass circulation of the phrase came to be part of the meaning of the phrase. That this should happen, moreover, was the deliberate design of the advertising firm that

25. Ketcham describes this phenomenon in *Transparent Designs*, 130.

designed the commercial—in this case, one DDB Worldwide, part of what is called "the Omnicom Group."

> The team uses sophisticated research and old-fashioned legwork—like checking out new art forms or going to underground film festivals—to anticipate what is about to become hip to its target audience of mostly men in their 20's and 30's. The language, styles and attitudes it finds are then packaged in ad campaigns that are broadcast so often that they become part of the public consciousness.[26]

The company sells this circulatory effect to its clients as "talk value." When office workers use catchphrases to joke around the coffee machine, they unwittingly realize the talk value that has already been sold to the corporation whose products were advertised. Indeed, DDB Worldwide has registered the phrase *talk value* as a trademark. As the phrase suggests, talk value allows a structured but mobile interplay between the reflexivity of publics (the talk) and the reflexivity of capital (the value). Neither is reducible to the other, and the DDB strategy works only if the relation between the popular idiom and the sale of beer is indirect, a process of mutual feedback experienced by individuals as a medium for improvisation.

Public reflexivity and market reflexivity have been interarticulated in a variety of ways from the beginning. In the case of the Whig booksellers, consciousness of a public created a new and expansive circulation for text commodities. With the *Spectator*, a greater range of dialectical stances opened up as the reflex consciousness of a public turned its critical attention on the reflex consumption of commodities in such forms as fashion. In contemporary mass culture, the play between these different ways of rendering the field of circulation reflexive has created countless nuances for the performance of subjectivity. To take only the

26. Patricia Winters Lauro, "Whassup? America's Asking," *New York Times*, 16 February 2001, C1, C4.

> After being beamed up to an alien spaceship, a family pet takes off his dog suit to reveal that he is an alien creature himself. "What have you learned?" his leader asks. The creature pauses to think, then responds "Whassup?" with his tongue lolling out of his mouth. . . . The Whassup campaign has won practically every award in advertising, including the prestigious international Grand Prix. . . . And, most important to Anheuser-Busch, the nation's largest brewer, the campaign has helped it sell more beer, not just Budweiser but its light beer, Bud Light. The company's worldwide sales grew by 2.4 million barrels, to 99.2 million barrels last year, according to Beer Marketer's Insights, a trade newsletter in Nanuet, N.Y.

Note, by the way, the *Times*'s headline to the story. The idea that all this circulation can be heard as "America" talking is the distinctive contribution made by news media in the layering of reflexivity on a circulation in which, after all, the *Times* story is otherwise merely one more example.

most obvious examples, we speak of a "mainstream," of "alternative" culture, of "crossover" trends, naming and evaluating stylistic affinities by characterizing the field in which they circulate.

Talk value has an affective quality. You don't just mechanically repeat signature catchphrases. You perform through them your social placement. Different social styles can be created through different levels of reflexivity in this performance. Too obvious parroting of catchphrases—for example, walking into the office on the morning after Budweiser runs its commercial and grabbing the first opportunity to say "Whassup?"—can mark you in some contexts as square, unhip, a passive relay in the circulation. In other contexts, it could certify you as one of the gang, showing that you too were watching the show with everyone else. Stylistic affinities can perform many functions, of course, but in mass culture they always involve adopting a stance toward the field of their circulation. Characterizations of that field are the stuff of performed stances that can range from immersion to irony or even aggressivity, in a way that always has some affective charge—hipness, normalcy, hilarity, currency, quaintness, freakishness, and so on. What is called "vernacular" performance is therefore in reality structured by a continually shifting field of artfulness in managing the reflexivity of mass circulation. (Many U.S. critics, seeing only one side of this process, like to interpret such artfulness as evidence of a folk or popular style in the "appropriation" of mass culture; for them, this counts as evidence against the Frankfurt School analysis of mass culture.)

The use of such pseudovernaculars or metavernaculars helps create the impression of a vital feedback loop despite the immense asymmetry of production and reception that defines mass culture. It helps sustain the legitimating sense that mass texts move through a space that is, after all, an informal lifeworld. That the maintenance of this feedback circuit so often takes the form of humor suggests that, as with all joking, there is a lively current of unease powering the wit. Unease, perhaps, on both sides of the recurring dialectic: to be hip is to fear the mass circulation that feeds on hipness and which, in turn, makes it possible; while to be normal (in the "mainstream") is to have anxiety about the counterpublics that define themselves through performances so distinctively embodied that one cannot lasso them back into general circulation without risking the humiliating exposure of inauthenticity.

Number 34 of the *Spectator*, by Steele, neatly illustrates how these feedback provisions combine with the punctual temporality of the daily form and an emergent ideology of polite sociability to produce the understanding of a public structured by its own discourse:

> The Club of which I am a Member, is very luckily compos'd of such
> Persons as are engag'd in different Ways of Life, and deputed as it were
> out of the most conspicuous Classes of Mankind: By this Means I am fur-
> nish'd with the greatest Variety of Hints and Materials, and know every
> thing that passes in the different Quarters and Divisions, not only of this
> great City, but of the whole Kingdom. My Readers too have the Satisfac-
> tion to find, that there is no Rank or Degree among them who have not
> their Representative in this Club, and that there is always some Body
> present who will take Care of their respective Interests, that nothing may
> be written or publish'd to the Prejudice or Infringement of their just
> Rights and Privileges.

Mr. Spectator relates that the members of the club have been relaying to him
"several Remarks which they and others had made upon these my Speculations,
as also with the various Success which they had met with among their several
Ranks and Degrees of Readers." They act as his field reporters, allowing the
Spectator to reflect on his own reception.

What follows is a fable of reading. Will Honeycomb, the ladies' man, reports
that some ladies of fashion have been offended by criticisms of their taste;
Andrew Freeport, the merchant, responds that those criticisms were well deserved,
unlike those directed against merchants; the Templar defends those, but objects
to satires of the Inns of Court, and so on. Every member of the Club inflects his
reception of the essays with the interests that define the social class of which
he is a typification. In the aggregate, each cancels out the others. It is left to the
clergyman—a character who scarcely appears anywhere else in the essay series
—to explain "the Use this Paper might be of to the Publick" precisely in challenging the interests of the orders and ranks. The result is a sense of a *general*
public, by definition not embodied in any person or class, but realized by the
scene of circulation as the reception context of a common object.

"In short," concludes Mr. Spectator, "If I meet with any thing in City, Court, or
Country, that shocks Modesty or good Manners, I shall use my utmost Endeav-
ours to make an Example of it." He continues:

> I must however intreat every particular Person, who does me the Honour
> to be a Reader of this Paper, never to think himself, or any one of his
> Friends or Enemies, aimed at in what is said: For I promise him, never to
> draw a faulty Character which does not fit at least a Thousand People; or
> to publish a single Paper, that is not written in the Spirit of Benevolence
> and with a Love to Mankind.

Steele here coaches his readers in the personal/impersonal generic conventions of public address: I never speak to you without speaking to a thousand others. This form of address is tightly knit up with a social imaginary: any character or trait I depict typifies a whole social stratum. Individual readers who participate in this discourse learn to place themselves, as characterized types, in a world of urbane social knowledge, while also detaching themselves ethically from the particular interests that typify them—turning themselves, by means of a "Spirit of Benev-olence" and "Love of Mankind," into the reading subjects of a widely circulating form.

And not just reading subjects. The achievement of this cultural form is to allow participants in its discourse to understand themselves as directly and actively belonging to a social entity that exists historically in secular time and has con-sciousness of itself—although it has no existence outside of the activity of its own discursive circulation. In some contexts, this form can even be understood to act in the world, to claim moral authority, to be sovereign. To be sure, a great deal must be postulated in order for it to work in the world: not only the material con-ditions of a circulating medium, but also corresponding reading or consuming practices as well as the sort of social imaginary in which stranger-sociability could become ordinary, valuable, and in some ways normative. Such a normative horizon was, by the historical point marked by the *Spectator*, well articulated in England. An ethical disposition, a social imaginary, an extremely specialized set of formal conventions, and a temporality—each could seem to imply and follow from the others.

The discourse of a public is a linguistic form from which the social conditions of its own possibility are in large part derived. The magic by which discourse conjures a public into being, however, remains imperfect because of how much it must presuppose. And because many of the defining elements in the self-under-standing of publics are to some extent always contradicted by practice, the sor-cerer must continually cast spells against the darkness. A public seems to be self-organized by discourse, but in fact requires preexisting forms and channels of circulation. It appears to be open to indefinite strangers, but in fact selects partic-ipants by criteria of shared social space (though not necessarily territorial space), habitus, topical concerns, intergeneric references, and circulating intelligible forms (including idiolects or speech genres).

These criteria inevitably have positive content. They enable confidence that the discourse will circulate along a real path, but they limit the extension of that path. Discourse addressed to a public seeks to extend its circulation—otherwise, the public dwindles to a group—yet the need to characterize the space of circulation means that the public is also understood as having the content and differentiated belonging of a group, rather than simply being open to the infinite and unknowable potential of circulation. Reaching strangers is public discourse's primary orientation, but to be a public these unknowns must also be locatable as a social entity, even a social agent. Public discourse circulates, but it does so in struggle with its own conditions.

The *Spectator* is understood as circulating to indefinite strangers, but of course the choice of language and the organization of markets for print make it seem natural that those strangers will be English. The closing peroration of the essay cited above coaches its readers in an ethical disposition of impartial publicness; but it is also the ethos of a social class. The essay's style—a landmark in the history of English prose—moderates all the interests and characters of its reception context, enabling a voice that can simultaneously address the merchant, the squire, the courtier, the servant, the lady; but it is also the marker of a social type (masculine, bourgeois, moral urbanity) itself. In these and similar ways, although the language addresses an impersonal, indefinite, and self-organized expanse of circulation, it also elaborates (and masks as unmarked humanity) a particular culture, its embodied way of life, its reading practices, its ethical conventions, its geography, its class and gender dispositions, and its economic organization (in which the serial essay circulates as it does because it is, after all, a commodity within a market).

The *Spectator* is not unusual in having these limitations. If anything, it is unusual in the degree of its social porousness, the range of voices that it makes audible, and the number of contexts that it opens for transformation. Even in the best of cases, some friction inevitably obtains between public discourse and its environment, given the circularity in the conventions and postulates that make the social imaginary of the public work. To some degree, this friction is unavoidable because of the chicken-and-egg problem with which I began: the imaginary being of the public must be projected from already circulating discourse.

One result is a special kind of politics, a kind that is difficult to grasp in terms of the usual framework of politics as a field of interested strategic actors in specific relations of power and subordination. In such a framework, the contradiction between the idea of a public and its realization might be said to be more or less ideological. Evidence will not be wanting for such a view. When, in *Spectator* no. 34, the reading audience is characterized as "Mankind," we have a rather obvious example.[27] Because the positive identity of a public always remains partly covert

27. Paula McDowell, in her otherwise excellent study *The Women of Grub Street: Press, Politics, and Gender in the London Literary Marketplace, 1678–1730* (Oxford: Clarendon, 1998), goes so far

—given the premises of address to strangers, self-organization through discourse, and membership through mere attention—the limitations imposed by its speech genres, medium, and presupposed social base will always be in conflict with its own enabling postulates. When any public is taken to be *the* public, those limitations invisibly order the political world.

Many critiques of the idea of the public in modern thought rest on this covert content. It is one of the things people have in mind when they say, for example, that the public is essentially white or essentially male.[28] It has become customary, in the wake of arguments over Habermas's *Structural Transformation of the Public Sphere,* to lament or protest the arbitrary closures of the publics that came into being with the public sphere as their background. The peculiar dynamic of postulation and address by which public speech projects the social world has been understood mainly in terms of ideology, domination, or exclusion. And with reason—the history of the public sphere abounds with evidence of struggle for domination through this means and the resulting bad faith of the dominant public culture. What the critiques tend to miss, however, is that the tension inherent in the form goes well beyond any strategy of domination. The projection of a public is a new, creative, and distinctively modern mode of power.

One consequence of this tension in the laws of public discourse is a problem of style. In addressing indefinite strangers, public discourse puts a premium on accessibility. But there is no infinitely accessible language, and to imagine that there should be is to miss other, equally important needs of publics: to concretize the world in which discourse circulates, to offer its members direct and active membership through language, to place strangers on a shared footing. For these purposes language must be concrete, making use of the vernaculars of its circulatory space. So in publics, a double movement is always at work. Styles are mobilized, but they are also framed as styles. Sometimes the framing is hierarchical, a relation of marked to unmarked. Sometimes the result can be more relativizing. Quite commonly, the result can be a double-voiced hybrid. The differential

---

as to depict the representational conventions of the *Spectator* as a strategy for displacing and silencing the female authors with whom Addison and Steele were in competition—an interpretation that has some force, but in my view misses the distinctive features of the public as a form and shows the limiting effect of our conception of politics as strategic.

28. See, for example, Joan Landes, *Women and the Public Sphere in the Age of the French Revolution* (Ithaca, N.Y.: Cornell University Press, 1988); and the essays by Mary Ryan, Nancy Fraser, and Geoff Eley in *Habermas and the Public Sphere,* ed. Craig Calhoun (Cambridge: MIT Press, 1992). On Landes's claim that the public sphere was "essentially, not just contingently, masculinist," see Keith Michael Baker's astute discussion in "Defining the Public Sphere in Eighteenth-Century France," in Calhoun, *Habermas and the Public Sphere.*

deployment of style is essential to the way public discourse creates the consciousness of stranger-sociability. In this, it closely resembles the kind of double-voicing of speech genres classically analyzed by Mikhail Bakhtin: "For the speakers . . . generic languages and professional jargons are directly intentional—they denote and express directly and fully, and are capable of expressing themselves without mediation; but outside, that is, for those not participating in the given purview, these languages may be treated as objects, as typifactions, as local color."[29] Bakhtin calls this the "critical interanimation of languages."[30]

Perhaps for this reason, the *Spectator* obsessively represents scenes on the margin of its own public, places where its own language might circulate but that it cannot (or will not) capture as its addressee. One example is a hysterical moment in *Spectator* no. 217. Mr. Spectator has received a letter, signed "Kitty Termagant," which turns out to be another of the many letters describing clubs similar to the Spectator's own—in this case, the Club of She-Romps. Its members meet once a week, at night, in a room hired for the purpose (i.e., a place that is significantly public, though also secluded from open view). "We are no sooner come together," writes Kitty, "than we throw off all that Modesty and Reservedness with which our Sex are obliged to disguise themselves in publick Places. I am not able to express the Pleasure we enjoy from ten at Night till four in the Morning, in being as rude as you Men can be, for your Lives. As our Play runs high the Room is immediately filled with broken Fans, torn Petticoats, lappets of Head-dresses, Flounces, Furbelows, Garters, and Working-Aprons" (2: 345).

The She-Romps seem to be designed almost as an inverted image of the Spectator's own club. His is all male, theirs female. His is regulated by an ethic of bourgeois moral urbanity—differences of class and self-interest correct each other through the general discussion. Theirs throws off the restraints of decorum. Differences are not balanced through equable conversation but unleashed through raw physical play. It's a bitch fight. And although men might have their own pleasures in fantasizing such a scene, the *Spectator* more than hints at some antipathy. Kitty Termagant tells us that the She-Romps refer to the rags and tatters of their discarded clothing as "*dead Men*" (2: 346; emphasis in original).

Women, of course, are hardly excluded directly from the public of the *Spectator*. Quite the contrary; in no. 4, Mr. Spectator announces: "I shall take it for the greatest Glory of my Work, if among reasonable Women this Paper may furnish *Tea-Table Talk*" (1: 21). Women readers are crucial to the *Spectator*'s sense of its

29. Mikhail Bakhtin, *The Dialogic Imagination: Four Essays*, trans. Caryl Emerson and Michael Holquist (Austin: University of Texas Press, 1981), 289.

30. Bakhtin, *Dialogic Imagination*, 296.

public, and gender relations are made the subject of critical reflection in a way that must have felt dramatic and transformative. The *Spectator* represents the Club of She-Romps to highlight, by contrast, the urbanity and restraint of its own social ethic. Mr. Spectator neither excludes women outright nor frankly asserts male superiority. He does, however, draw attention to what he regards as the essentially unpublic character of the She-Romps' interaction. He uses an uneasy mix of mocking humor, male fear, and urbane scandal to remind the reader of the polite sociability required for his own confidence in a public composed of strangers.

The She-Romps cannot afford that confidence. For this and other reasons, the Club of She-Romps cannot really be called a public at all. It is a finite club of members known to one another, who would not be able to secure the freedom to meet without the security of mutual knowledge. Like most gossip, which is strictly regulated by a sense of group membership and social position, the She-Romps' discourse is not oriented to strangers. It is not that the She-Romps are unpublic simply in being a closed club; the Spectator's club, after all, is equally closed. Rather, we are given to understand that the She-Romps cannot open onto a public, the way the Spectator's club does within his essays. They express a style of sociability too embodied, too aggressive, and too sexualized to be imagined as the indefinite circulation of discourse among strangers. These women are not content to be "reasonable Women" whose highest mode of publicness is "Tea-Table Talk"; they want their publicness to be modeled on something other than mere private acts of reading. "We are no sooner come together," writes Kitty, "than we throw off all that Modesty and Reservedness with which our Sex are obliged to disguise themselves in publick Places." It is this refusal of any familiar norm for stranger sociability, rather than simple femaleness, that makes them a counterimage to the public.

The She-Romps, however, clearly want to alter the norms of "publick Places" so as to allow themselves the same physical freedoms as men, as well as an ability to meet with other women who share their history of frustration. They aspire to a public or quasi-public physicality. But dominant gender norms are such that this quasi-public physicality looks like intimacy out of place. It looks most antipublic when it looks like sexuality: "Once a month we *Demolish a Prude*, that is, we get some queer formal Creature in among us, and unrig her in an instant. Our last Month's Prude was so armed and fortified in Whale-bone and Buckram that we had much ado to come at her, but you would have died with laughing to have seen how the sober awkard [*sic*] thing looked, when she was forced out of her Intrenchments" (2: 346).

79

How exactly *did* the queer creature look? Thrilled? Appalled? Or simply speechless? Kitty says no more. Why does description falter here, at just the point where the transformative intent of the club runs up against shame, intimate exposure, and the sexual body? Could discourse go no further? The scene can be taken as representing the necessary involvement of strangers in the subjective life of any public, but with its tone raised first to an anxious pitch and then to muteness by the idea that such involvement might also be corporeal and intimate.

Interestingly, it is at just this moment that Kitty invites the Spectator to open her club's scenes to public discourse as he does with his own: "In short, Sir, 'tis impossible to give you a true Notion of our Sport, unless you would come one Night amongst us; and tho' it be directly against the Rules of our Society to admit a Male Visitant, we repose so much Confidence in your Silence and Taciturnity, that 'twas agreed by the whole Club, at our last Meeting, to give you Entrance for one Night as a Spectator" (2: 346). The women seek, in effect, to open the transformative intent of their coming together onto the critical estrangement of public discourse.

The Spectator refuses. "I do not at present find in my self any Inclination to venture my Person with her and her romping Companions . . . and should apprehend being *Demolished* as much as the *Prude*" (2: 346). This is a bit of a joke, as Mr. Spectator has only a ghost's body to demolish; he is an allegorical form of the reading eye. But he has something to demolish nonetheless: his own enabling ideology of polite publicness, the norms that offer confidence in circulation among strangers.

The *Spectator* essays contain many odd and diverting moments like this one, but few that say more about its public. One has to read this passage only slightly against the grain to see it as the ghost image of a counterpublic: it is a scene in which a dominated group aspires to re-create itself as a public and, in doing so, finds itself in conflict not only with the dominant social group, but also with the norms that constitute the dominant culture as a public. The *Spectator* goes so far as to represent the scene in order to clarify the norms that establish its own confident posture. In fact, the challenge so comically imagined in its pages would soon enough find actual, historical expression. Even in the years of the essays' appearance, the public places and stranger-sociability of London were giving rise to clubs of all kinds of She-Romps, including the so-called molly houses where something like a modern homosexual culture was developing—though it was not until rather later that such scenes could really articulate themselves through discourse as a coherent and freely circulating public.[31]

31. See Rictor Norton, *Mother Clap's Molly House: The Gay Subculture in England, 1700–1830* (London: Gay Men's Press, 1992).

Over the past three centuries, many such scenes have organized themselves as publics, and because they differ markedly in one way or another from the premises that allow the dominant culture to understand itself as a public, they have come to be called counterpublics. Yet we cannot understand counterpublics very well if we fail to see that there are contradictions and perversities inherent in the organization of *all* publics, tensions that are not captured by critiques of the dominant public's exclusions or ideological limitations. Counterpublics are publics, too. They work by many of the same circular postulates. It might even be claimed that, like dominant publics, they are ideological in that they provide a sense of active belonging that masks or compensates for the real powerlessness of human agents in capitalist society. But here I merely leave this question aside; what interests me is the odd social imaginary that is established by the ethic of estrangement and social poesis in public address. The cultural form of the public transforms She-Romps and Spectators alike.

In a public, indefinite address and self-organized discourse disclose a lived world whose arbitrary closure both enables that discourse and is contradicted by it. Public discourse, in the nature of its address, abandons the security of its positive, given audience. It promises to address anybody. It commits itself in principle to the possible participation of any stranger. It therefore puts at risk the concrete world that is its given condition of possibility. This is its fruitful perversity. Public discourse postulates a circulatory field of estrangement that it must then struggle to capture as an addressable entity. No form with such a structure could be very stable. The projective nature of public discourse—which requires that every characterization of the circulatory path become material for new estrangements and recharacterizations—is an engine for (not necessarily progressive) social mutation.

Public discourse, in other words, is poetic. By this I mean not just that a public is self-organizing, a kind of entity created by its own discourse, or even that this space of circulation is taken to be a social entity. Rather, I mean that all discourse or performance addressed to a public must characterize the world in which it attempts to circulate, projecting for that world a concrete and livable shape, and attempting to realize that world through address.[32]

---

32. Even if the address is indirect. The most insightful study I know of the tight relation between a public form and a mode of life is an example of the indirect implication of a reception context by a form that refuses to address it outright: D. A. Miller's *Place for Us: Essay on the Broadway Musical* (Cambridge: Harvard University Press, 1998).

7. A public is poetic world-making.

There is no speech or performance addressed to a public that does not try to specify in advance, in countless highly condensed ways, the lifeworld of its circulation. This is accomplished not only through discursive claims, of the kind that can be said to be oriented to understanding, but also at the level of pragmatics, through the effects of speech genres, idioms, stylistic markers, address, temporality, mise-en-scène, citational field, interlocutory protocols, lexicon, and so on. Its circulatory fate is the realization of that world. Public discourse says not only: "Let a public exist," but: "Let it have this character, speak this way, see the world in this way." It then goes out in search of confirmation that such a public exists, with greater or lesser success—success being further attempts to cite, circulate, and realize the world-understanding it articulates. Run it up the flagpole, and see who salutes. Put on a show, and see who shows up.

This performative dimension of public discourse, however, is routinely misrecognized. Public speech contends with the necessity of addressing its public as already existing real persons. It cannot work by frankly declaring its subjunctive-creative project. Its success depends on the recognition of participants and their further circulatory activity, and people do not commonly recognize themselves as virtual projections. They recognize themselves only as already being the persons they are addressed as being, and as already belonging to the world that is condensed in their discourse.

The poetic function of public discourse is misrecognized for a second reason as well, one noted above in a different context. In the dominant tradition of the public sphere, address to a public is ideologized as rational-critical dialogue. The circulation of public discourse is consistently imagined—in folk theory and in sophisticated political philosophy alike—as dialogue or discussion among already present interlocutors, as within Mr. Spectator's club. The image that prevails is something like parliamentary forensics. I have already noted that this way of imagining publics causes their constitutive circularity to disappear from consciousness: publics are thought to be real persons in dyadic author-reader interactions, rather than multigeneric circulation. I have also noted that the same ideologization makes possible the idea that publics can have volitional agency: they exist so as to deliberate and then decide. The point here is that this perception of public discourse as conversation obscures the importance of the poetic functions of both language and corporeal expressivity in giving a particular shape to publics. The public is thought to exist empirically and to require persuasion rather than poesis. Public circulation is understood as rational discussion writ large.

This constitutive misrecognition of publics relies on a particular ideology of language. Discourse is understood to be propositionally summarizable; the poetic or textual qualities of any utterance are disregarded in favor of *sense*. Acts of reading, too, are understood to be replicable and uniform.[33] So are opinions, which is why private reading is felt to be directly connected to the sovereign power of public opinion. Just as sense can be propositionally summarized, opinions can be held, transferred, restated indefinitely. (The essential role played by this kind of transposition in the modern social imaginary might help to explain why modern philosophy has been obsessed with referential semantics and fixity.) Other aspects of discourse, including affect and expressivity, are not thought to be fungible in the same way. The development of such a language ideology has, without doubt, helped make possible the modern confidence placed in the stranger-sociability of public circulation. Strangers are less strange if you can trust them to read as you read, or if the sense of what they say can be fully abstracted from the way they say it.

I also suspect that the development of the social imaginary of publics, as a relation among strangers that is projected from private readings of circulating texts, has exerted over the past three centuries a powerful gravity on the conception of the human, elevating what is understood to be the faculties of the private reader as the essential (rational-critical) faculties of man. If you know and are intimately associated with strangers to whom you are directly related only through the discursive means of reading, opining, arguing, and witnessing, then it might seem natural that other faculties recede from salience at the highest levels of social belonging. The modern hierarchy of faculties and the modern imagination of the social are mutually implying. The critical discourse of the public corresponds as sovereign to the superintending power of the state. So the dimensions of language singled out in the ideology of rational-critical discussion acquire prestige and power. Publics more overtly oriented in their self-understandings to the poetic-expressive dimensions of language — including artistic publics and

33. In all the literature on the history of reading, the development of this ideology remains an understudied phenomenon. Adrian Johns makes a significant contribution in *The Nature of the Book: Print and Knowledge in the Making* (Chicago: University of Chicago Press, 1998); see especially 380–443. Johns's study suggests that the idea of reading as a private act with replicable meaning for strangers dispersed through space emerged in the very period that gave rise to publics in the modern form analyzed here; support for this conjecture can also be found in Kevin Sharpe, *Reading Revolutions: The Politics of Reading in Early Modern England* (New Haven, Conn.: Yale University Press, 2000); Guglielmo Cavallo and Roger Chartier, eds., *A History of Reading in the West* (Amherst: University of Massachusetts Press, 1999); and James Raven, Helen Small, and Naomi Tadmore, eds., *The Practice and Representation of Reading in England* (Cambridge: Cambridge University Press, 1996).

many counterpublics—lack the power to transpose themselves to the level of the generality of the state. Along the entire chain of equations in the public sphere, from local acts of reading or scenes of speech to the general horizon of public opinion and its critical opposition to state power, the pragmatics of public discourse must be systematically blocked from view.

Publics have acquired their importance to modern life because of the ease of these transpositions upward to the level of the state. Once the background assumptions of public opinion are in place, all discrete publics become part of *the* public. Though essentially imaginary projections from local exchanges or acts of reading and therefore infinite in number, they are often thought of as a unitary space. This assumption gains force from the postulated relation between public opinion and the state. A critical opposition to the state, supervising both executive and legislative power, confers on countless acts of opining the unity of public opinion; those acts share both a common object and a common agency of supervision and legitimation.

The unity of the public, however, is also ideological. It depends on the stylization of the reading act as transparent and replicable; it depends on an arbitrary social closure (through language, idiolect, genre, medium, and address) to contain its potentially infinite extension; it depends on institutionalized forms of power to realize the agency attributed to the public; and it depends on a hierarchy of faculties that allows some activities to count as public or general, while others are thought to be merely personal, private, or particular. Some publics, for these reasons, are more likely than others to stand in for *the* public, to frame their address as the universal discussion of the people.

But what of the publics that make no attempt to present themselves this way? There are as many shades of difference among publics as there are in modes of address, style, and spaces of circulation. Many might be thought of as subpublics, or specialized publics, focused on particular interests, professions, or locales. The public of *Field and Stream*, to take an example well within the familiar range of print genres, does not take itself to be the national people, nor humanity in general; the magazine addresses only those with an interest in hunting and fishing, who in varying degrees participate in a (male) subculture of hunters and fishermen. Yet nothing in the mode of address or in the projected horizon of this subculture requires its participants to cease for a moment to think of themselves as members of the general public as well; indeed, they might well consider themselves its most representative members.

Other publics mark themselves off unmistakably from any general or dominant public. Their members are understood to be not merely a subset of the public, but constituted through a conflictual relation to the dominant public. In an influential 1992 article, Nancy Fraser observed that when public discourse is understood only as a "single, comprehensive, overarching public," members of subordinated groups "have no arenas for deliberation among themselves about their needs, objectives, and strategies." In fact, Fraser writes, "members of subordinated social groups—women, workers, peoples of color, and gays and lesbians—have repeatedly found it advantageous to constitute alternative publics."[34] She calls these "subaltern counterpublics," by which she means "parallel discursive arenas where members of subordinated social groups invent and circulate counterdiscourses to formulate oppositional interpretations of their identities, interests, and needs."[35]

Fraser here names an important phenomenon. But what makes such a public "counter" or "oppositional"? Is its oppositional character a function of its content alone—that is, its claim to be oppositional? In that case, we might simply call it a subpublic, like that of *Field and Stream*, although characterized, to be sure, by a difference of degree: it is more likely to display a thematic discussion of political opposition. But there would be no difference of kind, or of formal mediation, or of discourse pragmatics, between counterpublics and any other publics. Fraser's description of what counterpublics do—"formulate oppositional interpretations of their identities, interests, and needs"—sounds like the classically Habermasian description of rational-critical publics with the word *oppositional* inserted.

Fraser's principal example is "the late-twentieth-century U.S. feminist subaltern counterpublic, with its variegated array of journals, bookstores, publishing companies, film and video distribution networks, lecture series, research centers, academic programs, conferences, conventions, festivals, and local meeting places."[36] This description aptly suggests the constitution of a public as a multicontextual space of circulation, organized not by a place or an institution but by the circulation of discourse. But this is true of any public, not only counterpublics. Fraser writes that the feminist counterpublic is distinguished by a special idiom for social reality, including such terms as *sexism*, *sexual harassment*, and *marital*, *date*, and *acquaintance rape*. This idiom can now be found anywhere—not always embodying a feminist intention, but circulating as common terminology. Is the feminist counterpublic distinguished by anything other than its program of reform?

34. Nancy Fraser, "Rethinking the Public Sphere: A Contribution to the Critique of Actually Existing Democracy," in Calhoun, *Habermas and the Public Sphere*, 122–23.
35. Fraser, "Rethinking the Public Sphere," 123.
36. Fraser, "Rethinking the Public Sphere," 123.

Furthermore, why would counterpublics of this variety be limited to "subalterns"? How are they different from the publics of U.S. Christian fundamentalism, or youth culture, or artistic bohemianism? Each of these is a similarly complex metatopical space for the circulation of discourse; each is a scene for developing oppositional interpretations of its members' identities, interests, and needs. They are structured by different dispositions or protocols from those that obtain elsewhere in the culture, making different assumptions about what can be said or what goes without saying.

In the sense of the term that I am advocating here, such publics are indeed *counterpublics*, and in a stronger sense than simply comprising subalterns with a reform program. A counterpublic maintains at some level, conscious or not, an awareness of its subordinate status. The cultural horizon against which it marks itself off is not just a general or wider public, but a dominant one. And the conflict extends not just to ideas or policy questions, but to the speech genres and modes of address that constitute the public and to the hierarchy among media. The discourse that constitutes it is not merely a different or alternative idiom, but one that in other contexts would be regarded with hostility or with a sense of indecorousness. (This is why the She-Romps seem to anticipate counterpublicness: "We throw off all that Modesty and Reservedness with which our Sex are obliged to disguise themselves in publick Places.") Friction against the dominant public forces the poetic-expressive character of counterpublic discourse to become salient to consciousness.

Like all publics, a counterpublic comes into being through an address to indefinite strangers. (This is one significant difference between the notion of a counterpublic and the notion of a bounded community or group.) But counterpublic discourse also addresses those strangers as being not just anybody. Addressees are socially marked by their participation in this kind of discourse; ordinary people are presumed to not want to be mistaken for the kind of person who would participate in this kind of talk or be present in this kind of scene. Addressing indefinite strangers in a magazine or a sermon has a peculiar meaning when you know in advance that most people will be unwilling to read a gay magazine or go to a black church. In some contexts, the code-switching of bilingualism might do similar work in keeping the counterpublic horizon salient—just as the linguistic fragmentation of many postcolonial settings creates resistance to the idea of a sutured space of circulation.

Within a gay or queer counterpublic, for example, no one is in the closet: the presumptive heterosexuality that constitutes the closet for individuals in ordinary speech is suspended. But this circulatory space, freed from heteronormative speech protocols, is itself marked by that very suspension: speech that addresses any participant as queer will circulate up to a point, at which it is certain to meet intense resistance. It might therefore circulate in special, protected venues, in limited publications. The individual struggle with stigma is transposed, as it were, to the conflict between modes of publicness. The expansive nature of public address will seek to keep moving that frontier for a queer public, to seek more and more places to circulate where people will recognize themselves in its address; but no one is likely to be unaware of the risk and conflict involved.

In some cases, such as fundamentalism or certain kinds of youth culture, participants are not subalterns for any reason outside of their participation in the counterpublic discourse. In others, a socially stigmatized identity might be predicated, but in such cases a public of subalterns only constitutes a counterpublic when its participants are addressed in a counterpublic way—as, for example, with African Americans who are willing to speak in a racially marked idiom. The subordinate status of a counterpublic does not simply reflect identities formed elsewhere; participation in such a public is one of the ways its members' identities are formed and transformed. A hierarchy or stigma is the assumed background of practice. One enters at one's own risk.

Counterpublic discourse is far more than the expression of subaltern culture and far more than what some Foucauldians like to call "reverse discourse." Fundamentally mediated by public forms, counterpublics incorporate the personal/impersonal address and expansive estrangement of public speech as the condition of their own common world. Perhaps nothing demonstrates the fundamental importance of discursive publics in the modern social imaginary more than this—that even the counterpublics that challenge modernity's social hierarchy of faculties do so by projecting the space of discursive circulation among strangers as a social entity, and in doing so fashion their own subjectivities around the requirements of public circulation and stranger-sociability.[37]

If I address a queer public, or a public of fellow She-Romps, I don't simply express the way I and my friends live. I commit myself, and the fate of my world-making project, to circulation among indefinite others. However much my address to them might be laden with intimate affect, it must also be extended impersonally, making membership available on the basis of mere attention. My world must be one of strangers. Counterpublics are "counter" to the extent that

37. For an interesting limit case, see Charles Hirschkind, "Civic Virtue and Religious Reason: An Islamic Counterpublic," *Cultural Anthropology* 16 (2001): 3–34. Hirschkind analyzes complex modes of commentary and circulation in contemporary Egypt; what remains unclear is the extent to which this emergent and reactive discourse culture can still be called a public.

they try to supply different ways of imagining stranger-sociability and its reflexivity; as publics, they remain oriented to stranger-circulation in a way that is not just strategic, but also constitutive of membership and its affects. As it happens, an understanding of queerness has been developing in recent decades that is suited to just this necessity; a culture is developing in which intimate relations and the sexual body can in fact be understood as projects for transformation among strangers. (At the same time, a lesbian and gay public has been reshaped so as to ignore or refuse the counterpublic character that has marked its history.)[38] So also in youth culture, coolness mediates a difference from dominant publics and, in so doing, a subjective form of stranger-sociability. Public discourse imposes a field of tensions within which any world-making project must articulate itself. To the extent that I want that world to be one in which embodied sociability, affect, and play have a more defining role than they do in the opinion-transposing frame of rational-critical dialogue, those tensions will be acutely felt.

I cannot say in advance what romping will *feel like* in my public of She-Romps. Publicness is simply this space of coming together that discloses itself in interaction. The world of strangers that public discourse makes must be made of further circulation and recharacterization over time; it cannot simply be aggregated from units that I can expect to be similar to mine. I risk its fate. This necessity of risked estrangement, though essential to all publics, becomes especially salient in counterpublic discourse and is registered in its ethical-political imagination. Dominant publics are by definition those that can take their discourse pragmatics and their lifeworlds for granted, misrecognizing the indefinite scope of their expansive address as universality or normalcy. Counterpublics are spaces of circulation in which it is hoped that the poesis of scene making will be transformative, not replicative merely.

Counterpublics face another obstacle as well. One of the most striking features of publics, in the modern public sphere, is that they can in some contexts acquire agency. Not only is participation understood as active, at the level of the individual whose uptake helps to constitute a public, it is also sometimes possible to attribute agency to the virtual corporate entity created by the space of circulation as a whole. Publics act historically. They are said to rise up, to speak, to reject false promises, to demand answers, to change sovereigns, to support troops, to give mandates for change, to be satisfied, to scrutinize public conduct, to take role models, to deride counterfeits. It's difficult to imagine the modern world

38. See Michael Warner, *The Trouble with Normal: Sex, Politics, and the Ethics of Queer Life* (New York: Free Press, 1999), especially chap. 2.

without the ability to attribute agency to publics, although doing so is an extraordinary fiction. It requires us, for example, to understand the ongoing circulatory time of public discourse as though it were a process of discussion leading up to a decision.

The attribution of agency to publics works, in most cases, because of the direct transposition from acts of private reading to the figuration of sovereign opinion. All of the verbs for public agency are verbs for private reading, transposed upward to the aggregate of readers. Readers may scrutinize, ask, reject, opine, decide, judge, and so on. Publics can do exactly these things. And nothing else. Publics—unlike mobs or crowds—remain incapable of any activity that cannot be expressed through such verbs. Even activities that are part of reading but do not fit its ideologized image as a practice of silent, private, replicable decoding—curling up, mumbling, fantasizing, gesticulating, ventriloquizing, and writing marginalia, for example—are bereft of counterparts in public agency.

Counterpublics tend to be those in which this ideology of reading does not have the same privilege. It might be that embodied sociability is too important to them; they might not be organized by the hierarchy of faculties that elevates rational-critical reflection as the self-image of humanity; they might depend more heavily on performance spaces than on print; it might be that they cannot so easily suppress from consciousness their own creative-expressive function. How, then, will they imagine their agency? Can a public of She-Romps romp?

It is, in fact, possible to imagine that almost any characterization of discursive acts might be attributed to a public. A queer public might be one that throws shade, prances, disses, acts up, carries on, longs, fantasizes, throws fits, mourns, "reads." To take such attributions of public agency seriously, however, we would need to inhabit a culture with a different language ideology, a different social imaginary. It is difficult to say what such a world would be like. It might need to be one with a different role for state-based thinking; as things stand now, it might be that the only way a public is able to act is through its imaginary coupling with the state.

This is one of the things that happen when alternative publics are cast as social movements—they acquire agency in relation to the state. They enter the temporality of politics and adapt themselves to the performatives of rational-critical discourse. For many counterpublics, to do so is to cede the original hope of transforming, not just policy, but the space of public life itself.

Michael Warner is a professor of English at Rutgers University. His most recent works include the forthcoming collection *Publics and Counterpublics*, *The Trouble with Normal: Sex, Politics, and the Ethics of Queer Life* (1999), and *American Sermons: The Pilgrims to Martin Luther King, Jr.* (1999).

Modern Social Imaginaries

Charles Taylor

The number one problem of modern social science has been modernity itself. By *modernity* I mean that historically unprecedented amalgam of new practices and institutional forms (science, technology, industrial production, urbanization), of new ways of living (individualism, secularization, instrumental rationality), and of new forms of malaise (alienation, meaninglessness, a sense of impending social dissolution).

In our day, the problem needs to be posed again from a new angle: Is there a single phenomenon here, or do we need to speak of *multiple* modernities, the plural reflecting the fact that non-Western cultures have modernized in their own ways and cannot be properly understood if we try to grasp them in a general theory that was originally designed with the Western case in mind?

This essay seeks to shed light on both the original and contemporary issues about modernity by defining the self-understandings that have been constitutive of it. Western modernity in this view is inseparable from a certain kind of social imaginary, and the differences among today's multiple modernities are understood in terms of the divergent social imaginaries involved. This approach is not the same as one that might focus on the *ideas* as against the *institutions* of modernity. The social imaginary is not a set of ideas; rather it is what enables, through making sense of, the practices of a society. This crucial point is expanded in part 3.

My aim here is a modest one. I would like to sketch an account of the forms of

Public Culture 14(1): 91–124

social imaginary that have underpinned the rise of Western modernity. This is an essay in Western history; it does not engage the variety of today's alternative modernities.[1] But I hope that a closer definition of the Western specificity may help us see more clearly what the different paths of contemporary modernization hold in common. In writing this, I have obviously drawn heavily on the pioneering work of Benedict Anderson in *Imagined Communities*, as well as on work by Jürgen Habermas, Michael Warner, Pierre Rosanvallon, and others, which I shall acknowledge as the argument unfolds.[2]

My hypothesis is that central to Western modernity is a new conception of the moral order of society. At first this moral order was just an idea in the minds of some influential thinkers, but later it came to shape the social imaginary of large strata, and then eventually whole societies. It has now become so self-evident to us, we have trouble seeing it as one possible conception among others. The mutation of this view of moral order into our social imaginary is the development of certain social forms that characterize Western modernity: the market economy, the public sphere, the self-governing people, among others.

I.

I will start with the new vision of moral order. This was most clearly stated in the new theories of natural law that emerged in the seventeenth century, largely as a response to the domestic and international disorder wrought by the Wars of Religion (1562–98). Hugo Grotius and John Locke are the most important theorists of reference for our purposes here.

Grotius derives the normative order underlying political society from the nature of its constitutive members. Human beings are rational, sociable agents who are meant to collaborate in peace to their mutual benefit. Since the seventeenth century, this idea increasingly has come to dominate our political thinking and the way we imagine our society. It starts off in Grotius's version as a theory of what political society is—what it is in aid of, how it comes to be. But any theory of this kind also provides an idea of moral order; it tells us something about how we ought to live together in society.[3]

1. Cf. Dilip Parameshwar Gaonkar, ed., *Alternative Modernities* (Durham, N.C.: Duke University Press, 2001).
2. Benedict Anderson, *Imagined Communities: Reflections on the Origin and Spread of Nationalism*, rev. ed. (London: Verso, 1991).
3. Grotius's *De Jure Belli ae Pacis* [The law of war and peace] is the relevant work for our discussion.

The picture of society is that of individuals who come together to form a political entity against a certain preexisting moral background and with certain ends in view. The moral background is one of natural rights; these people already have certain moral obligations toward one another. The ends sought are certain common benefits, of which security is the most important.

The underlying idea of moral order stresses the rights and obligations that individuals have in regard to one another, even prior to or outside of the political bond. Political obligations are seen as an extension or application of these more fundamental moral ties. Political authority itself is legitimate only because it was consented to by individuals (the original contract), and this contract creates binding obligations in virtue of the preexisting principle that promises should be kept.

It is Locke who first uses this theory as a justification of "revolution" and as a ground for limited government. Rights can now be seriously pleaded against power. Consent is not just an original agreement to set up government, but a continuing right to agree to taxation. Although the contract language may fall away and be used only by a minority of theorists, for the next three centuries the underlying idea of society as existing for the (mutual) benefit of individuals—and the defense of their rights—takes on increasing importance. That is, it not only comes to be the dominant view, pushing older theories of society or newer rivals to the margins of political life and discourse, but it also generates more and more far-reaching claims on political life. The requirement of original consent, via the halfway house of Locke's consent to taxation, becomes the full-fledged doctrine of popular sovereignty under which we now live. The theory of natural rights ends up spawning a dense web of limits to legislative and executive action by way of the entrenched charters that have become an important feature of contemporary government. The presumption of equality, implicit in the starting point of the state of nature, where people stand outside of all relations of superiority and inferiority, has been applied in a growing number of contexts, resulting in equal opportunity or nondiscrimination provisions, which are an integral part of most entrenched charters of rights.

In other words, during these last four centuries, the idea of moral order implicit in this view of society has undergone a double expansion: (1) in extension—more people live by it, it has become dominant; and (2) in intensity—the demands it makes are heavier and more ramified. The idea has gone through a series of "redactions," as it were, each richer and more demanding than the previous one, up to the present day.

It is clear that the images of moral order which descend through a series of transformations from that inscribed in the natural law theories of Grotius and

Locke are rather different from those embedded in the social imaginary of the premodern age.

Two important types of premodern moral order are worth singling out, because we can see them being gradually taken over, displaced, or marginalized by the Grotian-Lockean strand during the transition to political modernity. One is based on the idea of the *law* of a people, a law that has existed "time out of mind," and which in a sense defines a group as a people. This idea seems to have been widespread among the Indo-European tribes who at various stages erupted into Europe. It was very powerful in seventeenth-century England, under the guise of the ancient constitution, and became one of the key justifying ideas of the rebellion against the king in the civil war of the 1640s. From this example it is clear that these notions are not always conservative in import, but we should also include in this category the sense of normative order that seems to have been carried on through generations in peasant communities and out of which they developed a picture of the "moral economy," from which they could criticize the burdens laid on them by landlords or the exactions levied on them by state and church.[4] Here again, the recurring idea seems to have been that an original acceptable distribution of burdens had been displaced by usurpation and should be rolled back.

The other type of premodern moral order is organized around a notion of a hierarchy in society that expresses and corresponds to a hierarchy in the cosmos. These were often theorized in language drawn from the Platonic-Aristotelian concept of Form, but the underlying notion also emerges strongly in theories of correspondence (e.g., the king is in his kingdom, as the lion among animals, the eagle among birds, and so forth). From these theories the idea emerges that disorders in the human realm will resonate in nature, because the very order of things is threatened. The night on which Duncan was murdered was disturbed by "lamentings heard i' th' air, strange screams of death," and it remained dark even though day should have started. On the previous Tuesday, a falcon had been killed by a mousing owl, and Duncan's horses turned wild in the night, "contending 'gainst obedience, as they would make / War with mankind."[5]

In both these cases—and particularly in the second—we have an order that tends to impose itself by the course of things: violations are met with backlash that transcends the merely human realm. This is a very common feature of pre-

4. The term *moral economy* is borrowed from E. P. Thompson, *The Making of the English Working Class* (New York: Pantheon, 1964).

5. *Macbeth* 2.3.56; 2.4.17–18.

modern ideas of moral order. Greek philosopher Anaximander likens any deviation from the course of nature to injustice; he says that things that resist it must eventually "pay penalty and retribution to each other for their injustice according to the assessment of time."[6] And certainly the Platonic forms are active in shaping the things and events in the world of change.

In these cases, it is very clear that a moral order is more than just a set of norms; it also contains what we might call an "ontic" component, identifying features of the world that make the norms realizable. In contrast, the modern order that descends from Grotius and Locke is not self-realizing in the sense invoked by Hesiod or Plato or by the cosmic reactions to Duncan's murder. It is therefore tempting to think that our modern notions of moral order lack altogether an ontic component. But this would be a mistake, as I hope to show later. Realization is also an element of the modern moral order—but the emphasis is on humans rather than on God or the cosmos.

To recognize what is peculiar to our modern understanding of order, it will help to look at how the idealizations of natural law theory differ from those that were dominant before. Premodern social imaginaries, especially those of the second type mentioned above, were structured by various modes of hierarchical complementarity. Society was seen as being made up of different orders that needed and complemented one another. This didn't mean that their relations were truly mutual, because they didn't exist on the same level. Rather, they formed a hierarchy in which some had greater dignity and value than the others. An example is the often repeated medieval idealization of the society of three orders: *oratores*, *bellatores*, and *laboratores*—those who pray, those who fight, and those who work. It was clear that each needed the others, but there was also a descending scale of dignity; some functions were intrinsically higher than others.

The distribution of functions is itself a key part of the normative order. It is not just that each order ought to perform its characteristic function for the others, assuming they have entered these relations of exchange. No, the hierarchical differentiation itself is seen as the proper order of things. It was part of the nature or form of society. In the Platonic and neo-Platonic traditions, as I have just mentioned, this form was already at work in the world, and any attempt to deviate from it turned reality against itself. Society would be denatured in the attempt. Hence the tremendous power of the organic metaphor in these earlier theories. The organism seems to be the paradigmatic locus of forms at work, striving to

6. Quoted in Louis Dupré, *Passage to Modernity: An Essay in the Hermeneutics of Nature and Culture* (New Haven, Conn.: Yale University Press, 1993), 19.

heal its wounds and cure its maladies. And at the same time, the arrangement of functions that it exhibits is not simply contingent, it is "normal" and right. That the feet are below the head is how it should be.

In contrast, the basic point of the new normative order was the mutual respect and mutual service of the individuals who make up society. The actual structures were meant to serve these ends, and were judged instrumentally in this light. The difference might be obscured by the fact that the older orders also ensured a kind of mutual service: the clergy pray for the laity, and the laity defend and work for the clergy. The crucial point, however, is the hierarchical division into types. With the new normative order, we start with individuals and their debt of mutual service; the divisions emerge as a way to most effectively discharge this debt.

We can see the difference between new and old orders, if we look at how Plato, in book 2 of the *Republic*, starts out by reasoning from the non-self-sufficiency of the individual to the need for an order of mutual service. Quite rapidly it becomes clear that the basic point is the structure of this order. And any doubt is removed when we see that this order is meant to stand in analogy and interaction with the normative order in the soul. By contrast, in the modern ideal, the whole point is the mutual respect and service, however achieved.

Moreover, our primary service to one another was the provision of collective security (to use the language of a later age), to render our lives and property safe under law. But we also serve one another in practicing economic exchange. These two main ends, security and prosperity, are now the principal goals of organized society, which itself can be seen as a type of profitable exchange between its constituent members. The ideal social order is one in which our purposes mesh, and each in furthering oneself helps the others.

This ideal order was not thought to be a mere human invention: it was designed by God, and everything within it coheres according to God's purposes. Later in the eighteenth century, the same model is projected on the cosmos in a vision of the universe as a set of perfectly interlocking parts, in which the purposes of each kind of creature mesh with those of all the others. This God-given order sets the goal for our constructive activity insofar as it lies within our power to upset it or realize it. Of course, when we look at the whole, we see how much the order is already realized, but when we cast our eye on human affairs, we see how much we have deviated from it and upset it; it becomes the norm to which we should strive to return.

This order was thought to be evident in the nature of things. Of course, if we consult Revelation, we will also find the demand formulated there that we abide by it. But reason alone can tell us God's purposes. Living things, including ourselves, strive to preserve themselves. This is God's doing. As Locke writes,

> God having made Man, and planted in him, as in all other Animals, a strong desire of Self-preservation, and furnished the World with things fit for Food and Rayment and other Necessaries of Life, Subservient to his design, that Man should live and abide for some time upon the Face of the Earth, and not that so curious and wonderful a piece of Workmanship by its own Negligence, or want of Necessities, should perish again. . . . God . . . spoke to him, (that is) directed him by his Senses and Reason, . . . to the use of those things, which were serviceable for his Subsistence, and given him as means of his Preservation. . . . For the desire, strong desire of Preserving his Life and Being having been planted in him, as a Principle of Action by God himself, Reason, which was the voice of God in him, could not but teach him and assure him, that pursuing that natural Inclination he had to preserve his Being, he followed the Will of his Maker. . . .[7]

Being endowed with reason, we see that not only our lives but those of all humans are to be preserved. And in addition, God made us sociable beings. So that "every one as he is bound to preserve himself, and not quit his Station wilfully; so by the like reason when his Preservation comes not in competition, ought he, as much as he can, to preserve the rest of Mankind."[8]

Similarly Locke reasons that God gave us our powers of reason and discipline so that we could most effectively go about the business of preserving ourselves. It follows that we ought to be "Industrious and Rational."[9] The ethic of discipline and improvement is itself a requirement of the natural order that God had designed. Even the need for human will to impose order is an integral part of God's scheme.

We can see in Locke's formulation that he views mutual service in terms of profitable exchange. "Economic" (that is, ordered, peaceful, productive) activity has become the model for human behavior and the key for harmonious coexistence. In contrast to the theories of hierarchical complementarity, we meet in a zone of concord and mutual service, not to the extent that we transcend our ordinary goals and purposes, but rather in the process of carrying them out according to God's design.

7. Locke *Two Treatises of Civil Government* 1.86.
8. Locke *Two Treatises* 2.6; see also 2.135 and Locke *Some Thoughts Concerning Education* par. 116.
9. Locke *Two Treatises* 2.26.

This idealization of mutual benefit was at the outset profoundly out of sync with the way things in fact ran, thus with the effective social imaginary on just about every level of society. Hierarchical complementarity was the principle on which people's lives operated in practice, all the way from the kingdom, to the city, to the diocese, to the parish, to the clan and the family. We still have some lively sense of this disparity in the case of the family, because it is really only in our time that the older images of hierarchical complementarity between men and women are being comprehensively challenged. But this is a late stage on a "long march," a process in which the modern idealization has connected up with and transformed our social imaginary on virtually every level, with revolutionary consequences.

The very revolutionary nature of the consequences ensured that those who first took up this theory would fail to see its application in a host of areas that seem obvious to us today. The powerful hold of hierarchically complementary forms of life—in the family, between master and servant in the household, between lord and peasant on the domain, between educated elite and the masses —made it seem "evident" that the new principle of order ought to be applied only within certain bounds. This was often not even perceived as a restriction. What seems to us flagrant inconsistency, when eighteenth-century Whigs defended their oligarchic power in the name of the "people," for instance, was for the Whig leaders themselves just common sense.

In fact, they were drawing on an older understanding of "people," one stemming from a premodern notion of order, of the first type I mentioned above, in which a people is constituted as such by a law that always already exists, time out of mind. This law can confer leadership on some elements, who thus quite naturally speak for the people. Even revolutions (as we would term them) in early modern Europe were carried out under this understanding—as for instance, the antimonarchists in the French Wars of Religion, who accorded the right to rebel not to the unorganized masses but to the "subordinate magistrates." This was also the basis of Parliament's rebellion against Charles I.

And this long march is perhaps ending only today. Or perhaps we too are victims of a mental restriction, for which our posterity will accuse us of inconsistency or hypocrisy. In any case, some very important stages of this journey happened very recently. I have mentioned contemporary gender relations in this regard. But we should also remember that it wasn't very long ago when whole segments of our supposedly modern society remained outside of this modern social imaginary. As Eugen Weber has shown, many communities of French peasants were transformed only late in the nineteenth century and inducted into France as a nation of 40 million individual citizens.[10]

This history is easy to forget, because once we are well installed in the modern social imaginary, it seems the only possible one, the only one that makes sense. After all, are we not all individuals? Do we not associate in society for our mutual benefit? How else to measure social life?

Our limited perspective makes it very easy for us to entertain a quite distorted view of the process in two respects. First, we tend to read the march of this new principle of order and its displacing of traditional modes of complementarity as the rise of "individualism" at the expense of "community." As a result, we fail to recognize that the inevitable flip side of the new understanding of the individual is a new understanding of sociality: the society of mutual benefit, whose functional differentiations are ultimately contingent and whose members are fundamentally equal. This is what I have been insisting on in these pages, precisely because it generally gets lost from view. The individual seems primary because we read the displacement of older forms of complementarity as the erosion of community as such. We seem to be left with a standing problem of how to induce or force the individual into some kind of social order, make him or her conform and obey the rules.

This recurrent experience of breakdown is real enough. But it need not mask the fact that modernity is also the rise of new principles of sociality. As we can see with the case of the French Revolution, breakdown occurs when people are expelled from their old forms, through war, revolution, or rapid economic change, before they can find their way in the new structures, that is, connect some transformed practices to the new principles to form a viable social imaginary. But this doesn't show that modern individualism is by its very essence a solvent of community or that the modern political predicament is that defined by Hobbes: How do we rescue atomic individuals from the prisoner's dilemma? The real, recurring problem has been better defined by Tocqueville, or in our day François Furet.

The second distortion is a familiar one. The modern principle seems to us so self-evident—are we not by nature and essence individuals?—that we are tempted by a "subtraction" account of the rise of modernity. We just needed to liberate ourselves from the old horizons, and then the mutual service conception of order was the obvious remaining alternative. It needed no inventive insight or con-

---

10. Eugen Weber, *Peasants into Frenchmen: The Modernization of Rural France, 1870–1914* (London: Chatto and Windus, 1979), chap. 28.

structive effort. Individualism and mutual benefit are the evident residual ideas that remain after you have sloughed off the older religions and metaphysics.

But the reverse is the case. Humans have lived for most of their history in modes of complementarity, mixed with a greater and lesser degree of hierarchy. There have been islands of equality, like that of the citizens of the polis, but they are set in a sea of hierarchy once you replace them in the bigger picture. And these societies were certainly alien to modern individualism. What is rather surprising is that it was possible to achieve modern individualism—not just on the level of theory, but also transforming and penetrating the social imaginary. Now that this imaginary has become linked with societies of unprecedented power in human history, it seems impossible and mad to try to resist. But we must not commit the anachronism of thinking that this was always the case. The best antidote to this error is to recall some of the phases of the long and often conflictual march by which this theory has ended up achieving such a hold on our imagination.

Summing up, we can say that (1) the order of mutual benefit holds between individuals (or at least moral agents who are independent of larger hierarchical orders); (2) the benefits crucially include life and the means to live, however securing these relates to the practice of virtue; (3) it is meant to secure freedom, and easily finds expression in terms of rights. To these we can add a fourth point: these rights, this freedom, this mutual benefit is to be secured to all participants equally. Exactly what is meant by equality will vary, but that it must be affirmed in some form follows from the rejection of hierarchical order. These are the crucial features, the constants that recur in the modern idea of moral order, through its varying "redactions."

2.

I mentioned above that this new notion of order brought about a change in the understanding of the cosmos as the work of God's Providence. We have here in fact one of the earliest examples of the new model of order moving beyond its original niche and reshaping the image of God's providential rule.

The notion that God governs the world according to a benign plan was ancient, even pre-Christian, with roots in Judaism as well as Stoicism. What is new is the way of conceiving his benevolent scheme. We can see this in arguments ranging from the design of the world to the existence of a good creator God. Formerly, these arguments insisted on the magnificent design of the whole framework in which our world was set (e.g., the stars, the planets), and then on the admirable microdesign of creatures, including ourselves, with our organs fitted for their functions, as well as on the general way in which life was sustained by the processes of nature. These elements certainly remain part of the conception of a moral order, but what is added in the eighteenth century is an appreciation of the way in which human life is designed so as to produce mutual benefit. Emphasis is sometimes laid on mutual benevolence, but very often the happy design is identified in the existence of what one might call "invisible hand" factors. By this I mean actions and attitudes that we are "programmed" for, which have systematically beneficent results for the general happiness, even though these are not part of what is intended in the action or affirmed in the attitude. In *The Wealth of Nations*, Adam Smith has provided us with the most famous of these mechanisms, whereby our search for our own individual prosperity redounds to the general welfare. But there are other examples: in his *Theory of Moral Sentiments* Smith argues that nature has made us admire greatly rank and fortune because social order is much more secure if it rests on the respect for visible distinctions, rather than on the less striking qualities of virtue and wisdom.[11]

The order here is that of a good engineering design, in which efficient causation plays the crucial role. In this it differs from earlier notions of order, where the harmony comes from the consonance between the ideas or forms manifested in the different levels of being or ranks in society. The crucial thing in the new conception is that our purposes mesh, however divergent they may be in the consciousness of each of us. They involve us in an exchange of advantages. We admire and support the rich and well-born, and in return we enjoy the kind of stable order without which prosperity would be impossible. God's design is one of interlocking causes, not of harmonized meanings.

We can also see this order as an exchange of services. The fundamental model seems to be what we have come to call an economy. This new understanding of Providence is already evident in Locke's formulation of natural law theory in the *Second Treatise*. Here we begin to glimpse the great importance of the economic dimension in the new notion of order. There are two facets to this economic dimension. The first is metaphoric: the main goals of organized society were security and economic prosperity, but because the whole theory emphasized a kind of profitable exchange, one could begin to see political society itself through a quasi-economic metaphor.

Indeed no less a personage than Louis XIV, in the advice he offers to his dauphin, subscribes to something like an exchange view: "All these different

---

11. Leslie Stephen, *History of English Thought in the Eighteenth Century* (Bristol: Thoemmes, 1991), 2:72.

conditions that compose the world are united to each other only by an exchange of reciprocal obligations. The deference and respect that we receive from our subjects are not a free gift from them but payment for the justice and protection they expect to receive from us."[12]

This example, incidentally, points to an important transition stage on the long march of the order of mutual benefit into our social imaginary. There was a rival model of order based on command and hierarchy. Louis and his contemporaries can be seen as offering a compromise between the new and the old. The basic justifying reasoning of the different functions—in this case of ruler and subject—is new; it's given in terms of the necessary and fruitful exchange of services. But what is justified is still a hierarchical society and, above all, the most radical hierarchical relation, that of absolute monarch to subject. The justification is more and more in terms of functional necessity, but the master images still reflect something of inherent superiority, an ontological hierarchy. The king, by being above everyone else, can hold society together and sustain everything. He is like the sun, to use Louis's favorite image.[13]

We might call this the "baroque" solution, except that its most spectacular example—Versailles—saw itself in "classical" terms. It is this compromise that reigns for a while over most of Europe, sustaining regimes with much of the pomp, ritual, and imagery of hierarchical complementarity, but on the basis of a justification drawn increasingly from the modern order. Jacques-Bénigne Bossuet's defense of Louis's absolute rule is delivered in the same register.

The second facet of the new order's economic dimension is more than metaphoric. A strong economy eventually came to be seen as the collective goal of society. Contemporary with Louis's memoir of advice, Antoine de Montchrétien offers a theory of the state that sees it primarily as the orchestrating power which can make an economy flourish. (It is he, incidentally, who seems to have coined the term *political economy*.) Merchants act for love of gain, but good policy by the ruler (a still visible hand) can draw this toward the common good.[14]

This second facet reflects feature two of the modern order in my sketch above: the mutual benefit we are meant to confer on one another gives a crucial place to the securing of life and the means to live. This is not an isolated change within

12. *Mémoires de Louis XIV: Ecrit par lui-même et addressés à son fils* (Paris: Imprimerie Daragnes: Nouvelles Editions Publicataires, 1957), 63, cited in Nannerl Keohane, *Philosophy and the State in France: The Renaissance to the Enlightenment* (Princeton, N.J.: Princeton University Press), 248.

13. Keohane, *Philosophy and the State in France*, 249–51.

14. See the discussion of Montchrétien in Keohane, *Philosophy and the State in France*, 164–67.

theories of Providence; it goes along with a major trend of the age. This trend is often understood in terms of the standard "materialist" explanations; for instance, the old Marxist account that business classes, merchants, and later on, manufacturers were becoming increasingly numerous and powerful. This simple materialist account could be augmented with a reference to the changing demands of state power. Governing elites gradually became aware that increased production and favorable exchange were key elements of political and military power. The experiences of Holland and England demonstrated that. And, of course, once some nations began to "develop" economically, their rivals were forced to follow suit, or be relegated to dependent status. These sorts of political calculations, as much if not more than growing numbers and wealth, were responsible for the enhanced position of commercial classes.

These materialist accounts are important, but following Max Weber, I don't believe they take us to the origins of this change. In other words, I think that more production came about first, and then its military/political advantages began to be plain for all to see, and hence it became an object of policy.

What started us on this path, I believe, were certain political and even spiritual changes. Here I think Weber is right, even if not all the detail of his theory can be salvaged. The original importance of people working steadily in a profession came from the fact that they thereby placed themselves in "settled courses." If ordered life became a demand, not just for a military or spiritual/intellectual elite, but for the mass of ordinary people, then they had to become ordered and serious about what they were doing and of necessity had to be working in some productive occupation. A really ordered society requires that one take these economic occupations seriously and prescribe a discipline for them. This was the "political" ground.

But in Reformed Christianity, and to a growing extent among Catholics as well, there was a spiritual reason, which was the one Weber picked up on. To put it in the Reformed variant: If we reject the Catholic idea that there are some higher vocations (e.g., the monastic life) and claim that all Christians must be 100 percent Christian, regardless of vocation, then one must claim that ordinary life, the life of the vast majority, the life of production and the family, work, and sex is as hallowed as any other. Indeed, it is more sanctified than monastic celibacy, which is based on the vain and prideful claim to have found a higher way.

This is the basis for the sanctification of ordinary life, which I want to claim has had a tremendous and formative effect on our civilization, spilling beyond the original religious variant into myriad secular forms. It has two facets: (1) it promotes ordinary life, as a site for the highest forms of Christian life; and (2) it has an anti-elitist thrust: it takes down those allegedly higher modes of existence, whether in the Church (monastic vocations), or in the world (ancient-derived ethics that place contemplation higher than productive existence). The mighty are cast down from their seats, and the humble and meek are exalted. Both these facets have been formative of modern civilization. The first is indicated by the central place given to the economic in our lives and the tremendous importance we put on family life or "relationships." The second underlies the fundamental importance of equality in our social and political lives.

All these factors, material and spiritual, help explain the gradual promotion of the economic to its central place, a promotion already clearly visible in the eighteenth century. And at that time, another factor enters—or perhaps it is simply an extension of the "political" one above. The notion that economic activity is the path to peace and orderly existence gains more widespread acceptance. *Le doux commerce* is contrasted with the wild destructiveness of the aristocratic search for military glory. The more a society turns to commerce, the more "polished" and civilized it becomes, the more it excels in the arts of peace. The impetus to make money is seen as a "calm passion." When it takes hold in a society, it can help to control and inhibit the violent passions. Or put in other language, money-making serves our "interest," and interest can check and control passion.[15] Kant even believed that as nations become republics, and hence more under the control of their ordinary, economic-minded taxpayers, recourse to war will become rarer and rarer.

The new economic-centered notion of natural order underlies the doctrines of harmony of interest. It is even reflected in the eighteenth-century vision of cosmic order, not as a hierarchy of forms-at-work, but as a chain of beings whose purposes mesh with one another. Things cohere, because they serve each other in their survival and flourishing. They form an ideal economy. As Alexander Pope writes:

> See dying vegetables life sustain,
> See life dissolving vegetate again:
> All forms that perish other forms supply,
> (By turns we catch the vital breath, and die)
> Like bubbles on the sea of Matter born,

15. Albert Hirschman, *The Passions and the Interests: Political Arguments for Capitalism before Its Triumph* (Princeton, N.J.: Princeton University Press, 1977). I am greatly indebted to the discussion in this extremely interesting book.

They rise, they break, and to that sea return.
Nothing is foreign: Parts relate to whole;
One all-extending, all preserving Soul
Connects each being, greatest with the least;
Made Beast in aid of Man, and Man of Beast;
All served, all serving: nothing stands alone;
The chain holds on, and where it ends, unknown.

. . . .

God, in nature of each being, founds
Its proper bliss, and sets its proper bounds;
But as he framed a Whole, the Whole to bless,
On mutual Wants built mutual Happiness:
So from the first, eternal ORDER ran,
And creature linked to creature, Man to Man.[16]

From all this, Pope triumphantly concludes "that true SELF-LOVE and SOCIAL are the same."[17]

And so perhaps the first big shift wrought by this new idea of order, both in theory and in social imaginary, consists in our coming to see society as an "economy," an interlocking set of activities of production, exchange, and consumption, which form a system with its own laws and dynamic. Instead of being merely the management, by those in authority, of the resources we collectively need, in household or state, the economic now defines a way in which we are linked together, a sphere of coexistence that could in principle suffice to itself, if only disorder and conflict didn't threaten. Conceiving of the economy as a system is an achievement of eighteenth-century theorists (e.g., the Physiocrats and Adam Smith), but coming to see the most important purpose and agenda of society as economic collaboration and exchange is a drift in our social imaginary, which begins in that period and continues to this day. From that point on, organized society is no longer equivalent to the polity; other dimensions of social existence are seen as having their own forms and integrity. The very shift in this period of the meaning of the term *civil society* reflects this.

3.

I have just invoked the move from theory to social imaginary in connection with this new consciousness of society as an economy. But the eighteenth century sees

16. Pope *Essay on Man* 3.15–26, 109–14.
17. Pope *Essay on Man* 4.396.

other, perhaps even more fateful such moves. I want to describe two of these moves, which have helped shape our world. But first I will have to clarify my key term.

I have several times used the term *social imaginary* in the preceding pages. The time has come to make what is involved a little clearer. What I'm trying to get at with this term is something much broader and deeper than the intellectual schemes people may entertain when they think about social reality in a disengaged mode. I am thinking rather of the ways in which people imagine their social existence, how they fit together with others, how things go on between them and their fellows, the expectations that are normally met, and the deeper normative notions and images that underlie these expectations.

I want to speak of social imaginary here, rather than social theory, because there are important—and multiple—differences between the two. I speak of *imaginary* because I'm talking about the way ordinary people "imagine" their social surroundings, and this is often not expressed in theoretical terms; it is carried in images, stories, and legends. But it is also the case that theory is usually the possession of a small minority, whereas what is interesting in the social imaginary is that it is shared by large groups of people, if not the whole society. Which leads to a third difference: the social imaginary is that common understanding that makes possible common practices and a widely shared sense of legitimacy. In addition, we should note that what start off as theories held by a few people may come to infiltrate the social imaginary, first that of elites, perhaps, and then of society as a whole. This is what has happened, *grosso modo*, to the theories of Grotius and Locke, although the transformations have been many along the way, and the ultimate forms are rather varied.

Our social imaginary at any given time is complex. It incorporates a sense of the normal expectations that we have of one another, the kind of common understanding which enables us to carry out the collective practices that make up our social life. This incorporates some sense of how we all fit together in carrying out the common practice. This understanding is both factual and "normative"; that is, we have a sense of how things usually go, but this is interwoven with an idea of how they ought to go, of what missteps would invalidate the practice. Take our practice of choosing governments through general elections. Part of the implicit knowledge that makes sense of each act of voting is our awareness of the whole action, involving all citizens, each choosing individually, but from among the same alternatives, and the compounding of these microchoices into one binding, collective decision. Essential to our understanding of what is involved in this kind of macrodecision is our ability to identify what would constitute a foul: certain kinds of influence, buying votes, threats, and the like. In other words, this kind of macrodecision has to meet certain norms, if it is to be what it is meant to be. For instance, if a minority could force all others to conform to its orders, it would cease to be a democratic decision.

Implicit in this understanding of the norms is the ability to recognize ideal cases, for example, an election in which each citizen exercised to the maximum his or her judgment autonomously or in which everyone was heard. And beyond the ideal stands some notion of a moral or metaphysical order, in the context of which the norms and ideals make sense.

What I'm calling the social imaginary extends beyond the immediate background understanding that makes sense of our particular practices. This is not an arbitrary extension of the concept, because just as the practice without the understanding wouldn't make sense for us and thus wouldn't be possible, so this understanding necessarily supposes a wider grasp of our whole predicament, how we stand in relationship to one another, how we got where we are, how we relate to other groups.

This wider grasp has no clear limits. That's the very nature of what contemporary philosophers have described as the "background."[18] It is in fact that largely unstructured and inarticulate understanding of our whole situation, within which particular features of our world become evident. It can never be adequately expressed in the form of explicit doctrines because of its very unlimited and indefinite nature. That is another reason for speaking here of an imaginary, not a theory.

The relation between practices and the background understanding behind them is therefore not one-sided. If the understanding makes the practice possible, it is also true that the practice largely carries the understanding. At any given time, we can speak of the "repertory" of collective actions at the disposal of a given sector of society. These are the common actions that they know how to undertake, all the way from the general election, involving the whole society, to knowing how to strike up a polite but uninvolved conversation with a casual group in the reception hall. The discriminations we have to make to carry these off, knowing whom to speak to and when and how, carry an implicit map of social space, of what kinds of people we can associate with, in what ways, and under what circumstances. Perhaps I don't initiate the conversation at all, if the

18. See the discussion in Hubert L. Dreyfus, *Being-in-the-World: A Commentary on Heidegger's Being and Time, Division I* (Cambridge: MIT Press, 1991), drawing on the work of Martin Heidegger, Ludwig Wittgenstein, and Michael Polanyi.

group members are all socially superior to me, or outrank me in the bureaucracy, or are all women.

This implicit grasp of social space is unlike a theoretical description of this space, distinguishing different kinds of people, and the norms connected to them. The understanding expressed in practice stands to social theory the way that my ability to get around a familiar environment stands to a (literal) map of this area. I am able to orient myself without ever having adopted the standpoint of overview that the map offers me. And similarly, for most of human history and most of social life, we function through the grasp we have on the common repertory, without benefit of theoretical overview. Humans operated with a social imaginary well before they ever got into the business of theorizing about themselves.[19]

Another example might help make the width and depth of this implicit understanding more palpable. Let's say we organize a demonstration. This means that this act is already in our repertory. We know how to assemble, pick up banners, and march. We know that this is meant to be within certain bounds, spatially (don't invade certain spaces), and in the way it impinges on others (this side of a threshold of aggressivity; no violence). We understand the ritual.

The background understanding that makes this act possible for us is complex, but part of what makes sense of it is the picture of ourselves as speaking to others to whom we are related in a certain way—say, compatriots or the human race. There is a speech act here, addresser and addressees, and some understanding of how they stand in this relation to each other. There are public spaces; we are already in some kind of conversation with each other. Like all speech acts, this one is addressed to a previously spoken word, in the prospect of a to-be-spoken word.[20]

19. The way in which the social imaginary extends well beyond what has been (or even can be) theorized is illustrated in Francis Fukuyama's interesting discussion of the economics of social trust. Some economies find it difficult to build large-scale, nonstate enterprises, because a climate of trust that extends wider than the family is absent or weak. The social imaginary in these societies marks discriminations—between kin and nonkin—for purposes of economic association; these sorts of categorizations have gone largely unremarked in theories of the economy. And governments can be induced to adopt policies, legal changes, and incentives on the assumption that forming enterprises of any scale is there in the repertory and just needs encouragement. But the sense of a sharp boundary of mutual reliability around the family may severely restrict the repertory, however much it might be possible to people that they would be better off changing their way of doing business. The implicit "map" of social space has deep fissures, which are profoundly anchored in culture and imaginary, beyond the reach of correction by better theory. See Francis Fukuyama, *Trust: The Social Virtues and the Creation of Prosperity* (New York: Free Press, 1996).

20. Mikhail Bakhtin, *Speech Genres and Other Late Essays* (Austin: University of Texas Press, 1986).

The mode of address says something about the footing we stand on with our addressees. The action is forceful; it is meant to impress, perhaps even to threaten certain consequences if our message is not heard. But it is also meant to persuade; it remains on this side of violence. It figures the addressee as one who can and must be reasoned with.

The immediate sense of what we're doing (e.g., getting the message to the government and our fellow citizens that the budget cuts must stop) makes sense in a wider context, in which we see ourselves as standing in a continuing relation with others, in which it is appropriate to address them in this manner, and not, for example, by humble supplication or threats of armed insurrection. We can gesture quickly at all this by saying that this kind of demonstration has its normal place in a stable, ordered, democratic society. This does not mean that there are not cases where armed insurrection would be perfectly justified—Manila 1985, Tiananmen 1989. Indeed, the point of this act in those circumstances is to invite tyranny to open up to a democratic transition.

We can see here how the understanding of what we're doing right now (without which we couldn't be doing *this* action) makes the sense it does because of our grasp on the wider predicament: how we stand in relation to others and to power. There is also a space and time component to this predicament. We are concerned about our relationship to other nations and peoples, for example, with regard to external models of democratic life we are trying to imitate or of tyranny from which we are trying to distance ourselves. We are participating in the narrative of our becoming, whereby we recognize this capacity to demonstrate peacefully as an achievement of democracy, hard-won by our ancestors, or as a capability to which we aspire through this common action. This sense of standing in a global arena and in history is exemplified in the iconography of the demonstration itself, as in Tiananmen 1989, with its references to the French Revolution and its citation of the American case through the erection of a replica of the Statue of Liberty.

The background that makes sense of any given act is thus wide and deep. It doesn't include everything in our world, but the relevant sense-giving features can't be circumscribed. Indeed, the sense-giving draws on our whole world, that is, our sense of our whole predicament in time and space, among others and in history.

An important part of this wider background is what I called above a sense of moral order. By this I mean more than just a grasp of the norms underlying our social practice, which are part of the immediate understanding that makes this practice possible. There also must be a sense, as I stated above, of what makes these norms realizable. This too is an essential part of the context of action. People don't demonstrate for the impossible, for the utopic—or if they do, then this becomes ipso facto a rather different action.[21] Part of what we're saying as we march on Tiananmen is that a (somewhat more) democratic society is possible for us, that we could bring it off in spite of the skepticism of our gerontocratic rulers.

This confidence that we and other human beings can sustain a democratic order together, that it is within our range of possibilities, is based on images of moral order through which we understand human life and history. It ought to be clear from the above that our images of moral order, although they make sense of some of our actions, are by no means necessarily tilted toward the status quo. They may also infuse revolutionary practice, as at Manila and Beijing, just as they may underwrite the established order.

What I want to do, in the following pages, is sketch the changeover process in which the modern theory of moral order gradually infiltrates and transforms our social imaginary. In this process, what is originally just an idealization grows into a complex imaginary through being taken up and associated with social practices, in part traditional ones, which are often transformed by the contact. This is crucial to what I called above the extension of the understanding of moral order. It couldn't have become the dominant view in our culture without this penetration and transformation of our imaginary.

We see transitions of this kind happening, for instance, in the contemporary Western world's great founding revolutions, the American and the French. The transition was much smoother and less catastrophic in one case, because the idealization of popular sovereignty connected relatively unproblematically with an existing practice of popular election of assemblies. In the other case, the inability to "translate" the same principle into a stable and agreed set of practices was an immense source of conflict and uncertainty for more than a century. But in both these great events, there was some awareness of the historical primacy of theory—central to the modern idea of a "revolution"—whereby we set out to remake our political life according to agreed-upon principles. This "constructivism" has become a central feature of modern political culture.

21. This does not mean that utopias do not deal in their own kind of possibility. They may describe far-off lands or remote future societies that cannot be imitated today, which we may never be able to imitate. But the underlying idea is that these things are really possible, in the sense that they lie in the bend of human nature. This is what the narrator of Thomas More's *Utopia* (1516) thinks: the Utopians are living according to nature (Bronislaw Baczko, *Les imaginaires sociaux: Mémoires et espoirs collectifs* [Paris: Payot, 1984], 75). Plato thought this as well; he provided one of the models for More's book and for many other "utopian" writings.

What exactly is involved when a theory penetrates and transforms the social imaginary? For the most part, people take up, improvise, or are inducted into new practices. These practices are made sense of by the new outlook, the one first articulated in the theory; this outlook is the context that gives sense to the practices. And hence the new understanding comes to be accessible to the participants in a way it wasn't before. It begins to define the contours of their world and may eventually become the taken-for-granted shape of things, too obvious to mention.

But this process isn't just one-sided, a theory making over a social imaginary. In making sense of the action, the theory is "glossed," as it were, given a particular shape in the context of these practices. Rather like Kant's notion of an abstract category becoming "schematized" when it is applied to reality in space and time, the theory is schematized in the dense sphere of common practice.[22] Nor need the process end here. The new practice, with the implicit understanding it generates, can be the basis for modifications of theory, which in turn can inflect practice, and so on.

What I'm calling the "long march" is a process whereby new practices, or modifications of old ones, either developed through improvisation among certain groups and strata of the population (e.g., the public sphere among educated elites in the eighteenth century, trade unions among workers in the nineteenth century) or were launched by elites in such a way as to recruit a larger base (e.g., the Jacobin organization of the "sections" in Paris). Or alternatively, a set of practices in the course of their slow development and ramification gradually acquired a new meaning for people and hence helped to constitute a new social imaginary (e.g., the "economy"). The result in all these cases was a profound transformation of the social imaginary in Western societies and of the world in which we live.

4.

There are three important transitions that must figure in our account: the rise of (1) the economy, (2) the public sphere, and (3) the practices and outlooks of democratic self-rule. Each of these represents a penetration/transformation of the social imaginary by the Grotian-Lockean theory of moral order. I have already discussed the first transition and turn now to the other two.

The economic was perhaps the first dimension of "civil society" to achieve an identity independent from the polity. But it was soon followed by the public

22. Immanuel Kant, *The Critique of Pure Reason*, trans. and ed. Paul Guyer and Allen W. Wood (Cambridge: Cambridge University Press, 1998).

111

sphere. The term *public sphere* refers to a common space in which the members of society meet through a variety of media: print and electronic as well as face-to-face encounters, wherein they discuss matters of common interest and thus are able to form a common mind about these. I say *a* common space because although the media are multiple, as are the exchanges that take place in them, they are deemed to be in principle intercommunicating. The discussion we're having on television now takes account of what was said in the newspaper this morning, which in turn reports on the radio debate yesterday, and so on. That's why we usually speak of the public sphere in the singular.

The public sphere is a central feature of modern society. So much so, that even where it is in fact suppressed or manipulated it has to be faked. Modern despotic societies have generally felt compelled to go through the motions. Editorials appear in the party newspapers, allegedly expressing the opinions of the writers, offered for the consideration of their fellow citizens; mass demonstrations are organized, purporting to give vent to the felt indignation of large numbers of people. All this is meant to suggest that a common mind is indeed being formed through exchange, even though the result is carefully controlled from the beginning.

In this discussion, I want to draw in particular upon two very interesting books, Jürgen Habermas's *The Structural Transformation of the Public Sphere*, which deals with the development of public opinion in eighteenth-century western Europe, and Michael Warner's *The Letters of the Republic*, which describes the analogous phenomenon in the British American colonies.[23] A central theme of Habermas's book is the emergence of a new concept of public opinion. Dispersed publications and small group or local exchanges come to be construed as one big debate from which the "public opinion" of a whole society emerges. In other words, it is understood that widely separated people sharing the same view have been linked in a kind of space of discussion, wherein they have been able to exchange ideas together with others and reach this common end point.

What is this common space? It's actually a rather strange thing. The people involved have likely never met. But they are seen as linked in a common space of discussion through media—print media, in the eighteenth century. Books, pamphlets, newspapers circulated among the educated public, conveying theses,

23. Jürgen Habermas, *The Structural Transformation of the Public Sphere: An Inquiry into a Category of Bourgeois Society*, trans. Thomas Burger with Frederick Lawrence (Cambridge: MIT Press, 1989); originally published as *Strukturwandel der Öffentlichkeit* (Neuwied, Germany: Luchterhand, 1962); and Michael Warner, *The Letters of the Republic: Publication and the Public Sphere in Eighteenth-Century America* (Cambridge: Harvard University Press, 1990).

analyses, arguments, counterarguments, referring to and refuting one another. These were widely read and often discussed in face-to-face gatherings, in drawing rooms, coffeehouses, salons, and in more (authoritatively) public places, like Parliament. Any perceived general view that resulted from all this counted as "public opinion," in this new sense.

I have described the conditions under which something gets "counted as" public opinion. This reflects the fact that a public sphere can exist only if it is imagined as such. Unless all the dispersed discussions are seen by their participants as linked in one great exchange, there can be no sense of a resultant "public opinion." I'm not suggesting that imagination is all-powerful. There are objective conditions, both internal (e.g., that the fragmentary local discussions inter-refer) and external (e.g., the need for printed materials, circulating from a plurality of independent sources, as a basis for common discussion). As is often said, the modern public sphere relied on "print capitalism" to get going.[24] But as Warner shows, printing itself, and even print capitalism, didn't provide a sufficient condition. They had to be taken up in the right cultural context, where the essential common understandings could arise.[25] The public sphere was a mutation of the social imaginary, one crucial to the development of modern society. It was an important step on the long march.

We are now in a slightly better position to understand what a public sphere is and why it was new in the eighteenth century. It is a kind of common space, I have been saying, in which people who never meet understand themselves to be engaged in discussion and capable of reaching a common mind. Let me introduce some new terminology. We can speak of "common space" when people come together for a particular purpose, be it ritual, conversation, the enjoyment of a play, or the celebration of a major event. Their focus is common, as against merely convergent, because they are attending to the common object or purpose together, as opposed to each person just happening, on his or her own, to be concerned with the same thing. This kind of common space, in which people are assembled for some purpose—be it on an intimate level for conversation or on a larger, more "public" scale for a deliberative assembly or the enjoyment of a football match or an opera—is intuitively understandable. I want to call common space arising from assembly in some locale "topical common space."

But the public sphere, as we have been defining it, is something different. It transcends such topical spaces. We might say that it knits a plurality of spaces

24. See Anderson, *Imagined Communities*.
25. Warner, *Letters of the Republic*, chap. 1.

into one larger space of nonassembly. The same public discussion is deemed to pass through our debate today, and someone else's earnest conversation tomorrow, and the newspaper interview Thursday, and so on. I want to call this larger kind of nonlocal common space "metatopical." The public sphere that emerges in the eighteenth century is a metatopical common space.

Metatopicality is not new. The Church, the state were already existing metatopical spaces. But there are three novel features of the public sphere that mark it as a step in the long march, a mutation in the social imaginary, inspired by the modern idea of order.

One of these features is mentioned above: the identity independent of the polity. The second is its force as a benchmark of legitimacy. We can see the novelty in these two respects if we compare a modern society's public sphere with an ancient republic or polis. In the latter, we can imagine that debate on public affairs may be carried on in a host of settings: among friends at a symposium, between those who meet in the agora, and then of course in the *ekklesia* (general assembly) where the thing is finally decided. The debate swirls around and ultimately reaches its conclusion in the competent decision-making body. The discussions outside this body prepare for the action ultimately taken by the same people within it. The "unofficial" discussions are not set apart, given a status of their own, nor seen as constituting a kind of metatopical space.

But that is what happens with the modern public sphere. It is a space of discussion that is self-consciously seen as being outside power. It is supposed to be listened to by power, but it is not itself an exercise of power. Its extrapolitical status is crucial; it links the public sphere with other facets of modern society that also are seen as essentially extrapolitical. The extrapolitical status is not just defined negatively, as a lack of power. It is also seen positively: because public opinion is not an exercise of power, it can be ideally rational and disengaged from partisan spirit.

In other words, with the modern public sphere comes the idea that political power must be supervised and checked by something external. What was new, of course, was not that there was an outside check but rather the nature of it. It is not defined as the will of God or the law of nature (although it could be thought to articulate these), but as a kind of discourse emanating from reason, not from power or traditional authority. As Habermas puts it, power was to be tamed by reason. The notion was that *veritas non auctoritas facit legem.*[26]

---

26. Habermas, *Structural Transformation of the Public Sphere*, 82.

This brings us to the third novel feature. It is obvious that an extrapolitical, even international society, which could challenge the state, was not an unknown phenomenon in European history. The public sphere was preceded by the Stoic cosmopolis and, more immediately, by the Christian church. Europeans were used to living in a dual society, one organized by two mutually irreducible principles. So the third facet of the newness of the public sphere has to be defined as its radical secularity.

Here I am recurring to a very particular use of this term, one close to its original meaning as an expression for a certain kind of time. It is obviously intimately related to the one common meaning of secularity, which focuses on the removal of God or religion or the spiritual from public space. What I am talking about here is not exactly that, but something that has contributed to it, namely, a shift in our understanding of what society is grounded on. In spite of all the risks of confusion, there is a reason to use the term *secular* because it marks in its very etymology what is at stake here, which has something to do with the way human society inhabits time.[27]

The notion of secularity I'm using here is radical, because it stands in contrast not only with a divine foundation for society, but also with any idea of society as constituted in something that transcends contemporary common action. For instance, some hierarchical societies conceive themselves as bodying forth some part of the chain of being. Behind the empirical fillers of the slots of kingship, aristocracy, and so on, lie the ideas, or the persisting metaphysical realities, that these people are momentarily embodying. The king has two bodies, only one being the particular, perishable one, which is now being fed and clothed, and will later be buried.[28] Within this outlook, what constitutes a society as such is the metaphysical order it embodies.[29] People act within a framework that exists prior to and independent of their actions.

But secularity contrasts not only with divinely established churches, or great chains. It is also different from an understanding of our society as constituted by a law that has been ours from time immemorial. This type of understanding places our action within a framework, one that binds us together and makes us a

---

27. I have developed this change in time consciousness in "Die Modernität und die säkulare Zeit," in *Am Ende des Milleniums: Zeit und Modernitäten*, ed. Krzysztof Michalski (Stuttgart: Klett-Cotta, 2000).

28. See Ernest Hartwig Kantorowicz, *The King's Two Bodies: A Study in Medieval Political Theology* (Princeton, N.J.: Princeton University Press, 1957).

29. For an extra-European example of this kind of thing, see Clifford Geertz's *Negara* (Princeton, N.J.: Princeton University Press, 1980) and his discussion of the preconquest Balinese state.

society, and which transcends our common action. The public sphere, however, is an association that is constituted by nothing outside of the common action we carry out within it: coming to a common mind, where possible, through the exchange of ideas. It exists as an association simply through our acting together in this way. This common action is not made possible by a framework that needs to be established in some action-transcendent dimension: either by an act of God or in a great chain or by a law that comes down to us time out of mind. It is an agency grounded purely in its own common actions. This is what makes it radically secular. And this, I want to claim, gets us to the heart of what is new and unprecedented in it.

✦ ✦ ✦

I will now try to draw my comments together and state what the public sphere *was* and continues to be. It was a new metatopical space, in which members of society could exchange ideas and come to a common mind. As such it constituted a metatopical agency but one that was understood to exist independent of the political constitution of society and completely in profane time. An extrapolitical, secular, metatopical space—this is what the public sphere was and is. And the importance of understanding this lies partly in the fact that it was not an isolated entity, that it was part of a development that transformed our whole understanding of time and society, so that we have trouble recalling what it was like before.

5.

There are two other such extrapolitical, secular spaces that have played a crucial role in the development of society: (1) society considered as extrapolitically organized in a (market) economy, which I mentioned above; and (2) society as a "people," that is, as a metatopical agency that is thought to preexist and found the politically organized society. We have to see these three as linked in their development and also as interwoven with other kinds of social spaces that were also emerging at this time.

The citizen state is the third in the great connected chain of mutations in the social imaginary that have helped constitute modern society. It too starts off as a theory and then gradually infiltrates and transmutes social imaginaries. We can see how older ideas of legitimacy are colonized, as it were, with the new understandings of order and then transformed—without a clear break, in some cases.

The United States is a case in point. The reigning notions of legitimacy in Britain and America, the ones that fired the English civil war, for instance, as well as the beginnings of the colonies' rebellion, were basically backward-look-ing. They pivoted on the idea of an "ancient constitution," an order based on law from time immemorial, in which Parliament had its rightful place beside the king. This was typical of one of the most widespread premodern understandings of order, which referred back to a "time of origins"—a time separate from ordinary time.[30]

This older idea emerges from the American Revolution transformed into a full-fledged foundation in popular sovereignty, whereby the U.S. Constitution is put in the mouth of "We the people." This was preceded by an appeal to the ide-alized order of natural law in the invocation of "truths held self-evident" in the Declaration of Independence. What was understood as the traditional law privi-leged elected assemblies and their consent to taxation; this, in turn, facilitated the transition to popular sovereignty. All that was needed was to shift the balance in these institutions so as to make elections the only source of legitimate power.

But what makes this change a possibility is a transformed social imaginary, in which the idea of foundation is taken out of the mythical early time and seen as something that people can do today. In other words, it becomes something that can be brought about by collective action in contemporary, purely secular time. This happened sometime in the eighteenth century, but really more toward its end than its beginning. Elites propounded *theories* of founding action beforehand, but these hadn't adequately sunk into the general social imaginary for them to be acted on. So that 1688, radical departure as it may seem to us in retrospect, was presented as an act of continuity, of return to a preexistent legality. (We are fooled by a change in semantics. The Glorious Revolution had the earlier sense of a return to the original position, not the modern sense of an innovative turnover. Of course, its *Wirkungsgeschichte*, that is, its impact on later historical events, helped to alter the meaning.)

This fit between theory and social imaginary is crucial to the outcome. Popu-lar sovereignty could be invoked in the American case, because it had a generally agreed-upon institutional meaning. All colonists agreed that the way to found a new constitution was through some kind of assembly, perhaps slightly larger than the normal one, such as in Massachusetts in 1779. The force of the old represen-tative institutions helped to "interpret" the new concept in practical terms.

Quite different was the case in the French Revolution, with fateful effects. The impossibility remarked by all historians of "bringing the Revolution to an

30. "Time of origins" is Mircea Eliade's phrase; see his book, *The Sacred and the Profane: The Nature of Religion* (New York: Harcourt Brace, 1959).

end"[31] came partly from the fact that any particular expression of popular sovereignty could be challenged by some other, with substantial support. Part of the terrifying instability of the first years of the Revolution stemmed from this negative fact, that the shift from the legitimacy of dynastic rule to that of the nation had no commonly accepted meaning in a broadly based social imaginary.

This is to be understood not as the global "explanation" of this instability, but as telling us something about the way in which the different factors we cite to explain it worked together to produce the result we know. Of course, the fact that substantial parts of the king's entourage, the army, and the nobility did not accept the new principles created a tremendous obstacle to stabilization. And even those who were for the new legitimacy were divided among themselves. But what made these latter divisions so deadly was the absence of any agreed-upon understanding of the institutional meaning of the sovereignty of the nation.

Edmund Burke's advice to the revolutionaries was to stick to their traditional constitution and amend it piecemeal. But this was already beyond their powers. It was not just that the representative institutions of this constitution, the Estates General, had been in abeyance for 175 years. They were also profoundly out of sync with the aspiration to equal citizenship that had developed among the educated classes, the bourgeoisie, and a good part of the aristocracy, which found expression in a number of ways: negatively through the attack on aristocratic privilege and positively in the enthusiasm for republican Rome and its ideals.[32] That is why virtually the first demand of the Third Estate in 1789 was to abolish the separate chambers and bring all the delegates together in a single National Assembly.

Even more gravely, outside of these educated elites, there was very little sense of what a representative constitution might mean. True, masses of people responded to the calling of the Estates General with their *cahiers de doléance* (lists of grievances), but this whole procedure supposed the continuance of royal sovereignty; it wasn't at all suited to serve as a channel for the popular will.

What the moderates hoped for was something along the lines of Burke's prescription: an evolution of the traditional constitution to fashion the kind of representative institutions that would be understood by all as the expression of the nation's will, through the votes of the citizens. This is what the House of Commons had become in the eighteenth century, even though the "people" here con-

31. François Furet and Denis Richet, *La Révolution française* (Paris: Hachette Littératures, 1999).
32. See Simon Schama, *Citizens: A Chronicle of the French Revolution* (New York: Knopf, 1989), chap. 4.

stituted a small elite, deemed to speak for the whole through various kinds of virtual representation. This representation contributed to the sense of self-rule that was part of the broader society's social imaginary. Thus we find that in England, demands for broader popular participation took the form of proposals to extend the franchise. The people wanted entry into the established representative structure, as, most notably, in the Chartist agitation of the 1830s and 1840s. The American case discussed above was a stage ahead on this same evolution; their representative assemblies were generally elected on the basis of manhood suffrage.

These forms of self-rule through elected assembly were part of the generally available repertory in the Anglo-Saxon societies. The popular classes in France, however, had developed their own forms of popular protest, which were structured by a quite different logic. When things became intolerable, French peasants and city dwellers had their own way of making their needs known: the peasant or urban uprising. For example, when the price of wheat soared and local merchants were suspected of hoarding grain to make a large profit, riots ensued, targeting the municipal authorities and/or the offending merchants. Often these offenders were killed, casualties of a partly ritualized violence that the modern sensibility finds gruesome (e.g., once decapitated, their heads were carried around on pikes and displayed). The royal government would react, send in soldiers, restore order, and effect some exemplary punishments (more killing, with the ritual elements accompanying public executions under the ancien régime).[33] But they would also be sure to take measures to lower the price of grain, imposing ceilings and importing stocks from elsewhere.

From one point of view, the whole bloody process appears as an exchange between the base and the summit where power resides, the enacting of a *cahier de doléance* in unmistakable terms. But the background understanding that enframes the whole exchange is that power remains at the summit; it's the very opposite of the understanding defining popular sovereignty. Popular classes that function in this way have to transform their repertory before they can act as a sovereign people.

A good part of what was involved in "bringing the Revolution to an end" was this transformation of the popular repertory, the development of a new social imaginary that would confer on regular, ordered elections the meaning of expres-

33. Just how elaborate and horrifying (to us) these could be one can glean from the description of the execution of Damiens, who made an attempt on the life of Louis XV in 1757, in the riveting opening pages of Michel Foucault's *Surveiller et punir: Naissance de la prison* (Paris: Gallimard, 1975).

sions of popular will. In the meantime, as always, there was a struggle to reinterpret old practices in a new way.

Take the storming of the Bastille on 14 July 1789. This was in many ways an old-style popular insurrection. It had a particular, limited goal: getting hold of the arms that were supposedly stored in the Bastille in order to defend Paris against the threat of the Swiss mercenaries. And it ended in a very traditional ritual of violence: the execution of the governor and the displaying of his head on a pike. But just as the revolt of the colonies in the name of their traditional, established rights was later reinterpreted as the innovative act of a sovereign people, so here the taking of the Bastille was seen as an assertion of popular power. The building's importance was no longer the particular, contingent fact that it contained arms (actually it did not, but that is what was believed), but its essential, symbolic nature as a prison in which people were arbitrarily confined by royal fiat.

This creative misremembering has played a big part in the transformation of the social imaginary. It was ritually referred to in the *fête de la fédération* exactly a year later, through which Lafayette hoped to stabilize the revolution in the more moderate form of a constitutional monarchy. And it has become, of course, *the* symbolic date of the turnover to popular rule, the annual national feast of the French republic. But in the nature of things this kind of transformation couldn't be effected right away, in the immediate aftermath of the Revolution. Moreover, any chance of doing this was undermined by the fact that the leading elites couldn't agree on the representative forms that they wanted to have accepted as the normal channels of the popular will.

For the great battle among the different revolutionary factions turned on this question: What was the correct institutional expression for the sovereignty of the nation? This issue defined the terms of the struggle among these groups. Each had its formula to offer as the proper way of realizing this principle: whether through a republic or constitutional monarchy, through indirect representation or some more immediate relation of people and deputy, through the representation of different interests, or the undivided expression of a general will. The undecidable issue among these different institutions and procedures had in the end to be determined at the boundary of all of them, through *coups de force*. Thus the members of the Convention elected by the "people" were eventually purged in 1793 under threat of the activists from the Paris sections, and that in the name of the "people." The immediate consequences are too horrible and too well known to be repeated.

The terms of this struggle, its peculiarly intense ideological nature, the immense importance placed on theoretical justifications and models of right government, during those days when the urgent practical dangers of foreign invasion and internal counterrevolutionary insurrection seemed to demand their place at the top of the agenda; these are to be understood in this context. The discourse wasn't simply a cover for the hard reality of group interest and military defense (though this diagnosis does describe conditions under the Directory [1795–99]). In fact, all this talk was for real, its goal being to establish that one's own group was carrying out the only legitimate realization of the sovereignty of the people. And this meant that however dotty the content of the discourse, generally it was meant in deadly earnest—even in the case of the Jacobins, where the criteria of genuine representation of the people turned crucially on the virtue of the leaders, standing foursquare for the whole against the self-interested, divisive "factions." For the Jacobins, the expression "deadly earnest" is especially appropriate. As Furet has argued, the murderous craziness of the revolutionary crisis cannot be considered a kind of rhetorical froth thrown up by the real battles for national survival, or between groups. We have to allow for its centrality.[34]

The problem of "ending the Revolution" continued to haunt French society into the Restoration and well into the nineteenth century.[35] The return to some stability in the aftermath of the Revolution could come only through some generally accepted forms of representative government. And this meant solving the double problem that the whole revolutionary period had left unresolved: coming to an agreement among political elites on representative institutions, which could at the same time become part of the popular social imaginary.

Once again, during the Restoration, the opposition of the royalist ultras made things exceedingly difficult. And the growing social divisions that came with the growth of the working class made it all the more difficult to bridge the gap between elite constitutionalism and popular repertory. On the contrary, the Revolution remained alive for a number of radicals not just as the gateway to a proper institutional order, but as itself the paradigm moment of popular sovereignty. Something like a revolutionary scenario, what Robert Tombs calls "the Revolutionary passion play," haunted the radical imagination and remained in the popular memory, waiting to be reenacted in order to realize finally the promise of 1789.[36] In these circumstances, the specter of renewed revolution could never be laid to rest, however often the claim was made to have "ended the Revolution."

But as François Guizot, the Doctrinaires, Adolphe Thiers, and later Léon

34. François Furet, *Penser la Révolution française* (Paris: Gallimard, 1978).
35. See Pierre Rosanvallon, *Le moment Guizot* (Paris: Gallimard, 1985), especially 16–17 and 285.
36. Robert Tombs, *France: 1814–1914* (London: Longman, 1996), 20–26.

Gambetta saw, the only solution would be the evolution of forms that would come to be generally recognized as the obviously appropriate realization of the new principle of legitimacy. Guizot and the Doctrinaires understood that this required the growth of a new, widely shared social imaginary, but their own elite representative institutions, with their narrow franchise, could never crystallize this around themselves, as gradually became clear after 1830.[37] Over time, republican France found such forms, but only after it had gone over to manhood suffrage. Gambetta saw that the only way the people could develop a new social imaginary around ordered representative institutions was by participating in their election.[38]

The forms that "took" in France turned out to be interestingly different from the Anglo-American mode. Pierre Rosanvallon has traced the peculiar path by which universal suffrage was achieved in France, and he brings to light the different shape of the social imaginary in this republican tradition.[39]

6.

After the economy and the public sphere, the last of the three great mutations involves "inventing the people" as a new collective agency.[40] In the forms that have emerged from these mutations, we can recognize the lineaments of our understanding of moral order in contemporary liberal democracies. The way we imagine our social life is articulated in these forms. The society in which we live is not just the politically structured order; we also belong to *civil society*. We are linked in an economy, can seek access to a public sphere, and move in a world of independent associations.

37. Rosanvallon, *Le moment Guizot*, 80, and chap. 9.

38. See Gambetta's speech of 9 October 1877, quoted in Rosanvallon, *Le moment Guizot*, 364–65:

Je parle pour ceux qui, parmi les conservateurs, ont quelque souci de la stabilité quelque souci de la légalité, quelque souci de la modération pratiquée avec persévérance dans la vie publique. Je leur dis, à ceux-là: comment ne voyez-vous pas qu'avec le suffrage universel, si on le laisse librement fonctionner, si on le respecte, quand il s'est prononcé, son indépendance et l'autorité de ses décisions, comment ne voyez-vous pas, dis-je, que vous avez là un moyen de terminer pacifiquement tous les conflits, de dénouer toutes les crises, et que, si le suffrage universel fonctionne dans la plénitude de la souveraineté, il n'y a plus de révolution possible, parce qu'il n'y a plus de révolution a tenter, plus de coup d'État à redouter quand la France a parlé.

39. Pierre Rosanvallon, *Le sacre du citoyen: Histoire du suffrage universel en France* (Paris: Gallimard, 1992).

40. Edmund S. Morgan, *Inventing the People: The Rise of Popular Sovereignty in England and America* (New York: Norton, 1988).

Moreover, action in the political sphere has to take account of the integrity of the other forms and the goals people seek in them. It is true that the idea of politics as purely instrumental to, say, economic prosperity is hotly contested in the Western world (and rightly so, I believe). In fact, the emergence of popular sovereignty has given politics a new importance, which partly expressed itself in the retrieval of forms and ideals from the ancient republics and poleis, in which political activity stood at the apex of the citizen's life. But even so, the integrity of the other spheres cannot be gainsaid. The drive to override them, to control all other aspects of life in the name of some radiant future, has become familiar to us as the totalitarian temptation, visible early on at the height of the Jacobin terror and latterly in Soviet Communism and its offshoots. Not only do these attempts run counter to certain fundamental features of our understanding of moral order—most notably the demand for individual freedom and moral autonomy— but they themselves have generally been undertaken in the hope (vain, as it turns out) that this hypercontrol would bring forth a world of nonconstraint. For Marxism, the ultimate end was the withering away of the state. Here, indeed, is an eloquent testimony to the profound anchoring of the prepolitical in a modern understanding as limit and goal of politics.[41]

This sense of the modern age as one that gives a crucial place to the nonpolitical was articulated early on by Benjamin Constant in his famous lecture on ancient and modern liberty.[42] The error of Jacobinism (and of Rousseau), according to Constant, was to think that the only freedom which matters is that of political participation, prized by the ancients. But we have become people for whom economic prosperity and the satisfactions of private life also have a crucial importance. We cannot just apply the ancient models to our political life.

To the three forms of social existence we have already identified in our modern imaginary—economy, public sphere, and a polity ruled by the people—we should add a fourth, which has been articulated in bills and charters of rights. Here is a crucial feature of the original Grotian-Lockean theory that has become embedded in our understanding of normative order. It has come to structure our

41. In the case of the other great totalitarian temptation of our century, fascism, we do in fact have a frontal assault on our understanding of moral order. This is one facet of the reaction against this order, which I want to characterize more fully in another work. It is important to see that this order has been and will continue to be contested. But it is hard to imagine its being replaced. We were lucky in that fascism was eliminated by military defeat in the first half of the century. But even if it had not suffered this fate, I doubt that fascist regimes could have indefinitely resisted the demands for greater freedom that are so anchored in Western culture.

42. Benjamin Constant, "De la liberté des anciens, comparée à celle des modernes," in *Écrits politiques* (Paris: Gallimard, 1997).

social imaginary in somewhat the same way and by the same process as has popular sovereignty. That is, earlier practices were given a new sense, and thus came to be structured differently.

Just as the practices of getting consent from elected assemblies were transformed during the American Revolution into a new definition of political legitimacy, so too did the practices embodying the primacy of law begin to change their sense at the same time and through the same political changes. Instead of enshrining merely the rights of Englishmen, they began to be seen as reflections of the natural right of which the great seventeenth-century theorists had spoken. These were invoked in the Declaration of Independence. The primacy of rights is given a further push by the first ten amendments to the Constitution.

This whole development reaches its culmination in our time, in the period after the Second World War, in which the notion of rights that are prior to and untouchable by political structures becomes widespread—although they are now called "human" rather than "natural" rights. This consciousness is given expression in the entrenchment of charters of rights, by which ordinary legislation can be set aside when it violates these fundamental norms.

These declarations of rights can be seen as the clearest expression of our modern idea of a moral order underlying the political—the ideal of order as mutual benefit—which the political has to respect.

Charles Taylor is a professor emeritus of philosophy at McGill University. He is the author of *Sources of the Self: The Making of Modern Identity* (1989) and *The Ethics of Authenticity* (1992).

The Liberal Civil Subject and the Social in Eighteenth-Century British Moral Philosophy

Mary Poovey

Harnessed to so many theoretical paradigms, "the social" is a phrase that no longer conjures a common set of assumptions about society, culture, representation, or the methods by which we write history. Nevertheless, whether one uses the social to invoke an objective infrastructure that underwrites culture, as members of the *Annales* school did, or to suggest a gradual, continuously changing process that establishes threshold conditions for cultural and political events, as Marx and Tocqueville did, or to identify one in the series of relatively autonomous domains that compose modern life, as Niklas Luhmann tended to do, deploying the social as a noun automatically mobilizes certain theoretical claims implicit in the term's grammatical status. It is possible to use the social as a noun phrase that designates an objectified abstraction because of a historical process that has made such abstractions seem as real as material entities. As a consequence of the general acceptance of what Thomas Nagel (1986: 3–27) calls a "view from nowhere," which is organized from the standpoint of a nonparticipating, objectifying observer, it has become possible to think about social structures, relationships, and processes as entities, as relatively autonomous, and as sufficiently systematic to warrant scientific descriptions—which are systematic as well. Whatever individual theorists mean by the term, "the social" has become thinkable as part of the long history of reification that we call modernity.

I would like to thank Routledge for permission to publish this essay, which will also appear in *The Social in Question: New Bearings*, edited by Patrick Joyce (Routledge, in press).

Public Culture 14(1): 125–145

In this essay, I discuss one phase of this historical process: the forging of a link between philosophical theories about a specific objectified abstraction—human nature—and the legitimation of a new form of governmentality in early eighteenth-century Britain. This episode is relevant to the history of the social for three reasons. First, the endeavors of eighteenth-century British philosophers to theorize human nature constituted some of the earliest attempts to position a law-governed abstraction at the intersection between a providential order that was presumed to exist and the institutions of society. In so doing, philosophical theories about human nature advanced a *method* for studying what-can-be-seen through an abstract intermediary, which also functions as the implicit focal point of a disembodied, nonparticipating, and objectifying point of view that facilitates the basis for understanding (or acknowledging) what-cannot-be-observed (the "view from nowhere"). This method lies at the heart of all modern uses of the social to explain observable practices and relationships by reference not only to this point of view but also to an infrastructure that can only be theorized through the objectifying perspective that creates the mediating abstraction in the first place.

Second, experimental moral philosophers advanced a theory about the dynamics of human interaction that resembles the *content* of some modern theories about the social. According to this theory, individuals produce a secular code or semantic system in the process of living and working together, but the code that individuals collectively generate is said to be delimited by something that lies beyond both consciousness and individual human beings. For the eighteenth-century philosophers, this "something" was providential order, which was thought to manifest itself in human nature, among other places. For modern theorists, this "something" is comprehensible through one or more classificatory categories (class, race, gender) or one or more transindividual structures or processes (class relations, capitalism, urbanization), which are also comprehensible through interpretive categories.

Third, in theorizing that government emanates from human nature instead of being imposed on it, eighteenth-century moral philosophers implied that another abstraction, which Michel Foucault called governmentality, was as law-governed as human nature (and the providential order that informs it). This idea reemerges in one modern theory of governmentality which maintains that the ideal (liberal) state is not coercive but wields power indirectly by inciting the voluntary cooperation of individuals.[1]

Before embarking on a more detailed account of eighteenth-century British

1. See Burchell 1991.

moral philosophy, I address two theoretical issues that help clarify the concept of the social more generally. The first concerns the migration of the term *social* from adjectival to nominal status. The second is the theoretical benefit that might accrue from positioning discussions of the social within a consideration of what Charles Taylor and others call "social imaginaries." I suggest that identifying the social as one product of a specifically modern social imaginary helps illuminate some of the complexities that many theorists of the social have overlooked. These complexities include: (1) the relationship between interpretive abstractions, with their objectifying perspective, and the claims that can be made about and with these abstractions; (2) how modern uses of the social convey the theological connotations implicit in this concept's providential predecessor.

Etymological Migrations

In Samuel Johnson's *Dictionary of the English Language* and the *Oxford English Dictionary*, *social* is almost always an adjective. Neither of the two definitions the latter gives for the noun illuminates modern usage: the first ("a companion, an associate") is no longer current; the second ("a social gathering or a party") is too narrow to capture the theoretical work performed by nineteenth- and (especially) twentieth-century analysts. However, if we pay close attention to the changes that the *OED* tracks in the adjective's usage, we see how the appearance of *social* in certain contexts might have encouraged social scientists to nominalize the lowly adjective by appending the definite article *the*.[2]

From the Latin *socialis* or *socius*, meaning friend, ally, or associate, *social* came into the English language in the mid–sixteenth century as a modifier that described individuals' ability to form relationships. In 1562 *social* was defined as "*capable* of being associated or united with others" (my emphasis) (*OED*, 2d ed.). In citing capability, this definition of *social* assumes that individuals are monads, which can—but do not have to—relate to other monads. In so doing, the 1562 definition departs from the Platonic idea, which assumed that human beings are integral parts of a greater whole, not isolatable units. When William Wolloston (*OED*, 2d ed.) referred to "man" as "a Social creature" in 1722, he elaborated the individualism implicit in the mid-sixteenth-century usage as well

2. This discussion of the etymology of *the social* draws upon entries from Johnson's *Dictionary of the English Language,* 4th ed., and the *Compact Oxford English Dictionary,* 2d ed. All future references to the *Dictionary of the English Language* and the *Oxford English Dictionary* are abbreviated as *DEL* and *OED*, respectively.

as the ethical burden introduced by this individualism. In the second sentence of Wolloston's passage, what initially seems to be a definition ("man is a Social creature") proves to imply judgment, when Wolloston yokes the adjective *social* to the noun *Society*, which he uses in Johnson's sense of "company": "a single man, or a family, cannot subsist, *or not well*, alone out of all Society" (my emphasis) (*DEL*, 4th ed.).

Later in the 1720s, Joseph Butler drew out the complexities inherent in conceptualizing individuals as monads charged with ethical choice. In 1729 Butler (*OED*, 2d ed.) explained that "the nature of man considered in his . . . social capacity leads him to a right behaviour in society." This sentence suggests that by the late 1720s, social had come to seem like one attribute of an objectified abstraction—human nature—viewed as given to all individuals by God. As one among several God-given capacities, moreover, "social capacity" could only actualize human nature's virtuous potential if the individual exercised this capacity and controlled the others, including the capacity for what contemporaries called "self-love."[3]

By 1785 the connotations of divine provenance in Butler's "nature of man" had been minimized by Thomas Reid's ascription of "social" and "solitary" to "operations of the mind" (*OED*, 2d ed.). By opposing this pair of mental "operations," Reid not only naturalized capacities that had once been thought of in theological terms. He also offered a picture of a mind whose dynamics could be conceptualized in isolation from ethical considerations. In Reid's objectified "mind," the social "operation" is an object of study in its own right, regardless of the context in which an individual lives, the motives that inspire behavior, and the consequences that actions produce.

In the 1840s, the objectification implied by Reid's reference to mental operations was taken to another level when *social* began to appear in noun compounds that were themselves secular abstractions. Charles Bray's 1841 reference to "Social Reform" (*OED*, 2d ed.) and Archer Polson's 1845 invocation of "Social Economy" (*OED*, 2d ed.) reveal that what was first conceptualized as an ethical capacity of a nature given by God, then as the property of a naturalized mental operation, had been liberated altogether from individual humans. The migration of *social* from its adjectival relation to an abstraction that implicitly invoked God, to an integral position in a noun-compound detached from human agents, suggests the twin processes of alienation and reification that modern uses of the

3. "Self-love" is the central emotion represented by Bernard Mandeville in *The Fable of the Bees* (1714) and discussed by Alexander Pope in his *Essay on Man* (1722–24).

social assume: in order to imagine that "social reform" and "social economy" are relatively autonomous secular projects or areas of analysis, one must conceptualize "reform" and "economy" as separable from the individuals who engage in these activities, as amenable to scientific (rather than theological) analysis, and as relatively concrete projects or objects of study. This conceptualization, in turn, was only possible once "society" came to be understood not from a particular participant's point of view, but as an objective order with its own regulated dynamics. These mid-nineteenth-century compound nouns thus convey the atomism implicit in the adjectival uses of *social* since the mid–sixteenth century, but in such a way as to isolate not the individual human being but activities that human beings collectively pursue as expressions of the regulations of society. These mid-nineteenth-century noun-compounds thus signify the autonomy and materiality of abstractions that have been separated from human actors. At the same time, they also imply that the dynamics of what were once considered God-given human capacities or mental operations had come to be considered sufficiently lawful in their own right to be conceptualized as parts of the large, objectified process that was populated by its own abstract actors and that particular individuals could describe but not judge. This complexity is indicated by Polson's definition of "Social Economy" as the study of the "*laws* which directly consult the health, wealth, convenience or comfort of *the public*" (my emphasis) (*OED*, 2d ed.).

When modern theorists use *social* as a noun, they draw upon the theoretical assumptions captured in Polson's definition. These assumptions include: (1) that a relatively autonomous and objectified society exists; (2) that the dynamics of this objectified set of practices or structures are lawful and, when manifested in institutions and practices, amenable to systematic analysis; (3) that this domain of sociality both informs the institutions that its dynamics help explain and, in turn, refers to some invisible but law-abiding system; and (4) that aggregates, which are also abstractions (the public, labor), constitute the agents of more foundational abstractions like the social. Since the mid–nineteenth century, these aggregates have most often been constructed so as to be amenable to representation in the languages of quantification and classification (enumeration and statistics). Constructing these aggregates and translating them into forms that can be represented in numbers or statistics has been the characteristic work of late-nineteenth- and twentieth-century social scientists.

These etymological changes allude to what has been called the rise of modern abstraction, that complex series of theoretical and institutional developments by which the old conceptualization of society as one or more normative orders grasped from the standpoints of participants (the political polity, the Christian *sociatas*) was gradually replaced by a non-participant-based understanding of one or more law-governed domains (the economy, the political), which were interpreted as objective and thought to be organized by their own characteristic dynamics.[4] As society came to be viewed as a complex of law-governed, objectified domains, these domains were conceptualized from the standpoints specific to each (i.e., those of production and distribution), even though advocates for these points of view represented the perspectives as Nagel's objectifying views from nowhere. The perspectives and the domains they organized were also represented —for the purposes of analysis—as agent- or objectlike abstractions. When they are treated as such—as agents or as objects of analysis in their own right (as the social often is)—these abstractions carry with them connotations of both the standpoint articulated and the objectifying view from nowhere that is theoretically represented. To understand abstractions like the social, which populate the objectified domains of modern society, and to grasp the historical provenance of this abstraction in particular, it is helpful to turn to what Taylor and others have referred to as the social imaginary of modern societies.

The *Social* and Social Imaginaries

In theorizing the concept of a social imaginary, Taylor follows Cornelius Castoriadis (1987: 143), who uses the term to refer to "the final articulations the society in question has imposed on the world, on itself, and on its needs, the organizing patterns that are the conditions for the representability of everything that the society can give to itself."[5] In its most basic sense, the concept of the social imaginary refers not to particular representations or actions but to the foundational assumptions about what counts as an adequate representation or practice in the first place. Thus defined, the social imaginary is a concept that modern analysts use to describe the most foundational conceptual conditions of possibility for a society's operation, even if the society in question lacks a theoretical formulation that describes its operation in the abstract for its participants.

Let us turn to a specific example. Elsewhere I describe one component of modern Western societies' social imaginary as the reliance on the concept of the modern fact (Poovey 1998). The modern fact is an epistemological unit rather than a content. It links individual claims about specific observations with generaliza-

4. For discussions of the history of abstraction, see Poovey 1995: 25–54; Lefebvre 1991: 229–91; and Williams 1977: 55–71.
5. Craig Calhoun initially alerted me to Castoriadis's influence on Taylor. See Calhoun's essay in this issue.

tions about "larger" or "deeper" principles that presumably lie behind the observed phenomena. The modern fact thus anchors an epistemology that assumes a syntagmatic relationship between the part and the whole, an ordered universe of natural objects, and a dichotomy between the observing subject and the object that is observed. While this way of knowing the world now seems like common sense, the kind of reasoning implicit in the modern fact was developed in the fifteenth and sixteenth centuries, when it was institutionalized as a mode of writing particular to one occupational group (Italian merchants in their capacity as bookkeepers). In the seventeenth century, members of another social group, the British natural philosophers who bonded together as the Royal Society, appropriated the epistemological assumptions implicit in the modern fact to authorize another set of social behaviors—that is, to convince the king that the knowledge they produced about the natural world was reliable because nonsectarian. During the next century, the assumptions and representational practices associated with the modern fact were gradually taken up by increasing numbers of theorists and lay people as the method associated with this epistemological unit—the scientific method —gained more general cultural authority. While the way of thinking associated with the modern fact continued (and continues) to vie with other explanatory paradigms, it gained sufficient ascendancy by the end of the eighteenth century to be considered the dominant social imaginary of all western European societies that embraced the principles of scientific knowledge.

Taylor helps illuminate the general principles behind this specific example, although his brief exposition can also benefit from the kind of elaboration I offer here. Taylor stresses, for example, that a social imaginary is not simply a theory developed by specialists. Instead it is at least partly generated by ordinary people for use in everyday life, and it reveals itself in stories, myths, and commonplaces as well as theoretical narratives. According to Taylor (2000: 1), a social imaginary "is what enables, through making sense of, the practices of a society."[6] Taylor (20) also helpfully points out that a social imaginary is not simply descriptive; it also has a normative or prescriptive function, which guides the evaluation of practices as well as the practices themselves.

> It incorporates a sense of the normal expectations that we have of each
> other; the kind of common understanding which enables us to carry out
> the collective practices which make up social life. This incorporates some

6. In this essay I discuss Taylor's paper "Modern Social Imaginaries," delivered in August 2000 at the New Social Imaginaries conference in Montreal. A revised version of that paper is included in this issue.

sense of how we all fit together in carrying out the common practice. This understanding is both factual and "normative"; that is, we have a sense of how things usually go, but this is interwoven with an idea of how they ought to go, of what mis-steps would invalidate the practice.

Because they align description with prescription, social imaginaries also perform a legitimating function: "the social imaginary is that common understanding which makes possible common practices, and a widely shared sense of legitimacy."

Taylor's understanding of social imaginaries, which is explicitly indebted to Benedict Anderson's notion of imagined communities, has affinities with the concept of ideology, which also attempts to explain representations and collective practices by reference to a more capacious abstraction. Unlike most uses of ideology, however, Taylor's treatment of social imaginary does not hold that there is a preexisting foundation on which society's representations and practices rest, nor does it suggest that one could identify this foundation as independent of the representation created by ideology. Instead, as I understand Taylor's account, social imaginaries are self-authenticating (if not self-generating); they produce the terms by which they can be understood in producing the conditions in which some understandings count more than others. While a theorist can identify the imaginary that governs a given society's representations and practices, he or she cannot be said to reveal a "deeper" truth in doing so. In making some explanatory paradigms (and not others) available and credible in the first place, a particular social imaginary makes theoretical statements about "deeper" causes possible, but does not stipulate that there are truths that lie outside the imaginary that produces them.

In eliminating ideology's dichotomy between surface and depth—and between subjective delusion and the objective understanding offered by experts—Taylor's concept allows us to conceptualize social imaginaries as a feedback loop. In this loop, all of the elements inform one another, so that causation flows in multiple directions simultaneously. Thus, particular representations can influence institutional practices and vice versa, and explanatory paradigms that depend on abstractions can also be said to derive their power partly from the concrete images and stories these abstractions purport to explain. Because it describes a recursive structure rather than a dichotomy, Taylor's account allows us to connect the theoretical formulations that experts produce with the common understandings that ordinary people generate in living together. We can conceptualize this relationship temporally, as if images pass from theory to common sense (or vice versa), or spatially, as if the images produced by one group of social participants are variants of the images produced by another. It is impossible to know whether the temporal account is more accurate than the spatial account—or even to be certain that these are not just two ways of viewing a process whose complexities can be theorized only in temporary isolation from their unfolding in time and space. Since we know that the terms in which we conceptualize a given social imaginary are generated by the practices that institutionalize its assumptions, all we can know is that the claim to know helps create the conditions in which (some kinds of) knowledge is accorded truth-value.

To be fair, Taylor does not emphasize the self-authenticating nature of individual social imaginaries as much as I have, nor does he detail the recursive dynamic that I associate with the self-authenticating nature of this concept. I have emphasized self-authentification in seeking to liberate the concept of social imaginary from the dichotomies generally associated with ideology. This is important because it enables us to conceptualize dichotomies, such as the split between "objective" and "subjective," as products of a particular social imaginary, not a natural relation between terms that somehow stand outside a society's way of understanding and organizing itself.

Even as Taylor's concept would benefit from being further distinguished from most uses of ideology, I think that it would also help to embellish it with the internal differentiation that Raymond Williams has introduced into the concept of ideology. Rather than viewing ideology as homogeneous, and therefore totalizing, Williams discriminates among the emergent, dominant, and residual ideologies that may coexist in a single society. At any given moment, the dominant ideology must compete with new collective understandings that are just beginning to gain credibility as well as with lingering traces of old ideological formations (Williams 1977: 121–27). Combining Taylor's idea of social imaginaries with Williams's model of competing ideologies encourages us to think of a society's social imaginary as an ensemble of ideas and practices, including germs of models that will eventually assume greater definition as well as understandings that belong to older conceptualizations of social relations.[7]

Taylor (2000: 1) does suggest that social imaginaries are plural geographi-

---

7. That Williams's discussion seems compatible with Taylor's is clear from the latter's discussion of the various stages in "the long march" from idea to social imaginary. According to Taylor (2000: 24), it is "a process whereby new practices, or modifications of old ones, either developed through improvisation among certain groups and strata of the population . . . ; or else were launched by elites in such a way as to recruit a larger and larger base. . . . Or alternatively, a set of practices in the course of their slow development and ramification gradually changed their meaning for people, and hence helped to constitute a new social imaginary."

cally. Emphasizing the synchronic multiplicity of geographically separated social imaginaries helps prevent us from generalizing the social imaginary a particular theorist or citizen inhabits (and whose terms he or she necessarily uses) to all of the societies on earth. When imagined as synchronically and geographically plural, the concept of social imaginaries even suggests the limitations of the abstraction *modernity*. The existence of multiple, coeval social imaginaries implies that there is no single way of being modern. It also suggests that we need further clarification about the relationship between the development of particular social imaginaries—including those characterized by ever-more-finely discriminated levels of abstraction—and the term *modernity*, which is intended to characterize a general phase of historical and epistemological achievement.

However we think about the limitations of generalizing modernity, we can use Taylor's concept of social imaginaries to clarify how abstractions like *the social* function within societies that have embraced the epistemology of the modern fact. According to Taylor, the social imaginary that fosters such secular abstractions rests on two more foundational abstractions: an ideal of order and a normative image of human nature. The distinctive modern accomplishment, Taylor contends, has been to separate the former from its Platonic predecessor and to secularize the latter. As part of the reworking of these old categories, the modern social imaginary casts social order as exclusively deriving from and also benefiting human beings, who are by nature capable of relationship but required to create and maintain the affiliation that sustains monadic individuals. In Taylor's (2000: 61) succinct phrase, (Western) modernity is characterized by an "ideal of order as mutual benefit." As part of this ideal of order as mutual benefit, second-order analytic categories like the social have been generated to explain how the more foundational abstractions—such as order and human nature—"naturally" produce the precise relationship (of mutual benefit, ideally) that characterizes society. In so doing, the social plays the role for the modern theorist that Providence did for philosophers of an earlier age: it explains why this relationship is necessary or natural, not arbitrary or simply a projection of wishful thinking.[8]

8. Here the comments of Fredric Jameson (1981: 323) are illuminating. Jameson argues that the most fully theorized version of the social—historical materialism—makes the same assumption about necessity that providentialism did: "The idea of Providence is the distorted anticipation, within the religious and figural master-code, of the idea of historical necessity in historical materialism. . . . This concept is . . . simply the enabling presupposition of the historian herself, and [it] governs the form with which historiography endows the events of the past, the things that have already happened once and for all. The concept of historical necessity is simply the assumption that things happened the way they did because they had to happen that way and no other, and that the business of the historian is to show why they had to happen that way."

The concept of the social, like the commonplace images and stories to which it is related and with which it competes, ultimately functions to legitimate social arrangements that are no longer seen as resting on a providential ground.[9]

It is important to acknowledge the legitimating function that such abstractions play. According to John Finnis (1980: 43), a historical crisis in legitimacy (and faith) provoked theorists like Hugo Grotius and Samuel von Pufendorf to elaborate the work of mid-fourteenth-century writers like Francisco Suárez and Gabriel Vázquez into a theory of natural law. It is this theory of natural law that anchors our modern secular abstractions. In Taylor's account of Grotius and his contemporaries, the particular conceptualizations of order and human nature that eventually came to organize a new social imaginary were elaborated in a rather specialized conversation among theorists trying to rethink the legitimacy of governments and the rules of peace in the wake of the Religious Wars (Taylor 2000: 3). This conversation drew upon and reformulated not only the work of Suárez and Vázquez but also older theological ideas about relations between idealism and civil society (Pinkstock, in press). And from it emerged the modern idea that social order emanates from the human nature it also serves—an idea that gradually began to influence the terms of other discussions intended to legitimate other activities, such as the spread of Western commerce or the printing press's dissemination of secular knowledge.

Taylor's account of the modern social imaginary helpfully positions this ensemble of ideas and practices in relation to three large historical "events." Following Jacques Lezra (1997: 35–76), I place *events* in quotation marks to designate the mixed nature of these concepts/institutions: each "event" is both an analytic abstraction (and thus a product of the historical process I am describing) and a set of institutions and practices that materialize that abstraction and thus make descriptions of it credible. In Taylor's narrative, the three "events" that simultaneously accompanied and could be explained by the emergent modern social imaginary were the consolidation of "the economy," the appearance of what Jür-

---

9. This is true even when the analyst's specific use of the social is highly critical of modern social relations or when the point of the social-historical account is to show how modern social relations are *not* mutually beneficial. Thus, Marxists emphasize that the economic relations of production systematically enslave some individuals for the advantage of others; for many Marxists, capitalism exists on the horizon of the social. In this account, however, the tendencies Adam Smith attributed to human nature are simply being transferred to another abstraction (capitalism), which presumably still articulates "natural" human proclivities. "Mutual benefit" is obviously not achieved under capitalism, but the animating idea of Enlightenment models of mutual benefit is being carried forward by capitalism because this system allows for the expression of what Smith (1937: 13) described as individuals' "natural" inclination to "truck, barter, and exchange one thing for another."

gen Habermas has called the "public sphere," and the codification of the practices and outlooks of democratic self-rule, which Foucault calls "liberal governmentality" (Taylor 2000: 25).

Temporally, the consolidation of the economy constitutes the first of these large historical "events." In seventeenth-century England, in the wake of the civil war, ordered life and work were seen as newly important to individuals' ability to achieve self-realization and serve God, and commerce was viewed as crucial to domestic and religious peace. Gradually, using imagery generated by merchants and political theorists, common individuals began to think of daily production and consumption, as well as the nation's prosperity and strength, in terms of an "economy." According to Taylor (2000: 19): "Instead of being merely the management, by those in authority, of the resources we collectively need, in household or state, the 'economic' [began to define] a way in which [individuals] are linked together, a sphere of coexistence which could in practice suffice to itself, if only disorder and conflict didn't threaten."[10]

The images, theoretical paradigms, and institutions that composed the economy had attained sufficient visibility and regularity by the end of the seventeenth century to help fill the vacuum left by the obliteration of absolute monarchy in England. As John Brewer (1995a) has argued, the civil war, the Commonwealth, and the Protectorate virtually destroyed the court culture that had once represented itself as the legitimating ground of the British nation. Charles II and James II tried to resurrect the monarchy's old glory but did not succeed, and, under the rule of the house of Hanover, the prestige of the court deteriorated even further. At the same time, because of royal cupidity and the Reformation's repudiation of images, the Church also lost the public credibility and economic power essential to legitimate its rule. As a consequence, the basis of the nation's authority and the new dynasty's novel compound of rule by party politics and rule by finance needed to be justified to early-eighteenth-century Britons.

The press—the primary instrument of the emergent public sphere—helped supply these legitimating terms in images of politeness and a civilizing process of exchange appropriate to the new economy of paper credit and party politics. Periodicals like the *Spectator* enabled a newly empowered "public" to imagine itself as a single entity, whose rules were those of polite and rational discourse and whose legitimacy was founded not on the king or Church but on its members' ability to disagree without overt conflict. This public, as Brewer, Habermas, and

10. I also describe various components of the consolidation of "the economy" in Poovey 1998: 1–143.

others have emphasized, came to self-understanding not merely through elite individuals reading philosophical theories in formal educational settings but also through the larger literate populace discussing news and other matters in coffee-houses and over tea (Brewer 1995a: 344). The resulting "polite culture of the public sphere" functioned to constitute and instruct "a body of arbiters of taste, morality, and policy" (Brewer 1995a: 344; Habermas 1989: 57–88). As suggested by the mixed nature of the three large concepts/institutions Taylor identifies, the public sphere was partly constructed by the shared understandings and images of itself that were generated through print and conversation, and partly by the institutions that enabled these ideas about politeness to circulate and acquire social prestige. This public sphere generated a new sense of public order and of the public nature and accountability of political behaviors. "With the modern public sphere comes the idea that political power must be supervised and checked by something outside," Taylor explains (2000: 29). "What was new, of course, was not that there was an outside check, but rather the nature of this instance. It is not defined as the will of God, or the Law of Nature (although it could be thought to articulate these), but as a kind of discourse, emanating from reason and not from power or traditional authority."

This public sense of authority legitimated by rational discourse permeated a society of individuals conceptualized as both interchangeable and newly unique. The individuals who composed the public sphere seemed to contemporaries both more public and more private than ever before (as we have seen in eighteenth-century definitions of *social*). On the one hand, the new emphasis on commerce and public participation in politics placed a burden on individuals to perform socially, in the glare of the publicity they consumed and generated. On the other hand, the new emphasis on personal freedom and the sanctity of everyday life urged a new valuation of privacy and the elaboration of what Habermas (1989: 151–59) calls the sphere of intimacy. In the new social imaginary, publicness and privacy were actually two sides of a single coin. Periodicals like the *Spectator* provided rules for the individual's most solitary behaviors, such as how to make morally instructive extracts from books, but, because they were promoted in print, these rules brought the sphere of intimacy into the glare of public norms. Books of correspondence, as well as the innumerable letters printed in popular periodicals, generated the paradoxical image of a sphere of privacy simultaneously enforced by and evacuated of the very autonomy that was supposed to insulate it from the public.[11] The paradoxical formation of the sphere of intimacy had

11. John Brewer (1995b: 13) notes that "the first series of the *Spectator*, which consisted of 555 essays issued between March 1711 and December 1712, included 250 such letters."

a particularly powerful effect on women (see discussion below), but for men too it was arguably one of the most prominent and inescapable features of this new social imaginary.

Scottish Moral Philosophy and the Liberal Civil Subject

The admittedly overly schematic narrative I have just provided is intended to remind readers of the kind of story that uses "the modern ideal of order as mutual benefit" to distinguish modern societies from their predecessors and contemporary rivals. To make this narrative less schematic would require not only more historical detail but also a continuous emphasis on the way that various standpoints and abstractions were created to explain and legitimate the institutions and practices that materialized this ideal. This dimension of historical narratives is the one most frequently omitted, but without it we too often imagine that a narrative of the past provides a vantage point somehow superior to our analytic object, instead of thinking of our analytic terms as themselves products of a historical process. In the space remaining, I can offer only a brief description of what I take to be a critical phase in the rise of modern abstraction: in this phase, philosophers began to elaborate a new theory of governmentality by reworking their understanding of providential order, which was the predecessor of the social; they reworked providential order, in turn, by developing an understanding of human nature that entailed the nuanced dynamics of such abstractions as *desire*, *social capacity*, and *self-love*. I intend my brief account of this elaboration as a contribution to other scholarly work on this process, which I encourage interested readers to consult.[12]

During the first half of the eighteenth century, British moral philosophers began to justify the mode of government inaugurated by the Glorious Revolution with theoretical accounts of human nature that stressed human beings' natural tendency to benefit one another as they advanced their own interests.[13] Initially, philosophical accounts of human nature referred this natural tendency to God's design, although, as the *OED*'s exemplary quotations reveal, conceptualizing

12. See McKeon 1987: xiii–xviii and 26–28; Kramnick 1999: 189–90, 204–5; and Siskin 1988: 67–1147.

13. It should be noted that moral philosophy was not the only kind of writing that sought to discriminate among kinds of feelings or to delineate a descriptive-normative relationship among feelings. In imaginative writing, novelists and poets also developed these discriminations, and a modern reader would be hard-pressed to decide which kind of writing was more influential. Indeed, the recursive nature of the relationship between moral philosophical texts and novels or poetry is a good example of the internal dynamics of a social imaginary.

human capacity as an articulation of the providential order embedded in the nature of man cleared the way for marginalizing, then dispensing with, the providential explanation altogether. The kind of naturalization we saw in Reid's reference to "operations of the mind" (*OED*, 2d ed.) was arguably facilitated by the philosophical elevation of new abstractions—including, centrally, *human nature*—to an intermediary position between behaviors that could be observed and the providential order that was presumed to inform them. Using secular abstractions to think about what could not be seen but was assumed to exist, as well as about the observable behaviors the abstractions theoretically explained, laid the groundwork for thinking about interpretive abstractions apart from the original providential scheme. This was partly true because foundational abstractions such as human nature were amenable to—indeed called out for—the kind of theoretical elaboration that generated additional abstractions. By illuminating the dynamic relationship between derivative and foundational abstractions, theorists enabled people to understand how these abstractions functioned, either as articulations of God's order or as orderly (and relatively autonomous) entities independent of a providential framework. Thus, as theorists such as Francis Hutcheson, Adam Ferguson, George Turnbull, David Hume, and Adam Smith began to elaborate how "the social capacity" worked, they helped their contemporaries imagine that such a capacity actually existed, experience their own emotions as expressions of (or impediments to) "the social capacity," and seek institutional guarantees for the regular expression of this capacity by as many people as possible.

The foundational abstraction in which early-eighteenth-century philosophers anchored their defenses of liberal governmentality was not completely new at the turn of the century, but, as Roger Smith (1995: 94–95) has observed, human nature had never before received the kind of attention the moral philosophers paid it. Human nature served the same explanatory function as the sixteenth-century idea of natural law, but, as the difference between the two terms suggests, focusing on human nature meant supplementing the idea of law, which could be said to originate outside of individuals, with reflections on human subjectivity, which was experienced as originating within the individual. This shift from an abstraction that refers to concrete relations or external necessity to one that conjures internal experience informed the general project the British moral philosophers undertook: to explain why individuals could be counted on to produce a mutually beneficial society in the process of gratifying themselves.

To explain why individuals could be trusted to govern themselves—and why, as an extension of this mutually beneficial self-government, the party- and market-governed character of the new British nation was legitimate—philosophers began to conceptualize the dynamics of interiority more precisely than ever before, both distinguishing, as we have already seen, among various "capacities" (the "social capacity," the "capacity for self-love," and so on) and charting the relationships among these capacities (as in Pope's *Essay on Man* [3.318]: "Self-love and Social [are] the same"). In order to discriminate among the feelings that had once been classified according to broad theological categories like "good" and "evil," British moral philosophers appropriated a variant of the apparently nonjudgmental method that natural philosophers had developed to study the particulars of the natural world. This method, which depended upon observation and experiment, had enabled natural philosophers such as Robert Boyle to argue that the knowledge they produced was "objective," in the sense of nonsectarian. Appropriating this method allowed moral philosophers to argue that the observations they made about the dynamics of subjectivity were as reliable—because as systematic—as the observations about nature for which natural philosophers had already established social credibility. Because they were making claims about the "moral" domain, the eighteenth-century philosophers were understandably less eager to disavow judgment than their natural philosophical counterparts, but what we might call interested judgments were represented by the moral philosophers as unbiased descriptions of realizable norms. We see this characteristic coincidence of description and normative prescription in Hutcheson's comment that the "*moral sense*," which every individual supposedly possesses, reveals the "*End* or *Design*" of God's plan even in behaviors that are not self-evidently moral. In other words, according to Hutcheson (1969: xvi–xvii), the moral sense enables us to intuit "what is required of us by the Author of our nature" to realize God's plan, even when our ocular sense perceives no order and no plan at all.

The complete title of Hume's *Treatise* exemplifies the use of the natural philosophical method to support the descriptive/normative elaborations of the capacities that compose "human nature"; the work is titled *A Treatise of Human Nature: Being an Attempt to Introduce the Experimental Method of Reasoning into Moral Subjects*. Yet, as Hume also suggested, only the establishment of a reciprocal relationship between the two variants of philosophy could authenticate the common project of finding informing principles, whether one sought those principles in nature or in "man." "As the science of man is the only solid foundation for the other sciences," Hume (1984: 43) declares, "so the only solid foundation we can give to this science itself must be laid on experience and observation." Even when Hume replaces *experience* with the narrower term *experiment*, as he does in the last paragraph of his introduction, it is not clear how he intends to move from observation of discrete particulars to their informing principles *except* by assuming that such systematic principles exist. In other words, as Hume famously observed, we must take for granted that order exists before we can ascribe order to what we actually see, and this ascription of order to what we see follows our ability to create and elaborate systematic abstractions. Mediating abstractions such as human nature legitimate this foundational assumption—and paradoxically help make it a commonplace—because they can be elaborated systematically and in relation to other abstractions like *providential design* and *social capacity*.

The assumption that principles of order exist and can be described was essential to the entire moral philosophical project because the ability to produce systematic knowledge was what made moral philosophy a science, and the claim to explain why individual behaviors would guarantee social order anchored the philosophers' bid for social authority. Various philosophers suggested ways to raise the assumption that order exists to the level of explicit knowledge: Smith invoked the observable but "invisible hand" of the market as well as "sympathy"; Hutcheson described a "moral sense" that functions like one of the five physical senses; Hume used the analogy of billiard balls to endorse an inflexible model of "association"; and Turnbull cited mathematical reasoning as proof of an orderly universe. Aside from Hume, all of these philosophers invoked providential design as the source of order. Only later in the century, as the science of man was divided into more specialized, nontheological practices, did the providential narrative have to compete with the naturalized explanations that eventually displaced it.

While the explanatory content of the moral philosophers' early-eighteenth-century claims was eventually displaced by other explanatory paradigms, their foundational assumption persisted. The idea that the orderly dynamics of philosophical abstractions refer to existing principles of order has proved more resilient than any particular account of that order. This is the assumption, in fact, that informs modern invocations of the social, which attempt to explain observable institutions and practices by reference to some invisible but determining "logic," "structure," or "dynamic." Combined with the epistemology epitomized by the modern fact, this assumption of an underlying order lies at the heart of the modern social imaginary. If we did not collectively assume that such order exists—no matter what we call it—no systematic organization of knowledge (i.e., no science) would be credible, no observations about the past could purport to predict the future, and our ability to create and differentiate abstractions would have no explanatory power.

Coda

If we turn from philosophical discussions of abstractions like human nature to the accounts and practices of ordinary individuals, we find an even more nuanced rendering of the modern social imaginary's internal complexities. Capturing this internal complexity seems a desirable goal of contemporary accounts of the past not because it reveals some deeper explanatory truth that the moral philosophers could not see but because these philosophical formulations constitute only one part of a social imaginary. The other part was produced—and lived—by people positioned at different points in the hierarchy of eighteenth-century British society. By examining the practices of the individuals who were marginalized by theorists' writings, we obtain a more textured image of the modern social imaginary: the work of these marginalized individuals often constitutes the anomalies that philosophical writing is intended to smooth over. This is certainly true of women of virtually all social ranks in the early eighteenth century. As Paula McDowell (1998: 285–301) and others have observed, the rise of domestic norms, which played a central role in legitimating the institutional arrangements that stabilized eighteenth-century market society and the public sphere, functioned to stigmatize or even outlaw the activities of women who did not conform to what emerged as a cultural norm.

An examination of the activities and writing of women in this period enriches our chronicle of the rise of modern abstraction. The moral philosophers' efforts to discriminate abstractions such as *the social capacity* and *desire* helped construct a normative picture of human nature that relegated women to a single set of social functions: child rearing and moral governance. Not all women accepted this assignment however. Particularly in the first decade of the eighteenth century, as McDowell (1998: 176–79, 180–82) has demonstrated, women not only participated actively in the print industry as authors, booksellers, and publishers; they also articulated a community-oriented sense of self that did not conform to the philosophers' norm of an individualized self naturally directed to the mutual benefit of the community. By the same token, even after the domestic component of the modern social imaginary began to seem natural, some women continued to question or even defy it openly. We only have to look at the late-eighteenth-century writing of Mary Wollstonecraft and Mary Hays to see that alternative opinions were still possible. If social imaginaries were internally self-consistent and self-policing, or if philosophers were the only ones whose formulations counted, then it would have been impossible for anyone to voice—or even imagine—such radical critiques.

Of course, even a critique as radical as Wollstonecraft's *Vindication of the Rights of Woman* (1792) deployed abstractions to explain a "human nature" that seemed to her to have been misrepresented by the philosophers. Like the philosophers she scorned, Wollstonecraft advanced her critique by means of abstractions, and she did so at least partly to defy the philosophers' claims that women were incapable of making generalizations. Willing to question virtually every other social and intellectual convention of her day, Wollstonecraft was not willing to disturb what had by then become a cornerstone of her society's social imaginary: authoritative knowledge-production depends on and proceeds by means of abstractions that mediate between what everyone can see and what everyone believes. Wollstonecraft believed that to change our understanding of these abstractions would be to alter the institutions in which we live because it would reveal the truth about the order God had written into the world. Wollstonecraft's confidence is not so different from the enthusiasm of modern theorists, as they replace providential order with other abstractions like the social. With every claim to identify a law-abiding abstraction that explains what-can-be-seen by reference to what cannot, we reinscribe the social imaginary that positions the human capacity to imagine order at the foundation of society itself.

Mary Poovey is a professor of English and director of the Institute for the History of the Production of Knowledge at New York University. Her recent publications include *A History of the Modern Fact: Problems of Knowledge in the Sciences of Wealth and Society* (1998).

References

Brewer, John. 1995a. "The most polite age and the most vicious": Attitudes towards culture as a commodity, 1660–1800. In *The consumption of culture, 1600–1800: Image, object, text*, edited by Ann Bermingham and John Brewer. London: Routledge.

———. 1995b. This, that, and the other: Public, social, and private in the seventeenth and eighteenth centuries. In *Shifting the boundaries: Transformation of the languages of public and private in the eighteenth century*, edited by Dario Castiglione and Lesley Sharpe. Exeter: University of Exeter Press.

Burchell, Graham. 1991. Peculiar interests: Civil society and governing "the system of natural liberty." In *The Foucault effect: Studies in governmentality*, edited by Graham Burchell, Colin Gordon, and Peter Miller. Chicago: University of Chicago Press.

Castoriadis, Cornelius. 1987. *The imaginary institution of society*, translated by Kathleen Blamey. Cambridge: MIT Press.

Finnis, John. 1980. *Natural law and natural rights*. Oxford: Clarendon.

Habermas, Jürgen. 1989. *The structural transformation of the public sphere: An inquiry into a category of bourgeois society*, translated by Thomas Burger with Frederick Lawrence. Cambridge: MIT Press.

Hume, David. 1984. *A treatise of human nature*, edited by Ernest C. Mossner. London: Penguin.

Hutcheson, Francis. 1969. *Essay on the nature and conduct of the passions and the affections with illustrations on the moral sense*, edited by Paul McReynolds. Gainesville, Fla.: Scholars' Facsimiles and Reprints.

Jameson, Fredric. 1981. Religion and ideology. In *1642: Literature and power in the seventeenth century: Proceedings of the Essex conference on the sociology of literature, July 1980*, edited by Francis Barker. Colchester: University of Essex Press.

Kramnick, Jonathan. 1999. Locke's desire. *Yale Journal of Criticism* 12: 189–208.

Lefebvre, Henri. 1991. *The production of space*, translated by David Nicholson-Smith. Oxford: Blackwell.

Lezra, Jacques. 1997. *Unspeakable subjects: The genealogy of the event in early modern Europe*. Stanford, Calif.: Stanford University Press.

McDowell, Paula. 1998. *The women of Grub Street: Press, politics, and gender in the London literary marketplace, 1678–1730*. Oxford: Clarendon.

McKeon, Michael. 1987. *The origins of the English novel, 1600–1740*. Baltimore, Md.: Johns Hopkins University Press.

———. 2000. Introduction. In *The theory of the novel: A historical approach*, edited by Michael McKeon. Baltimore, Md.: Johns Hopkins University Press.

Nagel, Thomas. 1986. *The view from nowhere*. New York: Oxford University Press.

Pinkstock, Catherine. In press. The medieval origins of the social. In *The social in question: New Bearings*, edited by Patrick Joyce. London: Routledge.

Pope, Alexander. 1951. *Alexander Pope: Selected poetry and prose*, edited by William K. Wimsatt Jr. New York: Holt, Rinehart and Winston.

Poovey, Mary. 1995. *Making a social body: British cultural formation, 1830–1864*. Chicago: University of Chicago Press.

———. 1998. *A history of the modern fact: Problems of knowledge in the sciences of wealth and society*. Chicago: University of Chicago Press.

Siskin, Clifford. 1988. *The historicity of romantic discourse*. New York: Oxford University Press.

Smith, Adam. 1937. *An inquiry into the nature and causes of the wealth of nations*, edited by Edwin Cannan. New York: Modern Library.

Smith, Roger. 1995. The language of human nature. In *Inventing human science: Eighteenth-century domains*, edited by Christopher Fox, Roy Porter, and Robert Wokler. Berkeley: University of California Press.

Taylor, Charles. 2000. Modern social imaginaries. Paper presented at conference, New Social Imaginaries, Montreal, 3–6 August.

Williams, Raymond. 1977. *Marxism and literature*. Oxford: Oxford University Press.

Imagining Solidarity:
Cosmopolitanism,
Constitutional Patriotism,
and the Public Sphere

Craig Calhoun

Globalization and the coming of postnational and transnational society are often presented as matters of necessity. Globalization appears as an inexorable force—perhaps of progress, perhaps simply of a capitalist juggernaut, but in any case irresistible. European integration, for example, is often sold to voters as a necessary response to the global integration of capital. In Asia, Latin America, and elsewhere, a similar economistic imaginary is deployed to suggest that globalization moves of itself, and governments and citizens have only the option of adapting. Even where the globalist imaginary is not overwhelmingly economistic, it commonly shares in the image of a progressive and imperative modernization. Many accounts of the impact and implications of information technology exemplify this.

Alternatives to globalization, on the other hand, are generally presented in terms of inherited identities and solidarities in need of defense. Usually this means nations and cultural identities imagined on the model of nations; sometimes it means religions, civilizations, or other structures of identity presented by their advocates as received rather than created. The social imaginary of inherited cultural tradition and social identity is prominent in ideologies like Hindutva and

Earlier versions of parts of this text were presented as a Benjamin Meaker Lecture at the University of Bristol in June 2000 and to the Center for Transcultural Studies in July 2000. I am grateful for discussion from both audiences and especially to colleagues in the Center for their sustained challenges to and shaping of my ideas over many years.

Public Culture 14(1): 147–171

essential Ethiopianness, for example, as well as widespread notions of "cultural survival." These are denigrated by proponents of transnational society, who see national and many other local solidarities as backward or outmoded, impositions of the past on the present. Both nationalist economic protectionism and Islamist movements, thus, are seen as being simply the regressive opposite of globalization. In each case, such a perspective leaves obscure the transnational organization of the resistance movement.

In many settings, the economistic, or technologistic, imaginary of globalization is embraced by the very political leaders who advocate nationalist, religious, or other imaginaries that emphasize inherited cultural identity. The contradiction is avoided by assigning these to separate spheres. The Chinese phrase *ti-yong* has long signaled this, a condensation of "Western learning for material advancement, Eastern learning for spiritual essence." Similarly divided imaginaries inform many Asian, Middle Eastern, and other societies. Even in Canada, a recent *Financial Times* article reported, "the country wants to become a lean global competitor while maintaining traditional local values."[1]

In this essay, I take up two aspects of this discourse of globalization. First, I want to call attention to the dominance it grants social imaginaries that emphasize necessity and obscure options for political choice. Second, I want to address the inadequacy of most approaches to social solidarity in this literature. I will focus especially on the work of advocates of "cosmopolitan" approaches to transnational politics, including Jürgen Habermas with his notion of "constitutional patriotism."

I don't mean to denigrate cosmopolitanism—in which I hope I share—but to problematize its acceptance of economistic, modernizing imaginaries without giving adequate attention to the formation of solidarity and the conditions that enable collective choices about the nature of society. In addition to questioning whether "thin identities" are adequate underpinnings for democracy, I will suggest that the public sphere be conceptualized not simply as a setting for rational debate and decision making—thus largely disregarding or transcending issues of identity—but as a setting for the development of social solidarity as a matter of choice, rather than necessity. Such choice may be partly rational and explicit, but is also a matter of "world-making" in Hannah Arendt's sense. The production of new culture is as important as inheritance (and distinctions between the two are less clear than common usage implies). We should accordingly broaden the sense

1. Scott Morrison and Ken Warn, "Liberals Strive to Sharpen Competitive Edge," in "Canada Survey," *Financial Times*, 11 June 2001, 1–2.

of constitutional patriotism to include culture-forming and institution-shaping senses of *constitution*, as well as narrowly legal-political ones. New ways of imagining identity, interests, and solidarity make possible new material forms of social relations. These in turn underwrite mutual commitments. The moment of choice can never be fully separated from that of creativity or construction.

Cosmopolitanism and Constitutional Patriotism

Contemplating simultaneously the questions of German integration and European integration, Habermas has called for grounding political identity in constitutional patriotism.[2] This is an important concretization of a more general and increasingly widespread but not uncontested cosmopolitanism. The concept suggests both constitutional limits to political loyalty and loyalty to the legally enacted constitution as such. In the latter dimension, which Habermas emphasizes, the constitution provides both a referent for public discussion and a set of procedural norms to organize it and orient it to justifiable ends. The specific contents of any conception of the good life may vary, then, and modern societies will always admit of multiple such conceptions. Constitutional patriotism underwrites no single one of these, but rather a commitment to the justification of collective decisions and the exercise of power in terms of fairness. It is thus compatible with a wide range of specific constitutional arrangements, and with a variable balance between direct reference to universal rights and procedural norms on the one hand and a more specific political culture on the other.

Similarly, ideas of rights and justice underpin a new movement of calls for cosmopolitan democracy, democracy not limited by nation-states.[3] Though this is

2. Habermas's abstract theoretical formulations are not altogether separate from his contributions to German public debate—notably, in this case, in relation to the incorporation of the East into a united but West-dominated Germany; to the "historians' debate" over the legacy of the Third Reich; and to the debate over changes in the citizenship law, enacted in watered-down form to grant the children of immigrants naturalization rights. See, among many others, the essays collected in Jürgen Habermas, *The Inclusion of the Other: Studies in Political Theory*, ed. Ciaran Cronin and Pablo De Greiff (Cambridge: MIT Press, 1998).

3. For thoughtful examples, see essays in Daniele Archibugi and David Held, eds., *Cosmopolitan Democracy: An Agenda for a New World Order* (Cambridge, Mass.: Polity, 1995); and Daniele Archibugi, David Held, and Martin Köhler, eds., *Re-Imagining Political Community: Studies in Cosmopolitan Democracy* (Stanford, Calif.: Stanford University Press, 1998); and the more sustained exposition in David Held, *Democracy and the Global Order: From the Modern State to Cosmopolitan Governance* (Stanford, Calif.: Stanford University Press, 1995). Habermas issues a similar call in *Inclusion of the Other*. See also the essays connecting the present to Kant's cosmopolitan project in James Bohman and Matthias Lutz-Bachmann, eds., *Perpetual Peace: Essays on Kant's Cosmopolitan Ideal* (Cambridge: MIT Press, 1997).

not a uniquely European development, there is a notable link between the cosmopolitan message and a certain sense of "movement" in European intellectual life. It harks back directly to the Enlightenment (complete with residual echoes of eighteenth-century aristocratic culture). It also commonly expresses a sense of what Europeans have learned about living together in a multinational region and of how Europeans may take on a civilized (if not precisely civilizing) mission in a conflict-ridden larger world. Cosmopolitanism is potentially consonant with a vision of a Europe of the nations—preserving not only cultural difference but also political autonomy—so long as nationalism is not ethnically communitarian and is subordinated to human and civil rights. But it has a stronger affinity with visions of confederation or of an even greater degree of integration, although it emphasizes the outward obligations of Europeans. What it eschews most is nationalism—especially in its separatist forms, but also any application of the nationalist vision of cultural community to supranational polities. What it claims most, in the spirit of Kant, is that people should see themselves as citizens of the world, not just of their countries.

Central to both cosmopolitanism and constitutional patriotism is an image of "bad nationalism." Nazi Germany is paradigmatic, but more recent examples, like Slobodan Milosevic's Serb nationalism, also inform the theories. At the core of each instance, as generally understood, is an ethnic solidarity that triumphs over civility and liberal values and ultimately turns to horrific violence. Indeed, the negative force of the nationalist imaginary is so strong that each of these theoretical positions is defined more than its advocates admit by its opposition to nationalism—by the Other it would avoid.

But advocates of "postnational" society do themselves, and theory, no favors by equating nationalism with ethnonationalism and understanding the latter primarily through its most distasteful examples. Nations have often had ethnic pedigrees and employed ethnic rhetorics, but they are modern products of shared political, cultural, and social participation, not mere passive inheritances. To treat nationalism as a relic of an earlier order, a sort of irrational expression, or a kind of moral mistake is to fail to see both the continuing power of nationalism as a discursive formation and the work—sometimes positive—that nationalist solidarities continue to do in the world. As a result, nationalism is not easily abandoned even if its myths, contents, and excesses are easily debunked.[4] Not only this, the attempt to equate all nationalism with problematic ethnonationalism

4. I discuss nationalism as a discursive formation in Calhoun, *Nationalism* (Minneapolis: University of Minnesota Press, 1997).

sometimes ends up placing all "thick" understandings of culture and the cultural constitution of political practices, forms, and identities on the nationalist side of the dichotomy. Only quite thin notions of "political culture" are retained on the attractive, postnationalist side.[5] The problem here is that republicanism and democracy depend on more than narrowly political culture—they depend on richer ways of constituting life together.

Recognizing this, Habermas suggests that "the question arises of whether there exists a functional equivalent for the fusion of the nation of citizens with the ethnic nation."[6] He is right that democracy has depended on national identities to a greater degree than many critics of nationalism recognize. His formulation, however, tends to equate all nationalism with ethnic nationalism. "The nation-state owes its historical success to the fact that it substituted relations of solidarity between the citizens for the disintegrating corporative ties of early modern society. But this republican achievement is endangered when, conversely, the integrative force of the nation of citizens is traced back to the prepolitical fact of a quasi-natural people, that is, to something independent of and prior to the political opinion- and will-formation of the citizens themselves."[7] It is true that nationalist rhetoric often invokes the notion of a prepolitical people as the basis for all legitimate politics. Relying only on the negative image, though, leads Habermas to neglect the importance of other nationalist imaginaries to the nurturance of democratic politics. The founding of the United States and subsequent U.S. constitutionalism offer one useful example. It is true that the colonists-turned-nationalists thought of themselves largely as bearers of "the rights of free-born Englishmen." But their appeal was not, in the main, to an ethnic identity. Crucially, in fact, it was an appeal to an identity forged by public discourse itself.[8]

5. See, for example, "Struggles for Recognition in the Democratic Constitutional State," Jürgen Habermas's surprisingly fierce response to Charles Taylor's "The Politics of Recognition," both in *Multiculturalism: Examining the Politics of Recognition*, rev. ed., ed. Amy Gutmann (Princeton, N.J.: Princeton University Press, 1994). On the cosmopolitan side, see Janna Thompson's distorting examination of "communitarian" arguments, "Community Identity and World Citizenship," in Archibugi, Held, and Köhler, *Re-Imagining Political Community*.

6. Habermas, *Inclusion of the Other*, 117.

7. Habermas, *Inclusion of the Other*, 115.

8. Michael Warner, *The Letters of the Republic: Publication and the Public Sphere in Eighteenth-Century America* (Cambridge: Harvard University Press, 1990), is especially informative on the ways in which debate in print informed the constitutive U.S. public. For a discussion of the surprising asymmetry between the intensive and intellectually vital public discussion that informed the founding of the United States and the relative absence of such debate in contemporary Europe, see Larry Siedentop, *Democracy in Europe* (London: Penguin, 2000). It is in this sense, I am suggesting here, that Europe is being given shape and solidarity by economic integration, political institutions, and even certain growing cultural commonalities far more than by any foundational public sphere.

This is part of what Arendt celebrated, seeing the Revolution as a prime example of the capacity of public life for world-making, founding.[9] In this sense, the nation seems more a common project, mediated by public discourse and the collective formation of culture, than simply an inheritance.

The U.S. example could inform a different conception of constitutional patriotism, stronger than that advocated by Habermas. Although, in this new formulation, the emphasis on the norms that underwrite a justifiable life together would remain, this would no longer appear so much to be a matter of getting the abstractly "right" procedures in place on an abstract level. Rather, the idea of a basic law (especially a written document) would be complemented first by the Arendtian notion of founding. This idea of constitution as world-making helps clarify the role of the social imaginary. This is not simply about the imagining of counterfactual possibilities—utopias, for example—however instructive. Rather, it foregrounds ways of imagining social life that actually make it possible. World-making is a way of approaching culture that emphasizes agency and history in the constitution of the languages and understandings by which populaces give shape to social life. To speak of the social imaginary is to assert that there are no fixed categories of external observation adequate to all history; that ways of thinking and structures of feeling make possible certain social forms, and that such forms are thus products of action and historically variable.[10] It follows that cultural creativity can be seen to be basic even to such seemingly "material" forms as the corporation or the nation. These exist precisely because they are imagined; they are real because they are treated as real; and new, particular cases are produced through the recurrent exercise of the underlying social imaginary.

The notion of *constitution as legal framework* thus needs to be complemented by the notion of *constitution as the creation of concrete social relationships*: of bonds of mutual commitment forged in shared action, of institutions, and of

9. Hannah Arendt, *On Revolution* (New York: Penguin, 1977); see also Arendt, *The Human Condition* (Chicago: University of Chicago Press, 1958).

10. The idea of a social imaginary is prominent in the work of Cornelius Castoriadis, although my own usage is different. For Castoriadis, the concept addresses the dimensions of society not graspable as a functional system or a network of symbols, but crucial to the idea that there can be a collective choice about the functional and symbolic order of social life. The imaginary includes "significations that are not there *in order to* represent something else, that are like the final articulations the society in question has imposed on the world, on itself, and on its needs, the organizing patterns that are the conditions for the representability of everything that the society can give to itself." Castoriadis, *The Imaginary Institution of Society*, trans. Kathleen Blamey (Cambridge: MIT Press, 1987), 143. Cf. Charles Taylor: "The social imaginary is not a set of ideas; rather it is what enables, through making sense of, the practices of a society." Taylor, in this issue.

shared modalities of practical action. This expanded sense of constitution would, I think, be much richer. It would also imply an understanding of "peoplehood" much stronger than that acknowledged in Habermas's account of constitutional patriotism (or in the common variants of cosmopolitanism). This is important, as Charles Taylor argues forcefully, because of "the need, in self-governing societies, of a high degree of cohesion."[11]

Democratic states, in other words, require a form and level of "peopleness" that is not required in other forms of government. They offer a level of inclusion that is unprecedented—the government of *all* the people—but they place a new pressure on the constitution of this people in sociocultural and political practice. This makes it clear, I think, that—although not all aspects of constructing peoplehood can be brought into explicit political contention—constructing the relevant people should not be treated as a prepolitical process, as simply a taken-as-given basis for politics. Of course, this is precisely what much nationalist discourse does, and it is also what much political philosophy does—even in classic forms like John Rawls's theory of justice.[12] It says, in effect, "given a people, how should it be governed or socially organized?" It is important to see the constitution of "the people" as much more theoretically, and practically, problematic. One of the consequences of doing so, however, is that such a move entails rejection of any purely external or objective approach to resolving questions of political identity.

Neo-Kantian and, more generally, liberal models of collective life run into difficulties in grappling with the reliance of democracy on a strong notion of "the people." Yet, as Habermas's question about the functional equivalent of the ethnic nation implies, it is crucial to understand not simply which constitutional arrangements are in some abstract sense good, but what makes them have force for specific people. Attempts to resolve this question without addressing how a population conceived as many individuals can constitute itself as a people are deeply problematic, perhaps fatally flawed. This is because it is crucial to account not only for closure in relation to outsiders (so long as the polity is not a single-world polity), but also for mutual commitments among the members of the polity—including commitments to the constitution. Citizens need to be motivated by solidarity, not merely included by law.

In particular, external approaches to identifying "the people" fail to provide an understanding of why and when the definition of the whole becomes a political

11. Taylor, in this issue.
12. John Rawls, *A Theory of Justice* (Cambridge, Mass.: Belknap, 1971).

problem, and which issues become the key signifiers in debate. Why, for example, are there contexts where race matters less than language, and others in which that ordering is hard to imagine? Why are religious identities sometimes critical and at other times trivial? Belonging to (or being excluded from) "the people" is not simply a matter of large-scale political participation in modern society. It is precisely the kind of question of personal identity that produces passions that escape conventional categories of the political. We can see this is so, following Taylor, because of the extent to which ideas and feelings about "the people" are woven into the moral frameworks of "strong evaluation" in relation to which we establish our senses of self.[13]

There is thus an important Hegelian relation at work here, a dialectic of the whole and its parts. Without grasping this dialectic, we can understand neither of its polar terms—*nation* and *individual*. We are also especially apt to be misled into seeing them as opposites, rather than terms that are complicit with each other. But in fact, the ideas of nation and individual developed together in Western history and continue to inform each other. Far from being an objective distinction of collective from singular, the opposition of nation and individual reflects a relation laden with tension. Nations are themselves treated as individuals—by ideologues, of course, but also by diplomats, lawyers, and comparative sociologists. Moreover, the relation between human persons and nations is commonly constructed as immediate, so that intermediate associations and subsidiary identities—family, region, trade—are displaced by it. In this way, nations commonly appear in rhetorical practice as categories of similar individuals as well as organic wholes.[14]

An external account of peoplehood is apt to rely on identity (cultural similarity) and/or interest (and, implicitly or explicitly, a social contract). Identity and/or interest can then be invoked to explain why people accept shared institutions and, indeed, accept each other. The dominant discourses about membership in a European polity work on these bases. Either people are Europeans because they are culturally similar to one another, or they are Europeans because to be so is in their interest (usually described in economic terms). In either case, the emphasis is on passive preconditions, not projects; on adaptation to external necessity, not creative pursuit of an attractive solidarity. The implication is that the persons in question are already formed as either similar or different in cultural terms; as

13. Charles Taylor, *Sources of the Self: The Making of the Modern Identity* (Cambridge: Harvard University Press, 1989).

14. I explore these issues in *Nationalism*.

either having or lacking common interests. Such accounts rely on a notion of the public sphere as a setting in which such ready-constituted people exercise reason, and on that basis debate what institutions and policies they should have. It is understood crucially as the setting in which people transcend differences in identity and particularities of interests. What is missing from such accounts is the role of public life in actually constituting social solidarity and creating culture.

Taking ethnic nationalism as his model, Habermas treats the attempt to ground European unity in some form of peoplehood as tantamount to ethnic exclusion. He sees peoplehood, in other words, as necessarily a matter of some preestablished, passive cultural affinity rather than as the potential result of an active process of public engagement. Habermas hopes the public sphere will produce a rational agreement that can take the place of preestablished culture as the basis for political identity. He works, however, with an overly sharp dichotomy between inherited identity and rational discourse. He identifies voluntary public life entirely with the latter, and thus obscures the extent to which it is necessarily also a process involving modes of cultural creativity and communication not the less valuable for being incompletely rational.

This model allows for a decidedly thin form of identity, to be produced by the rational discourse of the cosmopolitan public sphere. It is thus hard to see how the cosmopolitan public can overcome the disjuncture between such favored sources of legitimation—which are, ideally, rational—and the too commonly irrational sources of integration. "Whereas the voluntary nation of citizens is the source of democratic legitimation, it is the inherited or ascribed nation founded on ethnic membership that secures social integration."[15] As I have argued, in Habermas's dichotomous view, the alternative to such ascription is conscious, rational agreement. But such a formulation neglects the extent to which not only common culture but also all sorts of politically significant agreements are produced and reproduced in social action—as opposed to being either consciously chosen or passively inherited.

For similar reasons, the actual conditions of membership are not restricted to a choice between thick but irrationally inherited identities on the one hand and thin but rationally achieved ones on the other. First, neither of these ideal types fits well with how identities are actually produced and reproduced in society. Second, the opposition obscures the possibilities for producing new and different, but still relatively thick, common identities. Third, we should take care not to reduce social solidarity to common identity—and especially not to naturalize or

15. Habermas, *Inclusion of the Other*, 115.

essentialize its sources by locating them as somehow anterior to political action or its legitimation.

The problem with which Habermas is grappling is real, for there is indeed a widespread tendency to treat common culture as always inherited, and to separate the normative analysis of legitimacy from the givenness or facticity of actually existing collectivities. But his solution to the problem is inadequate. In the first place, however common in political argument it may be to treat cultural similarity as the basis of solidarity, this is not a sociologically adequate account. Common membership of such a category may be one source of solidarity, but hardly the only one. Functional integration, concrete social networks, and mutual engagement in the public sphere are also sources or dimensions of solidarity. Moreover, there is no reason to accept the rhetoric of ethnic nationalists who treat tradition as "the hard cake of culture," simply to be affirmed on the basis of its prepolitical antiquity. Culture is subject to continual reformation or it dies; reproduction involves an element of creative practice.

It is important to emphasize that ethnicity is not the whole of the nationalist imaginary. Nations are also imagined through representations of collective action —the taking of the Bastille, for example. They are constituted through images of collective participation in processes of nation-building. Nationalism does not just provide democracy with a vocabulary for establishing what counts as "the people" on a priori grounds (e.g., ethnicity). It also provides an account of the subjectivity of ordinary people, the collective action of the people, processes of self-making, and the popular guidance of government. In this sense, the honor of membership in the nation is not simply ascribed but achieved; ethnic members can fail when called upon to live up to nationalism, and nonethnic members can be assimilated by active choice.

The nineteenth-century historian Ernest Renan's famous description of the nation as a "daily plebiscite" is expressive of the close relation between nationalism and democracy.[16] But it presents this link in interestingly ambiguous terms, placing individuals in the position of responding (or choosing not to respond) to the calls of the nation. It doesn't clearly describe individuals as authoring the nation through participation in collective action—including, sometimes, public discourse. For Renan, the idea of democracy as genuine self-rule and self-making demands political participation as a good in itself. It is not met simply by government purporting expertly to serve the interests of the people (let alone determin-

16. Ernest Renan, "What Is a Nation?" in *Nation and Narration*, ed. Homi Bhabha (London: Routledge, 1990).

ing in nondemocratic ways what the people's interests ought to be). Varying degrees of constitutional patriotism may thus also be incorporated into nationalist self-imagining, as normative ideals or substantive features of collective life.

A collective European identity may thus be growing, but although this process involves creativity, the extent to which it involves widespread choice is questionable (and no doubt will be widely debated). Marketing, product design, food, and leisure activities all convey images of a European identity. Although news media are not effectively organized on a European scale, entertainment is a bit more so. And both news and entertainment media carry more and more content about an integrated Europe—and, implicitly, a European culture.

Participation in democratic public life is not, however, separate from the processes through which culture is produced and reproduced in modern societies; it is integral to them, and likewise part of the process by which individual and collective identities are made and remade. The problem with which Habermas rightly wrestles remains insoluble so long as culture is treated as inheritance and placed in sharp opposition to reason, conceived in terms of voluntary activity. I have invoked the notion of the social imaginary partly to suggest an approach that recognizes culture as activity, not simply inheritance. It is a figuration that also marks the impossibility of fully disembedding reason from culture. At work in the choice of social institutions is not only an exercise of abstract reason in relation to phenomena outside itself; simultaneously, there is an imaginative constitution of those very institutions in the process of the formation and reformation of culture.

Habermas's call for constitutional patriotism—like most appeals to cosmopolitanism—tries to establish political community on the basis of thin identities and normative universalism. The key questions to ask here are not simply whether such a community would be ordered by good principles, but whether it would achieve a sufficient solidarity to be truly motivating for its members.[17] There is no intrinsic reason why constitutional patriotism could not work on a European scale, but the project courts questions about whether it can stand alone as an adequate source of belonging and mutual commitment. It is therefore important to address legitimacy and solidarity as related issues.

This need not involve a reduction of the normative content of arguments about

---

17. Emphasis on the public sphere also suggests a greater freedom in the important sense that it treats culture-forming activity as an open-ended process. As Arendt suggested, it is never entirely possible to know where activity in public will lead, what will be created. Just as culture is produced and reproduced, not simply inherited, so creativity, not simply tolerance, mediates cross-cultural relations.

legitimacy to a mere recognition of the facticity of existing solidarities. On the contrary, it could involve the development of a stronger normative analysis of the legitimacy of different forms and concrete organizations of solidarity. Attending to the dynamic processes by which culture is produced and reproduced also makes it easier to conceptualize the introduction into public space of other kinds of identities besides those that unify the polity as a whole. To take such a position is not to deny the challenge posed by multiculturalism, but it does question its characterization as the introduction of radically new elements into a previously unproblematic uniformity and fixity of collective identity. The key is to reject the notion—which nationalist ideologies indeed commonly assert—that the cultural conditions of public life, including both individual and collective identities, are established prior to properly public discourse itself.

The Public Sphere and Solidarity

Can we conceive of public discourse as (among other things) a form of social solidarity? Such a framing flies to some extent in the face of common usage. Solidarity or integration is treated as a question distinct from, and generally prior to, that of collective decision-making or legitimate action. The implication is that the collective subject is formed first, and activity in the public sphere is about steering it, not constituting it.

One reason for this is that in the most influential early modern works of political theory—and not just the extreme example of Hobbes—the collective subject was conceived, to a great extent, not as "the people," but as the state. Or, more precisely, the people were arguably the subject of *legitimacy* (in a modern, "ascending" approach to the question of legitimacy, as distinct from a medieval, "descending" approach emphasizing divine right or heredity). But the state was the subject of collective *action*, which was either legitimate, or not. So in a sense, states were actors, and public discourse—where it was influential—steered states. The collective action of the people might have created states in the mythical past of social contract theory or in the language of the U.S. Declaration of Independence. But both for liberals in the tradition of Locke and conservatives like Hegel, the state became the proper collective subject, either ensuring the freedom of individual actors within it or subsuming them into its larger whole. Legitimacy came in some combination from serving the interests of the people or from the process by which the people contributed to the steering of the state. But in approaches deriving from this sort of account (notably, for example, Habermas's classic exposition) a clear distinction was made between the public sphere and the state.[18]

The public sphere appeared, then, as a dimension of civil society, but one that could orient itself toward and potentially steer the state. In this sense, the public sphere did not itself appear as a self-organizing form of social solidarity, although another crucial part of civil society—the market (or economic system)—did. Rather than a form of solidarity, the public sphere was a mechanism for influencing the state. Civil society provided a basis for the public sphere through nurturing individual autonomy. But the public sphere did not steer civil society directly; rather, it influenced the state. The implication, then, was that social integration was accomplished either by power (the state) or by self-regulating systems (the economy). If citizens were to have the possibility of collective choice, they had to act on the state—which could then, in turn, act on the economy (although too much of the latter would constitute a problematic dedifferentiation of spheres according to many analysts, including the later Habermas). What was not developed in this account was the possibility that the public sphere was effective not only through informing state policy, but also through forming culture—that through the exercise of social imagination and the forging of social relationships the public sphere could constitute a form of social solidarity.

The public sphere is important as a basic condition of democracy. But it signals more than simply the capacity to weigh specific issues in the court of public opinion. The public sphere is also a form of social solidarity. It is one of the institutional forms in which the members of a society may be joined together with one another. In this sense, its counterparts are families, communities, bureaucracies, markets, and nations. All of these are arenas of social participation. Exclusion from them is among the most basic definitions of alienation from contemporary societies. Among the various forms of social solidarity, though, the public sphere is distinctive because it is created and reproduced through discourse. It is not primarily a matter of unconscious inheritance, of power relations, or of the usually invisible relationships that are forged as a by-product of industrial production

18. Jürgen Habermas, *The Structural Transformation of the Public Sphere: An Inquiry into a Category of Bourgeois Society*, trans. Thomas Burger with Frederick Lawrence (Cambridge: MIT Press, 1989). It is worth noting that the classical vision of the public sphere that Habermas presents does stress that citizens forge a public sphere through their interactions with one another; it is not simply called into being top-down by subjection to a common power. Indeed, in line with a long tradition of political theory that includes Locke, in Habermas, subjects of a state become citizens by virtue of their capacity for lateral communication.

and market exchanges. People talk in families, communities, and workplaces, of course, but the public sphere exists uniquely in, through, and for talk. It also consists specifically of talk about other social arrangements, including but not limited to actions the state might take. The stakes of theories and analyses of the public sphere, therefore, concern the extent to which communication can be influential in producing or reshaping social solidarity.

What are some of the other choices? Let me borrow Emile Durkheim's famous distinction of mechanical from organic solidarity to illustrate two main alternatives.[19] Mechanical solidarity, Durkheim suggested, obtains in societies where people and social units are basically similar to each other; it is produced, above all, by a shared *conscience collective*. Organic solidarity, on the other hand, is characteristic of differentiated societies with a complex division of labor, considerable variation among individuals, and constituent groups formed on different principles. Durkheim used the distinction largely to analyze the contrast between "traditional" and "modern" societies.[20] It may be more helpful, however, to think of these as suggesting two dimensions of solidarity formation at work in modern societies.

We can rename organic solidarity "functional interdependence," encompassing within this category market relations as well as other ways in which different social institutions and groups depend on each other. Perhaps less intuitively, we can rename mechanical solidarity "categorical identity," with nationalism as a prime example. Think of it as describing the ideology of equal membership in a whole defined by the similarity of its members—complete, in the nationalist case, with a strong sense of the whole's primacy over its members, such that they will die for it and kill for it. Both forms of solidarity are at work in every country today: material relations of interdependence, more or less managed by states and markets; and collective identities, reflecting various combinations of inheritance and energetic reproduction and shaping by intellectuals and cultural producers. Neither of these types of solidarity describes a process of choice, however. Both are externally determined.

Let me round out this discussion by incorporating these categories in a list of four forms of social solidarity:[21]

19. Emile Durkheim, *The Division of Labor in Society*, trans. W. D. Halls (New York: Free Press, 1975).

20. Durkheim has puzzled a century of commentators by insisting that, in principle, organic solidarity knits people together more tightly than mechanical solidarity, and all the failures of modern social integration are merely exceptions to the rule. What is clear is that organic solidarity can knit together larger populations.

21. Note that power is not in itself the basis for a conception of social solidarity; subjection as such is not solidarity, although it may create a polity. This is why the ideal cases of pure despotism place a premium on the absence of active unity among subjects.

1. *Functional interdependence.* This is loosely analogous to "system" in the sense in which Habermas employs the term, as informed by Niklas Luhmann and Talcott Parsons. An interdependence based on various kinds of flows—for example, of goods—joins people in a mutuality that is not primarily manifest in their common recognition of it but instead can operate, as it were, behind their backs. Much of modern life depends on such quasi-autonomous systems. While in principle it may be possible to "unmask" systems of functional integration as products of human choices, in social practice, they are not chosen as such.

2. *Categorical identities.* Nation is the primary example here, but race, class, and a range of other identities work in the same way. They posit a set of individuals equivalent to each other insofar as they share a crucial category of similarity. This is not the same as sharing culture (despite some attempts to treat it so, by nationalist ideologues, among others), because it refers to sharing a specific dimension of culturally significant similarity; how well that stands for participation in a common way of life is an empirical question. While those who try to mobilize others on the basis of categorical identities commonly claim that one identity is a kind of "trump" against other possible identities or interests, there is in fact always some element of choice as to which identity one accepts as salient.[22]

3. *Direct social relations.* Here, the referent is concrete networks of actual connections between people who are identifiable to each other as concrete persons. Much reference to *community* privileges such worlds of direct relations, although when the term is used to refer to solidarity in nation-states, scale dictates that this cannot be the primary meaning and that some other sense of solidarity is at least implicitly being invoked. Referring to *direct relations* also avoids the implication of harmony or affection common to some usages of *community*.[23] While

22. By the same token, interests are not fixed or objectively ascertainable. They vary with the salience of different identities to individuals. Not all individual identities reflect categories of similarity to others, of course, and while there may be an element of choice at work, much identification happens outside conscious choice or recognition.

23. On the effort to distinguish networks of relations from shared sentiments, see Craig Calhoun, "Community: Toward a Variable Conceptualization for Comparative Research," *Social History* 5 (1980): 105–29. On the problematic extension of the concept of community from networks of concrete, interpersonal relationships to broad cultural or political categories, see Calhoun, "Nationalism, Political Community, and the Representation of Society: Or, Why Feeling at Home Is Not a Substitute for Public Space," *European Journal of Social Theory* 2 (1999): 217–31. Such networks are sharply limited in their capacity to constitute the social order of a complex, large-scale society, which is necessarily shaped much more by the mediation of markets, formal organizations, and impersonal communications. See Calhoun, "Imagined Communities and Indirect Relationships: Large Scale Social

social structure and other largely external conditions shape patterns of direct relations substantially, there is also room for choice. This occurs both directly, as people choose relationships, and indirectly, as they choose forms of social participation (say, social movements or jobs) that introduce them to particular populations of potential network partners.

4. *Publics.* Publics are self-organizing fields of discourse in which participation is not based primarily on personal connections and is always in principle open to strangers.[24] A public sphere comprises an indefinite number of more or less overlapping publics, some ephemeral, some enduring, and some shaped by struggle against the dominant organization of others. Engagement in public life establishes social solidarity partly through enhancing the significance of particular categorical identities and partly through facilitating the creation of direct social relations. Beyond this, however, the engagement of people with each other in public is itself a form of social solidarity. This engagement includes, but is not limited to, rational-critical discourse about affairs of common concern. Communication in public also informs the sharing of social imaginaries, ways of understanding social life that are themselves constitutive of it. Both culture and identity are created partly in public action and interaction. An element of reasoned reflection, however, is crucial to the idea of choice as a dimension of this form of solidarity—to the distinction of public culture from the simple expression of preexisting identity.

Emphasizing the public sphere thus presents a challenge to speaking of institutions as though they were produced simply by adaptation to material necessity (as neoliberal and other market ideologies would suggest). It presents a no less powerful challenge to the ways in which nationalists present membership in France, say, or Serbia or China, as being an undifferentiated and immediate relationship between individuals and a collective whole that is always already there

---

Integration and the Transformation of Everyday Life," in *Social Theory for a Changing Society*, ed. Pierre Bourdieu and James S. Coleman (Boulder, Colo., Westview, 1991), and "The Infrastructure of Modernity: Indirect Social Relationships, Information Technology, and Social Integration," in *Social Change and Modernity*, ed. Hans Haferkamp and Neil J. Smelser (Berkeley: University of California Press). My conception of categories and networks is indebted to Siegfried Nadel, *The Theory of Social Structure* (London: Cohen and West, 1957), and Harrison White, *Identity and Control: A Structural Theory of Social Action* (Princeton, N.J.: Princeton University Press, 1992). White, however, sees networks as basic and categories as more typically epiphenomenal, and believes a structural network theory can dispense with the need for separate reference to functional integration. He does not consider publics.

24. In his "Publics and Counterpublics," in this issue, Michael Warner identifies seven criteria for defining publics.

and about which there are few legitimate variations in opinion. The public sphere is an arena simultaneously of solidarity and choice.

This duality is brought out more clearly in Arendt's account of public action and public spaces than in Habermas's. The term "public," she writes, "signifies two closely interrelated but not altogether identical phenomena: It means, first, that everything that appears in public can be seen and heard by everybody and has the widest possible publicity. . . . Second, the term "public" signifies the world itself, in so far as it is common to all of us and distinguished from our privately owned place in it."[25] Public action, moreover, is the crucial terrain of the humanly created, as distinct from the natural world; of appearance and memory, of talk and recognition. We hold in common a world we create in common, in part by the processes through which we imagine it. It is these processes that the social imaginary shapes.

Arendt emphasizes creativity, including the creation of the forms of common political life through founding actions—as in revolution and constitution-making. But imagination is involved not only in founding moments but in all social action, and the notion of a social imaginary points our attention to broad patterns of stability in imagination as well as to occasional, more or less radical, changes. Equally important, Arendt's account of public space approaches people as radically plural: not necessarily similar, but bound to one another by promises that are explicit or implicit in their lives together.[26]

In the accounts of both Arendt and Habermas, the emphasis is on political publics, but in Arendt, the notion of politics is extended to include all public action. The public sphere is a crucial site for the production and transformation of politically salient identities and solidarities—including the basic category and practical manifestation of "the people" that is essential to democracy.[27] In his

25. Arendt, *Human Condition*, 50, 52.

26. The plurality Arendt emphasizes extends not only to subjects but also to public spaces, which she thought would inevitably need to be many and imperfectly integrated in modern, large-scale societies. See Hannah Arendt, *Crises of the Republic: Lying in Politics, Civil Disobedience on Violence, Thoughts on Politics, and Revolution* (New York: Harcourt Brace Jovanovich 1972), 232; see also Craig Calhoun, "Plurality, Promises, and Public Spaces," in *Hannah Arendt and the Meaning of Politics*, ed. Calhoun and John McGowan (Minneapolis: University of Minnesota Press, 1997).

27. There has been debate over whether Habermas's theory implies a unitary public sphere or multiple publics: see Nancy Fraser, "Rethinking the Public Sphere: A Contribution to the Critique of Actually Existing Democracy," in *Habermas and the Public Sphere*, ed. Craig Calhoun (Cambridge: MIT Press, 1992); and Warner, "Publics and Counterpublics." Clearly, in several senses, publics may be multiple, but where public discourse addresses, and/or is occasioned by, a state, there is pressure for reaching integration at the level of that state. It is necessary for plural publics to sustain relations with one another if they are to facilitate democracy within that state by informing its actions.

classic early account of the public sphere, Habermas works with a narrower, state-centered notion of politics, although he recognizes the ways in which a literary public sphere foreshadows, shapes, and overlaps with the political one — making the distinction between the two an analytic one, at best, rather than a purely empirical one.[28]

Recognizing politics at work at sites beyond or outside the state is especially important to seeing how transnational public spheres might be effective. The questions of how a European public sphere might be organized and what influence it might have are as basic to Europe's future as the rise of democratic institutions within nation-states was to its past. Indeed, Habermas himself has returned to this theoretical framework recently in considering the relations among nation, rule of law, and democracy in a changing Europe:

> The initial impetus to integration in the direction of a postnational society is not provided by the substrate of a supposed "European people" but by the communicative network of a European-wide political public sphere embedded in a shared political culture. The latter is founded on a civil society composed of interest groups, non-government organizations, and citizen initiatives and movements, and will be occupied by arenas in which the political parties can directly address the decisions of European institutions and go beyond mere tactical alliance to form a European party system.[29]

This is clearly a statement of hopes and conditions for a desirable future as much as a description of trends. Such a European public sphere is a question more than a reality, as is an integrated European party system. But the conceptual point is clear. The creation of such a public sphere is the condition of a democratic, republican integration of Europe and the safeguard against a problematically nationalist one.[30]

28. Habermas reaffirms this emphasis in more recent work: "The 'literary' public sphere in the broader sense, which is specialized for the articulation of values and world disclosure, is intertwined with the political public sphere" (Jürgen Habermas, *Between Facts and Norms: Contributions to a Discourse Theory of Law and Democracy*, trans. William Rehg [Cambridge: MIT Press, 1996], 365). However, it may be noted that his recent work is less centered on the state.

29. Habermas, *Inclusion of the Other*, 153.

30. In *Structural Transformation of the Public Sphere*, Habermas's attention is focused not just on the ideals of public life but on the question of why apparently democratic expansions in the scale of public participation had brought a decline in the rational-critical character of public discourse, a vulnerability to demagogic and mass media manipulation, and sometimes a loss of democracy itself. The distorted publicity of American-style advertising, public relations, and political campaigns was a manifest focus, but an underlying concern was also the way in which German public life lost its links to both democracy and rational-critical understanding under the Third Reich.

The production of a flourishing public sphere, thus, along with a normatively sound constitution, offers a good answer to Habermas's orienting question: "When does a collection of persons constitute an entity—'a people'—entitled to govern itself democratically?" But as Habermas notes, the answer most commonly provided is much less promising: "In the real world, who in each instance acquires the power to define the disputed borders of a state is settled by historical contingencies, usually by the quasi-natural outcome of violent conflicts, wars, and civil wars. Whereas republicanism reinforces our awareness of the contingency of these borders, this contingency can be dispelled by appeal to the idea of a grown nation that imbues the borders with the aura of imitated substantiality and legitimates them through fictitious links with the past. Nationalism bridges the normative gap by appealing to a so-called right of national self-determination."[31]

At the heart of the notion of a democratic public sphere lie differences, both among participants and among possible opinions. If a public sphere is not able to encompass people of different personal and group identities, it can hardly be the basis for democracy. If people have the same views, no public sphere is needed—or at least none beyond a space for plebiscites or ritual affirmations of unity. Differences among opinions challenge not only nationalist pressures to conform, but also technocratic insistence on the application of expertise, as though such expertise (or the science that might lie behind it) embodies perfect, unchanging, and disinterested solutions to problems.

Differences among participants also pose a challenge. If a public sphere needs to include people of different classes, genders, even nations, it also requires participants to be able—at least some of the time—to adopt perspectives distanced from their immediate circumstances, and thus carry on conversations that are not determined strictly by private interest or identity. The point is not that any interlocutors escape influences from their personal lives, but that none are strictly determined by those influences, unable to see the merits in good arguments presented by those who represent competing interests or worldviews. If there are no meaningful differences within the public sphere, the lack may reaffirm solidarity and *conscience collective*, but it cannot address choices about how solidarity and institutional arrangements could be other than what they are.

The differences within a public sphere may be bases for the development of multiple publics (specific fields of discourse) and public spaces (settings for discourse). We can speak of a public sphere to the extent that examples of both of

31. Habermas, *Inclusion of the Other*, 141.

these categories overlap and produce an open-ended discourse that addresses some common concerns—for example, about how people should live together or what a state should do. Some of the multiple publics may claim to represent the whole, while others oppose dominant discursive patterns, and still others are neutral.

Nancy Fraser has influentially emphasized the importance of "subaltern counterpublics" such as those framed by race or gender.[32] In thinking about the multiplicity of publics forming a public sphere, however, it is important to be critical about the distinction of some publics as marked while others remain unmarked. Unmarked does not automatically equal either universal or univocally dominant. If the attempt to establish closure to outsiders is sometimes a strategy of counterpublics, as Michael Warner has suggested, the deployment of claims on an unmarked public as *the* public sphere is also a strategy, generally a strategy of the powerful.[33] In speaking of counterpublics, it should be kept in mind both that their existence as such presupposes engagement in some larger public sphere and that individuals may participate in multiple publics. Thus, a newspaper opinion essay by a gay rights activist, for example, may address simultaneously members of a specifically gay public—and even a queer counterpublic within that—and participants in the unmarked broader public.[34]

Furthermore, the segmentation of a distinct public from the unmarked larger public may be a result of exclusion, not choice. During the classic heyday of the eighteenth- and early-nineteenth-century British public sphere, many artisans and workers were denied participation in the public sphere. But such subalterns should not be regarded simply and unambivalently as members of a separate, proletarian public sphere, although they did develop their own media and organiza-

---

32. Fraser, "Rethinking the Public Sphere."

33. Warner, "Publics and Counterpublics." Warner rightly questions Fraser's identification of counterpublics with subalterns, noting that many groups not clearly in subaltern positions identify themselves by contraposition to the dominant culture or institutions of a society and may constitute counterpublics opposed to the dominant patterns of the public sphere. His chief example is the Christian right in the United States. The new populist right wing in Europe seems largely similar in this respect. Electoral victors take pride in describing themselves as outsiders to dominant institutions, even while claiming to be the ultimate insiders within, and defenders of, national traditions.

34. I distinguish the idea of a gay public from a queer counterpublic to make two points. First, per Michael Warner, *The Trouble with Normal: Sex, Politics, and the Ethics of Queer Life* (New York: Free Press, 1999), there is a tension among gay men and lesbians—at the levels of both practical politics and discursive practices—over the question of whether to demand reduction of the demarcation of gay from straight or to assert queer identities in a potentially disruptive (and/or liberating) fashion. Second, distinguishing a gay public from a queer counterpublic reminds us that not all demarcation of publics is necessarily the production of counterpublics.

tions and to some extent constitute a counterpublic. They simultaneously claimed the right to participate in the dominant, unmarked public sphere and challenged those who introduced restrictive measures to make it a specifically bourgeois (or, in more general terms, propertied) public sphere.[35] The very people who excluded those with less wealth from the public sphere were nevertheless claiming it, in unmarked form, as simply *the* British public.

The issue of *democratic inclusiveness* is not just a quantitative matter of the scale of a public sphere or the proportion of the members of a political community who may speak within it. While it is clearly a matter of stratification and boundaries (e.g., openness to the propertyless, the uneducated, women, or immigrants), inclusiveness is also a matter of how the public sphere incorporates and recognizes the diversity of identities that people bring to it from their manifold involvement in civil society. It is a matter of whether, for example, to participate in such a public sphere, women must act in ways previously characteristic of men and avoid addressing certain topics defined as appropriate to the private realm (the putatively more female sphere). Marx criticized the discourse of bourgeois citizenship for implying that it fit everyone equally, when in fact it tacitly presumed an understanding of citizens as property owners; the same sort of false universalism has presented citizens in gender-neutral or gender-symmetrical terms without in fact acknowledging underlying conceptions that are highly gendered. Moreover, the boundaries between public and private are part of the stakes of debate in the public sphere, not something neatly settled in advance.[36]

35. Habermas famously focused on the "bourgeois" public sphere, contrasting it with an earlier aristocrat-dominated public, an emphasis that has sparked complaints that he neglected the proletarian public sphere. See Oskar Negt and Alexander Kluge, *The Public Sphere and Experience: Toward an Analysis of the Bourgeois and Proletarian Public Sphere*, trans. Peter Labanyi, Jamie Daniel, and Assenka Oksiloff (Minneapolis: University of Minnesota Press, 1993); see also Geoff Eley, "Nations, Publics, and Political Cultures: Placing Habermas in the Nineteenth Century," in Calhoun, *Habermas and the Public Sphere.* Their differences notwithstanding, Habermas and Negt and Kluge alike accept the separation between bourgeois and proletarian as already established, a distinction based on objective economic conditions rather than something forged largely in contestation within and above the public sphere. For Habermas, the issue of inclusion is thus tied to a later broadening of the public sphere rather than posited as a formative theme from the start. Tactics such as raising taxes on newspapers to discourage the popular press—or disparaging workers as insufficiently rational—were then, in a sense, counterpublic mobilizations from above.

36. Salient examples of this large literature include: Nancy Fraser, *Unruly Practices: Power, Discourse, and Gender in Contemporary Social Theory* (Minneapolis: University of Minnesota Press, 1989), and *Justice Interruptus: Critical Reflections on the "Postsocialist" Condition* (New York: Routledge, 1997); Jean Bethke Elshtain, *Public Man, Private Woman: Women in Social and Political Thought* (Princeton, N.J.: Princeton University Press, 1993); and Michael Warner, "Public and Private," in *The Blackwell Companion to Gender Studies*, ed. Catharine R. Stimpson (Cambridge, Mass.:

All attempts to render a single public discourse authoritative privilege certain topics, certain forms of speech, certain ways of constructing and presenting identities, and certain speakers. This is partly a matter of emphasis on the single, unitary whole—the discourse of *all* the citizens rather than of subsets, multiple publics—and partly a matter of specific demarcations of public from private. If sexual harassment, for example, is seen as a matter of concern to women, but not men, it becomes a sectional matter rather than a matter for the public in general; if it is seen as a private matter, then, by definition, it is not a public concern. The same goes for a host of other topics that are inhibited from receiving full recognition in a public sphere conceptualized as a single discourse about matters consensually determined to be of public significance.

The classical liberal model of the public sphere, on Habermas's account, pursues discursive equality by disqualifying discourse about the differences among actors. These differences are treated as matters of private, but not public, interest.[37] The best version of the public sphere was based on "a kind of social intercourse that, far from presupposing the equality of status, disregarded status altogether."[38] It worked by a "mutual willingness to accept the given roles and simultaneously to suspend their reality."[39] This "bracketing" of difference as merely private and irrelevant to the public sphere was undertaken, Habermas argues, in order to defend the genuinely rational-critical notion that arguments must be decided on their merits rather than on the identities of the arguers. This was, by the way, as important a factor as the fear of censorship in the anonymous or pseudonymous attributions of authorship that were a prominent feature of the eighteenth-century public sphere.[40] Yet bracketing has the effect of excluding some of the most important concerns of the members of any polity—both those whose existing identities are suppressed or devalued and those whose exploration of possible identities is truncated. If the public sphere exists in part to relate individual life histories to public policies—as Habermas himself suggests

---

Blackwell, forthcoming). See also the early response to Habermas and the very different development of the idea of the public sphere in Negt and Kluge, *Public Sphere and Experience*.

37. In a similar sense, many approaches to multiculturalism treat ethnicity and community as domains of "privacy"—protected precisely because they are not public. The discourse of rights encourages both advocates of communitarianism and liberal critics to ask what kind of private right—of individuals or groups—might protect differences, rather than questioning what kind of public good difference may serve or what kind of public claim supports it.

38. Habermas, *Structural Transformation of the Public Sphere*, 36.

39. Habermas, *Structural Transformation of the Public Sphere*, 131.

40. See Warner, *Letters of the Republic*.

—then bracketing issues of identity is seriously impoverishing.[41] In addition, the bracketing of differences also undermines the self-reflexive capacity of public discourse. If it is impossible to communicate seriously about basic differences among members of a public sphere, then it will also be impossible to address the difficulties of communication across such lines of basic difference.

Conclusion

Constitutional patriotism depends on a vital public sphere. It is entirely possible, however, to achieve collective identity without an effective public sphere. Such solidarity might be based on nationalism or religion, or grow out of economic relations and marketing. To undergird democracy, however, more than mere inheritance or a thin identity is required. Democracy depends on a public sphere, and must be realized largely within it. Public life must offer a realm of social solidarity and culture formation as well as critical discourse. This is needed for the nurturance of a democratic social imaginary as much as for informing any specific policy decisions.

Given the recent wave of celebrating civil society as the potential cure to all the ills of democracy, it is important to recall that the dominant forces in transnational civil society remain businesses and organizations tied to business and capital. Businesses are important in ways that distinguish them from markets—as institutions, they organize much of the lives of their employees, and they coordinate production as well as exchange across continents. The business dimension of global civil society is not limited to multinational corporations: it includes NGOs that set accountancy standards and provide for arbitration and conflict resolution, as well as the business press, lawyers, and a range of consultants. The point is not whether this is good or bad, but that this is civil society—on a global scale, to be sure, but not totally unlike what such pioneer theorists as Adam Smith and Adam Ferguson saw on a local and national scale in the late eighteenth century. Civil society meant then, and still means, the extension of more or less self-organizing relationships on a scale beyond the intentional control of individual actors and outside of the strict dictates of states. It offers many freedoms—but so do states. Neither is automatically liberal or democratic. The development of an effective public sphere lags behind functional integration and powerful organizations in constituting civil society.

At the same time, it is equally important to remember the extent to which life

41. See Habermas, *Between Facts and Norms*, chap. 8.

together is made possible not simply by systemic integration, the construction of formal organizations, and rational-critical discourse. It is made possible, as Arendt argued, by promises that bind people to one another. This is a crucial dimension of constitution-making. Collective life is made possible also by acts of imagination, communicated and incorporated into common culture.

Think for a moment of the ways in which such acts of promising and imagining are implicated in the creation of the institutions of our shared world. Not only the nation but also the business corporation, for example, exists as the product of such imagining (and is none the less real and powerful for that). How is the corporate whole called into being, granted legitimacy in law and the capacity to act, in contracts, suits, or property holding? It is a product of the social imaginary. But—as with ideas of the individual self and the nation—the acceptance of corporations is deeply rooted in much modern culture. It is reproduced in a host of quotidian practices as well as in more elaborate legal procedures. This is indeed part of what turns a merely formal organization into an institution. Such a process can be grasped only from within the very culture that makes it possible, not externally to it. It can never, therefore, be rendered altogether objective.

The most helpful conception of the public sphere is thus one that includes within it *both* a dimension of rational-critical discourse and a dimension of social imagination and promising. Among the many virtues of the former is the capacity to challenge and potentially to improve existing culture, products of social imagination, and social relations. But among its limits is the fact that in itself it cannot create them.

Alternative imaginaries are operative in the constitution of global culture and social relations. From Islamism to deep ecology, there are multiple ways of imagining the possible institutions of a new and different social order. A common humanity is imagined most prominently in discourses of human rights. And in fact the most powerful postnational or cosmopolitan social imaginary is that of the market.[42] Affirmation of global society comes less from the expression of some positive value than from the notion that the market demands it. *The market* in such discourse is always represented in external and deterministic terms, as a force of necessity rather than an object of choice.

And this raises the basic issue. The speed with which global civil society is

---

42. Bruce Robbins notes that the first cited usage under "cosmopolitan" in the *Oxford English Dictionary* comes from John Stuart Mill's treatise of 1848, *Political Economy*: "Capital is becoming more and more cosmopolitan" (Robbins, *Secular Vocations: Intellectuals, Professionalism, Culture* [New York: Verso, 1993], 182).

gaining the capacity to self-organize autonomously from the state may be debated. But there is little doubt that the global public sphere lags dramatically behind the less democratic, less choice-oriented dimensions of global society. Among the many questions to ask about global society is: What kinds of identity and solidarity will orient participation within it? Are there attractive forms of collective identity that offer nationalism's potential to integrate large populations and produce mutual commitment—without assuming its tendencies of external exclusion and the rejection of internal difference?

Fear of bad nationalism leads many to hope that relatively thin identities will predominate. Cosmopolitans and constitutional patriots may presumably orient themselves to multiple spheres of action, from the very local to the global. But are these forms of identity that can create a new social imaginary that will commit people to each other on a global scale? Further, are they by their nature restricted to elites, and meaningful only in relation to the nationalism of others? Or are they attractive possibilities that follow from, rather than lay the basis for, more democratic public institutions?

I have argued that the idea of constitution is deepened by attending to the question of what kind of social imaginary underpins the creation of institutions and the organization of solidarity—that is, what ways of understanding life together actually make possible specific forms of social relations. Not least in this regard, it is important to conceive of solidarity not only in terms of common economic interests, but also in terms of a range of relations of mutual interdependence, including engagement in shared projects of imagining a better future.

The importance of the public sphere lies not only in achieving agreement on legal forms and political identity, but in achieving social solidarity as such. For this to happen, it needs to be a realm of cultural creativity as well as rational discourse, and a realm of mutual engagement. For nationalism to give way to some postnational organization of social life will not simply be a matter of new formal structures of organization, but of new ways of imagining identity, interests, and solidarity. A key theme will be the importance of configurations of mutual commitment—solidarity—that are more than reinscriptions of preestablished interests or identities. Can shared participation in the public sphere anchor a form of social solidarity in which the nature of life together is chosen *as it is constructed*?

Craig Calhoun is president of the Social Science Research Council and a professor of sociology and history at New York University. A longer version of his argument on constitutional patriotism will appear in the forthcoming volume *Transnational Politics*, edited by Pablo De Greiff and Ciaran Cronin.

Islam in Public:
New Visibilities and
New Imaginaries

Nilüfer Göle

Islam has acquired new forms of visibility over the last two decades as it has made its way in the public avenues of both Muslim and European societies. New faces of Muslim actors using both secular and religious idiom are appearing in public life; the terms of public debate are being transformed by the eruption of religious issues; Islamic films and novels are becoming popular subjects of cultural criticism; new spaces, markets, and media are opening up in response to the rising demands of recently formed Muslim middle classes. Islam carves out a public space of its own as new Islamic language styles, corporeal rituals, and spatial practices emerge and blend into public life. On the one hand, public Islam testifies to a shift in the orientation of the Islamic movement from macropolitics toward micropractices, and on the other hand, it challenges the borders and the meanings of the secular public sphere.

As Islam makes a move into national public spheres, the consensual principles and homogeneous structure of the national public spheres are unsettled, but so are those of the Islamic movement. Indeed two different phases of contemporary Islamism can be distinguished.[1] The first phase, starting at the end of the 1970s

---

1. In speaking of Islamism, we are differentiating between *Muslim*, which expresses religious identity, and *Islamist*, which refers to a social movement through which Muslim identity is collectively reappropriated as a basis for an alternative social and political project. Thus Islamism implies a critique and even a discontinuity with the given categories of Muslim identity; it is an endeavor to rename and reconstruct Muslim identity by freeing it from traditional interpretations and by challenging assimilative forces of modernism.

Public Culture 14(1): 173–190

and reaching its peak with the Iranian Islamic revolution in 1979, is characterized by mass mobilizations, Islamic militancy, a quest for an Islamic collective identity, and the implementation of a political and religious rule. In the second phase, the revolutionary fervor declines, the ideological chorus gives way to a multiplicity of voices, and a process of distancing and individuation from the collective militancy takes place leading to an "exit from religious revolution."[2] In this phase, after the assertion of a collective and exacerbated form of difference, Muslim identity is in the process of "normalization." In the "second wave" of Islamism, actors of Islam blend into modern urban spaces, use global communication networks, engage in public debates, follow consumption patterns, learn market rules, enter into secular time, get acquainted with values of individuation, professionalism, and consumerism, and reflect upon their new practices. Hence we observe a transformation of these movements from a radical political stance to a more social and cultural orientation, accompanied by a loss of mass mobilization capacity, which led some researchers to pronounce the end of Islamism and the "failure of political Islam."[3] But a more cultural orientation does not mean a less political one. Indeed, instead of disappearing as a reference, Islam penetrates even more into the social fiber and imaginary, thereby raising new political questions, questions not addressed solely to Muslims but concerning the foundational principles of collective life in general.

An analytical concern at the level of ideologies (such as Islamism) or of political formations (such as the state) cannot explain this process of interpenetration and dialogical relation. The public visibility of Islam and the specific gender, corporeal, and spatial practices underpinning it trigger new ways of imagining a collective self and common space that are distinct from the Western liberal self and progressive politics. Exploring these Islamic makings of the self and the micropractices associated with it will lead us to understand new social imaginaries and the transformations of the public sphere in a non-Western context.

Non-Western Publics

Although the idea of the public is Western in its origins and its basic features are understood as universal access, individualism, equality, and openness (*Öffentlichkeit*), it circulates and moves into contexts other than the West. The ways in which these concepts, ideas, and institutions travel and are adopted in non-

2. Farhad Khosrokhavar and Olivier Roy, *Iran: Comment sortir d'une révolution religieuse* (Paris: Seuil, 1999); Fariba Adelkhah, *Etre moderne en Iran* (Paris: Karthala, 1998).

3. Olivier Roy, *L'échec de l'Islam politique* (Paris: Seuil, 1992); Gilles Kepel, *Jihad: Expansion et déclin de l'Islamisme* (Paris: Gallimard, 2000).

Western contexts depend on local agencies and cultural fields. The experience of colonization in India, for example, or voluntary modernization in Turkey have shaped the ways in which the public sphere is imagined and institutionalized. Studying the adoption of modern concepts at the level of language, their entry, translations, and transformations—namely the history of concepts (*Begriffsgechichte*)—can reveal the diversity of meanings and trajectories and hint at the particular conjunctions between the universal definitions of the public sphere and homegrown practices and idioms.[4] The articulations and tensions between two different cultural codes, modern and indigenous, intervene in distinguishing and defining public and private spheres, interior and exterior spaces, licit and illicit practices. Sometimes they are simply juxtaposed in mutual indifference, sometimes they compete with each other, and sometimes they engage in a dialogue that produces interpenetrations and displacements. Conception of the exterior space, civility in the European sense of order and discipline can therefore take on a different meaning and form in non-Western contexts. To indicate the differences between a Brahmanical concept of cleanliness and purity and a Western concept of hygiene, Sudipta Kaviraj describes how the exteriors of houses in India are abandoned to an intrinsic disorderliness, while the interiors are kept impressively clean.[5] The interior, intimate, gendered space is similarly valorized and highly disciplined in Muslim societies, leading to different conceptualizations and institutionalizations of the modern public and city life. Although the cultural program of modernity has a great capacity to influence and circulate, the encounter between the two cultural codes leads not to a simple logic of emulation or rejection but to improvisations in social practices and cultural meanings. Studying the public sphere as a social imaginary may offer new clues to map out these improvisations in a non-Western context.

The social imaginary is, as Cornelius Castoriadis tells us, "the creation of significations and the creation of the images and figures that support these significations."[6] There is an "essential historicity of significations: apparently similar 'institutions' can be radically other, since immersed in another society, they are caught up in other significations."[7] Institutions are not to be conceived as external

4. On the history of concepts, see Reinhart Koselleck, *Futures Past: On the Semantics of Historical Time* (Cambridge: MIT Press, 1985); originally published as *Vergangene Zukunft: Zur Semantik geschichtlicher Zeiten* (Frankfurt am Main: Suhrkamp, 1979).

5. Sudipta Kaviraj, "Filth and the Public Sphere: Concepts and Practices about Space in Calcutta," *Public Culture* 10 (1997): 98.

6. Cornelius Castoriadis, *The Imaginary Institution of Society*, trans. Kathleen Blamey (Cambridge: MIT Press, 1987), 238.

7. Castoriadis, *Imaginary Institution*, 367–68.

to social imaginaries and social practices. There is no institution without signification, but the signification is not legitimate without shared practices. Although the "original" European code of modernity has constituted the crucial starting point and continual reference point, it is continuously and creatively appropriated and altered; consequently these distinct cultural foundations and institutional formations should be analyzed, as Shmuel N. Eisenstadt and Wolfgang Schluchter remind us, "not only in terms of their approximation to the West but also in their own terms."[8] An analysis of the public sphere as a social imaginary can illustrate the circulation of a universal code of modernity as well as the particular significations and practices. Approaching the public sphere as a social imaginary in Castoriadis's sense emphasizes its dynamic aspect, as an ongoing process, a creation of significations and practices rather than an "imagined" and "preestablished" frame. Furthermore it defies the thesis of time lag and "deficiency of modernity"[9] for non-Western countries and gives intellectual credibility to societal practices in historical contexts other than the West; it suggests the possibility for "*l'institution imaginaire de la société.*"[10]

The public sphere in a non-Western context is neither identical with its counterparts in the West nor totally different, but manifests asymmetrical differences as it is continuously altered by a field of cultural meanings and social practices. Modern social imaginaries, as Charles Taylor reminds us, are social in the sense that they are widely and commonly shared.[11] They may have explicit theoretical formulations, but unlike ideas and ideologies they are not in the hands of a few. Social imaginaries are embedded in the habitus of a population or carried in implicit understandings that underlie and make possible common practices. Even in cases where the public sphere is introduced by colonizing agents or adopted by modernizing elites, it cannot be understood as an alien structure or as an imposed idea from the above. As a social imaginary, the public sphere works in a social field and penetrates and blends into cultural significations.

In the Turkish context of voluntary modernization, the public sphere is institutionalized and imagined as a site for the implementation of a secular and progressive way of life. An authoritarian modernism—rather than bourgeois, indi-

---

8. Shmuel N. Eisenstadt and Wolfgang Schluchter, "Introduction: Paths to Early Modernities—A Comparative View," *Daedalus* 127, no. 3 (1998): 4–7.

9. Nilüfer Göle, "Global Expectations, Local Experiences, Non-Western Modernities," in *Through a Glass, Darkly: Blurred Images of Cultural Tradition and Modernity over Distance and Time*, ed. Wil Arts (Boston: Brill, 2000).

10. This is the original French title of Castoriadis's book *The Imaginary Institution of Society*.

11. See Taylor's essay in this issue.

vidualist liberalism—underpins this public sphere. Religious signs and practices have been silenced as the modern public sphere has set itself against the Muslim social imaginary and segregated social organization; modern codes of conduct have entered public spaces ranging from Parliament and educational institutions to the street and public transportation. In a Muslim context, women's participation in public life, corporeal visibility, and social mixing with men all count as modern. The modern gendered subject has been constituted through women role models and repetitive performances, including language styles, dress codes, modes of habitation, and modes of address.

Here we see the social imaginary of the public sphere at work. While it adheres to some of the basic universal principles of the Western public sphere, these principles are selectively highlighted, coupled, and translated into social practices that are creatively altered as well. The central stakes of the modern subject are worked out in tension with Muslim definitions of self; consequently the access of women to public life and gender equality acquires a more salient signification in the public imaginary of Muslim societies. Moreover, in non-Western contexts, the public sphere provides a stage for the didactic performance of the modern subject in which the nonverbal, corporeal, and implicit aspects of social imaginaries are consciously and explicitly worked out. Because the public sphere provides a stage for performance rather than an abstract frame for textual and discursive practices, the ocular aspect in the creation of significations and the making of social imaginaries becomes of utmost importance. Social imaginaries are carried by images. The body, as a sensorial and emotional register, links the implicit nonverbal practices and learned dispositions (namely habitus) into a public visibility and conscious meaning. Public visibility refers to the techniques of working from inside out, transforming implicit practices into observable and audible ones. This essay explores the centrality of gender as well as related corporeal regimens and spatial protocols in the making of the public sphere.

The ways in which Islam emerges into the public sphere defy modernist aspirations for a civilized (read Westernized) and emancipated self yet follow a similar pattern in regard to gender, body, and space issues. The covered woman deputy walking into the Turkish Parliament and walking out the same day serves as an icon: an image that crystallizes the tensions emanating from two different cultural programs in the making of the self and the public. A visibility that by the same token reveals the ways in which Parliament as a secular public sphere is imagined, constructed, and instituted in the Turkish Republican context. Therefore a two-layered reading is required. One concerns the modern self-presentation and its migration into the Turkish context of modernity. The second concerns the counterattack of Islamic practices as a competing form of pious self-making and social imaginary. And with this second reading, through an examination of the ways in which Islam is problematized in the public sphere, we become aware of the unspoken, implicit borders and the stigmatizing, exclusionary power structure of the secular public sphere.

The Headscarf in the Parliament: A "Blowup"

For the first time in its Republican history, Turkey witnessed the election of a "covered" Muslim woman, an Istanbul deputy from the pro-Islamic party (Fazilet Partisi) during the last general elections (18 April 1999). But it was Merve Kavakçı's physical presentation in the Parliament, not her election, that provoked a public dispute, a blowup. On the very day of its opening on 2 May 1999, when Kavakçı, a thirty-one-year-old woman wearing a white headscarf with fashionable frameless eyeglasses and a long-skirted, modern two-piece suit, walked (over-)confidently into the meeting hall of the National Assembly for the opening session of the new Parliament. The men and women deputies stood up and protested against Kavakçı's presence with such vehemence—especially twelve women from the Democratic Left Party (DSP)—shouting "Merve out, ayatollahs to Iran," "Turkey is secular, will remain secular," that she was obliged to leave the Parliament without taking the oath.[12] Kavakçı's Islamic covering challenged the unwritten laws of the Parliament and enraged the deputies as well as (secular) public opinion.[13] The best-known secular women's association organized meetings and condemned the headscarf in the Parliament as an "ideological uniform of Islamic fundamentalism," challenging republican state power and secular reforms.[14] She was treated as an "agent provocateur" in the Turkish press, which accused her of having close links with the Palestinian group Hamas and working for foreign powers such as Iran and Libya. It was discovered that Kavakçı had become a U.S. citizen shortly after becoming a parliamentary candidate. As she had not officially noted that she was holding another passport,

12. "The Revolt of Women," *Hürriyet*, 4 May 1999, 1. According to a survey on political and social values conducted in October 1999 by the Foundation of Political Science in Istanbul (IMV-SAM), 61 percent of the Turkish population thought that Kavakçı should have taken off her headscarf while in the Parliament. Another covered woman deputy, from the Nationalist Party (MHP), had taken off her headscarf to attend the National Assembly and while giving her oath was applauded.

13. Nicole Pope, "Parliament Opens amid Controversy," TurkeyUpdate (Web publication at www.TurkeyUpdate.com), 3 May 1999.

14. "The Revolt of Women," 1.

authorities were able to use this legal pretext to strip Kavakçı of her Turkish citizenship.[15]

The above story cannot be narrated as merely a political incident. At a microlevel, instantaneous social reality and the significant tensions that generate history can be condensed and concealed. The trivial can be revealed as meaningful. In Georg Simmel's words, in these "momentary images," snapshots (*Moment-bilder*), fragments of social reality, we are able to glimpse the meaning of the whole.[16] We can unpack the nature of the social discord between the secular and religious practices compressed in this political incident if we first take it as it is, that is, frame it as a picture or snapshot. Visualizing the story and the players will bring into focus the corporeal, gendered, and spatial aspects of the social cleavages. Second, we need to defamiliarize our gaze. The picture is taken from the present day. It is widely and commonly shared. Its accessibility makes its understanding even more difficult because it appears as "ordinary" and "natural" to the common eye, duplicating the given terms of public controversy. This trompe l'oeil poses a challenge to sociology. A sign must be interpreted using "thick description" and placed in historical perspective if we want to reveal all of its possible meanings.[17] We need to go back and forth between micro- and macro-levels of analysis, between empirical practices and theoretical readings.[18] If we introduce anthropological unfamiliarity, historical distance, and the shift between micro- and macrolevels, the ordinary will appear less ordinary, and the still picture will turn into a movie. In his film *Blow Up* (1966), Michelangelo Antonioni tells the story of a photographer who by chance takes a picture that appears at first incoherent and incomprehensible. But he then enlarges a detail of the photograph, and that detail leads him to read the whole picture differently.[19] Let us enlarge—"blow up"—the picture of the veiled deputy taken in the secular Turkish Parliament.

Merve Kavakçı's portrait is both representative and distinctive in relation to

---

15. Nicole Pope, "Islamist Deputy Stripped of Her Turkish Citizenship," TurkeyUpdate (Web publication at www.TurkeyUpdate.com), 17 May 1999.

16. David Frisby, *Fragments of Modernity: Theories of Modernity in the Work of Simmel, Kracauer, and Benjamin* (Cambridge, England: Polity, 1985), 6.

17. Clifford Geertz, "Thick Description: Toward an Interpretative Theory of Culture," in *The Interpretation of Cultures: Selected Essays* (New York: Basic Books, 1973).

18. Jacques Revel, "Micro-analyse et construction du social," in *Jeux d'échelles: La micro-analyse à l'expérience*, ed. Revel (Paris: Gallimard: Seuil, 1996).

19. Revel, *Jeux d'échelles*, 36. Revel uses this example to establish a parallelism with microhistory. Rather than privileging one scale over the other, he argues that the methodological principle is the variations between them.

other Muslim women in the Islamic movement. The trajectory of the Muslim woman deputy follows a social dynamic similar to that of Islamic female students who have sought the right to attend university classes wearing headscarves since the beginning of the 1980s.[20] Access to higher education, daily experience of urban city life, and use of political idiom and action expose new female Islamic actors to modernity; this exposure is problematic for both secular actors and religious ones. The case of Merve Kavakçı, although not an exception, serves as an example that carries the process of interaction with a program of modernity to its extreme limits; it thereby blurs the oppositional boundaries. Kavakçı had access to higher education, became a computer engineer, trained at the University of Texas (the headscarf was banned in Turkish universities), lived in the United States, had two children, divorced her Jordanian-American husband, returned to Turkey, and became a member of the pro-Islamic party. She had access therefore to powerful symbols of modernity and was simultaneously engaged in Islamic politics. Living in the United States (not in Saudi Arabia), speaking English fluently, using new technologies, fashioning a public image (light-colored headscarf and frameless eyeglasses)—these are all cultural symbols of distinction in a non-Western context of modernity. And Islamists are not insensitive to acquiring such cultural capital. In fact, though they are in an oppositional political struggle with the modern secularists, they often mirror them and search for public representatives who speak foreign languages and belong to the professional and intellectual elite. Even Kavakçı's choice of a two-piece suit rather than an overcoat is a duplication of the Republican women's dress code. With all of her elite credentials, Kavakçı could have been used to bolster Islamic pride—if only she was not so "foreign."[21]

Her trajectory is not only a sign of distinction, it also distinguishes her from other Muslim women and brings her socially closer to the Western-oriented, secular elites of Turkey. It's a closeness that creates more enmity than sympathy. The appropriation of social signs of modernity, such as language, comportment, politics, public exposure, and being in contact with secular groups without giving up the Islamic difference (marked by the headscarf)—this is the source of trou-

20. Nilüfer Göle, *The Forbidden Modern: Civilization and Veiling* (Ann Arbor: University of Michigan Press, 1996).

21. For an analysis of the foreigner in terms of distance from and proximity to the social group, see Simmel's notion of "l'étranger": Georg Simmel, "Digressions sur l'étranger," in *L'école de Chicago: Naissance de l'écologie urbaine*, ed. Yves Grafmeyer and Isaac Joseph (Paris: Editions du Champ Urbain, 1979); for an English translation, see *The Sociology of Georg Simmel*, trans. Kurt Wolff (New York: Free Press, 1950).

ble. It is the "small difference" and the small distance between her and the secular women that ignites political passion. Only when there is this feeling of a stranger's intrusion into one's own domain, places, and privileges is there an issue of rejection or recognition of difference. The figure of the stranger, in a Simmelian approach, represents the ambivalent relation of proximity and distance, identity and difference, through which a group reproduces social life and structures hierarchically social space.[22] This is why the small difference is so crucial in understanding the rejection of those that are closest.

In Turkey, one of the arguments widely used against the headscarf is that it has been appropriated as a political symbol, so the desire to wear it is not a disinterested one. Many will say they are not against their grandmother's headscarf, that on the contrary they remember it with affection and respect. This is certainly true to the extent that "grandmothers" either sat in their corners at home and didn't step into the sites of modernity or took off their headscarves as they walked out from indoors. Such behavior is in conformity with the scenario of national progress and emancipation of women, key elements of the modern social imaginary in a non-Western context. But today the play has changed and so have the actors. The Islamic headscarf is deliberately appropriated, not passively carried and handed down from generation to generation. It is claimed by a new generation of women who have had access to higher education, notwithstanding their modest social origins (many come from the periphery of the big cities or from small towns). Instead of assimilating to the secular regime of women's emancipation, they press for their embodied difference (e.g., Islamic dress) and their public visibility (e.g., in schools, in Parliament) and create disturbances in modern social imaginaries. Islamic women hurt the feelings of modern women and upset the status quo; they are playing with ambivalence, being both Muslim and modern without wanting to give up one for the other. They are outside a regime of imitation, critical of both subservient traditions and assimilative modernity. One can almost twist the argument and say that they are neither Muslim nor modern. The ambiguity of signs disturbs both the traditional Muslim and the secular modernist social groups. And this goes further than a question of abstract identity. It takes place in the public sphere, it involves a face-to-face relation, which means that difference is marked on the body; it is an embodied difference, one that is visible to others. Islamic visibility (and not solely the identity) creates such a

22. Simonetta Tabboni, "Le multiculturalisme et l'ambivalence de l'étranger," in *Une société fragmentée? Le multiculturalisme en débat*, ed. Michel Wieviorka et al. (Paris: Editions La Découverte, 1997), 239–40.

malaise because it has a corporeal, ocular, and spatial dimension. These dimensions are only intensified in the case of Merve Kavakçı.

Kavakçı is both a local and a "foreigner" (in a literal sense as well, given that she became a U.S. citizen); she is from here but also from elsewhere. Her popular background and her choice to wear a headscarf recall the indigenous yet premodern Turkey, while her education, individualistic posture, and political language belong to the modern world; she is a woman who follows an Islamic dress code yet does not adopt the traditional dress, behavior, and representations. Professional and political ambitions as well as divorce are all indicators of a nontraditional life and personality. Furthermore, that she did not collapse into tears under heavy pressure and criticism, and does not speak the collective language of those who were persecuted, interposes a psychological distance between her and the Muslim community. The latter uses widely the idiom of suffering and victimization and through common emotional practices, such as crying and lamenting, reproduces a repertoire of cultural signs, a sense of social belonging, and a collective social movement. Meanwhile, Kavakçı's individualist and composed self-presentation creates trouble in the Islamic social imaginary. Secular women, too, were no less suspicious of her "cold-blooded attitude"; it was taken as one more strike against her, revealing her militant discipline and premeditated behavior at the service of a political conspiracy. Kavakçı cannot be situated in terms of geographical location, communitarian belonging, or cultural coding; as she crosses the boundaries, circulates among different locations—thereby placing them in "disjunctive" relation to one another—new social imaginaries are being shaped.[23]

Kavakçı's fearlessness in the face of intimidation and her insensitivity to established relations of domination between Muslim and secularist women are perceived as arrogant, but at the same time her carriage and discourse change the codes of interaction. Her political language is that of constitutional rights, which resonates more in a U.S.-style democracy than in Turkey, where the constitution tends to provide more trouble than rights. Her language makes reference to an ultramodern space, whereas her covered body suggests Muslim privacy and modesty. Again, she is from here but also from elsewhere; she is neither a replica of a local Muslim nor a Western other. On the one hand, she is no less modern than the Turkish women defending the secular national public sphere. On the other hand, her persistent wearing of the Islamic headscarf displays her embodied difference and reproduces and deepens the cleavage. The ambiguous signs carried by her presence create confusion and disturbance among Muslims and

23. For global circulations and modern social imaginaries, cf. Arjun Appadurai, *Modernity at Large: Cultural Dimensions of Globalization* (Minneapolis: University of Minnesota Press, 1996).

also among secularists (including journalists from CNN to whom her U.S.-inflected language was more familiar). The fact that she comes from "elsewhere" and makes reference to another mental space disturbs—and also helps to transgress—the social rules of conduct and interaction. As Erving Goffman writes, the rupture of the framework is used by those from below, trying to discredit and disturb an adversary.[24] Such surprising crossovers bring into question the fixity of categories and boundaries.

The social dispute generated by the public visibility of Islam is carried by corporeal performances and self-presentations rather than by textualized forms of subjectivities and discursive practices. The public sphere is not simply a preestablished arena; it is constituted and negotiated through performance. In addition to constituting the public sphere, these micropractices enact a way of being public. We can speak of what Victor Turner calls "performative reflexivity," "a condition in which a sociocultural group, or its most perceptive members acting representatively, turn, bend, or reflect back upon themselves, upon the relations, actions, symbols, meanings, and codes, roles, statuses, social structures, ethical and legal rules, and other sociocultural components which make up their public 'selves.' "[25] Islamic performance has a reflexive character to the extent that the codes and symbols embedded in the religious culture are critically appropriated and distanced from the traditional culture. The Islamic dress code exemplifies this performative reflexivity. The practice of veiling restores a link with past traditions; it signifies the immutability of religion and nonsecular time. Through repetition, rehearsal, and performance, the practice of veiling is reproduced again and again, acquiring legitimacy and authority and contributing to the making of a modest pious self. But veiling is not derived directly from prevailing cultural habits and preestablished conventions. On the contrary, it bears a new form, the outcome of a selective and reflexive attitude that amplifies and dramatizes the performative signs of "difference." It is transgressive with respect to Muslim traditions as well as to modern self-presentations. Consequently, the new covering suggests a more rather than less potent Islam, which accounts for secular counterattacks against the headscarf for being not an "innocent" religious convention but a powerful "political symbol."

Let us look back to secularist counterattacks. A brief detour to the linkage between women and the making of the public sphere will introduce a historical perspective into the picture without which we cannot explain the destabilizing force of Islam in secular social imaginaries. One has to remember that secularist

---

24. Erving Goffman, *Les cadres de l'expérience* (Paris: Minuit, 1991), 417; originally published as *Frame Analysis: An Essay on the Organization of Experience* (New York: Harper and Row, 1974).

25. Victor Turner, *The Anthropology of Performance* (New York: PAJ Publications, 1986), 24.

women have entered into modernity through emancipation from religion, which was symbolized by taking off the veil. They have experimented with modernity as a tangible entity inscribed on their bodies, clothes, and ways of life —not exclusively as an abstract and distant category of citizenship. They are products of a historical, emotional, corporeal fracture with the Muslim identity; a fracture with the past that made it possible for them to have access to modernity.

Public Site As Visual Secularism

The grand narratives on modernity typically describe the elements of modernity in non-Western contexts as insufficient. However, when the concepts of Western modernity travel into different contexts, they often acquire not only different meanings but also an unexpected intensity. Secularism is an example of this phenomenon. Secularism, because of its origins in the Western historical development, is expected to be a marginal element in other contexts, especially in Muslim ones. Yet in the Turkish case, for instance, we observe not only its role in nation-state building and its penetration into civil and military elite ideology but also its emergence in civil society and in particular in women's associations. Secularism works as a social imaginary.

It is possible to speak of an excess of secularism, when secularism becomes a fetish of modernity. Modern social imaginaries cross boundaries and circulate but take a different twist and a slightly modified accent in non-Western contexts— they take on a sense of extra. We can read *extra* both as external to the West and as additional and unordinary. The evolutionary concept of historical change can hardly imagine that there can be a surplus or excess of modernity in some domains of social life in non-Western contexts. Modernity functions as a fetish. In non-Western contexts, modernity's manifestations are overemphasized, as are the performances of belonging to modernity.[26] The excess of secularism in Muslim contexts of modernity is such an example. The public sphere becomes a site for modern and secular performances. In contrast with the formation of the public sphere in the West, characterized initially as a bourgeois sphere that excluded the working classes and women, in Muslim contexts of modernity, women function as a pivotal sign/site in the making and representing of the public sphere.[27]

26. The concept of "extra-modernity" is developed in Göle, "Global Expectations."

27. On the public sphere in the West, see Jürgen Habermas, *The Structural Transformation of the Public Sphere: An Inquiry into a Category of Bourgeois Society*, trans. Thomas Burger with Frederick Lawrence (Cambridge: MIT Press, 1989); on the public sphere in a Muslim context, see Nilüfer Göle, "The Gendered Nature of the Public Sphere," *Public Culture* 10 (1997): 61–81.

In a Muslim context, women's visibility and the social mixing of men and women attest to the existence of a public sphere. Women as public citizens and women's rights are more salient than citizenship and civil rights in the Turkish modern imaginary. The removal of the veil, the establishment of compulsory coeducation for girls and boys, civil rights for women that include eligibility to vote and to hold office, and the abolition of Islamic family law guarantee the public visibility and citizenship of women. Women's participation in public life as citizens and as civil servants, their visibility in urban spaces, and their socialization with men all define the modern secular way of life and indicate a radical shift from the social organization and gender roles framed by Islam. In other words, in a Muslim context, secularism denotes a modern way of life, calling for the "emancipation" of women from religion, the removal of the veil, and the end of the spatial separation of sexes. Women are symbols of the social whole: home and outside, interior and exterior, private and public. They stand in for the making of the modern individual, for the modern ways of being private and public. Women's corporeal and civic visibility as well as the formation of heterosocial spaces underpin the stakes of modernity in a Muslim society.

Secularism is enacted as a modern social imaginary through gendered, corporeal, and spatial performances. In that respect, some common spaces are transformed as they gain additional symbolic value and become public sites of visual modernity and gendered secular performances. In addition to Parliament, schools, and the workplace, spaces such as beaches, opera and concert halls, coffeehouses, fashion shows, public gardens, and public transportation all become sites for modern self-presentations. They are instituted and imagined as public spaces through these daily micropractices in which men and women rehearse and improvise in public their new self-presentations, dress codes, bodily postures, aesthetic and cultural tastes, and leisure activities.

The implicit dimensions of modern social imaginaries, namely, the aspects that are embodied in the habitus of a population, in the modes of address, living, habitation, and taste, all become explicit features of performative modernity in a non-Western context. The public sphere denotes a space for the making of the new modern self while it excludes others, namely, those who do not conform to this "new life" and new habitus—Muslims, for example. Acts of performance as well as space are not socially neutral concepts; indeed, they are situated in and produced by social relations of domination and exclusion.

As Henri Lefevbre puts it, the notion of space refers not to an empty space but to a space of production of social relations, defining boundaries of exclusion and inclusion, of the licit and illicit.[28] Social space, moreover, implies virtual or actual assembling at a point; urban space brings together the masses, products, markets, acts, and symbols. It concentrates them, accumulates them. Speaking about urban space invokes as well a center and a centrality, actual or possible.[29] Through its invocation of the possibility of assembly and commonality, public space establishes its link with democracy.

The issue of recognition arises when the Other, perceived as different, becomes closer in proximity—spatially, socially, and corporeally. Recognition of difference is possible only when one finds similitude and commonality with the other. One has to discern the "concrete other"—single individuals with life histories—in order to be able to tolerate difference as part of a social bond.[30] Overpoliticized definitions of identity and arguments of conspiracy exclude the possibility of finding semblance and familiarity; indeed they reinforce the demoniacal definitions of the adversary. In Merve Kavakçı's case, she is not recognized as a woman, an individual, a Muslim, a deputy, and a citizen but is rejected and stigmatized as a militant, an Islamist, and an outsider.

The question of a social bond with the stigmatized and excluded is the essential problem of democracy.[31] In the case of Islam in the public sphere, there is a double movement that causes uneasiness: Islamists seek to enter into spaces of modernity, yet they display their distinctiveness. There is a problem of recognition to the extent that Islamists start sharing the same spaces of modernity, such as the Parliament, university classes, television programs, beaches, opera halls, and coffeehouses, and yet they fashion a counter-Islamic self. In contrast with being a Muslim, being an Islamist entails a reflexive performance; it involves collectively constructing, assembling, and restaging the symbolic materials to signify difference. The symbols of Muslim habitus are reworked, selectively processed, and staged in public. Performative acts of religious difference in the secular public space defy the limits of recognition and of social bonds and unsettle modern social imaginaries.

28. Henri Lefebvre, *La production de l'espace*, 3d ed. (Paris: Editions Anthropos, 1986), 35.

29. Lefebvre, *Production de l'espace*, 121.

30. Seyla Benhabib, *Situating the Self: Gender, Community, and Postmodernism in Contemporary Politics* (London: Routledge, 1992).

31. Danilo Martuccelli, *Sociologies de la modernité: L'itinéraire du XXe siècle* (Paris: Gallimard, 1999), 447.

The Islamic critique of modernity can be interpreted as a new stage in the process of the indigenization of modernity in non-Western contexts. The Islamic subject is formed both through liberation from traditional definitions and roles of Muslim identity and through resistance to a cultural program of modernity and liberalism. Alain Touraine claims that the subject owes her existence to a social conflict or collective action that criticizes the established order, expected roles, and logic of power.[32] Thus the Islamic subject is created by a collective action that is critical of the subjugation of Muslim identity by both community (religious and otherwise) and modernity. The search for difference and authenticity expresses a critical resistance to the assimilative strategies and homogenizing practices of modernity. Especially in non-Western contexts, the reflexive nature of modernity, the critical capacity to surpass its limits, is weak.[33] Criticism of modernity is engendered when modernity becomes an indigenous, everyday practice. Indigenously defined modernity not only is a discursive regime that shapes subjectivity but also is constituted and negotiated through performances.[34] The Habermasian model of bourgeois public sphere as worked out by "rational-critical debate" does not always provide a frame to understand the performative basis of the indigenously defined modernity. In distinction from the Enlightenment notion of the public sphere, which endorsed gender blindness, gender movements and other identity-based movements display and make public sexual differences.[35] Performance of difference through corporeal and spatial practices requires a new reading of nonverbal communication, embodied information, and sensorial interaction.

The nonverbal "embodied information" and its link to "naked senses" provides one of the crucial communication conditions, according to Erving Goffman.[36] And of the sensory organs, the eye has a uniquely sociological function: the union and interaction of individuals is based upon mutual glances.[37] Espe-

32. Alain Touraine, *Critique de la modernité* (Paris: Fayard, 1992), 337.

33. On reflexivity and modernity, see Ulrich Beck, Anthony Giddens, and Scott Lasch, *Reflexive Modernization: Politics, Tradition, and Aesthetics in the Modern Social Order* (Cambridge, England: Polity, 1994).

34. For a discussion of such an approach to performing modernity in the case of the Miao population in China, see Louisa Schein, "Performing Modernity," *Cultural Anthropology* 14 (1999): 361–95.

35. Michael Warner, "Public and Private," in *Critical Terms for the Study of Gender and Sexuality*, ed. Catharine R. Stimpson and Gil Herdt (Chicago: University of Chicago Press, in press).

36. Erving Goffman, *Behavior in Public Places: Notes on the Social Organization of Gatherings* (New York: Free Press, 1966), 15.

37. Goffman, *Behavior in Public Places*, 93.

cially where issues of religion and gender are in question, the vocabulary of gaze and spatial conventions acquire a greater salience. When Muslim women cross the borders between inside and out, multiple senses—sight, smell, touch, and hearing—feature in concerns over redefining borders, preserving decency, and separating genders. A public Islam needs to redefine and recreate the borders of the interior, intimate, illicit gendered space (*mahrem*).[38] The notion of modesty (*edep*) underpins the Muslim self and her relation to private and public spaces. The veiling suggests the importance of the ocular (avoiding the gaze, casting down one's eyes), and the segregation of spaces regulates gender sociability. These acts, counteraesthetics, body postures, and modes of address are public performances; they seek to gain authority and legitimacy through their repetitions and rehearsals. They are not alien to Muslim memory and culture. They are rooted in past traditions and memory, in the religious habitus. But they are not simple conventions that have always been there and that are unconsciously handed down from generation to generation. The habitus provides, in Pierre Bourdieu's account, a source of improvisations; it allows for a process of continual correction and adjustment.[39] However, Islamic public visibilities are not implicitly embodied in Muslim habitus. They mark a break with traditions. Islamism is a political means for the exacerbation of Muslim difference. This process of exacerbation makes the habitus (both secular and religious) explicit and conscious. Grandmother's veiling is acceptable because it is "natural." Whereas the new veiling is seen as not so innocent because it is not a movement among religious or interior women. Secularists are not wrong to read it as a symbol. Although not rendered discursively, a nonverbal embodied communication in the veil conveys information; it disobeys both traditional and secular ways of imagining self-emancipation and becoming public.

Islamic public visibility presents a critique of a secular version of the public sphere. The work of Richard Sennett has shown that the initial development of the public sphere in the West was inseparable from the ways in which people were experiencing their bodies; the body was linked to urban space by religious rituals.[40] According to Sennett, the dematerialization of the public sphere and its

38. The title of the Turkish edition of my book on veiling, *The Forbidden Modern*, is *Modern mahrem*.

39. Craig Calhoun, "Habitus, Field, and Capital: The Question of Historical Specificity," in *Bourdieu: Critical Perspectives*, ed. Craig Calhoun, Edward LiPuma, and Moishe Postone (Chicago: University of Chicago Press, 1993), 61–89.

40. Richard Sennett, *Flesh and Stone: The Body and the City in Western Civilization* (New York: Norton, 1996).

separation from the body is the secular version of the public sphere. The divorce of urban experience from religious understanding inhibits the creation of intense civic bonds and "civic compassion" in a multicultural city.[41] Drawing upon this analysis, one can suggest that Islamic public display recuperates a phenomenon that has been repressed by secularism. This public display attempts to reconstruct the social link between subjectivity and public space through the reintroduction of religious self-fashionings, performances, and rituals. Women are the principal actors in this process as they display the boundaries between private and public, licit and illicit, body and imaginary. Islamism reinforces the boundaries in social relations through regulating bodily practices in public spaces; this regulation, in turn, serves as a public display of Islamic subjectivity. The Muslim body becomes, for actors of Islamism, a site for resistance to secular modernity. It is a site where both difference and prohibition are linked to the formation of a new subject (neither Muslim nor modern) and a new sociability. On the one hand, this new subject becomes modern; on the other hand, she incorporates the limits, the boundaries, the interdictions; hence it is a "forbidden modern." Self-limitation and self-disciplining go together with becoming modern. Ambivalence, a feeling that is normally alien to both the religious and the modern, undergirds the contemporary Muslim psyche. In *Another Modernity, a Different Rationality*, Scott Lash draws on Kant's "reflective judgment" to define ambivalence as a third space, the margin between the same and the other, where difference is more primordial than either presence or absence and instead exists as an aporetic space of ambivalence and undecidability.[42]

Castoriadis insists on the complementary nature of social representations—without this complementarity, he writes, society would not be possible. For example, the relation between serf and lord—and feudal society itself—is made possible through the institutions and representations that bind them.[43] However, Islamic social imaginaries and practices are worked out through ambivalence rather than complementarity. Surprising crossovers between Muslim and modernity and between secular and religious practices take place, unsettling the fixity of positions and oppositional categories. Turkish experience provides us with a privileged terrain for this choreography of ambivalence. Voluntary modernization means a processed and displaced form of Western modernity as well as the absence of a colonial Other against which to direct Islamic oppositional discourse. Mutu-

41. Sennett, *Flesh and Stone*, 370.

42. Scott Lash, *Another Modernity, a Different Rationality* (Oxford: Blackwell, 1999), 4.

43. Castoriadis, *Imaginary Institution*, 367.

ally inclusive categories create not binary oppositions, counterdiscourses, or emulations but multifaceted, intertwining modern performances. This ambivalence operates basically through crossing over, losing one's positionality, and circulating in different spaces, categories, and mental mappings. Rather than resulting in peaceful juxtapositions, hybridities, and augmentations, it is worked out in double negations (neither Muslim nor modern), ambiguities (forbidden and modern), resulting in fragmented subjectivities and transcultural performances. New social imaginaries are shaped by these circulatory, transcultured, and crossover performances. They are imagined, abstract, and implicit categories; they are carried in images, produced by bodily practices and in physical spaces. Islam displays a new "stage" in the making of modern social imaginaries; a stage in which ocular, corporeal, and spatial aspects underlie social action, confrontation, and cohabitation. It is the intrusion of senses, prelinguistic aspects of communication embodied in habitus, that makes the conflict between secularists and Islam so charged with corporeal stigma, affectivity, and political passion.

Nilüfer Göle is director of studies at the Centre d'Analyse et d'Intervention Sociologiques, Ecole des Hautes Etudes en Sciences Sociales, Paris. She is the author of *The Forbidden Modern: Civilization and Veiling* (1996).

Cultures of Circulation:
The Imaginations of Modernity

Benjamin Lee and Edward LiPuma

The speed, intensity, and extent of contemporary global transformations challenge many of the assumptions that have guided the analysis of culture over the last several decades. Whereas an earlier generation of scholarship saw meaning and interpretation as the key problems for social and cultural analysis, the category of *culture* now seems to be playing catch-up to the economic processes that go beyond it. Economics owes its present appeal partly to the sense that it, as a discipline, has grasped that it is dynamics of circulation that are driving globalization—and thereby challenging traditional notions of language, culture, and nation.

There is a certain historical irony to the contemporary discovery of the centrality of circulation to the analysis of the globalization of capitalism. The anthropologist Claude Lévi-Strauss (1969) inaugurated what would later be called the "linguistic turn" by applying Prague School linguistics to the analysis of circulation and exchange in precapitalist societies; by focusing on the structural analysis of the "total social fact" of exchange, he sought to overcome the dichotomy of economy and culture that is characteristic of modern thought. In hindsight, it can be seen that his use of phonology as the model for structural analysis raised fundamental issues about structure, event, and agency that con-

We would like to thank Arjun Appadurai, Dilip Gaonkar, Moishe Postone, Michael Silverstein, Charles Taylor, Michael Warner, and Robert Gooding-Williams for their help in formulating this essay.

Public Culture 14(1): 191–213

tinue to inform poststructuralist discussions of performative identity. One result is that performativity has been considered a quintessentially cultural phenomenon that is tied to the creation of meaning, whereas circulation and exchange have been seen as processes that *transmit* meanings, rather than as constitutive acts in themselves. Overcoming this bifurcation will involve rethinking circulation as a cultural phenomenon, as what we call *cultures of circulation*. An expanded notion of performativity would then become crucial for developing a cultural account of economic processes.

If circulation is to serve as a useful analytic construct for cultural analysis, it must be conceived as more than simply the movement of people, ideas, and commodities from one culture to another. Instead, recent work indicates that circulation is a cultural process with its own forms of abstraction, evaluation, and constraint, which are created by the interactions between specific types of circulating forms and the interpretive communities built around them. It is in these structured circulations that we identify cultures of circulation. Our idea draws from a variety of contemporary sources, including Benedict Anderson's (1991) account of nation, narration, and imagination; Jürgen Habermas's (1989) work on public opinion and the public sphere; Arjun Appadurai's (1996) conceptualizations of cultural flows and "-scapes"; and Charles Taylor's essay, in this issue, on the self-reflexive creation of modern social imaginaries. But our project also harks back to classic anthropological work on gifts and exchange such as studies by Marcel Mauss (1967) and Bronislaw Malinowski (1966), and their updatings by Pierre Bourdieu (1977), Annette Weiner (1992), and Jacques Derrida (1992), as well as Marxist analyses of money and capital (Postone 1993; Harvey 1982). The broad range of this legacy suggests that developing a critical perspective on circulation will require moving beyond disciplinary boundaries and placing it in a conceptual space that encompasses some of the most difficult and troubling issues in contemporary cultural and philosophical analysis: self-reflexivity, performativity, indexicality, metalanguage, objectification, and foundationalism, to name just a few.

Cultures of circulation are created and animated by the cultural forms that circulate through them, including—critically—the abstract nature of the forms that underwrite and propel the process of circulation itself. The circulation of such forms—whether the novels and newspapers of the imagined community or the equity-based derivatives and currency swaps of the modern market—always presupposes the existence of their respective interpretive communities, with their own forms of interpretation and evaluation. These interpretive communities determine lines of interpretation, found institutions, and set boundaries based principally on their own internal dynamics.

The three social imaginaries that Taylor (in this issue) suggests are crucial to Western modernity—the public sphere, the citizen-state, and the market—all presuppose a self-reflexive structure of circulation built around some reciprocal social action, whether that action be reading, as in the case of the public sphere and nationalism, or buying and selling, as in the case of the market. The ideological prototype for such creative social self-reflexivity is that of the social contract, in which individuals engaging in the reciprocal performative acts of promising and agreeing create a quasi-objective social totality that then governs their actions. The effectiveness of the social contract as a foundational ideology for Western modernity stems from the fact that its performative construction of collective agency is a crucial aspect not only of modern social imaginaries, but also of capital itself.

The concept of performativity has been very prominent in contemporary discussions of personal and sexual identity. But it is another line of inquiry, comprising anthropological studies of ritual and magic (Tambiah 1985; Silverstein 2000) and exchange (Lévi-Strauss 1969; Bourdieu 1977; Mauss 1967; Sahlins 1972; LiPuma 2000), that suggests that something like performativity is crucial for understanding any system of circulation and exchange. The analytical problem is how to extend what has been a speech act–based notion of performativity to other discursively mediated practices, including ritual, economic practices, and even reading. What is interesting about performatives is that they go beyond reference and description—indeed, they seem to create the very speech act they refer to. More important for our purposes in this essay, they allow for language to "objectify" its own praxis. Produced by their self-reflexive objectification, performative acts can thus be seen to be a presupposition for the very cultures of circulation of which they are a constitutive part.

Our analytical focus in this essay is the performative constitution of collective agency and the implications of this performativity for the imagination of social totality. Alongside the notion of social imaginaries, as discussed elsewhere in this issue, we will examine the performative construction of capital as a self-reflexive temporal agency that, in concert with mutually created/creating sociocultural phenomena, motivates the circulation of social forms characteristic of the modern. Capital appears in two objectified forms—historically as abstract labor time and surplus value, nowadays as risk and finance capital—and gives rise to a fundamental and decisive conception of social totality whose underlying performativity appears in different domains in the form of social imaginaries. That is, capital's performativity surfaces in fetishized figurations, such as the collective agencies of the market, the public sphere, and agentive peoplehood ("We the people"), which in turn are necessary components in the drive to totalization characteristic of capitalism. Moreover, modern social imaginaries depend on an objectified conception of totality itself that is at once an essential and a fetishized moment of the totalizing impulse of capital.

In the work of Anderson, Habermas, and Taylor, the critical context and dialectical partner of cultures of circulation is the modern capitalist nation-state. These thinkers inaugurated an inquiry into what kinds of culturally circulated forms were necessary under conditions of modernity for the development of a production-based capitalism within a procedurally democratic nation-state. Their insights provide a crucial dimension to our understanding of circulation because the export and installation of these cultural forms—through the absorption of new territories by Western nation-states and the construction of relations of dependency—are a necessary cultural component of the encompassment of others (Appadurai 2000), the ensuing construction of alternative modernities (Gaonkar 1999), and the continuation of the encompassment of others on new terms in the era of globalization. Institutional forms such as markets and administrative bureaucracies instigate and feed off a dialectic between a continuing project of objectification and the production of the forms of subjectivity necessary to produce culturally/historically specific types of collective identity. They contrast sharply with the forms circulated in noncapitalist, non-nation-state "societies"; under capitalism, cultures of circulation take a special turn in that the forms appear as self-reflexively created social agents that move in objective secular time, independently of the character of a specific culture or the actions of individual subjects.

Imagining Circulation

For the Euro-American world and increasingly for the world as a whole, the public sphere, the modern citizen-state, and the market are the basic components of the social imaginary of modernity. For reasons both social and historical, they are the counterparts, in cultural circulation, of capital in its emergence as the driving, self-reflexive subject of social life. In this capacity, they shape new forms of subjectivity and identity that are grounded in the everyday, in the habitus, through their inscription in specific social practices such as rational calculation, reading, and democratic voting—all of which require the development of requisite supporting institutions, whether they be coffeehouses and publishing firms or clearinghouses and banks.

It is usual for the citizens of a democratic nation-state to think of the three modern social imaginaries—the public sphere (public opinion), the citizen-state ("We the people"), and the market—as collective agents, created by the actions of the participants and moving in secular time. The performative dimension to each imaginary is located in a new form of collective agency through the coordination of specific social actions. These social actions can be approached as examples of what Charles Sanders Peirce (1960: 111) called "indexical icons," each of which contains a representation of the totality it is a part of. In Peirce's illustration, someone draws in the sand a map of the beach on which he or she is located, including the very map itself, and in the map there would be a map of the map, ad infinitum, in a telescoping of self-reflexivity. A full-blown performative is this figuration taken one step further: to draw the map is to create the beach. Stanley Tambiah (1985) extended Peirce's notion to describe ritual and magical actions. In Tambiah's analysis, the sequence of acts that constitute a ritual—especially one that engages the whole society, such as a coronation or a high-status marriage— often produces a microcosm of the very social totality it is supposed to invoke and bring into contact with the mundane world. In other words, the ritual process creates an instantiation of the very macrocosm it represents.

A performative would thus be a special, creative type of indexical icon: a self-reflexive use of reference that, in creating a representation of an ongoing act, also enacts it. From the standpoint of linguistics, performatives involve a delicate calibration between indexical and nonindexical structures of language, or between what might be termed "subjective" (first-person) versus "objective" (third-person) perspectives on discourse. These distinctions can be made not only in the case of discrete speech acts, but also at the level of genre. As Emile Benveniste (1971) has pointed out, "objective" genres, such as scientific and historiographical forms, tend to minimize the use of indexicals; on the other hand, as Mikhail Bakhtin (1984) emphasized in his work on "metalinguistics," indexicality and meta-indexicality lie at the heart of narration and the novelistic representation of subjectivity.

The extension of performativity beyond the level of the speech act to those of ritual, the interplay of genres, and even the process of reading provides a crucial insight to how self-reflexivity and circulation interact. The objectification of certain types of discursively mediated actions can provide the performative basis for complex cultures of circulation. For example, in the case of the public sphere and nationalism, critical aspects of the construction of these social imaginaries can be identified in what might be called a performative ideology of reading and discussion. In Anderson's (1991) account, readers of narratives disseminated trans-locally through print identify with both the audience addressed by the narrator and the narrated-about characters, and become aware of the existence of like-minded readers who share similar identifications. The "We" of nationalism is the tropic embodiment of these two identifications. Each act of reading is thus an indexical icon of the community that it performatively instantiates and re-creates (Silverstein 2000). From a Marxian perspective, the fetish is none other than the act of shared imagination in which agents apprehend, cognitively and precognitively, that the mutuality and performativity of their actions across a variety of domains is what produces society.

Both the citizen-state and public sphere can thus be seen as self-reflexive collective agencies created by an interplay between language and language about language—that is, metalanguage. The social imaginary of the market, on the other hand, combines buying and selling with formalized models of contract and exchange. According to Marx, the commodification of labor by objectified forms of financial calculation and time reckoning produces a dialectic of temporality and metatemporality, between concrete labor time and abstract labor time, that has an intrinsic dynamic of self-valorization and self-expansion. This dynamic expresses itself through a drive for totalization, for incorporating and transforming other societies in its own image—even as, in its creation of new versions of social totality, it creatively destroys itself. Marx's key insight, following Hegel, is that modern capitalism has two *performative subjects*: a self-reflexive subject constituted by value (abstract labor time) that is the "deep structure" of capital; and a fetishized locus of self-reflexive collective agency in the social imaginary of the market, ideologically connected to the public sphere and citizen-state through such notions as the social contract.

The Imaginary of the Market

Both the imaginaries of the public sphere and the citizen-state have first- and third-person, performative and constative components, as the terms *We* (first person, performative) and *the people* (third person, constative) suggest. The market is, however, different, in ways that are significant for understanding the relation between capital and the modern image of how the economy functions in society. Members of capitalist economies almost invariably think of "the market" as a third-person collective agent, to which first-person agents, such as "We the investors," respond but do not necessarily identify with. The covert asymmetries of agentive verbal ascriptions reflect this relationship. Thus, "the market" can *act, indicate, warn, hesitate, climb,* and *fall,* but is usually not able to take second-order verbs such as *reflect, assume guilt,* or *take responsibility* in the ways that a national people might.

In addition, investors think of the market as so fraught with risk and uncertainty that they deem it prudent and wise both to try to predict the action of the market and to deploy various investing strategies designed to reduce risk and uncertainty. Paradoxically, because the market by its nature leaves them uncoordinated, the interactions among these strategies can result not only in increasing the risks the strategies were meant to minimize but actually in creating new ones. As George Soros (1995: 311), the dean of hedge fund managers and thus an important player in the world of financial capital, puts it: "The generally accepted theory is that financial markets tend toward equilibrium and, on the whole, discount the future correctly. I operate using a different theory according to which financial markets cannot possibly discount the future correctly because they do not merely discount the future, they help to shape it."

The bifurcation of first-person and third-person agentive perspectives on the market is, of course, attributable to the mathematical and statistical nature of market transactions. In the citizen-state, the statistical enumeration of the population and the controlling of risk are subsumed within the first-person collective national identity. In the liberal state, the "We the people" of democratic institutions manage risks such as environmental hazards, nuclear warfare, or disease and illness via collective decision making. In the case of the market, the different and decentralized acts of buying and selling produce risk; market-focused institutions, such as clearinghouses, oversight committees, and mandated insurance, control a certain kind of risk by eliminating the possibility of default by a legal individual, but there is a clear line between the strategies of individual investors and the purported collective agency of the market. Financial indices, such as those operated by Standard and Poor's, Nasdaq, and Dow Jones, and the extraordinary emphasis that the media and the investing public place on them, reinforce the image of the collective agency of the market—this in marked contrast to early stock markets that had no averages, only listings for individual companies. That the public, from professionals to observers, uses these averages to determine the health of the economy, the strength of stocks generally, and the performance of the participants further reinforces the notion of animated and self-defining collective agency.

When we talk about "the market" today (at sites ranging from ordinary conversations to newspaper headlines), we usually mean the stock market and its counterparts. But this was not always the case. For most of mercantile history, "the market" designated institutions for exchanging valuables, commodities, and services. The stock market and its parallel institutions, such as commodity, options, and currency markets, are all part of what Marx would have characterized as nonproductive wealth; they produce wealth in the form of money but do not implicate productive labor. They therefore are not part of the mechanism for producing surplus value, but rather enable its distribution. Stocks and derivatives, in Marx's account, have no "value" per se.

At the same time, society is increasingly described in economic terms. Louis Dumont (1977) argues that while Adam Smith and other Enlightenment economists began to describe the economy as an autonomous, self-regulating system, it was Marx's labor theory of value that first explained society in terms of economic practices. In effect, Marx unifies two models of collective agency, one derived from economic discourses such as those of the Physiocrats, Smith and David Ricardo, the other from the social contract–based models proposed by Thomas Hobbes and John Locke. The French philosopher Jean Hyppolite sees the Hegelian dialectic as having its origins in Adam Smith and locates the crucial link in Hegel's transformation of Smith's "invisible hand" into the cunning of reason, a dialectic that opposes the aims that the individual sets up and the ends achieved. Hyppolite (1969: 76–77) writes: "It was in the course of tracing this concrete dialectic through the whole of human life and then translating it onto a logical plane that Hegel struggled to reconstruct the very notion of dialectic. . . . the course of the world is the outcome of the interaction between individuals which constitutes a universal individuality."

The contract exchange model represents the point of overlap between Smith and the social contract theorists. In Marx's hands, this will become the "objectified" surface model of human relations in capitalism, a particular moment within a larger, dialectical conception of social totality. Using Hegel's account of self-reflexivity, Marx creates a model of collective agency in which objectification and fetishism embed a third-person perspective on exchange relations within a first-person dialectical model of social totality. In his account of the fetish, Marx describes how capitalist societies treat relations between persons as if they were relations between things. Commodities are the product of the social mediation of labor, but this is disguised by the market; the money form objectifies all commodities by giving each a market price that appears to be a quasi-objective property of the commodity—independent of its origins in productive labor (value as abstract labor time). Price is thus the (third-person) objectification of value; yet it is precisely value, as abstract labor time, that is the self-valorizing subject of capitalism; the identical subject-object that, in positing itself, self-reflexively creates itself.

As is clear in numerous references in the *Grundrisse* and the opening volume of *Capital*, the model for such an identical subject-object is taken from Hegel's

Logic. In volume I of *Capital*, Marx shows that circulation can animate a drive toward social totality under specific historical circumstances: when labor itself becomes a commodity on the market. The totality is constituted by value, realized as abstract labor time, and is characterized by an internal dynamic that, in its "unfolding" or "self-positing," self-reflexively constitutes itself. Marx derived these properties of self-reflexivity and self-positing from Hegel's account of spirit (*Geist*) and concept (*Begriff*), both of which the latter had developed from a philosophical analysis of the first-person pronoun; indeed, Hegel's reasoning here had carried him so far as to argue that the free and concrete realization of the concept was none other than "I," or pure self-consciousness. Marx famously inverted the Hegelian position in order to relocate the dialectic in social reality. Thus, for Marx, the integration of first-person and third-person perspectives does not result in a transcendent point that anchors social totality, but instead produces a sociohistorically specific performative subject that produces the *notion of totality*.

Dumont observes that although Smith gave the first account of the internal consistency of the economy by linking individual and general interests, it was Marx who conceived of capitalist society as a self-organizing totality. Marx grasps that capitalism completely redefines the categories of value, social relations, and the commodity in its striving toward totality. Yet in so doing, he deploys the full Hegelian armature of self-reflexivity and self-reference to construct a historically specific identical subject-object. This identical subject-object emerges in a social formation that already has a commodity as its money form—that is, in a society in which money is the medium of exchange and the measure of value and in which labor power has become a commodity in the form of wage labor. The latter condition presupposes both a market for labor and a contract model of exchange.

> Labour-power can appear upon the market as a commodity only if, and in so far as, its possessor, the individual whose labour-power it is, offers it for sale, or sells it as a commodity. In order that its possessor may sell it as a commodity, he must have it at his disposal, he must be the free proprietor of his own labour-capacity, hence of his person. He and the owner of money meet in the market, and enter into relations with each other on a footing of equality as owners of commodities, with the sole difference that one is a buyer, the other a seller; both are therefore equal in the eyes of the law. (Marx 1976: 271)

In capitalism, according to Marx, labor is a self-reflexive, self-constituting subject. It is the only commodity whose use value possesses the property of producing value. The value of a commodity is the socially necessary abstract labor time needed to produce it. When labor is a commodity, a certain amount of labor time is necessary to produce it (i.e., the worker); the goal of capitalism is to produce a surplus between the value necessary to produce the labor power and the value produced by it.

Non-Capitalist Circulation and the Social Imaginary

The Western imaginaries of the public sphere, citizen-state, and the market all have explicit connections with social contract models of society. Against the backdrop of a "state of nature," individuals exchange promises and create a transcendent power to govern the social totality they create. This act of promising embodies the performative creation of society. The contract objectifies the result of first-person agreements as a "we" that then becomes the object of future identifications. In Marx, the commodification of labor via the contractual conditions of the market is what produces value as the performative subject of capitalism. Marshall Sahlins draws out the implications of this interplay between first- and third-person perspectives and the creation of social totality in his comparison of Marcel Mauss's work on gift exchange and the Hobbesian social contract model of the creation of the state. In both cases, exchange creates peace and constitutes a particular form of society; as Sahlins (1972: 168) puts it, "In place of Hobbes's war of every man against every man, Mauss substitutes the exchange of everything between everybody." But Sahlins notes a critical difference. In Mauss's case, the reciprocity between exchanging parties does not "dissolve the parties in a higher unity, but correlating their opposition, perpetuates it" (70). In Hobbes's case, the exchange of promises creates a transcendent authority, the sovereign or sovereign state, which subsumes the individuals within it. The sovereign is a third-person authority that transcends the "I-You" exchanges of promises that constitute it; the sovereign is not one of the parties of the contract that creates him as sovereign.

By contrast, in gift-based societies, there is no transcendent surplus. Surpluses are given away in agonistic ceremonial displays or ritualized gift-giving, or are the subject of constant redistribution. Moreover, because gifts encode culturally and historically specific modes of sociality in which gifts are aspects of agents in their relations to others, their trajectory is to transform one social relation into another. Relations of kinship and community are simultaneously canonically presupposed and indexically recalibrated in the performance of giving gifts. In economic and social terms, gifts neither presuppose a totality nor are necessarily instrumental in creating one. In a word, the existence of the *social* does not necessitate *society*. There is no necessity to reify the social as society except—crucially—under capitalism (LiPuma and Postone n.d.).

It is not surprising then that in the work of Mauss, Malinowski, and later commentators, the circulation and exchange of gifts and valuables presuppose and create the exchanging groups, but there is no transcendent "view from nowhere" that allows its participants to name, much less agentify, the totality of exchanges. Despite his repeated attempts, Malinowski could not elicit from his Trobriand informants any kind of objectification of the cycle of gift exchanges known as the "Kula ring," even as they described the different paths through which *kula* might circulate. Positing a typical Trobriand Islander, Malinowski (1996: 83) writes: "If you were to ask him what the Kula is, he would answer by giving a few details, most likely by giving his personal experiences and subjective views on the Kula . . . for the integral picture does not exist in his mind; he is in it, and cannot see the whole from the outside." There is no transcendent view from nowhere, and thus the imagination of totality plays no role in the meaning of an exchange or in the intentionality of the participants.

It is also a well-known phenomenon that in many noncapitalist forms of sociality, first-person plural identities are easily ascribed to clans, moieties, or group segments that can also be given a proper name or totemic designation; however, there will be no third-person auto-designation, such as a proper name, for the group as a whole (Urban 1996). Such auto-designations for the group are, in reality, characteristically produced in the context of encompassment, when local agents begin to interact and exchange with others whose habitus is the social epistemology of capitalism—for example, colonial officials, missionaries, expatriate entrepreneurs, and anthropologists (LiPuma 2000).

From these observations, we can begin to draw some interesting contrasts. In social systems dominated by gift exchange, there is no transcendent view of the social totality constituted by exchange. The capitalist notion of value that makes a striving toward totality possible is absent as a condition of the production of gift-based sociality. From an external perspective, the kind of totality constituted by gift exchange consists of homogeneous units differentiated by the exchange process, but from the point of view of the exchanging groups, other units appear different and heterogeneous. Within the contract model of exchange, by contrast, the social totality appears as a homogeneous agency that subsumes individuals who are in principle unique; at the same time, these transcendent homogeneous agencies are seen as mutually differentiating. Examples of this opposition are the modern citizen-state that is transcendent with respect to individual citizens but differentiated from other nation-states, or capital conceived as abstract labor time with respect to the particularities of use values, but differentiated from other, "competing," capitals.

The three social imaginaries of the public sphere, the citizen-state, and the market (capital) all require a third-person objectification of a transcendent "surplus" and a subsequent first-person "we" identification with it in order to generate their particular forms of self-reflexively constituted collective agency. A classic example is the Rousseauian notion of "the people," in which persons give up their freedom as individuals to create a greater, collective freedom. In the case of Marx, the "substance" whose mediation provides the very basis for value is time; abstract labor time is created in and through exchange, but becomes realized in practice only in a society in which labor is a commodity and commodity production has become so generalized as to subsume and preempt relations based on kinship and community.

By contrast, Pierre Bourdieu (1977) argues that "time itself" is the pivotal factor that "splits" the vision of social totality in social systems defined by the exchange of gifts. Here, the prestation and its reply/return must be separated by an interval of time. To reply immediately to a gift with a countergift is to insult the giver, to nullify the gift by treating it as though it were a commodity exchange between strangers; such an exchange is thus situated on the frontiers or margins of sociality. The interval between gift and return provides the basis for strategy, for the exercise of timing and the calculation of symbolic, as differentiated from economic, capital. The preconceptual structures of the habitus provide the phenomenological base for what from an objective perspective is a "misrecognition" that is constitutive of the social totality of exchange. The systems of reckoning time are also preconceptual; not the infinitely divisible, empty, homogeneous time of modernity in which all events take place, but the varying periodicities of seasonal and diurnal temporalities that intersect with indexically calibrated spatial patterns. Yet, even more important, if such circulations and exchanges are actually constitutive of the exchanging groups, then the temporal delay is also what creates the groups themselves and the social totality of exchange. In the final analysis, particular and particularistic modes of sociality — ways of constructing social units and imagining their integration — are intrinsically linked to a mode of temporality that is heterogeneous, contextual, and immune to any uniform standard of measurement.

Bourdieu's insights allow us to see more clearly what is revolutionary about Hobbes's social contract theory. By insisting that all the participants have to promise mutually and reciprocally to give up their right to everything, Hobbes annuls the temporal separation of giving, receiving, and exchanging that is at the heart of Bourdieu's analysis. At the same time, this simultaneous and reciprocal act also creates a surplus of authority that is the foundation for the authority of the sovereign. What is unconsciously separated in gift exchange is consciously aggregated in the contract.

Labor, Time, and the Derivative

In contrast with the case of precapitalist societies, it is exactly the contract model of exchange and the infinitely divisible and measurable time of modernity that Marx presupposes in his account of capital. The infinitely divisible continuum of price (money as a measure of value) mediates exchange (money as the medium of exchange) and becomes analogically projected onto productive labor itself, thus allowing labor time to be measured and given a price, that is, allowing the calculation of the value of labor power. Unlike concrete labor time, abstract labor time is infinitely divisible and denumerable and presupposes the existence of formal modes of calculation and measurement. When labor power becomes a commodity—that is, when wage labor becomes a necessary part of the production of commodities—the conditions have been set for the creation of surplus value, or capital. Capital creates a social totality that is in constant motion, that constantly destroys itself in creating and expanding itself, a dialectical dynamic that Moishe Postone (1993) describes as a "treadmill effect" particular to capitalism.

According to this reading of Marx, increased productivity increases the amount of value produced per unit of time until this productivity becomes generalized across the economy; at that point, the magnitude of value derived in that time period, because of its abstract and general temporal determination, will fall back to its previous level. The cycle of increases in productivity, followed by a return to the preexisting level of value formation, compels even those producers who had resisted adopting these new methods to do so (Postone 1993: 290). If the amount of labor time expended in production in a given society is held roughly constant, this treadmill effect of competitive productivity produces an increasing disparity between value—in the form of abstract labor time—and material and monetary wealth, a contradiction that intensifies as capital expands.

But does Marx's equation of abstract labor time, self-reflexivity, and collective agency still hold in an age of post-Fordist finance capital? The answer depends on the degree to which his "ethnography of value" in capitalism still holds true. There has been a major transformation over the last twenty years in the relations between finance capital and labor. From 1983 to 1998, daily trading in currency markets grew from $200 million to $1.5 trillion, with 98 percent of the 1998 figure intended for speculation; the growth was due in great part to the use of complicated currency derivatives. Trading in derivatives grew 215 percent per year from 1987 to 1997, and by the time of the Asian market crash in 1997, the annual value of traded derivatives was more than ten times the value of global production.

Derivatives are financial instruments that derive their monetary value from other assets, such as stocks, bonds, commodities, or currencies. The peculiarity of all derivatives is that they give individuals the right to buy or sell certain assets by a specified date. For example, one might purchase a call option for $500 to buy one hundred shares of IBM at some future date for $100 a share—the strike price. If at that future date IBM shares were valued at $120, the buyer would realize a profit of $1,500 ($2,000 minus the $500 option) on the initial investment of $500, for a 300 percent profit. A direct purchase of one hundred shares of IBM at $100 per share and sold at $120 would yield a profit of $2,000, but the rate of return would be only 20 percent of the initial investment of $10,000. Thus, for the price of an option, investors can partake in the profit (or loss) that might be realized in the value of the underlying assets without the cash layout required by direct purchase; the difference between the price of the underlying security and the strike price, and the price of the option is a measure of the leverage that derivatives provide. In addition, with an option, an investor's risk is limited to the price of the option, no matter what happens to the underlying security.

Originally used exclusively to hedge risk, derivatives have now become speculative instruments that circulate in their own universe. At the same time, derivatives represent a *metalevel* with respect to their underlying assets, a metalevel created by the fixed temporal interval in which they are exercisable, a fact captured in the famous Black-Scholes equations for pricing options (Black and Scholes 1973; these equations are examined in some detail further on). Besides leverage, options allow investors to create profitable positions that rely only on the volatility of the underlying security; for example, by using options strategies such as straddles or strangles, one can make money whether the stock goes up, down, or nowhere in price.

The advent of this new financial order might reasonably be dated at 1973. That year marked the end of the Bretton Woods agreement and of the gold standard, which cut currencies loose to float; the Middle East oil crisis, which signaled the declining influence of Fordist production on the U.S. economy; the creation of the Chicago options exchange, the first institutional market in the United States specializing in options trading; and the discovery, or invention, of the Black-Scholes equations governing price options and other derivatives. If we look at this nexus more closely, we can see a transformation from Marx's production-based dynamic of self-reflexivity, time, and labor to a metatemporally based dynamic of circulation. The demise of the gold standard and Fordist production, and the concomitant rise of economic globalization, represent a significant shift from Marx's account of capital.

In one sense, the three volumes of *Capital* could be said to have presented the "deep structure" of capital, unfolding it as a dynamic, self-reflexive subject that creates a specific type of social totality. On the other hand, *Capital* is also a socio-historically specific account of nineteenth-century English capitalism. Although the totalizing dynamic may be characteristic of any society in which there is a money equivalent, commodity production and exchange have been generalized, and labor is a commodity, Marx abstracted his formulation of capital from specifically English economic data and institutions—as, for example, with the specific forms of land rent and finance analyzed in volume 3. If we situate England within a global system of production, circulation, and consumption (Arrighi 1994; Frank 1998), globalization can be seen as the process of the integration and differentiation of multiple, alternative, and competing capitalisms, each subject to specific local, regional, and historical contingencies.

The globalization of capitalism builds upon and transforms preexisting global circulations and, with the decline of colonial regimes and empires, increasingly expresses itself as a competition between national capitalist economies whose strength is represented by their currencies. The end of Bretton Woods effectively decoupled national identifications (e.g., the U.S. dollar) from a fixed, universal equivalent in gold. Pegged exchange rates became increasingly difficult to maintain in a period of capital mobility inaugurated by the huge productivity gains and trading surpluses of countries such as Germany and Japan.

Of course, floating currencies introduced a new level of risk into the system, and it was within this newly volatile environment that currency derivatives began to play an increasingly important role as hedges, as the explosion in their use indicates. However, Marx's analysis affords no place for these new financial instruments. Derivatives would be valueless in his scheme, since they "derive" their monetary worth from assets that Marx had already located in the sphere of the distribution of surplus value rather than in production. But the fact is that the value of derivatives is created by their expiration at a fixed date—they could be said to "punctuate" the temporality implicit in their underlying assets—and as such they correspond to a metatemporal level. Within the speculative uses of derivatives, there develops an internal dynamic of competition, but the temporal measure appears to be the inverse of Marx's formulation of abstract labor time, which holds that more time expended produces more value. Instead, the invention of increasingly complex derivatives, the secrecy surrounding them, and the development of speculative strategies specifically designed to take advantage of arbitrage opportunities that quickly close as they become known (see Lowenstein 2000 for an account of strategies pursued by the firm Long-Term Capital Management) generate an internal dynamic that exhibits many of the characteristics of the treadmill effect of abstract labor time—but now in the sphere of "value-free" circulation.

In their hedged uses, currency derivatives can reduce risk by locking in a fixed exchange rate over a specific time period, thereby stabilizing costs for raw materials and other commodities. Though such currency fluctuations may be rather small in absolute terms, the enormous leverage provided by options such as these allows these fluctuations to be multiplied many times over and thus worth speculating on (in the case of Long-Term Capital Management, the leverage ratios exceeded 100 to 1). Currency hedging reduces individual risk by sharing and redistributing that risk, thereby increasing the convertibility and global mobility of capital. In fact, what is increasingly "objectified" in both hedged and speculative uses of derivatives is nothing other than risk itself.

Is there anything in the nature of derivatives that corresponds to value or abstract labor time and that might have a corresponding dynamic? A possible answer seems to lie in the aforementioned Black-Scholes equations, which are used to price derivatives. Formulated by the economists Fischer Black and Myron Scholes in 1973, these equations provide the standard method for pricing the relations between risk and temporality. Key factors in the formula are the asset price, the strike price, the risk-free interest rate, the time to expiration, and the volatility of the stock price. *Volatility* is a measure of the uncertainty of the returns provided by the stock: the greater the chances of the underlying stock or asset moving higher or lower over the time period of the option, the higher the price of the option. Volatility is thus a measure of risk, and derivatives can be used to control this risk through hedging or speculating on it using the leverage enabled by the fact of their expiration.

The fixed expirations of derivatives create a close-ended metatemporal level with respect to the more open-ended temporality of the underlying assets that also makes possible the leverage necessary for hedging and speculation. Currency hedging enhances the intertranslatability of currencies and capitals, while speculative practices increase both the quantity and velocity of the capital produced and a concomitant demand for its mobility. Increasing the mobility of capitals requires their interconvertibility, which in turn increases the need for hedging. In short, the structure of derivatives creates a break with the classic relationship between finance capital and value proposed by Marx; derivatives allow circulation to have a self-reflexive dynamic that parallels that of value but is distinct from it. Postone's image of the treadmill is applicable to this new dynamic that comes to characterize finance capital: a dynamic of constant expansion, in which labor's place is taken by risk.

Self-Reflexivity, Circulation, and Exchange

We can now begin to see how self-reflexivity, circulation, and exchange interact to create different types of collective agency. In social economies based on exchange and gifts, figurations of collective agency combining first-person (we) and third-person (discrete groups' proper names) designations may identify particular exchanging groups within the totality constituted by exchange, but there is no objectified "economic" surplus; nor is there an objectified limit to sociality, a boundary for the production of social totality. In classic social contract models, the existence of an objectified surplus within a self-limiting social entity provides the resources for collective identification. Yet almost all of these models are founded on concepts of communities of transacting individuals who alienate their property through the process of exchange—a distant cry from the types of societies that have dominated the anthropological literature.

The notion of exchange deployed in modern contract theory stands in relation to that of noncapitalist economies as the commodity form does to gifts. The creation of transcendent collective agencies built around homogeneous cores (essentialized notions of language and ethnicity) excludes other societies—even as international trade between them grows. If the first imaginings of the nation required the global circulation of printed material, the spread of print capitalism relied no less on a host of financial inventions: the joint stock company, double-entry bookkeeping, letters of credit, cost-benefit analysis, and corporate bonds, not to mention the modern transnational corporation (Poovey 1998; Arrighi 1994). By the end of the nineteenth century, the statistical enumeration of national populations (the first national U.S. census was held in 1790 for the purpose of determining the electorate and became a model for future statistical surveys) had come together with modern economic science to create the idea of competing national economies. If we trace the concept of modern collective agency from its origins in the American and the French Revolutions, through German idealism, Marx emerges as a crucial figure in linking mathematically measurable economic categories with the construction of a notion of social totality: in

Marx, capital as abstract labor time replaces Hegel's *Geist* as the subject of history (Postone 1993). Though now presupposed in academic and public discussion of social or economic policy, the statistical elaboration of social categories is a relatively new phenomenon; from a cultural and historical standpoint, the very separation of economics and culture (or the concomitant figuration of culture as rational choice writ large) can be seen to depend on the idea that social phenomena, such as class, race, and ethnicity, are statistical in nature—an idea that is itself the product of a long, historically contingent development (Hacking 1975; Stigler 1986).

Marx joined two hitherto separate lines of argument. The first was the idea of the economy as an autonomous, self-regulating system; the second was that of social contract theory and its arguments about social totality. In his inversion of Hegel, Marx posits a new relation among circulation, exchange, and self-reflexivity in which an objectified third-person structure of exchange—created by *price*—is embedded within a larger, self-reflexively constituted "subject," or *value*. This structure relies on a dynamic tension between price and value and occupies a sociohistorically specific conjunction among labor, exchange, and objectified forms of economic and mathematical calculation. Seen from a larger historical perspective, Marx's ethnography of capitalism uncovers a self-propelling treadmill structure to capital that manifests itself in different permutations in different societies; globalization is the process of the integration and differentiation of competing and alternative capitalisms by this dynamic. The contemporary decline of the nation-state as the relevant unit of analysis for global capitalism is reflected in two distinct circulatory movements: the increasingly transnational character of labor and the global mobility of finance capital.

With the acceleration of the mobility of capital by new communications technology (brought about, in no small part, by the mobilization of much capital to accelerate technology) and the invention of complex derivative structures (which represent, in no small part, capital's adjustment to new technology), the leading edge of capitalism is no longer the mediation of production by labor, but rather the expansion of finance capital. Capitalist social relations are no longer only mediated by labor, but also by risk. For these new financial instruments assume that particular forms of risk, no matter how incompatible or historically independent (e.g., that a software program will gain end-user acceptance *and* that corporate interest rates will remain steady during the introductory phase of its marketing), can be aggregated as an abstract form, determinable by mathematical calculation; combined within a single derivative; and then distributed to speculators, many of whom have collateralized their payment by making other wagers in the reverse direction (arbitrage). The circulation and redistribution of risk is also accentuated by the fact that corporate entities have a fiduciary responsibility not to assume their own risk with respect to capital and its monetized circulations.

The demise of the gold standard revealed the existence of multiple and competing capitalisms, as represented by the floating of national currencies against one another. The development of complex derivatives to hedge the risk of floating currencies has enhanced the intertranslatability of different finance capitals, increasing their mobility and expansion at the same time that their sale and speculative use create ever-expanding pools of finance capital. Just as the genesis of the modern social imaginaries of the nation, the public sphere, and the market was accompanied by the progressive creation of institutions such as national banks, which effectively extinguished local forms of money by establishing national currencies, and Security and Exchange Commissions, which in like fashion extinguished local forms of stock certification—so, too, the (post)modern transformation of social imaginaries is being accompanied by the emergence of intertranslatable transnational forms.

The metatemporal structure of derivatives marks a significant break with the temporalities of production that lie at the center of Marx's analysis of capital. It produces the leverage that makes the speculative uses of these instruments possible. Yet it is these very uses that increase the contradiction between value and wealth and have produced a situation in which it seems increasingly impossible to see how, even in the final instance, *value* could determine *price*. If productive labor once constituted the "reality" of the economy, in the age of finance and speculative capital it seems that instead of the economy driving the markets, the markets are driving the economy.

Circulating a Conclusion

The contemporary processes of globalization demonstrate that capitalism, in its cycles of creative destruction and resurrection, has again reinvented itself. It is in transition from a production-centric system to one whose primary dynamic is circulation. The process is occurring with unprecedented speed—an acceleration that is intrinsic to this reinvention. Marx's findings were developed in an age of industrial capitalism; simply to apply them to contemporary conditions is to leave an increasing inventory of events, phenomena, and socioeconomic relations unaccounted for. Derivatives, especially those having to do with currency exchanges, are one of a number of powerful examples that demonstrate the ascendance of these new structures of circulation. Production-based labor—the combining of materials, machines, and workers to produce commodities—is being displaced and dispersed. The labor that increasingly drives the system today is of a sort that has no value in a strictly production-based account.

Production-driven competition harnessed technological innovation as the integral mechanism for driving capital; a circulation-based capitalism harnesses technology for the extraction and manipulation of data that can then be converted into quantifiable measures of risk. The contemporary objectification, calculation, and distribution of risk rely on larger and more accurate data sets and increased computer power, all driven by competition among mathematically sophisticated quantitative experts. This is tightening the relation between technology and the "value-free" development of finance capital. These new information technologies demand a deep infrastructure of technology and talent, a development that is resulting in a global rush for technological training and education paralleling the expansion of global equity markets. On a broader canvas, global inequalities in access to information are also increasing asymmetries of knowledge and control over the economic forces directly affecting societies. There are considerable gaps in the distribution of expertise about these complicated new financial instruments; one of the contributing factors in the Asian currency crisis of 1997 was the lack of currency hedging in several Southeast Asian countries, which—when combined with the lack of restrictions on short-term capital flows—accentuated the severity, rapidity, and depth of the crisis. Since the fall of Bretton Woods, the vast majority of currency crises have occurred outside the G-10 (Group of Ten) countries; the catastrophic effects of the 1997 Asian crisis indicate that there are new forms of transnational violence that are now beyond the control of any single nation-state or government.

The advent of circulation-based capitalism, along with the social forms and technologies that complement it, signifies more than a shift in emphasis. It constitutes a new stage in the history of capitalism, in which the national capitalisms that were created from the seventeenth century through the concluding decades of the twentieth are being simultaneously dismantled and reconstructed on a global scale. The effect is to subordinate and eventually efface historically discrete cultures and capitalisms and to create a unified cosmopolitan culture of unimpeded circulation. The striving toward totality that has always characterized capitalism, and set it apart from pre- or noncapitalist exchange, has gone global in a way that is not imaginable from the perspectives of the imaginaries of the citizen-state and the national public sphere. There is here a process of the encompassment of others that is the successor of colonialism and other historical forms of domination—the simultaneous advent and intervention of something entirely new.

Semiotic analyses that fixate exclusively on cultural forms are inherently inadequate because the issue of capital cannot be ignored or bracketed. The same holds for traditional Marxist accounts that locate their social understanding in production-based capitalism and the surface form of the market. To hold fast to either model, ignoring the emergence of circulation, is to deny the leading role of finance capital in creating a transnational capitalism. Any contemporary account, to succeed, will have to theorize and thematize the historical transition we are undergoing: from production-centric capitalisms linked to modern social imaginaries privileging the nation-state, which seek to encompass rival capitalisms through the extension of production-based capitalism—to the emergent circulation-based capitalism and its concomitant, a transformed set of social imaginaries that privileges a global totality as it produces new forms of risk that may destroy it.

Benjamin Lee is co-director of the Center for Transcultural Studies and a professor of anthropology at Rice University. **Edward LiPuma** is a professor of anthropology and director of the Center for Social and Cultural Studies at the University of Miami and the author of *Encompassing Others: The Magic of Modernity in Melanesia* (2000). Currently they are working on a book manuscript titled "The Cultures of Circulation."

References

Anderson, Benedict. 1991. *Imagined communities: Reflections on the origin and spread of nationalism.* London: Verso.

Appadurai, Arjun. 1996. *Modernity at large: Cultural dimensions of globalization.* Minneapolis: University of Minnesota Press.

———, ed. 2000. *Globalization.* Special issue, *Public Culture* 12.

Arrighi, Giovanni. 1994. *The long twentieth century: Money, power, and the origins of our times.* London: Verso.

Bakhtin, Mikhail. 1984. *Problems of Dostoevsky's poetics,* translated and edited by Caryl Emerson. Minneapolis: University of Minnesota Press.

Benveniste, Emile. 1971. *Problems in general linguistics,* translated by M. Meek. Coral Gables, Fla.: University of Miami Press.

Black, Fischer, and Myron Scholes. 1973. The pricing of options and corporate liabilities. *Journal of Political Economy* 81: 637–54.

Bourdieu, Pierre. 1977. *Outline of a theory of practice,* translated by Richard Nice. Cambridge: Cambridge University Press.

Derrida, Jacques. 1992. *Given time. I, counterfeit money*, translated by Peggy Kamuf. Chicago: University of Chicago Press.

Dumont, Louis. 1977. *From Mandeville to Marx: The genesis and triumph of economic ideology*. Chicago: University of Chicago Press.

Frank, Andre Gunder. 1998. *Re-orient: Global economy in the Asian Age*. Berkeley: University of California Press.

Gaonkar, Dilip Parameshwar, ed. 1999. *Alter/native modernities*. Special issue, *Public Culture* 11.

Habermas, Jürgen. 1989. *The structural transformation of the public sphere: An inquiry into a category of bourgeois society*, translated by Thomas Burger with Frederick Lawrence. Cambridge: MIT Press.

Hacking, Ian. 1975. *The emergence of probability: A philosophical study of early ideas about probability, induction, and statistical inference*. Cambridge: Cambridge University Press.

Harvey, David. 1982. *The limits to capital*. Oxford: Blackwell.

Hegel, Georg Wilhelm Friedrich. 1989. *Science of logic*, translated by Arnold V. Miller. Atlantic Highlands, N.J.: Humanities Press.

Hyppolite, Jean. 1969. *Studies on Marx and Hegel*. New York: Basic Books.

Lévi-Strauss, Claude. 1969. *The elementary structures of kinship*, translated by James Harle Bell. London: Eyre and Spottiswoode.

LiPuma, Edward. 2000. *Encompassing others: The magic of modernity in Melanesia*. Ann Arbor: University of Michigan Press.

LiPuma, Edward, and Moishe Postone. N.d. *Gifts, commodities, and the encompassment of others*. Forthcoming.

Lowenstein, Roger. 2000. *When genius failed: The rise and fall of Long-Term Capital Management*. New York: Random House.

Malinowski, Bronislaw. 1966. *Argonauts of the western Pacific: An account of native enterprise and adventure in the archipelagoes of Melanesian New Guinea*. London: Routledge and Kegan Paul.

Marx, Karl. 1976. *Capital: A critique of political economy*, vol. 1, translated by Ben Fowkes. New York: Vintage.

Mauss, Marcel. 1967. *The gift: Forms and functions of exchange in archaic societies*, translated by Ian Cunnison. New York: Norton.

Peirce, Charles Sanders. 1960. *The collected papers of Charles Sanders Peirce*, vol. 8, edited by Charles Hartshorne and Paul Weiss. Cambridge, Mass.: Belknap.

Poovey, Mary. 1998. *A history of the modern fact: Problems of knowledge in the sciences of wealth and society*. Chicago: University of Chicago Press.

Postone, Moishe. 1993. *Labor, time, and social domination: A reinterpretation of Marx's critical theory*. Cambridge: Cambridge University Press.

Sahlins, Marshall. 1972. *Stone Age economics*. Chicago: Aldine-Atherton.

Silverstein, Michael. 2000. Language philosophy as language ideology: John Locke and Johann Gottfried Herder. In *Regimes of language*, edited by P. Kroskrity. Santa Fe, N.M.: School of American Research Press.

Soros, George. 1995. *Soros on Soros: Staying ahead of the curve*. New York: John Wiley and Sons.

Stigler, Stephen M. 1986. *The history of statistics: The measurement of uncertainty before 1900*. Cambridge: Harvard University Press.

Tambiah, Stanley Jeyaraja. 1985. *Culture, thought, and social action: An anthropological perspective*. Cambridge: Harvard University Press.

Urban, Gregory. 1996. *Metaphysical community: The interplay of the senses and the intellect*. Austin: University of Texas Press.

Weiner, Annette. 1992. *Inalienable possessions: The paradox of keeping-while-giving*. Berkeley: University of California Press.

Notes on Gridlock:
Genealogy, Intimacy, Sexuality

Elizabeth A. Povinelli

We're tired of trees. We should stop believing in trees, roots, and radicals.
They've made us suffer too much. . . . Thought is not arborescent, and the
brain is not a rooted or ramified matter.

Gilles Deleuze and Felix Guattari,
A Thousand Plateaus: Capitalism and Schizophrenia

W hy does the recognition of peoples' worth, of their human and civil rights, always seem to be hanging on the more or less fragile branches of a family tree? Why must we be held by these limbs?

The two archives prompting this meditation are not new to me or to anyone else. Moreover, the social worlds and visions of these two archives are, geographically speaking, worlds apart. Stacks of land claim documents sit to the left of me. Some of these documents concern an Australian indigenous claim I am currently working on. Others compose the archives of claims already heard that I hope to use as a precedent for what I am trying to argue in the current case. All of them demand a diagram of a "local descent group." That is what I am doing right now, drawing a genealogical diagram, a family tree, using now-standard icons for sex and sexual relationship: a diamond represents a man; a circle, a woman; an upside-down staple, sibling relations; a right-side-up staple, marriage; and a small perpendicular line between these two staples, heterosexual reproduction.

The book I am currently reading, *Family Values: Two Moms and Their Son*, lies to the right of me. *Family Values* is a first-person account of the radicalization

Public Culture 14(1): 215–238

of a lesbian mother as she fights to adopt her partner's son. The author, Phyllis Burke (1993: 6), figures lesbian motherhood in terms of a morbid chiasma: "Eight thousand gay men were prematurely dead in San Francisco by the time Jesse [Burke's son] was two, and yet behind what was almost a shadowy membrane there was a lesbian baby boom. Lesbians were giving birth, adopting children, and building families with gay men" (see also Lewin 1993). As I read across these texts I remember a T-shirt that the Society for Lesbian and Gay Anthropologists (SOLGA) printed a few years ago. It schematically represents gay families with the same kinship iconography I am using in these land claims. When I finish *Family Values*, I plan to reread *Querelle*, Jean Genet's (1974: 4) tale about a "sailor's mortal flesh," about the sea, murder, and criminality, and about love against nature. The values in *Querelle* are hardly about the families gay men build. Whenever I read Genet I think of Alexandre Kojeve's (1969: 6) carnal description of human desire: "Man 'feeds' on Desires as an animal feeds on real things. And the human I, realized by the active satisfaction of its human Desires, is as much a function of its 'food' as the body of an animal is of its food."

Clear differences separate the two family archives in which I am immersed. The family diagrams I am drafting for the land claim do not indicate the love, desire, affect, or intimacy that exist between indigenous persons reproductively related. Nor do they document nonsexual corporeal relations. There is no standard icon for "intimacy," "desire," or "love." What makes these indigenous families felicitous in law is the principle of descent that regiments them (e.g., patrilineality, matrilineality). In contrast, Burke argues that true families and just nations are made by love—not by laws of adoption and descent or social, sexual, and gender status. Can Genet's vision of a world of sailors take root in this queer kinship?

What follows are notes on how we might examine the presuppositions and global circulations of what I call genealogical and intimacy grids, some suggestions about their connectivities and irreducibilities, and a few comments on the social worlds made possible and interrupted by their functionings. Why are these the grids that appear across such diverse social and geographical spaces in the public struggle for recognition? How are they distributed across different populations in such a way that I can make sense of the two archives staring at me today? How, in their seeming oppositionality, have they more effectively colonized social imaginaries and territorialized regional social worlds? This essay looks at how these grids have made possible not only the thinking of sex acts as legitimate social acts, but also the restricting and recirculating of the imagination of a counterethics of national and everyday life. The end of this exercise is not the essay itself. The larger goal is to understand: the presuppositions of global forms of felicitous sexual activity, the history of these presuppositions' emergence, and the distribution of them across specific social groups.

Genealogical Grids

From the perspective of their roots, genealogical trees have been moving with Europeans for a very long time. The size and characteristics of these European trees, and how they may be legitimately planted, have changed dramatically as marriage reforms progressed from the fifteenth century onward, and as new market and civil forms displaced blood and rank as the defining grid of power and sociality (Goody 1983; Plakans 1984; Macfarlane 1986). The causal history of this transformation is well rehearsed, albeit in competing versions (Foucault 1980; Habermas 1989; Taylor, in this issue). Humanity as a concept was slowly freed from the grip of familial kinship, descent, and rank; and as a concept and practice it came to define emergent modern social orders. Membership in an abstract human order, rather than in a family (aristocratic) grid, increasingly defined civil, social, and political rights and obligations. As opposed to the social solidarity premised on a genealogical grid, the European diaspora seemed increasingly bent on stranger-sociability.

Of particular importance to this essay, for reasons indicated below, is the function that a specific characterization of nature played in disembedding the individuated human from his or her social role, function, and status. The infamous state of nature: Charles Taylor (in this issue) points to the role Hugo Grotius and John Locke played in producing a disembedded individual by projecting the individual against a natural world stripped of all social encumbrances. The meaning and use of this conceptual move continued to echo in the eighteenth century. Adam Smith (1976: 140–1), for instance, thought that people should not observe each other from the point of view of "something separate and detached" but as "Man . . . citizens of the world," made equal by being projected against "the vast commonwealth of nature."

I am not so interested here in whether this abstract individual emerged from new forms of market circulation ("the traffic in commodities and news"[1]) that broke down previous forms of social organization or from the migration of theoretical imaginings into broader social imaginings. Instead, I am interested in the alleyways of this progress narrative, in a set of genealogical intensions and extensions inside and outside Europe that accompanied the emergence of the individualized human and its polity. For instance, inside Europe the genealogical grid

1. Habermas 1989: 15.

did not simply disappear as a means of governmentality; rather it was imaginatively reduced, regrounded, and dispersed. For one thing, it is clear that citizenship continues to have a strong genealogical component in many nation-states (birth in the national body gives persons citizenship rights that then descend genealogically). Moreover, though the political relevance of family trees was narrowed and relocated, their social relevance was in fact democratized and dispersed into the life-world of ordinary people and the seams of homogenous national space-time (Anderson 1991).

We could argue that, in being democratized, the genealogical grid has become more vital and real to the political order, whether it is attacked or defended. Certainly, the genealogical grid ceased to function as a broadcast model in which concentric circles of genealogical ranks and associations radiated from the apical crown. Polity no longer unfolded out of the (fictive) ranked affiliations of the people from the point of view of the sovereign family. But now everyone could have a little heritage of his or her own—diagrammed as a personal tree—a stake in some plot that tracked generationally. And, remember, though a petite cosmology, the genealogical grid now organizes democratic state dispensations like inheritance, marriage, child welfare, and capital gains. And not only does it organize the distribution of material goods within each of these agencies, the genealogical grid also provides a mode of translation among them. Genealogy allows governments and social agencies to coordinate people across social practices (e.g., the regulatory fields of inheritance and welfare). Moreover, though the linkage between family and cosmology is of a very different order from that experienced by Duncan in Shakespeare's *Macbeth*, many Christian fundamentalists believe the connection to be as tight.

In its reduced and dispersed form, however, the genealogical grid that operates as the presupposition of national life is not the same grid that operated prior to the seventeenth century. Here Jacques Le Goff's (1989) discussion of the king's body and Jürgen Habermas's (1989) discussion of intimacy—"saturated and free interiority"—are crucial (see also Landes 1988 and Berlant 1997). The aristocratic genealogy was rich in distinctions of rank, role, and kinship that both ordered persons and allowed them multiple avenues for contestation, elaboration, and negotiation. The genealogical grid inherited by market society was only unevenly deracinated from social status and rearticulated to *humanity*, a term intended to suggest equivalence. Questions about the internal dynamic of hierarchy within the new bourgeois family arose almost immediately, as did questions about the grounds for building these new families. What forms of subordination should extend out of the reduced differences among men and women, parents and children? What could—and should—be the presuppositional grounds for forming these petite genealogies if not the social or religious status of the contracting members? Who should be included and excluded from the ranks of blood and money, property and inheritance, love and affection, and sex?

The emergence of democratic genealogies in the eighteenth and nineteenth centuries and debates about what could serve as their legitimate foundations do not provide the history of the genealogical grid, nor even the interior history of Western elaborations of their own genealogical imagination. Dynamic transpositions between old regimes of genealogy and new regimes of citizenship occurred in colonial and European worlds. Both of these worlds ramified into European conceptualizations of their own genea-

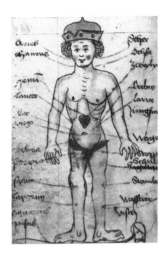

logical systems. Here we return to the complex and uneven deployment of the state of nature in Western social theory. Though the state of nature was originally the empty backdrop against which seventeenth-century legal theorists abstracted persons from all social relations of superiority and inferiority, eventually the state of nature was recollapsed into a genealogical grid through the mediating function of savage society. When applied to so-called savage societies, the state of nature was no longer empty. The savage slot, as Michel-Rolph Trouillot (1991) has called it, was identified as coterminous with nature. In other words, subjects of empire provided the site in which a family, a sexual form, and a governmentality based on them were naturalized. The social organization projected into this new state of nature was soon said to be dependent on the relations of superiority and inferiority projected out of "the elementary fam-

Figures 1 and 2
The king's body; the social body.

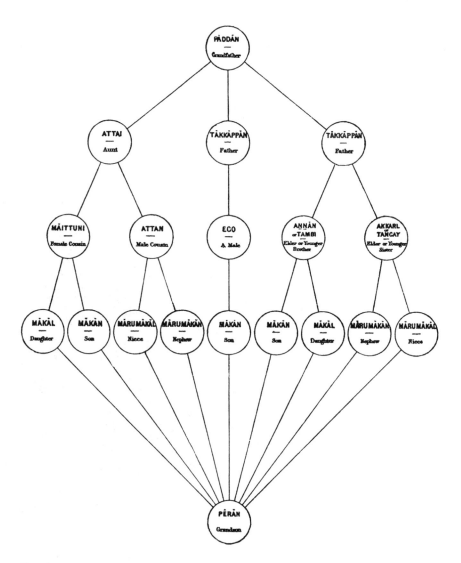

Figure 3
The imperial body.

ily" (Radcliffe-Brown 1965). Two histories need to be told in relation to these developments: one to examine the theoretical elaboration of human society as a divide between descriptive (real) and classificatory kinship societies and subsequent rewritings of the state of the state of nature, the other to examine the dissemination of the genealogical grid with empire, and the resulting territorializations and reterritorializations of metropole and colony. Let me sketch the contours of these two histories.

> Mr. G. F. Bridgman's native servant, before mentioned, who had travelled far and wide throughout Australia, told him that he was furnished with temporary wives by the various tribes with whom he sojourned in his travels; that his right to those women was recognized as a matter of course; and that he could always ascertain whether they belonged to the division into which he could legally marry, "though the places were 1000 miles apart, and the languages quite different." Many pages might be filled with similar testimony. (Fison and Howitt 1991: 53–54)

In Lorimer Fison and A. W. Howitt's slightly overheated reports, an infinitely extendable collectivity of possible female sexual partners exists for male indigenous Australians not because indigenous groups lacked orderly social relations ("marriage classes") but because the entire world was enclosed within them. So Fison and Howitt famously described the endless horizon of kinship and marriage in savage epistemology.

Kant's question of governance (How should we be governed once detached from the tutelage of social rank?) developed an imperial form: How are societies functionally held together and reproduced without the formal structures of government? In 1871, Lewis Henry Morgan, a lawyer from New York, published an account of how colonial societies ordered and reproduced themselves. Morgan began with the already deracinated ego: "Around every person there is a circle or group of kindred of which such person is the centre, the Ego, from which the degree of the relationship is reckoned, and to whom the relationship itself returns" (10). There were "but two radically distinct forms of consanguinity." On the one hand were descriptive systems, such as "the Aryan, Semitic, and Uralian families." This system recognized only the "primary terms of relationship . . . which are those for husband and wife, father and mother, brother and sister, and son and daughter, to which must be added, in such languages as possess them, grandfather, grandmother, and grandson and granddaugh-

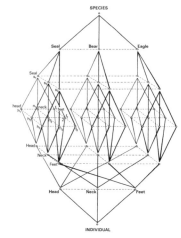

Figure 4
The totemic body.

ter. . . . Each relationship is thus made independent and distinct from every other."
On the other hand were the classificatory systems of consanguinity, such as the
Turanian, American Indian, and Malayan families. These rejected "descriptive
phrase in every instance, and reducing consanguinei to great classes by a series
of apparently arbitrary generalizations, [applied] the same terms to all the members of the same class. It thus confounds relationships, which, under the descriptive system, are distinct, and enlarges the signification both of the primary and
secondary terms beyond their seemingly appropriate sense" (12). In her 1989
Lewis H. Morgan lectures, Marilyn Strathern noted that Morgan's vision was
critical to the collapse of the state of nature into the state of colonial societies:
"Morgan conceived the contrast as between those closer to and more distant
from nature. . . . Indeed the draft opening chapter of *Systems of Consanguinity*
referred to family relationship existing in nature independently of human creation" (1992: 16; see also Fortes 1969 and Kuper 1988).

The comparative study of kinship was revitalized and made the foundation of
the emergent science of anthropology, when, in 1910, the British psychologist
W. H. R. Rivers announced a major methodological breakthrough in the study of
"savage" societies. Shortly after returning from a collaborative study of the Torres Strait Islanders off northeast Australia, Rivers announced new procedures for
collecting and analyzing data that allowed the scientific study of man to move
beyond conjectural history. Rivers recommended the genealogical method to the
emergent anthropological community on the basis of its simplicity and the minimal impact local systems of meaning would make on the collection of social data.
Rendered into its reduced modern and democratic form, the genealogical grid's
utility to social science was clear. A couple of assumptions about human beings

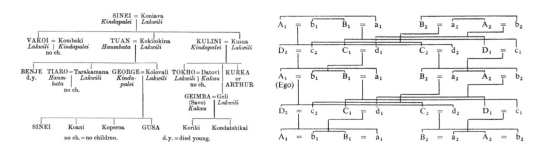

Figures 5 and 6
The genealogical body; the structural body.

(sex difference and heterosexual reproduction), assumptions that could be claimed to be the universal preconditions of human life, provided just enough structure for the maximal comparison among societies.[2] The comparative reach, the territorial possibilities of this new demographic method, stretched as far as the British Empire.

What was initially a research method soon became a full-fledged social theory, as Rivers's student, A. R. Radcliffe-Brown, transformed a tool for generating social data into a theory of the generative structure of social systems. Harking back to Morgan, Radcliffe-Brown posited that genealogy (kinship and affinity) provided the structural principle out of which a social system unfolded, operated, and was reproduced.

> The existence of the elementary family creates three special kinds of
> social relationship, that between parent and child, that between children
> of the same parents (siblings), and that between the husband and wife as
> parents of the same child or children. A person is born or adopted into a
> family in which he or she is son or daughter and brother or sister. When a
> man marries and has children he now belongs to a second elementary
> family, in which he is husband and father. This interlocking of elementary
> families creates a network of what I call, for lack of any better term,
> genealogical relations, spreading out indefinitely. . . . In any given society
> a certain number of these relationships are recognised for social purposes,
> i.e. they have attached to them certain rights and duties, or certain distinc-
> tive modes of behavior. (Radcliffe-Brown 1965: 51–52)

All the great and small societies of Africa, Australia, and the Americas provided clear demonstrations of the social elaborations of the "elementary family," a structure presupposing the same two principles: sex difference and heterosexual reproduction. These two principles provided the minimal dual pairs out of which all other social differences, such as rank, status, and duty, were built. Both principles had to be in play for a family to exist as such. Thus a childless couple fell off the genealogical grid for Radcliffe-Brown—just as they sometimes do in contemporary land claim practices in Australia, where consanguineous ancestors who did not reproduce are often left off the genealogies, for clarity's sake.

2. Rivers (1910: 1) writes:

The first point to be attended to is that, owing to the great difference between the systems of relationship of savage and civilised peoples, it is desirable to use as few terms denoting kinship as possible, and complete pedigrees can be obtained when the terms are limited to the following: father, mother, child, husband and wife.

In *The Elementary Structures of Kinship* (1969), dedicated to Lewis H. Morgan, Claude Lévi-Strauss goes one step further, seemingly decapitating the sovereign subject from the logic of kinship. Kinship systems were not projections out of the elementary family or the sovereign ego, but out of a deeper structural semantics of restricted exchange. Indeed, Lévi-Strauss transformed the possibility of associating the human being and natural being ("the state of nature") by arguing that the human existed not prior to but alongside kinship. Humanity and kinship, culture and nature, emerged as such in the transformation, or transition, marked by the advent of the first rule of exchange, first announced in a negative form: the prohibition of incest. This rule of rules is, of course, dependent on another: a "deep polygamous tendency, which exists in all men," which "always makes the number of available women seem insufficient" (38). Homosexuality, polyandry, and wife swapping were immediately transformed into solutions to the seeming scarcity of women. More social forms and relations fell off the grid or were recast as mere by-products of its logic, as the atom of kinship and the very nature of culture emerged as the dialectic of binary exchanges that constituted I and thou; man and woman; parent and child; and wife-givers and -takers.

Of course, this short overview simplifies the more complicated history of genealogy theory in the social sciences. The French schools argued with the British over generality and comparison (see, for instance, Leach 1966: 2). And in the United States, a generation of scholars argued heatedly whether kinship was a cultural category or whether it reflected a human universal—each proposition controversial in some way or another (Schneider 1968; Scheffler 2001; Strathern 1992; Collier and Yanagisako 1987). With every new argument, the interior complexity of the genealogical grid intensified. Indeed, building careers was one of the means by which the genealogical imaginary was elaborated and spread. New discursive contours, possibilities, and lines of flight emerged. And, insofar as scholars struggled to characterize the essential properties that determined the applicability of the genealogical grid, they cast the grid itself into the background.

Alongside this analysis of the theoretical intensions and extensions within the Western academy, we need an analysis of how the genealogical grid was inlaid into and diversified by the life-worlds of colonial subjects. Here we can return to the first of the two cases prompting my reflections in this essay. All the land claim documents I am shuffling through contain a description of the genealogical principles by which Australian indigenous persons are recruited into the "local descent group" said to own the land. The Australian Parliament and courts demand that indigenous people present some principle of descent as the grounds for a successful land claim. They do not demand any specific principle of descent. They simply demand descent, typically understood as "a relationship defined by connection to an ancestor (or ancestors) through a culturally recognized sequence of parent-child links" (Keesing 1975: 148; see also Sutton 1998). It is also generally understood that the relationships defined by these parent-child links provide the presuppositional grounds for a number of other social relations, such as property, affect, and ritual. Culture is conceived as an incrustation on the parent-child link. What, if any, presuppositions ground the self-evident social fact of the parent-child link is not typically discussed (that is, rarely does anyone query the universal application of the parent-child connection).

Putting aside this problem for now, we find an impressive variety of principles of descent that indigenous people and anthropologists have presented to the courts as local principles of social recruitment. Indeed, it is a lesson in the power of generative grammar, itself an analogical extension of the family tree. Based on nothing more than two assumptions—sex difference and heterosexual reproduction—anthropologists have introduced a range of descent models beyond the patrilineal clan, originally the only model of descent recognized as traditional by land commissioners and many anthropologists. Over the course of twenty-six years of land claim hearings, the tree has grown many branches: cognatic, ambilineal, patrilineal with one-step matrifiliation, matrilineal with one-step patrifiliation. Diversity in the content of the genealogical grammar is supported and sanctified by one influential strand of legal interpretation. In paragraph 89 of his 1982 report on the Finniss River Land Claim, Toohey J. stated that the land commissioner should base an understanding of recruitment into a local descent group "on a principle of descent deemed relevant by the claimants," not on anthropological theory or debate. The words *local*, *descent*, and *group* should be considered ordinary English words rather than anthropological terms. Of course, they have to be considered; that is, making the meaning of "local descent group" local did not relieve locals from the demand that they give these terms meaning. Recognition has an implicit command structure. The third land commissioner, Michael Maurice, sanctified descent, arguing in paragraph 92 of the 1985 Timber Creek Land Claim report that "it is [the] religious bond with the world . . . that the Parliament has endeavored to recognize by its definition of traditional Aboriginal owner with its three elements: family ties to land; religious ties; and economic rights, i.e., to forage."

Recognizing the local meanings of the local descent group, of family, and

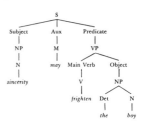

Figure 7

The linguistic body.

of family ties and the principles upon which they are constructed is one of the key means by which the genealogical grid is inlaid locally. Recognition connects the genealogical grid to simple human desires, such as the desire to live and be recognized as being worthy, to have personal and social value, and to reclaim lands once owned. The fulfillment of these large and small desires depends on the ability of indigenous people to produce a "descent group" recognizable as such by lawyers, land commissioners, and anthropologists. And insofar as they do, the law of recognition demonstrates the delicate processes by which local identities are constituted and mediated and the extraordinary delicacy with which local protocols for building and sustaining communities are displaced (see also Povinelli, in press).

But land claims were not the first forum in which the genealogical imaginary was localized. Before the *Aboriginal Land Rights (Northern Territory) Act 1976* was passed, other social practices like welfare and child care addressed colonial subjects through the genealogical imaginary and demanded a response in kind. And, not only were genealogical relations the presuppositional grounds for address, they were also the bureaucratic means by which administrators could coordinate colonial subjects. To be sure, the very nature of political administrative and scholarly practice, its open rather than closed structure, provided colonial subjects room to maneuver. For instance, administrative debates over social policy provided an opening through which subject populations could present countervisions of their social worlds. And, in the case of scholarly regimes, the conversation between ethnographer and subject often teetered between real and fictive dialogical partners. Nevertheless, the discursive protocols of asking, testing, and arguing about the difference between Western forms of genealogy and local practices of corporeality wove genealogical and nongenealogical modes of social organization firmly into the fabric of the possible (see also the exchange between Blowes and Secretary in Povinelli 1999).

Something else happened when Morgan projected European-based genealogical grids onto the empire. Insofar as colonial political and scholarly communities took advantage of differences the colony afforded to advance their own projects, a back draft was felt in the metropole. As Marilyn Strathern (1992) has noted, European forms of kinship and affinity could no longer be taken as singular or natural. They were simply a type of genealogical system, a type that was dissociated from the universal by queer forms of kinship. True, most kinship theorists distinguish between descriptive ("real") and classificatory kinship—from the nineteenth century onward. But the European heterosexual family became more explicitly theorized and politically elaborated as the core institution of the nation-state even while the genealogical surface of that family was being diversified. Eric Fassin's recent discussion of debates in France and the United States over the adoption of children by homosexual couples exemplifies this point, as does Kath Weston's ethnography, *Families We Choose* (Fassin 2001; Weston 1991). As Fassin relates, the French have grounded their arguments in Lévi-Straussian and Lacanian models of the linkage between the family, nature, and culture. But discussions about new reproductive technologies and kinship would do equally well (Franklin and Ragoné 1998; Ginsburg and Rapp 1995). In these new technologies, kinship and affinal relations proliferate, but this proliferation seems only to elaborate and more thoroughly disperse the genealogical grid. Indeed, we can hardly call kinship and affiliation a theory anymore, so thoroughly has it reterritorialized modern social life.

Intimacy Grids

Though saturated with intimations of the intimate sanctity that Aboriginal families share with their country, neither Maurice's commentaries nor those of any other land commissioner has concluded that the indigenous family is the result of anything more than an (un)conscious calculus of social inclusion and exclusion undertaken by indigenous people factoring their local principles of heterorelationality (kinship, affinity, and descent). Love does not make an indigenous family qua traditional family according to the Australian Parliament and the courts, nor do local notions of corporeality, proximity, affect, place, context, or spirituality. The Aboriginal family recognized by the Australian Parliament and courts as the basis of indigenous property is a typological projection of classic British structural-functional accounts of "kinship societies." The organization of social life is based on ever more elaborate extensions out of the elementary family (a man, his wife, and their children). The richness of indigenous social imaginations and practices arising out of local notions of the proximities and potencies of various bodies are not relevant to the state imaginaries informing material redistribution schemes. Indeed, practices and relations that fall off the genealogical grid receive very little attention in court hearings because they, like the nonreproductive ancestor, are thematized as irrelevant to the task at hand.

Although members of Australian courts and Parliament do not grant non-genealogical-based corporeal potencies a formative function in the making of indigenous social worlds, they nevertheless assume that social life depends on the exchange of intimate forms of recognition. The formative function of intimacy in state-based property negotiations reappears when we shift our focus away from what the courts recognize as the basis of an indigenous social order and toward what they presume is the basis of a just national order. At this level we see the rhetoric of recognition moving across juridical and public genres, filling the public sphere with calls for mutuality in cultural love, tolerance, intimacy, and understanding. We hear that the Australian nation is threatened by the interruption of mutual displays of cultural worth. The intimate recognition I am talking about here is not between an I and a Thou but between their abstracted plural counterparts: We-the-People distended from ourselves in being alienated from the best version of ourselves by You-the-Other.[3]

The constitutive character of intimate love in the formation of true families and just nations is, of course, a central debate within U.S. gay politics. The Australian case seems turned on its head: in mainstream America, it is said that love makes families elemental(ly). *Family Values*, for instance, hinges together family and nation through an argument about the value of intimate recognition. The dust jacket thematizes the story of *Family Values* as the threat posed to the nation by the denial of the fundamental role human love plays in family-formation (parent and child).

> Painfully aware of the fact that the law did not acknowledge her ties to the child she loved and helped raise like any other "natural" parent, Burke began adoption proceedings to win recognition as Jesse's second legal mother. The court's resistance to her request was a powerful blow to her ability to quietly endure the treatment lesbians and gays receive in mainstream society. Inspired by her love for and pride in her family, Burke, who had formerly been unnerved by the militant stance of gay activist groups like Queer Nation, now found their riotous tactics and "in your face" attitude a source of strength.

The limbs holding Burke and her family are the unexpected extensions of an army of love(rs). The polemic is fairly clear. State, public, and personal worth of a family should be based on the intimate recognition that occurs between two people, on the choice to love and the love that circulates through this choice. No matter that one of the major distinguishing features of modern intimacy is an expectation of a blurring of choice and compulsion in the context of love, of a

---

3. Note however that even this mode of address is fictional. In the public sphere of newspapers, talk shows, and government reportage, the Other is typically not addressed. Rather, the mode of address is oriented to the assumed and entailed We-the-People who beseech one another to incorporate or expel the nonperson plural They-the-Other. (The significance of the We-Them form is suggested by Benveniste 1971.)

dynamic among self-risk and self-elaboration, personal transcendence, and the fall back onto the self. Indeed, *love* thematizes and indicates the affective site where choice and compulsion are blurred. Still, *Family Values* and countless other public pronouncements in the United States make a similar argument. Love makes a family. And laws that stifle the natural connection between love and family by restricting reproductive technologies (with adoption as a legal reproductive technology) are therefore perverse and antidemocratic.

Of course, *Family Values* could easily be described as part of a conservative bent in American gaylesbian politics. Moreover, though it refers to gays and lesbians, the book does not capture the rich jargons, dialects, and speech genres characterizing contemporary gay and lesbian social life (much less the modern novel and some modern [auto]biographies). Genet offers a welcome alternative. The self-professed pied piper of criminality, Genet's goal never was "to gain entrance into your houses, your factories, your laws and holy sacraments, but to violate them"—and to help children violate them. Genet is well known in France for his support of the Algerian revolution, the PLO, and the Black Panther movement and, more generally, his anticolonial, antimilitary, and antiracist politics (Sartre 1964; White 1994; Le Sueur 2001). Still, for Genet, the act of love was not for self-recognition or for a pure relay of recognition with an other but for self-evacuation and self-murder through the murder of an other. A void created through the self-executing exercises of sexuality—this was the pure vision of Genet's sexuality. No surprise that it is difficult to produce a community out of Genet's work, or even a boatload of sailors. They just do not add up. Indeed, Genet's vision sometimes seems completely washed out of contemporary U.S. political discussions by the flood of discourse about whether it takes Adam and Eve to make a family or whether it just takes a little love.

Intimacy is not absent in *Querelle*. Reproduced throughout it are the private journal entries that Lieutenant Seblon of the *Vengeur* keeps on Georges Querelle, the protagonist of the book. These journal entries ache with the desire for intimacy. "I shall not know peace until he makes love to me, but only when he enters me and then lets me stretch out on my side across his thighs, holding me the way the dead Jesus is held in a pietà" (1974: 275). And yet Genet insists that Seblon is not "in the book." This claim is odd because we are reading selections from Seblon's journal, which Genet refers to as a book within the book, as a "book of prayers" and "meditations" on Querelle. There between the spines that signal the space of the book we find the soft pornographic interior of Lieutenant Seblon's languid stroll over Querelle's "muscles, his rounded parts, his teeth, his guessed-at genitals" (11). But Genet is careful to distinguish Seblon's mood from that of the other characters. "While the other characters are incapable of lyricism which we are using in order to recreate them more vividly within you, Lieutenant Seblon himself is solely responsible for what flows from his pen" (23). Seblon's lyricism, what could be wrong with that? Why does Genet write Seblon into *Querelle* only to deny him?

As we know, Habermas pivoted the rise of modern forms of the public sphere on the development and circulation of new forms of textually mediated intimate address, exemplified, in many ways, by the lyric genre. Intimacy came to mark a particular movement and elaboration of the deracinated ego in relation to a deracinated other. "From the beginning, the psychological interest increased in the dual relation to both one's self and the other: self-observation entered a union partly curious, partly sympathetic with the emotional stirrings of the other I. The diary became the letter addressed to the sender, and the first-person narrative became a conversation with one's self, addressed to another person. These were the experiments with the subjectivity discovered in the close relationships of the conjugal family" (Habermas 1989: 49). These experiments with subjectivity arose in the period when the grounds for building genealogy were detached from social status, rank, and religion. They provided a means, not of doing away with genealogy, but of hinging it onto emergent humanist narratives of the citizen/subject (the *I*) and his or her relationship to We-the-People. As a result, one of the questions that arose was: What could, and should, be the presuppositional foundations for forming petite genealogies once marriage on the basis of social, economic, or religious contracts was delegitimated? And one of the answers was: intimate recognition. *Intimate love* was the phrase used to refer to and entail the feelings associated with a person's worth based solely on his or her capacities and qualities as a human being. Eventually, *love* absorbed the semantics of *intimacy* and stood as if on its own, opposed to interested attachment, to use, to usury. To assert a bond of love was to assert simultaneously a rejection of social utility. And, simultaneously, nationalism absorbed the structures of this recognition: We-the-People emerged as a transposition and lifting-up (*Aufhebung*) of the dialectic of the intimate I and thou.

These experiments in subjectivity make specific narrative demands on the personal and national subject. We know some aspects of the form that modern intimacy demands. Intimacy, and personal sexual intimacy in particular, has come to be characterized by a form of pronominalized interiority. As numerous people have noted, the intimate interiority is characterized by a second-order critical reflexivity, by the *I* that emerges in the asking of the question, What do I feel toward you? In other words, the I who asks, What do I feel toward you? How do

I desire you? contours the intimate interior. Along with being a form of orientation and attachment, intimacy is the dialectic of this self-elaboration. Who am I in
relation to you?—this question and its cognates lift up a reflexive ego in the act
of asking and stitch it into the world of others. The question is a performative in
the strict sense. In the act of asking, Who am I? the I is constituted. This I and its
labor with an other provide the micropragmatic architecture out of which We-
the-People and other mass subjects unfold.[4] Indeed, the I of the modern self has
become so closely associated with this particular narrative form that challenges
to intimacy seriously threaten the modes of attachment the subject has to herself
and others, and thus challenge the basis of social coherence. Where would the I
be without this intimate form of reflexivity? Where would we be? At sea—cast
adrift, without nationality and without recognition?

"Where" is one way of asking the question; "when" is another. In other words,
crucial aspects of the intimate subject emerge when we examine the changing
temporalities of asking, Who am I in relation to you and what do I feel? And
when we ask, What are the changing stakes of my answer in relation to my social
bonds? Understanding the temporality of the intimate subject moves us away
from intimacy and toward what we might describe as the temporality of modern
sexual contract and consent. Taylor notes that Grotius and Locke disagreed about
the temporality of consent in the governance of man. According to Taylor,
Grotius understood political authority to be legitimate insofar as it was consented
to by individuals. This original contract created binding obligations by virtue of
the preexisting principle that promises ought to be kept. It is Locke who changed
the temporal rhythm of consent, setting government according to its clock and
justifying revolution when that timing is thrown off. "Consent is not just an original agreement to set up government, but a continuing right to agree to taxation"
(Taylor, in this issue). Consent must now be continually re-theatricalized in the
form of the franchise. We see an interesting parallel in Catholic and Protestant
approaches to the marriage contract. Does the original marriage contract create
binding obligations between the two persons, or must they continually reaffirm
their commitment? How does an approach to marriage that necessitates a continual consent as opposed to a "done deal" change the orientation of the I in relation
to itself and the other? Isn't the demand for a continual inspection of the intimate

4. If, according to Alexandre Kojeve (1969: 4), it is in, by, and as desire that man is formed and
revealed to himself and others as a (human) I—the I that is essentially different from, and radically
opposed to, the non-(human) I—then the intimate interior I is built on top of that, as the I that
reflects, discerns, and differentiates its desires.

contract one of the technologies producing, rather than resulting from, the intimate interiority? And how does the I of intimate love change (or not) in the light cast from the new temporalities figured within derivative contracts? Are some people called upon to re-contract to their commitments in a different way? Do some people conceptualize their intimacies as premised on a series of conditions, distributions of accountabilities, increasing or decreasing portfolios?

No matter how we answer these questions, it does seem clear that the intimacy grid is unevenly distributed across global populations. We must therefore follow the migration of intimacy with the European diaspora. Some scholars have already begun to track this history of sexual diaspora. The recent diasporic and transnational turn in queer studies has contested the history of sexuality as written in the West. This diasporic and transnational turn aspires to displace the history of sexuality by engaging its colonial and postcolonial scenes of circulation and inscription. But queer national and diasporic studies of sexuality share many common orientations. Both forms of queer studies turn away from the catalog of sex acts and identities toward a view of counternormative sex publics as a condition and site, where new political, social, and economic worlds are imagined and where the practices of world-building are elaborated. Insofar as they share this orientation, these scholars follow their subjects into rich worlds of sexual imaginings and new corporeal economies. The object, however, is not simply to enumerate the variety of gaylesbian worlds, but to understand the conditions of their intelligibility as human worlds within a larger liberal diaspora in which such intelligibility is increasingly demanded. To do this it is helpful to return to Genet's stance toward intimate recognition before we enter the postcolony.

It is clear that Genet was experimenting with subjectivity or, more precisely, desubjectification, in a way that was quite different from that of eighteenth- and nineteenth-century Europe and of many in the contemporary gaylesbian movement. His was an experiment in an unnatural love that emptied the body, devisaged the face. Genet's love betrayed its usury, and made intimacy, as a relay of recognition, impossible. Stirrings resonate throughout *Querelle*, but as waves that anesthetize the curious self or as positions that annul the possibilities that these emotional stirrings will move into human relationality. Thus when Querelle approaches his friend Vic to kill him after Vic has helped him smuggle opium off the ship: "No longer was any part of Querelle present within his body. It was empty. Facing Vic, there was no one. . . . He was free to leave his body, that audacious scaffolding for his balls. Their weight and beauty he knew. With one hand, calmly, he opened the folding knife he had in the pocket of his peacoat" (Genet 1974: 59). And, when Querelle symbolically executes himself for his murderous crime by allowing Norbert (the owner of the bar where Querelle will sell his drugs) to fuck him, the position of their act enables the momentary desire for a facial relation but bars its consummation. "In a vague way [Querelle] felt grateful toward Norbert for protecting him, in thus covering him. A sense of some degree of affection for his executioner occurred to him. He turned his head slightly, hoping, after all, and despite his anxiety, that Norbert might kiss him on the mouth; but he couldn't even manage to see his face" (75). These de-facializations enrich the social in a way that is different from the Hegelian fight for recognition. It is a richness of bogs, pungent with odors, stench, and despair.

Of course, Genet's experiment with desubjectification was made possible by the success of the earlier bourgeois experiment with intimate recognition. Habermas is surely right that "the jeopardy into which the idea of the community of love was thereby put, up to our day, occupied the literature (and not only the literature) as the conflict between marriage for love and marriage for reason, that is, for economic or social considerations" (Habermas 1989: 47). This conflict remains. For instance, I am surprised reading Burke's autobiography. It is less syrupy than I expected, and shot through with the cynical subjectivity of love (see also Williamson 1991). And yet, in the European diaspora that Genet addressed, this conflict between intimate love and instrumental marriage was unequally fought, for intimate love soon became the tender of the democratic marriage contract, the true grounds for the union between persons, and a necessary basis for a community of people. Love of persons and love of country are the twin contracts of modernity that sailors circumnavigate, or so Genet might say. Thus, Seblon's stylization of love, his lyrical, virile lassitude, is indeed the backdrop Genet wishes to bypass if not surpass, in the desubjectifying rituals of sailors. Gone is the sublimation of I and Thou into We-the-Couple or We-the-People. Kojeve's carnal construction of desire no longer seems an appropriate partner for Genet. No one is home in this unnatural sex. And no one is homesick. Two men having sex. What comes of sailors (de)facing thusly? In other words, if Genet was experimenting with desubjectification, what is the outcome of this experiment? To what would the social refer if the relay of recognition between you and me were cut, if *entre nous* were blocked by the practices of sex?

These are questions that numerous readers of Genet and his legacy have asked. Leo Bersani has argued quite definitely that Genet forecloses the possibility of a humanist answer to these questions. He argues that Genet refuses "cultural relationality" in order to imagine "a form of revolt that has no relation whatsoever to the laws, categories, and values it would contest and, ideally, destroy" (Bersani 1995: 152). This nonrelational ethics allows Genet to be radically alone, and absolutely distinguishes him from "the tame demand for recognition on the part of our own gay community" (161).

Genet and Bersani are not the only persons experimenting with or beyond intimacy. Candace Vogler has characterized certain modern styles of sex as seeking depersonalized intimacy; Michael Warner, stranger intimacy; Lauren Berlant, critical utopian intimacy (Vogler 1998; Warner, in this issue; Berlant 1998). When we supplement these forms of intimacy emerging in the United States with emergent styles and stylizations outside its hegemony, we see the edge of contemporary theoretical and social experimentation. And we see a vague glimmer of the dispersion of intimacy surrounding us.

The dispersion of the intimacy grid is especially apparent when we examine historical linkages among intimacy, sexuality, and recognition in the shadow of the postcolony. Remembering the lesson from Genet that to be human is to engage in practices of intimate recognition, let us return to the postcolony. There some people are foreclosed from entering the human realm in order that a nation can be made more human(e). It is in this light that we return to our earlier discussion of state forms of recognition of indigenous social organization, this time focusing on the dehumanizing gesture embedded within it. Remember, in legal precedents pertaining to traditional forms of tenure, indigenous persons are recognized as organizing their sexualities or socialities not on the basis of intimate recognition but rather on the basis of social status—kinship, religion, economic utility. Ashis Nandy (1983) has discussed with great insight the shattering of the intimate self in this colonial relation. Indeed, Western recognition of the worth of other cultures within the nation and among nations was meant, in one of its ideal forms, to repair these distensions. What irony then that state recognition of traditional forms of indigenous social organization works by acknowledging the humanity of indigenous social organization (the local descent group) even as it evacuates the prima facie indices of that humanity: intimacy (Habermas 1989: 47). The double bind in which persons are placed multiplies. It might not be the intent of legislators within the liberal Australian state, but in the context of indigenous Australia—where life chances are closely tied to state aid—indigenous persons must in fact dehumanize themselves into pure genealogy to gain the recognition of courts. And so tightly has the narrative *I* of intimacy become associated with the human and humanity that to be without it is to risk being dehumanized and subject to all the harms of the dehumanizing practices of modernity. What wonder that we now know that all people have feelings. We might conclude by noting that the gay families Burke promotes do not escape these binds. They just approach them from another angle. To be sure, intimate love makes a family human, but love must still culminate in a family, a domestic or communal plot, a social group that adheres. It is Genet who pulls apart the intimate and genealogical plot, by creating narrative spaces in which intimacy and the subjective *I* separate and in which love refuses to build into the grammar of genealogy. Thus, in the end,

> As soon as the thought crossed her mind, she felt deeply ashamed. Then, numbly, Madame Lysiane saw her own words written out in front of her, in her own inimitable grammar. "They is singing." Looking at Querelle, Madame Lysiane no longer felt what fencing masters call the hunger of the rapier. She was alone. (Genet 1974: 276)

Coda

The genealogical imaginary did not die when the sovereign's head tumbled. Nor was it replaced by intimacy as a new form of association and attachment. Something more—and less—interesting is happening. Both genealogy and intimacy have emerged as semiautonomous foundations for legitimating sex acts and other forms of corporeal sociality, even as both have been dispersed in and by colonial and postcolonial worlds. Sociality seems unthinkable not only without one or the other of these two grids, but without them working as twin pairs, intertwined, twisting, struggling against each other in the empty horizon of the Universal.

Elizabeth A. Povinelli is a professor in the Department of Anthropology and the Committee on the History of Culture at the University of Chicago. She is co-editor (with George Chauncey) of a special issue of *GLQ* titled *Thinking Sexuality Transnationally* (1999) and the author of *The Cunning of Reason: Indigenous Alterity and Australian Multiculturalism* (in press).

References

Anderson, Benedict. 1991. *Imagined communities: Reflections on the origin and spread of nationalism.* Rev. ed. London: Verso.

Benveniste, Emile. 1971. *Problems in general linguistics,* translated by Mary Elizabeth Meek. Coral Gables, Fla.: University of Miami Press.

Berlant, Lauren. 1997. *The queen of America goes to Washington City: Essays on sex and citizenship.* Durham, N.C.: Duke University Press.

———. 1998. Intimacy. *Critical Inquiry* 24: 281–88.

Bersani, Leo. 1995. *Homos*. Cambridge: Harvard University Press.

Burke, Phyllis. 1993. *Family values: Two moms and their son*. New York: Random House.

Collier, Jane Fishburne, and Sylvia Junko Yanagisako, eds. 1987. *Gender and kinship: Essays toward a unified analysis*. Stanford, Calif.: Stanford University Press.

Fassin, Eric. 2001. Same sex, different politics: "Gay marriage" debates in France and the United States. *Public Culture* 13: 215–23.

Fison, Lorimer, and A. W. Howitt. 1991. *Kamilaroi and Kurnai: Group-marriage and relationship, and marriage by elopement drawn chiefly from the usage of the Australian Aborigines; also, the Kurnai tribe, their customs in peace and war*. Canberra: Aboriginal Studies Press.

Fortes, Meyer. 1969. *Kinship and the social order: The legacy of Lewis Henry Morgan*. Chicago: Aldine.

Foucault, Michel. 1980. *The history of sexuality, volume 1: An introduction*, translated by Robert Hurley. New York: Vintage.

Franklin, Sarah, and Helena Ragoné, eds. 1998. *Reproducing reproduction: Kinship, power, and technological innovation*. Philadelphia: University of Pennsylvania Press.

Genet, Jean. 1974. *Querelle*, translated by Anselm Hollo. New York: Grove.

Ginsburg, Faye D., and Rayna Rapp, eds. 1995. *Conceiving the new world order: The global politics of reproduction*. Berkeley: University of California Press.

Goody, Jack. 1983. *Development of the family and marriage in Europe*. Cambridge: Cambridge University Press.

Habermas, Jürgen. 1989. *The structural transformation of the public sphere: An inquiry into a category of bourgeois society*, translated by Thomas Burger with Frederick Lawrence. Cambridge: MIT Press.

Keesing, Roger M. 1975. *Kin groups and social structure*. New York: Harcourt Brace Jovanovich College Publishers.

Kojeve, Alexandre. 1969. *Introduction to the reading of Hegel*, edited by Allan Bloom, translated by James H. Nichols. Ithaca, N.Y.: Cornell University Press.

Kuper, Adam. 1988. *The invention of primitive society, transformations of an illusion*. London: Routledge.

Landes, Joan B. 1988. *Women and the public sphere in the age of the French Revolution*. Ithaca, N.Y.: Cornell University Press.

Leach, Edmund. 1966. *Rethinking anthropology*. London School of Economics Monograph of Social Anthropology, no. 22. New York: Athlone.

Le Goff, Jacques. 1989. Head or heart? The political use of body metaphors in the

Middle Ages. In *Fragments for a history of the human body*, edited by Michael Feher. New York: Zone.

Le Sueur, James D. 2001. *Uncivil War: Intellectuals and identity politics during the decolonization of Algeria*. Philadelphia: University of Pennsylvania Press.

Lévi-Strauss, Claude. 1969. *The elementary structures of kinship*, translated by James Harle Bell. Boston: Beacon.

Lewin, Ellen. 1993. *Lesbian mothers: Accounts of gender in American culture*. Ithaca, N.Y.: Cornell University Press.

Macfarlane, Alan. 1986. *Marriage and love in England: Modes of reproduction, 1300–1840*. New York: Blackwell.

Morgan, Lewis Henry. 1871. *Systems of consanguinity and affinity of the human family*. Washington, D.C.: Smithsonian Institution Press.

Nandy, Ashis. 1983. *The intimate enemy: Loss and recovery of self under colonialism*. Oxford: Oxford University Press.

Plakans, Andrejs. 1984. *Kinship in the past: An anthropology of European family life, 1500–1900*. New York: Blackwell.

Povinelli, Elizabeth A. 1999. Settler modernity and the quest for indigenous traditions. *Public Culture* 11: 19–47.

———. 2001. Sexuality at risk: Psychoanalysis metapragmatically. In *Homosexuality and psychoanalysis*, edited by Tim Dean and Christopher Lane. Chicago: University of Chicago Press.

———. In press. The poetics of ghosts: Social reproduction in the archive of the nation. In *The cunning of recognition: Indigenous alterity and Australian multiculturalism*. Durham, N.C.: Duke University Press.

Radcliffe-Brown, A. R. 1965. The study of kinship systems. In *Structure and function in primitive society: Essays and addresses*. New York: Free Press.

Rivers, W. H. R. 1910. The genealogical method of anthropological inquiry. *Sociological Review* 3: 1–12.

Sartre, Jean-Paul. 1964. *Saint Genet: Actor and martyr*. New York: New American Library.

Scheffler, Harold W. 2001. *Filiation and affiliation*. Boulder, Colo.: Westview.

Schneider, David Murray. 1968. *American kinship: A cultural account*. Englewood Cliffs, N.J.: Prentice-Hall.

Smith, Adam. 1976. *The theory of moral sentiments*. Indianapolis, Ind.: Liberty Classics.

Strathern, Marilyn. 1992. *After nature: English kinship in the late twentieth century*. Cambridge: Cambridge University Press.

Sutton, Peter. 1998. *Native title and the descent of rights*. Perth, Australia: National Native Title Tribunal.

Trouillot, Michel-Rolph. 1991. Anthropology and the savage slot: The poetics and politics of otherness. In *Recapturing anthropology: Working in the present*, edited by Richard Fox. Santa Fe, N.M.: School of American Research.

Vogler, Candace. 1998. Sex and talk. *Critical Inquiry* 24: 328–65.

Weston, Kath. 1991. *Families we choose: Lesbians, gays, kinship*. New York: Columbia University Press.

White, Edmund. 1994. *Genet: A biography*. New York: Random House.

Williamson, Donald S. 1991. *The intimacy paradox: Personal authority in the family system*. New York: Guilford.

Figure Credits

Figures 1 and 2—Jacques Le Goff, *Fragments for a History of the Human Body*, ed. Michael Feher (New York: Zone, 1989), 12, 19.

Figure 3—Lewis Henry Morgan, *Systems of Consanguinity and Affinity of the Human Family* (Washington, D.C.: Smithsonian Institution, 1871), appendix, plate 11.

Figure 4—Claude Lévi-Strauss, *The Savage Mind* (Chicago: University of Chicago Press, 1966), 152.

Figure 5—W. H. R. Rivers, "The Genealogical Method of Anthropological Inquiry," *The Sociological Review* 3 (1910): 1.

Figure 6—Claude Lévi-Strauss, *The Elementary Structures of Kinship*, translated by James Harle Bell (Boston: Beacon, 1969), 165.

Figure 7—Noam Chomsky, *Aspects of the Theory of Syntax* (Cambridge: MIT Press, 1965), 69.

African Modes of Self-Writing

Achille Mbembe

translated by Steven Rendall

> *The only subjectivity is time. . . .*
> Gilles Deleuze, *Cinéma 2: L'image-temps*

Over the past two centuries, intellectual currents have emerged whose goal has been to confer authority on certain symbolic elements integrated into the African collective imaginaire. Some of these trends have gained a following, while others have remained mere outlines. Very few are outstanding in richness and creativity, and fewer still are of exceptional power.

At the intersection of religious practices and the interrogation of human tragedy, a distinctively African philosophy has emerged. But governed though it has been, for the most part, by narratives of loss, such meditation on divine sovereignty and African people's histories has not yielded any integrated philosophico-theological inquiry systematic enough to situate human misfortune and wrongdoing in a singular theoretical framework.[1] Africa offers nothing compara-

Ato Quayson and Ruth Marshall-Fratani critiqued an earlier version of this essay. Sarah Nuttall, Françoise Vergès, Carol Gluck, and Candace Vogler offered additional comments. Sustained encouragement came from Bogumil Jewsiewicki, Pierre Nora, Carol A. Breckenridge, Arjun Appadurai, and Dilip Parameshwar Gaonkar. Excerpts were presented at conferences in Cape Town in August 2000; Patna in February 2001; and Evanston, Illinois, in March 2001.

1. See, e.g., Fabien Eboussi Boulaga, *Christianisme sans fétiche: Révélation et domination* (Paris: Présence africaine, 1981); Jean-Marc Ela, *Le cri de l'homme africain: Questions aux chrétiens et aux églises d'Afrique* (Paris: L'Harmattan, 1980), and *Ma foi d'africain* (Paris: Karthala, 1985); and Valentin Y. Mudimbe, *Tales of Faith: Religion as Political Performance in Central Africa* (London: Athlone, 1997).

Public Culture 14(1): 239–273
Copyright © 2002 by Duke University Press

ble, for example, to a German philosophy that from Luther to Heidegger has been based not only on religious mysticism but also, more fundamentally, on the will to transgress the boundary between the human and the divine. Nor is there anything comparable to Jewish Messianism, which, combining desire and dream, confronted almost without mediation the problem of the absolute and its promises, pursuing the latter to its most extreme consequences in tragedy and despair, while at the same time treating the uniqueness of Jewish suffering as sacred at the risk of making it taboo.[2] It is true that, following the examples of these two metanarratives, contemporary African modes of writing the self are inseparably connected with the problematics of self-constitution and the modern philosophy of the subject. However, there the similarities end.

Various factors have prevented the full development of conceptions that might have explained the meaning of the African past and present by reference to the future, but chief among them may be named historicism. The effort to determine the conditions under which the African subject could attain full selfhood, become self-conscious, and be answerable to no one else soon encountered historicist thinking in two forms that led it into a dead end. The first of these is what might be termed *Afro-radicalism*, with its baggage of instrumentalism and political opportunism. The second is the burden of the metaphysics of difference (*nativism*).[3] The first current of thought—which liked to present itself as "democratic," "radical," and "progressive"—used Marxist and nationalist categories to develop an *imaginaire* of culture and politics in which a manipulation of the rhetoric of

2. See Gershom Scholem, *Aux origines religieuses du judaïsme laïque: De la mystique aux Lumières*, ed. Maurice Kriegel (Paris: Calmann-Lévy, 2000); Yitzhak F. Baer, *Galout: L'imaginaire de l'exil dans le judaïsme*, trans. Marc de Launay (Paris: Calmann-Lévy, 2000); Hannah Arendt, *The Jew as Pariah: Jewish Identity and Politics in the Modern Age* (New York: Grove, 1978); and Sylvie Anne Goldberg, *La Clepsydre: Essai sur la pluralité des temps dans le judaïsme* (Paris: Albin Michel, 2000).

3. To be sure, the two currents of thought adhere to no single theory of identity, politics, or culture. For different critiques, see Amady A. Dieng, *Hegel, Marx, Engels et les problèmes de l'Afrique noire* (Dakar: Sankoré, 1978); Bogumil Jewsiewicki, *Marx, Afrique et Occident: Les pratiques africanistes de l'histoire marxiste* (Montreal: McGill University, Centre for Developing-Area Studies, 1985); and Valentin Y. Mudimbe, *The Idea of Africa* (Bloomington: Indiana University Press, 1994), 41–46. See also Mudimbe, *Parables and Fables: Exegesis, Textuality, and Politics in Central Africa* (Madison: University of Wisconsin Press, 1991), 166–91. It can further be argued that in its attempt to reconceptualize the problem of the subject, African feminism does not fundamentally alter the dominant African Marxist, nationalist, or nativist understandings of subjectivity or concepts of human intentionality. See, e.g., Amina Mama, Ayesha Imam, and Fatou Sow, eds., *Engendering African Social Sciences* (Dakar: CODESRIA, 1997); and Ifi Amadiume, *Re-inventing Africa: Matriarchy, Religion, and Culture* (London: Zed, 1997).

autonomy, resistance, and emancipation serves as the sole criterion for determining the legitimacy of an authentic African discourse.[4] The second current of thought developed out of an emphasis on the "native condition." It promoted the idea of a unique African identity founded on membership of the black race.

Fundamental to both currents of thought are three historical events, broadly construed: slavery, colonization, and apartheid. A particular set of canonical meanings has been attributed to these three events. First, on the level of individual subjectivities, there is the idea that through the processes of slavery, colonization, and apartheid, the African self has become alienated from itself (*self-division*). This separation is supposed to result in a loss of familiarity with the self, to the point that the subject, having become estranged from him- or herself, has been relegated to a lifeless form of identity (*objecthood*). Not only is the self no longer recognized by the Other; the self no longer recognizes itself.[5]

The second canonical meaning has to do with property. According to the dominant narrative, the three events have led to dispossession, a process in which juridical and economic procedures have led to material expropriation. This was followed by a unique experience of subjection characterized by the falsification of Africa's history by the Other, which resulted in a state of maximal exteriority (*estrangement*) and deracination. These two phases—the violence of falsification and material expropriation—are said to be the main components of African history's uniqueness and of the tragedy that is at its foundation.[6]

Finally, there is the idea of historical degradation: slavery, colonization, and apartheid are supposed to have plunged the African subject not only into humiliation, debasement, and nameless suffering but also into a zone of nonbeing and

4. This approach contrasts with the politics of black radical activity in the United States during the twentieth century. In the latter case, attempts were made to organically conjoin Marxism and Black Nationalism, to develop a praxis that would attend to both *class* and *race* in promoting social transformation. See, for example, Cedric J. Robinson, *Black Marxism: The Making of the Black Radical Tradition* (Chapel Hill: University of North Carolina Press, 2000); and the essay by Brent Hayes Edwards, "The 'Autonomy' of Black Radicalism," *Social Text*, no. 67 (2001): 1–12.

5. Whether discussing it under the term *alienation* or *deracination*, it is francophone criticism that has most fully conceptualized this process. See, in particular, Frantz Fanon, *Black Skin, White Masks* [*Peau noire, masques blancs*], trans. Charles Lam Markmann (New York: Grove, 1967); Hamidou Kane, *L'aventure ambiguë* (Paris: Julliard, 1961); and Fabien Eboussi Boulaga, *La crise du Muntu: Authenticité africaine et philosophie* (Paris: Présence africaine, 1977), and *Christianisme sans fétiche*.

6. This is particularly applicable to English-language studies of Marxist political economy, anthropology, or history. Sometimes these also rely on nationalist and dependentist theses. See, e.g., Claude Aké, *A Political Economy of Africa* (Harlow, England: Longman, 1981); Walter Rodney, *How Europe Underdeveloped Africa* (Washington, D.C.: Howard University Press, 1981); and, on a more general level, Samir Amin, *Le développement inégal: Essai sur les formations sociales du capitalisme périphérique* (Paris: Editions de Minuit, 1973).

social death characterized by the denial of dignity, heavy psychic damage, and the torment of exile.[7] These three fundamental elements of slavery, colonization, and apartheid are said to serve as a unifying center of Africans' desire to know themselves, to recapture their destiny (*sovereignty*), and to belong to themselves in the world (*autonomy*).

By following the model of Jewish reflection on the phenomena of suffering, contingency, and finitude, these three meanings might have been used as a starting point for a philosophical and critical interpretation of the apparent long rise toward nothingness that Africa has experienced all through its history. Theology, literature, film, music, political philosophy, and psychoanalysis would have had to be involved as well. But such a synthesis did not occur.[8] In reality, the production of the dominant meanings of these events was itself colonized by the two ideological currents introduced above—the one instrumentalist, the other nativist—that claim to speak in the name of Africa as a whole.[9]

In the remarks that follow, I examine these two currents of thought and draw out their weaknesses. Throughout this discussion, I propose ways out of the dead end into which they have led reflection on the African experience of self and the world. Against the arguments of critics who have equated identity with race and geography, I show how current African imaginations of the self are born out of disparate but often intersecting practices, the goal of which is not only to settle factual and moral disputes about the world but also to open the way for *self-styling*. By emphasizing historical contingency and the process of subject formation, my aim is to reinterpret subjectivity as time.

---

7. On the problematics of slavery and reparation, see J. F. Ade Ajayi, "The Atlantic Slave Trade and Africa," and "Pan-Africanism and the Struggle for Reparation," in *Tradition and Change in Africa: The Essays of J. F. Ade Ajayi*, ed. Toyin Falola (Trenton, N.J.: Africa World Press, 2000). Cf., for a more subtle and sophisticated interpretation of slavery and its impact, Orlando Patterson, *Slavery and Social Death: A Comparative Study* (Cambridge: Harvard University Press, 1982); and, on "dispersion" as seen from the other side of the Atlantic, Paul Gilroy, *The Black Atlantic: Modernity and Double Consciousness* (Cambridge: Harvard University Press, 1993).

8. To be sure, attempts have occasionally been made at such a project. Apartheid has been the subject of constant biblical interpretation. See, among others, Allan Boesak, *Black and Reformed: Apartheid, Liberation, and the Calvinist Tradition: Sermons and Speeches*, comp. Mothobi Mutloatse, ed. John Webster (New York: Orbis, 1984); and Desmond Tutu, *Hope and Suffering* (Grand Rapids, Mich.: Eerdmans, 1984). Colonization has also been the subject of such interpretations. See, e.g., Oscar Bimwenyi-Kweshi, *Discours théologique négro-africain: Problème des fondements* (Paris: Présence africaine, 1981); and Ela, *Le cri de l'homme africain* and *Ma foi d'Africain*.

9. See, e.g., Thandika Mkandawire and Charles C. Soludo, *Our Continent, Our Future: African Perspectives on Structural Adjustment* (Trenton, N.J.: Africa World Press, 1999).

The Instrumentalist Paradigm: Primal Fantasies

The current of thought marked above as Marxist and nationalist is permeated by the tension between voluntarism and victimization. It has four main characteristics. First of all, it exhibits a lack of self-reflexivity and an instrumental conception of knowledge and science, in the sense that neither is recognized as autonomous. They are useful only insofar as they are mobilized for service in partisan struggle.[10] To this partisan struggle is attributed an intrinsic moral significance, since it is alleged to oppose revolutionary liberation to the forces of conservatism.[11]

The second characteristic is a mechanistic and reified vision of history. Causality is attributed to entities that are fictive and wholly invisible, but are nevertheless said to determine, ultimately, the subject's life and work. According to this point of view, the history of Africa can be reduced to a series of subjugations, narrativized in a seamless continuity. African experience of the world is supposed to be determined, a priori, by a set of forces—always the same ones, though appearing in differing guises—whose function is to prevent the blooming of African uniqueness, of that part of the African historical self that is irreducible to any other.

As a result, Africa is said not to be responsible for the catastrophes that are befalling it. The present destiny of the continent is supposed to proceed not from free and autonomous choices but from the legacy of a history imposed upon Africans—burned into their flesh by rape, brutality, and all sorts of economic conditionalities.[12] The African subject's difficulty in representing him- or herself as the subject of a free will is supposed to proceed from this long history of subjugation. This construction of history leads to a naive and uncritical attitude with regard to so-called struggles for national liberation and to social move-

10. See, e.g., Jacques Depelchin, "African Anthropology and History in the Light of the History of FRELIMO," *Contemporary Marxism*, no. 7 (1983): 69–88.

11. This tendency took shape during the last quarter of the twentieth century in ideological production issuing not only from national institutions, such as the University of Dar-es-Salaam (Tanzania), but also from regional ones, such as the Southern African Political Economy Series (SAPES) Trust, based in Harare (Zimbabwe), and continental ones, such as the Council for the Development of Social Science Research in Africa (CODESRIA), based in Dakar (Senegal). For a theorization, see Claude Aké, *Social Science as Imperialism: The Theory of Political Development* (Ibadan: Ibadan University Press, 1982), and *Revolutionary Pressures in Africa* (London: Zed, 1978).

12. See the ideological criticisms of structural adjustment programs and the continuous conceptual dependence on a developmentalist paradigm in Thandika Mkandawire and Adebayo Olukoshi, eds., *Between Liberalization and Oppression: The Politics of Structural Adjustment in Africa* (Dakar: CODESRIA, 1995).

243

ments; an emphasis on violence as the privileged avenue for self-determination; the fetishization of state power; the disqualification of the model of liberal democracy; and the populist and authoritarian dream of a mass society.[13]

The third characteristic is a desire to destroy tradition and the belief that authentic identity is conferred by the division of labor that gives rise to social classes, the proletariat—urban or rural—playing the role of the universal class par excellence.[14] The dictum that the working class is the only practical agency that can engage in universal emancipatory activity results in the denial of any possible multiplicity of foundations for the exercise of social power.[15]

Finally, this Marxist-nationalist school of thought relies on an essentially *polemical* relationship to the world, a relationship based on a troika of rhetorical rituals. The first ritual contradicts and refutes Western definitions of Africa and Africans by pointing out the falsehoods and bad faith they presuppose. The second denounces what the West has done (and continues to do) to Africa in the name of these definitions. And the third provides ostensible proofs that—by disqualifying the West's fictional representations of Africa and refuting its claim to have a monopoly on the expression of the human in general—are supposed to open up a space in which Africans can finally narrate their own fables. This is to be accomplished through the acquisition of a language and a voice that cannot be imitated because they are, in some sense, authentically Africa's own.[16]

Yet what might appear to be the apotheosis of voluntarism is here accompanied by a lack of philosophical depth and, paradoxically, a cult of victimization. Philosophically, the Hegelian thematics of identity and difference, as classically exemplified in the master-bondsman relationship, is surreptitiously reappropriated by the ex-colonized. In a move that replicates an unreflexive ethnographic practice, the ex-colonized assigns a set of pseudohistorical features to a geographical entity which is itself subsumed under a *racial name*. The features and

13. On social movements, see Mahmood Mamdani and Ernest Wamba-dia-Wamba, eds., *African Studies in Social Movements and Democracy* (Dakar: CODESRIA, 1995). On the populist critique of liberal democracy, see Claude Aké, *The Feasibility of Democracy in Africa* (Dakar: CODESRIA, 2000); and Issa G. Shivji, *The Concept of Human Rights in Africa* (London: CODESRIA, 1989), and *Fight My Beloved Continent: New Democracy in Africa* (Harare: SAPES Trust, 1988).

14. See, e.g., Mahmood Mamdani, ed., *Uganda: Studies in Labour* (Dakar: CODESRIA, 1996); Issa G. Shivji, *Class Struggles in Tanzania* (London: Heinemann, 1976).

15. One recent example is Mahmood Mamdani, *Citizen and Subject: Contemporary Africa and the Legacy of Late Colonialism* (Princeton, N.J.: Princeton University Press, 1996). See also Mamdani, *Politics and Class Formation in Uganda* (New York: Monthly Review Press, 1976).

16. See, e.g., Paul Tiyambe Zeleza, *A Modern Economic History of Africa*, vol. 1, *The Nineteenth Century* (Dakar: CODESRIA, 1993), and *Manufacturing African Studies and Crises* (Dakar: CODESRIA, 1997).

the name are then used to identify or make possible the recognition of those who, by virtue of possessing those features or bearing that name, can be said to belong to the racial collectivity and the geographical entity thus defined. Under the guise of "speaking in one's own voice," then, the figure of the "native" is reiterated. Boundaries are demarcated between the native and the nonnative Other; and on the basis of these boundaries, distinctions can then be made between the authentic and the inauthentic.

In the critique that follows, I will be arguing (1) that such nationalist and Marxist narratives of the African self and the world have been superficial; (2) that as a consequence of this superficiality, the formulations of self-government and autonomy they engender are founded, at best, on a thin philosophical base; and (3) that their privileging of victimhood over subjecthood is derived, ultimately, from a distinctively nativist understanding of history—one of history as sorcery.

Self-affirmation, autonomy, and African emancipation—in the name of which the right to selfhood is claimed—are not new issues. As the Atlantic slave trade came to an end in the middle of the nineteenth century, doubts among Europeans regarding Africans' ability to govern themselves—that is, according to Hegel, to control their predatory greed and their cruelty[17]—gained impetus. These doubts were connected with another, more fundamental doubt that was implicit in the way modern times had resolved the complex general problem of alterity and the status of the African sign within this economy of alterity. Both Western philanthropic movements and the African intelligentsia of the times responded to this doubt from within the paradigm of the Enlightenment.[18]

The Legacy of the Enlightenment   To draw out the political implications of these debates, I should perhaps first remark the project, central to Enlightenment thought, of defining human nature in terms of its possession of a generic identity. The rights and values to be shared by all are derived from this identity, universal in essence. It is identical in each human subject because it has reason at its center. The exercise of reason endows individuals with not only liberty and autonomy, but

17. See Georg Wilhelm Friedrich Hegel, *The Philosophy of History*, trans. John Sibree (Buffalo, N.Y.: Prometheus, 1991), 91–99.

18. To be sure, Enlightenment discourse on race was not univocal. Nevertheless, it can be said that, for the most part, its thinkers joined in debate on common discursive terrain. As Paul Gilroy shows, the extensive debate as to whether "Negroes" should be accorded membership in the human family was central to the formation of the modern episteme. See Gilroy, "Race Ends Here," *Ethnic and Racial Studies* 21 (1998): 838–47. See also Susan Buck-Morss, "Hegel and Haiti," *Critical Inquiry* 26 (2000): 821–65; and, more generally, Emmanuel Chukwudi Eze, ed., *Race and Enlightenment: A Reader* (Cambridge, Mass.: Blackwell, 1997).

245

also the ability to conduct life in accordance with moral principles and an idea of the good. The thing to note here is that outside this circle, there is no place for a politics of the universal. And for European thinkers of the period of abolition, the question was indeed whether Africans were to be situated inside or outside the circle—that is, whether they were human beings like all others. In other words: Could we find among Africans the same human person, merely disguised by different designations and forms? Could we consider Africans' bodies, languages, works, and lives as products of human activity, as manifesting a subjectivity—that is, a consciousness like our own—that would allow us to consider each of them, taken individually, as another self (*alter ego*)? The Enlightenment's response to these questions can be traced through three distinct intellectual moments with distinct political implications.

An initial set of answers suggested that Africans be kept within the limits of their presupposed ontological difference. This school of Enlightenment thought— as exemplified by positions taken by Hegel and Kant—identified in the African sign something unique, and even indelible, that separated it from all other human signs. The best testimony to this specificity was the black body, which was supposed not to contain any sort of consciousness and to have none of the characteristics of reason or beauty.[19] Consequently, it could not be considered a body composed of flesh like one's own because it belonged solely to the order of material extension and of the object doomed to death and destruction. It is this centrality of the body in the calculus of political subjection that explains the importance assumed, in the course of the nineteenth century, by theories of the physical, moral, and political regeneration of blacks and, later on, of Jews.

According to this darker side of the Enlightenment, Africans developed unique conceptions of society, of the world, and of the good that they did not share with other peoples. It so happened that these conceptions in no way manifested the power of invention and universality peculiar to reason. Nor did Africans' representations, lives, works, languages, or actions—including death—obey any rule or law whose meaning they could, on their own authority, conceive or justify. Because of this radical difference, it was deemed legitimate to exclude them, both de facto and de jure, from the sphere of full and complete human citizenship: they had nothing to contribute to the work of the universal.[20]

19. On the centrality of the body in Western philosophy and its status as the ideal unit of the subject, the site of the recognition of his or her identity, see Maurice Merleau-Ponty, *Phénoménologie de la perception* (Paris: Gallimard, 1945), 81–234. On the "weight" of the body of the colonized, see Fanon, *Black Skin, White Masks*, 110–13.

20. On this point and the preceding discussion, cf. Olivier Le Cour Grandmaison, *Les citoyennetés en Révolution, 1789–1794* (Paris: Presses universitaires de France, 1992); Pierre Pluchon, *Nègres et*

A significant shift occurred with the advent of the formal, state-directed colonization of Africa in the late nineteenth century. While the principle of ontological difference persisted, the concern for self-determination became connected with the imperative to "become civilized." A slight slippage thus was introduced within the old economy of alterity. The thesis of nonsimilarity was not repudiated, but it was no longer based solely on the emptiness of the sign as such. The sign was given a name: *custom*. If Africans were different kinds of beings, that was because they had an identity of their own. This identity was not to be abolished. On the contrary, difference was to be inscribed within a distinct institutional order, a native order forced to operate within the fundamentally inegalitarian and hierarchized colonial framework. In other words, difference was recognized, but only insofar as it implied inequalities that were, moreover, considered natural to the extent that it justified discrimination and, in the most extreme cases, segregation.[21]

Later, the colonial state went on to use this concept of custom—that is, the thesis of nonsimilarity, in a revised edition—as a mode of government in itself. Specific forms of knowledge were produced for this purpose; such was the case of statistics and other methods of quantification, as deployed in censuses and various other instruments like maps, agrarian surveys, and racial and tribal studies.[22] Their objective was to canonize difference and to eliminate the plurality and ambivalence of custom.[23] There was a paradox to this process of reification. On

---

Juifs au XVIIIe siècle: Le racisme au siècle des lumières (Paris: Tallandier, 1984); Charles de Secondat, Baron de Montesquieu, *De l'esprit des lois* (Paris: Garnier-Flammarion, 1979); Voltaire, *Oeuvres complètes* (Paris: Imprimerie de la Société littéraire et typographique, 1785); and Immanuel Kant, *Observations on the Feeling of the Beautiful and Sublime*, trans. John T. Goldthwait (Berkeley: University of California Press, 1965).

21. The most fully realized institutional form of this economy of alterity was the system of apartheid, in which the hierarchies were biological in nature. A less extreme version was "indirect rule," a not very onerous form of domination which, in the British colonies, made it possible to exercise authority over natives with few soldiers by making use of the natives' passions and vices. Cf. Lucy Philip Mair, *Native Policies in Africa* (London: Routledge, 1936); Frederick John Dealtry, Baron Lugard, *The Dual Mandate in British Tropical Africa* (London: Blackwood and Sons, 1980).

22. See "Number in the Colonial Imagination," chap. 6 in Arjun Appadurai, *Modernity at Large: Cultural Dimensions of Globalization* (Minneapolis: University of Minnesota Press, 1996). For a study of the appropriation of these techniques by postcolonial elites, see Thongchai Winichakul, *Siam Mapped: A History of the Geo-Body of a Nation* (Honolulu: University of Hawai'i Press, 1994).

23. This was done notwithstanding the fact that "custom" varied radically from place to place. As was the case elsewhere, "custom" became the trope for social order in African societies thought to be outside of history, devoid of individuals. It could, from the colonial moment on, be reproduced through the force of law. On similar experiences in a different part of the colonized world, see Nicholas B. Dirks, "The Policing of Tradition: Colonialism and Anthropology in Southern India," *Comparative Studies in Society and History* 39 (1997): 182–212.

the one hand, it looked like recognition. But on the other, it constituted a moral judgment, because ultimately, custom was only made specific the better to indicate the extent to which the world of the native, in its naturalness, failed to correspond with our own—that it was, in short, not part of our world, and thus could not serve as the basis for a praxis of living together in a civil society.

The third approach offered by the Enlightenment had to do with the politics of assimilation. Here, a comparison with the Jewish experience is worth making. Just as with the figure of the "blacks," the invocation of the figure of the Jews as an archetypal Other to the West was central to the Enlightenment notion of *Bildung* (the formative process by which the individual moves toward autonomy). Jews were perceived as the negation of the Enlightenment's promise of an emancipation through the use of reason. In principle, the concept of assimilation was based on the possibility of an experience of the world common to all human beings—or, rather, on the possibility of such an experience as premised on an *essential similarity* among human beings. But this world common to all human beings, this similarity, was not supposed to have been given a priori to all.

The black, especially, had to be *converted* to it. This conversion was the condition for his being perceived and recognized as a fellow human being and for his otherwise indefinable humanity to enter representation. Once this condition was met, the project of assimilation could proceed, with the recognition of an African individuality distinct from generic tribal identities. African subjects could have rights and enjoy them, not by virtue of their subordination to the rule of custom, but by reason of their status as autonomous individuals capable of thinking for themselves and exercising reason, the peculiarly human faculty.[24]

To recognize this individuality—that is, this ability to imagine goals different from those imposed by custom—was to do away with difference. The latter had to be erased or annulled if Africans were to become like us, if they were henceforth to be considered as alter ego. Thus, the essence of the politics of assimilation consisted in desubstantializing and aestheticizing difference, at least for a category of natives (*les évolués*) whose conversion and "cultivation" made them

24. In practice, the new subjects created by the politics of assimilation were cast as homogeneous reproductions of the metropolitan subject. Christopher Miller rightly states that the "theory and practice of assimilation stressed continuity with the metropolitan country and the reproduction of 'her' values, while ignoring or denying the truly profound break that colonial subjects were experiencing in relation to their own cultures" (Miller, *Nationalists and Nomads: Essays on Francophone African Literature and Culture* [Chicago: University of Chicago Press, 1998], 122). As Fanon makes clear, race would remain the barrier between the *assimilé* and Frenchness; the amount of Frenchness available to the colonized would be restricted by biology. See *Black Skin, White Masks*, chap. 5.

suitable for citizenship and the enjoyment of civil rights. Assimilation thus inaugurated a passage from custom into civil society, but by way of the civilizing mill of Christianity and the colonial state.[25]

During the nineteenth-century conjuncture of abolition and the advent of formal colonialism, when African criticism first took up the question of selfcraft in terms of self-government and self-imaging, it inherited these three moments, but did not subject them to a coherent critique. On the contrary, subscribing to the program of emancipation and autonomy, it accepted, for the most part, the basic categories then used in Western discourse to account for universal history.[26] The notion of "civilization" was one of these categories. It authorized the distinction between the human and the nonhuman—or the not-yet-sufficiently human that might become human if given appropriate training.[27] The three vectors of this process of domestication were thought to be conversion to Christianity, the introduction of a market economy, and the adoption of rational, enlightened forms of government.[28] In reality, it was less a matter of understanding what led to servitude and what servitude meant than of postulating, in the abstract, the necessity of liberating oneself from foreign rule.

To be sure, African thinkers took seriously the challenge of colonial disruption. Seeking to be their own masters, they at times interrogated the moralities of colonial modernity in vernacular accents. At other times, they sought to capture the material benefits of colonial rule for their own advantage. Leaders of resistance at one moment in history, many shuttled between principled options and dubious alliances. Following a "zigzag line of a hundred tacks," most inhabited the ambiguous and largely uncharted zones of dependence.[29] In their polemical use of the West's ideas, they imported new concepts and discursive models "in order to defend new frontiers of locality" and to tame what they perceived as modernity's threats. In the process, they invented a narrative of liberation built

25. Even when the postulate of equality among human beings was admitted, colonization was sometimes justified in the name of "civilization." See, among others, Alexis de Tocqueville, *De la colonie en Algérie* (Brussels: Editions Complexe, 1988). On the ambiguities of French assimilation policies, see Alice L. Conklin, *A Mission to Civilize: The Republican Idea of Empire in France and West Africa, 1895–1930* (Stanford, Calif.: Stanford University Press, 1997).

26. Cf. the essays in Henry S. Wilson, ed., *Origins of West African Nationalism* (London: Macmillan–St. Martin's Press, 1969).

27. Cf., e.g., Marie Jean Antoine Nicolas de Caritat, Marquis de Condorcet, "Réflexions sur l'esclavage des nègres," in *Oeuvres* (Paris: Firmin-Didot, 1849).

28. See Edward W. Blyden, *Christianity, Islam and the Negro Race* (Edinburgh: Edinburgh University Press, 1967).

29. See Shula Marks, *The Ambiguities of Dependence in South Africa: Class, Nationalism, and the State in Twentieth-Century Natal* (Johannesburg: Ravan, 1986).

around the dual temporality of a glorious—albeit fallen—past (tradition) and a redeemed future (nationalism).[30]

But for the first modern African thinkers, liberation from servitude was equivalent above all to acquiring formal power. The basic moral and philosophical question—that is, how to renegotiate a social bond corrupted by commercial relationships (the sale of human cargoes), the violence of endless wars, and the catastrophic consequences of the way in which power was exercised—was considered secondary. African criticism did not assume as its primary task a political and moral philosophical reflection on the nature of the internal discord that led to the slave trade and colonial domination. Still less did it concern itself with the modalities of reinventing a being-together in a situation in which, with regard to the philosophy of reason that it claimed to espouse, all the outward appearances of a possible human life seemed to be lacking, and what passed for politics had more to do with the power to destroy and to profit than with any kind of philosophy of life or reason.

To be sure, in the post–World War II period, African nationalisms came to replace the concept of "civilization" with that of "progress." But they did so the better to endorse the characteristic teleologies of the times.[31] Such was the case of Marxism.

In Marx's narrative, both the subject and the telos of history are known. In this tradition, the ultimate frontier of history is a commodity-free society. To decommodify economic and social relationships entails the abolition of the power of the market and the collapse of the distinction between state and society. Such processes, and the ensuing formation of new relations of production, may involve a coercive logic or even terror. The latter may be mobilized as a means to facilitate the passage of history. As for Marx's subject, he or she exists wholly as a mere reflection and effect of material production. Revolutionary violence is conceived as a force of cohesion, the purpose of which is to produce a moral refashioning of the subject, a transformation of his or her consciousness as well as material conditions.[32]

30. See Jomo Kenyatta, *Facing Mount Kenya: The Tribal Life of the Gikuyu* (London: Secker and Warburg, 1938); and John Lonsdale, "Jomo, God, and the Modern World," in *African Modernities? Duration and Disjuncture,* ed. Jan-Georg Deutsch, Peter Probst, and Heike Schmidt (London: James Currey, in press).

31. In later modernity, Western philosophical criticism has begun moving away from some of the most radical Enlightenment propositions. See Jürgen Habermas, *The Philosophical Discourse of Modernity: Twelve Lectures,* trans. Frederick Lawrence (Cambridge: MIT Press, 1987).

32. Karl Marx, *Capital, A Critique of Political Economy,* vols. 1 and 3, trans. Ben Fowkes (Harmondsworth, England: Penguin, 1976, 1981). On violence see Leon Trotsky, *Terrorism and Commu-*

If, in the Western experience, Marx's theory equated modernization with modernity and was conceived as a science, the same narrative in the African context soon became associated with politics as a sacramental practice. As such, politics required the total surrender of the individual to a utopian future and to the hope of a collective resurrection that, in turn, required the destruction of everything that stood opposed to it. Embedded within this conception of politics as pain and sacrifice was an entrenched belief in the redemptive function of violence. As an offering of one's life on the public altar of the revolution, violence could be expiatory or substitutive. It could also imply self-sacrifice—in which case the logic of sacrifice was linked with that of the gift. Expiatory, substitutive, or self-sacrificial, violence was deployed—and death unleashed—in the name of a Marxist telos. Murder itself was commuted and concealed through ascription to a final moral truth, while the proof of virtue and morality lay in pain and suffering.[33]

The possibility of a properly philosophical reflection on the African condition having been set aside, only the question of raw power remained: Who could capture it? How was its enjoyment legitimated? In justifying the right to sovereignty and self-determination and in struggling to wrest power from the colonial regime, two central categories were mobilized: on one hand, the figure of the African as a victimized and wounded subject, and on the other, the assertion of the African's cultural uniqueness.[34] Both required a profound investment in the idea of race and a radicalization of difference itself.

At the heart of the postcolonial paradigm of victimization, we find a reading of the self and the world as a series of conspiracies. Such conspiracy theories have their origins in both Marxist and indigenous notions of agency.[35] In African history, it is thought, there is neither irony nor accident. We are told that African history is essentially governed by forces beyond Africans' control. The diversity

nism: A Reply to Karl Kautsky, 2d English ed. (Ann Arbor: University of Michigan Press, 1961). For critiques, see Maurice Merleau-Ponty, Humanism and Terror: An Essay on the Communist Problem, trans. John O'Neill (Boston: Beacon Press, 1969); and Hannah Arendt, La crise de la culture; Huit exercices de pensée politique [Between Past and Future: Eight Exercises in Political Thought], trans. Patrick Lévy (Paris: Gallimard, 1972), 28–57.

33. See, for instance, the texts collected in Aquino de Bragança and Immanuel Wallerstein, eds., The African Liberation Reader (London: Zed, 1982).

34. See Nnamdi Azikiwe, Renascent Africa (London: Cass, 1969); Kwame Nkrumah, I Speak of Freedom: A Statement of African Ideology (London: Heinemann, 1961); Amilcar Cabral, Revolution in Guinea: Selected Texts (New York: Monthly Review Press, 1970).

35. This is especially the case with respect to notions of witchcraft. See Peter Geschiere, The Modernity of Witchcraft: Politics and the Occult in Postcolonial Africa, trans. Geschiere and Janet Roitman (Charlottesville: University Press of Virginia, 1997).

and the disorder of the world, as well as the open character of historical possibilities, are reduced to a spasmodic, unchanging cycle, infinitely repeated in accord with a conspiracy always fomented by forces beyond Africa's reach. Existence itself is expressed, almost always, as a stuttering. Ultimately, the African is supposed to be merely a castrated subject, the passive instrument of the Other's enjoyment. Under such conditions, there can be no more radical utopian vision than the one suggesting that Africa disconnect itself from the world—the mad dream of a world without Others.

This hatred of the world at large (which also marks a profound desire for recognition) and this paranoid reading of history are presented as a "democratic," "radical," and "progressive" discourse of emancipation and autonomy—the foundation for a so-called politics of Africanity.[36] Rhetoric to the contrary, however, the neurosis of victimization fosters a mode of thought that is at once xenophobic, racist, negative, and circular. In order to function, this logic needs superstitions. It has to create fictions that later pass for real things. It has to fabricate masks that are retained by remodeling them to suit the needs of each period.

The course of African history is said to be determined by the combined action of a diabolical couple formed by an enemy—or tormentor—and a victim. In this closed universe, in which "making history" consists of annihilating one's enemies, politics is conceived of as a *sacrificial process*, and history, in the end, is seen as participating in a great *economy of sorcery*.[37]

The Prose of Nativism

Parallel to this current of thought that seeks to found a politics of Africanity on the categories of Marxist political economy (while viewing politics as sacrifice and history as sorcery), a rhetorical configuration has developed whose central thematics has to do with cultural identity. This current of thought is characterized by a tension between a universalizing move that claims shared membership within the human condition (*sameness*) and an opposing, particularistic move.

36. See Archie Mafeje, "Africanity: A Combative Ontology," *CODESRIA Bulletin* 1 (2000): 66–71. For different views, see, in the same issue, Wambui Mwangi and André Zaiman, "Race and Identity in Africa: A Concept Paper," 61–63; Fabien Eboussi Boulaga, "Race, Identity, and Africanity," 63–66; and Mahmoud Ben Romdhane, "A Word from a Non-Black African," 74–75.

37. This is something that the vernacular language fully recognizes, but that the Marxist lexicon nevertheless prevents African intellectuals from naming as such. See, e.g., Ernest Wamba-dia-Wamba, "Mobutisme après Mobutu: Réflexions sur la situation actuelle en République Démocratique du Congo," *Bulletin du CODESRIA*, nos. 3, 4 (1998): 27–34.

This latter move emphasizes difference and specificity by accenting, not original-ity as such, but the principle of repetition (*tradition*) and the values of autoch-thony. The point where these two political and cultural moves converge is race. Let me briefly survey the history of its problematization in African thought.

To begin with, there is the notion of race and its long-privileged status in his-torically contingent practices of recognizing human attributes. Historically, most nineteenth-century theories established a close relationship between the human subject and the racial subject. Race was understood as a set of visible physiolog-ical properties and discernible moral characteristics. These properties and char-acteristics were supposed to mark distinct human species.[38] Moreover, such marks made it possible to classify these species within a hierarchy whose violent effects were at once political, economic, and cultural in nature.[39] As I have already indicated, the classifications dominant during the period of the Atlantic slave trade and its aftermath actually excluded Africans from the circle of humanity or, at best, assigned to them an inferior status in the hierarchy of races.

This denial of humanity (or attribution of inferiority) has forced African responses into contradictory positions that are, however, often concurrently espoused.[40] There is a universalistic position: "We are human beings like any others."[41] And there is a particularistic position: "We have a glorious past that testifies to our humanity."[42] Discourse on African identity has been caught in a dilemma from which it is struggling to free itself: Does African identity partake in the generic human identity?[43] Or should one insist, in the name of difference and uniqueness, on the possibility of diverse cultural forms within a single humanity—but cultural forms whose purpose is not to be self-sufficient, whose ultimate signification is universal?[44]

The apologetic density of the assertion "we are human beings like any others"

38. Cf. Immanuel Kant, *Anthropology from a Pragmatic Point of View*, trans. Victor Lyle Dowdell (Carbondale, Ill.: Southern Illinois University Press, 1978).

39. See Pierre Guiral and Emile Témime, eds., *L'idée de race dans la pensée politique française contemporaine: Recueil d'articles* (Paris: Editions du CNRS, 1977).

40. With regard to the other side of the Atlantic, see Brent Hayes Edwards, "The Uses of *Diaspora*," *Social Text*, no. 66 (2001): 45–75.

41. Cf. the importance of this theme in Fanon, *Black Skin, White Masks*. See also Aimé Césaire, *Discours sur le colonialisme* (Paris: Présence africaine, 1955); and, more generally, Léopold Sédar Senghor's poetry.

42. See, e.g., Cheikh Anta Diop, *Antériorité des civilisations nègres: Mythe ou vérité historique?* (Paris: Présence africaine, 1967).

43. On this, see Fanon's last pages, *Black Skin, White Masks*.

44. This is Léopold Sédar Senghor's thesis. See Senghor, *Liberté I: Négritude et humanisme* (Paris: Seuil, 1964), and *Liberté III: Négritude et civilisation de l'universel* (Paris: Seuil, 1977).

can be gauged only with respect to the violence of the denial that precedes it and makes it not only possible but necessary.[45] The reaffirmation of a human identity that has been denied by the Other belongs, in this case, to the discourse of rehabilitation and functions as a mode of self-validation.[46] But although the aim of the discourse of rehabilitation is to confirm that Africans too belong to humanity in general, it does not challenge the fiction of race.[47] The defense of the humanity of Africans is almost always accompanied by the claim that their race, traditions, and customs have a specific character.

In dominant African narratives of the self, the deployment of race is foundational not only to difference in general, but also to the idea of the nation, since racial determinants are supposed to serve as the moral basis for political solidarity. In the history of being African, race is the moral subject and at the same time an immanent fact of consciousness. The basic underpinnings of nineteenth-century anthropology, namely, the evolutionist prejudice and the belief in the idea of progress, remain intact; racialization of the (black) nation and the nationalization of the (black) race go hand in hand. Whether we look at negritude or the differing versions of Pan-Africanism, in these discourses the revolt is not against Africans' belonging to a distinct race, but against the prejudice that assigns this race an inferior status.

The next item to consider is tradition and the privileged place it occupies in this nativist current of thought. The starting point here is the claim that Africans have an authentic culture that confers on them a peculiar self irreducible to that of any other group. The negation of this self and this authenticity would thus constitute a mutilation. On the basis of this uniqueness, Africa is supposed to reinvent its relationship to itself and to the world, to own itself, and to escape from the obscure regions and the opaque world (the "Dark Continent") to which history has consigned it. Because of the vicissitudes of history, Africans are supposed to have left tradition behind them. Whence the importance, in order to recover it, of moving backward, which is the necessary condition for overcoming the phase of humiliation and existential anguish caused by the historical debasement of the continent.

45. Cf. the problematics of race in the United States as discussed in Charles W. Mills, *Blackness Visible: Essays on Philosophy and Race* (Ithaca, N.Y.: Cornell University Press, 1998), and Lewis R. Gordon, ed., *Existence in Black: An Anthology of Black Existential Philosophy* (New York: Routledge, 1997).

46. See Abiola Irele, "African Letters: The Making of a Tradition," *Yale Journal of Criticism* 5 (1991): 69–100.

47. Cf. Kwame Anthony Appiah's criticism of texts by Alexander Crummel and W. E. B. Du Bois in *In My Father's House: Africa in the Philosophy of Culture* (London: Methuen, 1992) chaps. 1–2. See also Appiah's "Racism and Moral Pollution," *Philosophical Forum* 18 (1986/87): 185–202.

PUBLIC CULTURE

Society for Transnational Cultural Studies

Please enter my one-year subscription (three issues) to *Public Culture* at the low subscription rate of $34 for individuals; $22 for students with photocopy of current I.D. Subscribers outside the U.S.: Please add $12 for postage. Canadian subscribers: Please add 7% GST to the subscription rate, in addition to outside-U.S. postage.

☐ Enclosed is my check, made payable to Duke University Press.

Please charge my   ☐ VISA   ☐ MasterCard   ☐ American Express

Account Number

Expiration Date   **Signature**

Name

Address

City/State/Zip   PC211

Send your orders to Duke University Press, Journals Fulfillment, Box 90660, Durham, NC 27708-0660.
To place your journal order using a credit card, call toll-free 1-888-387-5765 (within the U.S. or Canada) or
919-687-3602 (elsewhere). www.dukeupress.edu

Library request for a subscription/examination copy

Please enter our one-year subscription (three issues) to *Public Culture*.
Libraries and institutions: $108 (add $12 for postage outside the U.S.;
Canadian libraries add 7% GST to the subscription rate).

Institution

Address   PC211

☐ Purchase order enclosed.

☐ Please bill our agent:

☐ Please send a free examination copy to the address listed above (libraries only).

Volume 14, 2002 (3 issues)
ISSN 0899-2363

Send your orders to Duke University Press, Journals Fulfillment, Box 90660, Durham, NC 27708-0660.
To place your journal order using a credit card, call toll-free 1-888-387-5765 (within the U.S. and Canada) or
919-687-3602 (elsewhere). www.dukeupress.edu

BUSINESS REPLY MAIL

FIRST CLASS MAIL   **PERMIT NO. 1000**   **DURHAM, NC**

POSTAGE WILL BE PAID BY ADDRESSEE

Duke University Press
Journals Fulfillment
Box 90660
Durham, NC 27706-9942

NO POSTAGE
NECESSARY
IF MAILED
IN THE
UNITED STATES

BUSINESS REPLY MAIL

FIRST CLASS MAIL   **PERMIT NO. 1000**   **DURHAM, NC**

POSTAGE WILL BE PAID BY ADDRESSEE

Duke University Press
Journals Fulfillment
Box 90660
Durham, NC 27706-9942

The emphasis on establishing an "African interpretation" of things, on creating one's own schemata of self-mastery, of understanding oneself and the universe, of producing endogenous knowledge have all led to demands for an "African science," an "African democracy," an "African language."[48] This urge to make Africa unique is presented as a moral and political problem, the reconquest of the power to narrate one's own story—and therefore identity—seeming to be necessarily constitutive of any subjectivity. Ultimately, it is no longer a matter of claiming the status of alter ego for Africans in the world, but rather of asserting loudly and forcefully their alterity.

It is this alterity that must be preserved at all costs. In the most extreme versions of nativism, difference is thus praised, not as the symptom of a greater universality, but rather as the inspiration for determining principles and norms governing Africans' lives in full autonomy and, if necessary, in opposition to the world. Softer versions leave open the possibility of "working toward the universal" and enriching Western rationality by adding to it the "values of black civilization," the "genius peculiar to the black race." This is what Léopold Sédar Senghor calls *le rendez-vous du donner et du recevoir* (the meeting point of giving and receiving), one of the results of which is supposed to be the *métissage* of cultures.

Since the nineteenth century, those who maintain that Africans have their own cultural identity, that there is a specific African autochthony, have sought to find a general denomination and a place to which they could anchor their prose. The geographical place turns out to be a tropical Africa, bounded as a thoroughly fictional realm in opposition to the phantasmatic anatomy invented by Europeans and echoed by Hegel and others.[49] Somehow, the disjointed members of this imaginary polis must be glued back together. The dismembered body of the continent's history is therefore reconstituted in the light of myth. An attempt is made to locate Africanity in a set of specific cultural characteristics that ethnological

48. On these debates, see Julius Nyerere, *Ujamaa: Essays on Socialism* (London: Oxford University Press, 1968); Kwasi Wiredu, *Cultural Universals and Particulars: An African Perspective* (Bloomington: Indiana University Press, 1996), and "How Not to Compare African Thought with Western Thought," in *African Philosophy as Cultural Inquiry,* ed. Ivan Karp and D. A. Masolo (Bloomington: Indiana University Press, 2000), 187–214; Paulin Hountondji, ed., *Endogenous Knowledge: Research Trails* (Dakar: CODESRIA, 1997); Kwame Gyekye, *African Cultural Values: An Introduction* (Philadelphia: Sankofa, 1996), and *Tradition and Modernity: Philosophical Reflections on the African Experience* (New York: Oxford University Press, 1997); Ngugi wa Thiong'o, *Decolonising the Mind: The Politics of Language in African Literature* (London: James Currey, 1986).

49. See Hegel's geography of Africa in *Philosophy of History.*

research is expected to provide. Nationalist historiography sets out in quest of the missing remainder in ancient African empires and in pharaonic Egypt.[50]

In the prose of nativism (as well as in some versions of the Marxist and nationalist narratives), a quasi-equivalence is established between race and geography. Cultural identity is derived from the relationship between the two terms, geography becoming the privileged site at which the (black) race's institutions and power are supposed to be embodied.[51] Pan-Africanism in particular defines the *native* and the *citizen* by identifying them with black people. In this mythology, blacks do not become citizens because they are human beings endowed with political rights, but because of two particularistic factors: their color and a privileged autochthony. Racial and territorial authenticity are conflated, and Africa becomes the land of black people. Since the racial interpretation is at the foundation of a restricted civic relatedness, everything that is not black is out of place, and thus cannot claim any sort of Africanity. The spatial body, the racial body, and the civic body are thenceforth one, each testifying to an autochthonous communal origin by virtue of which everyone born of the soil or sharing the same color or ancestors is a brother or a sister.

The idea of an Africanity that is not black is simply unthinkable. Whence the impossibility of conceiving, for example, the existence of Africans of European, Arab, or Asian origin—or that Africans might have multiple ancestries. One result of the Atlantic slave trade is that blacks live in faraway places. How should we account for their inscription within a nation defined racially and geographically, when geography and history have cut them off from the place from which their ancestors came? Since the African geographical space constitutes the natural homeland of black people, those whom slavery has taken away from it must "return to the land of [their] fathers . . . and be at peace."[52]

The Shattered Mirror

We have just seen that dominant African discourses on the self developed within a racist paradigm. As discourses of inversion, they draw their fundamental cate-

50. See Joseph Ki-Zerbo, *Histoire de l'Afrique noire d'hier à demain* (Paris: Hatier, 1972); Cheikh Anta Diop, *L'unité culturelle de l'Afrique noire: Domaines du patriarcat et du matriarcat dans l'antiquité Classique* (Paris: Présence africaine, 1959); Théophile Obenga, *L'Afrique dans l'antiquité: Egypte pharaonique, Afrique noire* (Paris: Présence africaine, 1973).

51. Ironically, we find the same impulse and the same desire to conflate race with geography in the racist writings of white settlers in South Africa. For details, see J. M. Coetzee, *White Writing: On the Culture of Letters in South Africa* (New Haven, Conn.: Yale University Press, 1988).

52. Blyden, *Christianity, Islam and the Negro Race*, 124.

gories from the myths they claim to oppose and reproduce their dichotomies: the racial difference between black and white; the cultural confrontation between civilized peoples and savages; the religious opposition between Christians and pagans; the very conviction that race exists and is at the foundation of morality and nationality. They are inscribed within an intellectual genealogy based on a territorialized identity and a racialized geography, the myth of a racial polis obscuring the fact that while the rapacity of global capitalism may be at the origin of the tragedy, Africans' failure to control their own predatory greed and their own cruelty also led to slavery and subjugation.[53] More fundamentally, behind the dream of political emancipation and the rhetoric of autonomy, a perverse operation has been taking place, the result of which has only strengthened Africans' ressentiment and their neurosis of victimization.

Of all the attempts that have been made in the course of the twentieth century to break with this empty dream, this exhausted mode of thought, two are of particular interest for our discussion. First of all, there are the efforts to deconstruct tradition (and thereby Africa itself) by showing the latter to have been invented.[54] From this point of view, Africa as such exists only on the basis of the text that constructs it as the Other's fiction. This text is then accorded a structuring power, to the point that a self that claims to speak with its own, authentic voice always runs the risk of being condemned to express itself in a preestablished discourse that masks its own, censures it, or forces it to imitate.

This is as much to say that Africa exists only on the basis of a preexisting library, one that intervenes and insinuates itself everywhere, even in the discourse that claims to refute it—to the point that with regard to African identity and tradition, it is now impossible to distinguish the "original" from a copy.[55] The same can be said of any project aimed at disentangling Africa from the West. In a related vein, a second avenue has problematized African identity as an identity in formation.[56] From this point of view, the world is no longer perceived as a

53. See Joseph Miller, *Way of Death: Merchant Capitalism and the Angolan Slave Trade (1730–1830)* (Madison: University of Wisconsin Press, 1988).

54. In his study of the foundations of discourse about Africa, Mudimbe notices that "Western interpreters as well as African analysts have been using categories and conceptual systems which depend on a Western epistemological order. Even in the most explicitly 'Afrocentric' descriptions, models of analysis explicitly or implicitly, knowingly or unknowingly, refer to the same order" (Valentin Y. Mudimbe, *The Invention of Africa: Gnosis, Philosophy, and the Order of Knowledge* [Bloomington: Indiana University Press, 1988], x).

55. For a case study, see Carolyn Hamilton, *Terrific Majesty: The Powers of Shaka Zulu and the Limits of Historical Invention* (Cambridge: Harvard University Press, 1998).

56. See Appiah, *In My Father's House.* In a later study, Appiah denounces the narrowness of

threat. On the contrary, it is imagined as a vast network of affinities. In contrast to unanimist mythologies, the essential message here is that everyone can imagine and choose what makes him or her an African.

In large measure, both of these criticisms are driven by methodological considerations. They do not go to the heart of the matter: How to deal with the specters invoked by the nativists and so-called radicals in their respective attempts to hypostatize African identity—at the very time when the imaginative and social practices of African agents show that other orders of reality are being established. In other words, how should we conceive, creatively and in their heteronomy, the all-purpose signifiers constituted by slavery, colonization, and apartheid?

On the philosophical level, priority must be given to interrogating the imprisoning model of a history that is already shaped and that one can only undergo or repeat—and to addressing that which, in actual African experiences of the world, has escaped such determination. On a more anthropological level, the obsession with uniqueness and difference must be opposed by a thematics of sameness. In order to move away from ressentiment and lamentation over the loss of a *nom propre*, we must clear an intellectual space for rethinking those temporalities that are always simultaneously branching out toward several different futures and, in so doing, open the way for the possibility of multiple ancestries. Finally, on a sociological level, attention must be given to the contemporary everyday practices through which Africans manage to recognize and maintain with the world an unprecedented familiarity—practices through which they invent something that is their own and that beckons to the world in its generality.[57]

Let me briefly examine some of the genuinely philosophical inquiries neglected

---

nationalist positions, emphasizes the possibility of double ancestry, and affiliates himself with a "liberal cosmopolitanism." See Kwame Anthony Appiah, "Cosmopolitan Patriots," *Critical Inquiry* 23 (1997): 617–39.

57. In recent years, various studies have shown how, beyond claims to Africanness, Africans have constantly negotiated new positions in the spaces between cultures and have disrupted the signs of both identity and difference. See, among others, Karin Barber, ed., *Readings in African Popular Culture* (Bloomington: Indiana University Press, 1997); Sarah Nuttall and Cheryl-Ann Michael, eds., *Senses of Culture: South African Culture Studies* (Oxford: Oxford University Press, 2000); Jonathan Haynes, ed., *Nigerian Video Films* (Athens, Ohio: Ohio University Center for International Studies, 2000). For two case studies on the complex entanglements of so-called traditional and global intellectual traditions, see Peterson Bhekizizwe, *Monarchs, Missionaries, and African Intellectuals: African Theatre and the Unmaking of Colonial Marginality* (Johannesburg: Witwatersrand University Press, 2000); and Stephanie Newell, *Ghanaian Popular Fiction: "Thrilling Discoveries in Conjugal Life" and Other Tales* (Oxford: James Currey, 2000).

by African criticism in its reflection on slavery, colonization and apartheid. The first question that should be identified concerns the status of suffering in history—the various ways in which historical forces inflict psychic harm on collective bodies and the ways in which violence shapes subjectivity. It is here that a comparison with other historical experiences has been deemed appropriate. The Jewish Holocaust furnishes one such comparative experience.[58] Indeed, the Holocaust, slavery, and apartheid all represent forms of originary suffering. They are all characterized by an expropriation of the self by unnameable forces. In each case, the forces assume various forms. But in all, the central sequence is the same: to the orgiastic intoxication summoned by the administration of mass murder corresponds, like an echo, the placing of life between two chasms, so that the subject no longer knows if he or she is dead or alive. This combination of destructive animus and the dislocation of the self constitutes the Dionysian terrain shared by these three events. Indeed, at their ultimate foundation, the three events bear witness against life itself. On the pretext that origin and race are the criteria of any kind of valuation, they indict life. Whence the question: How can life be redeemed, that is, rescued from this incessant operation of the negative?

The second question has to do with the work of memory, with the function of forgetting, and with the modalities of reparation. Is it possible to lump together slavery, colonization, and apartheid as a memory? That is to say, not in a sort of distinction between before and after or past and future, but in what might be termed the *genetic power* of these events—their revelation of the impossibility of a world without Others and of the weight of the peculiar responsibility incumbent upon Africans themselves in the face of tragedy (which is not the only element!) in their history. It is here that the comparison between African and Jewish experiences reveals profound differences. In contrast to the Jewish memory of the Holocaust, there is, properly speaking, no African memory of slavery;[59] or, if there is such a memory, it is one characterized by diffraction.[60] At best, slavery is experienced as a wound whose meaning belongs to the domain of the uncon-

58. See Laurence Thomas, *Vessels of Evil: American Slavery and the Holocaust* (Philadelphia: Temple University Press, 1993).

59. On Jewish memory, see, among other studies, Dominick LaCapra, *History and Memory after Auschwitz* (Ithaca, N.Y.: Cornell University Press, 1998); Yosef H. Yerushalmi, *Zakhor: Jewish History and Jewish Memory* (Seattle: University of Washington Press, 1982). For a philosophical critique, cf. Paul Ricoeur, *La mémoire, l'histoire, l'oubli* (Paris: Seuil, 2000).

60. See Madeleine Borgomano, "La littérature romanesque d'Afrique noire et l'esclavage: 'Une mémoire de l'oubli'?" in *Esclavage et abolitions: Mémoires et systèmes de représentation*, ed. Marie-Christine Rochmann (Paris: Karthala, 2000), 99–112.

259

scious—in a word, witchcraft.[61] When efforts at conscious recollection have been made, they have scarcely escaped the ambivalence that characterizes similar gestures in other historical contexts.[62]

There are two reasons for this difficulty with the project of recuperating the memory of slavery. First, between African Americans' memory of slavery and that of continental Africans, there is a shadowy zone that conceals a deep silence—the silence of guilt and the refusal of Africans to face up to the troubling aspect of the crime that directly engages their own responsibility. For the fate of black slaves in modernity is not solely the result of the tyrannical will and cruelty of the Other, however well established the latter's culpability may be. The other primitive signifier is the murder of brother by brother, "the elision of the first syllable of the family name," in Jacques Lacan's phrase—in short, the divided polis. Along the trajectory of the events that led to slavery, this is the trail that dominant African discourses of the self try to erase.

The ablation here is significant, because it enables the functioning of the illusion that the temporalities of servitude and misery were the same on both sides of the Atlantic. This is not true. And it is this distance that prevents the trauma, the absence, and the loss from ever being the same on the two sides of the Atlantic.[63] As long as continental Africans neglect to rethink slavery—not merely as a catastrophe of which they were but the victims, but as the product of a history that they have played an active part in shaping—the appeal to race as the moral and political basis of solidarity will depend, to some extent, on a mirage of consciousness.[64]

61. See, e.g., Rosalind Shaw, "The Production of Witchcraft/Witchcraft as Production: Memory, Modernity, and the Slave Trade in Sierra Leone," *American Ethnologist* 24 (1997): 856–76. Cf. *Route et traces des esclaves*, special issue, *Diogène*, no. 179 (1997).

62. See T. A. Singleton, "The Slave Trade Remembered on the Former Gold and Slave Coasts," *Slavery and Abolition* 20 (1999): 150–69; and Edward M. Bruner, "Tourism in Ghana: The Representation of Slavery and the Return of the Black Diaspora," *American Anthropologist* 98 (1996): 290–304. In the postapartheid context, see the description of "township tours" by Steven Robins, "City Sites," in Nuttall and Michael, *Senses of Culture*, 408–25.

63. On the status of these categories in general and their role in Jewish consciousness in particular, cf. Dominick LaCapra, "Trauma, Absence, Loss," *Critical Inquiry* 25 (1999): 696–730.

64. In their "Trust, Pawnship, and Atlantic History: The Institutional Foundations of the Old Calabar Slave Trade," *American Historical Review* 104 (1999): 333–55, Paul E. Lovejoy and David Richardson show how African dealers in slaves and British merchants adapted the local institution of debt bondage, or "pawnship," as a way of securing credit (or goods advanced against the delivery of slaves). For a general discussion on human pawnship in Africa, see Toyin Falola and Paul E. Lovejoy, eds., *Pawnship in Africa: Debt Bondage in Historical Perspective* (Boulder, Colo.: Westview Press, 1994).

The second challenge to the recovery of memory is of another order. In certain parts of the New World, the memory of slavery is repressed by the descendents of African slaves. The family drama at the origin of the tragedy as well as the misery of their existence in the present are constantly denied. To be sure, this denial is not equivalent to forgetting as such. It is simultaneously a refusal to acknowledge one's ancestry and a refusal to remember an act that arouses feelings of shame. Under such conditions, the priority is not really to reestablish contact with oneself and with one's origins.[65] Nor is it a question of restoring a full and positive relationship to oneself, since this self has been damaged and humiliated beyond any limit. Because the narrative of slavery has been condemned to being elliptical, a ghost persecutes and haunts the subject and inscribes on his or her unconscious the dead body of a language that must constantly be repressed. For in order to exist in the present, it is considered necessary to forget the name of the father in the very act in which one claims to ask the question of origin and filiation. This is notably the case in the Antilles.[66]

A third lacuna in African philosophical reflection on the three events is presented by the question of the symbolism of exile. The metaphor of the concentration camp is used to compare the condition of slavery with the predicament of European Jewry as well as, on a more general level, relations between race and culture in modern consciousness. But there is something hasty and superficial about this comparison.[67] In fact, the Jewish imagination constantly oscillates between a plurality of contrasted myths and unresolved, but productive, tensions—the myth of autochthony versus the reality of forced displacement, the empirical fact of dislocation versus the promise of return—in short, a temporality in suspense, in which resides the twofold visage of the diaspora and Israel, the absence of territory in no way signifying the interruption of Jewish continuity. And finally, beyond contingency, fragmentation, and terror, there is a Book, the Torah, a text continuously reinscribed through a process of exegesis and commentary.

Beyond the appearance of fractures and diffraction, the experience of African

65. Compare Lucien Taylor, "Créolité Bites. A Conversation with Patrick Chamoiseau, Raphael-Confiant, and Jean Bernabé," *Transition* 74 (1998): 124–60, with Peter Hallward, "Edouard Glissant between the Singular and the Specific," *Yale Journal of Criticism* 11 (1998): 441–64.

66. On these questions, see Daniel Maragnes, "L'identité et le désastre: Origine et fondation," in *Mémoire juive, mémoire nègre: Deux figures du destin,* ed. Roger Toumson (Châteauneuf-le-Rouge, France: Vents des Iles, 1998).

67. Paul Gilroy, "Between Camps: Race and Culture in Postmodernity. An Inaugural Lecture," *Economy and Society* 28 (1999): 183–97.

slaves in the New World reflects a more or less comparable plenitude of identity, even if the forms of its expression differ, and even though there is no Book as such. Like Jews in the European world, they have to narrate the self and narrate the world, approaching this world from a position in which their lives, their work, and their way of speaking (*langage*) are scarcely legible, enveloped as they are in ghostly contours. They have to invent an art of existing in the midst of despoliation—even though, by this date, it is almost impossible to reenchant the past and cast a spell upon the present (except, perhaps, in the syncopated terms of a body that is constantly made to pass from being to appearance, from song to music).[68] But that said, the similarity ends. In contrast with the case of the Holocaust, black peoples' experiences of slavery in the New World and elsewhere have not been interpreted in any way—philosophically, politically, or culturally—that brings out the possibility of founding a universal telos.[69]

Marxist and nationalist criticism has underestimated the wide variety of African experiences of colonial conquest. Recent historiography has shown that Africans gave very different answers to the choices forced on them by European invasion. The social divisions constituted over the period of the Atlantic slave trade had sharpened under the test of colonialism. New sources of wealth acquired during the heyday of the slave trade and its aftermath overturned preexisting social orders. The two major monotheistic religions, Islam and Christianity, questioned the cosmological bases of local societies. As political violence and extortion intensified during the second half of the nineteenth century, the exercise of power was released from mediation by any discourse of political responsibility. The shifts in relations of power, exacerbated by local wars of succession, resulted in a comprehensive crisis of authority. In most places, the colonial advance across the interior of the continent could be said to have taken the character of a creeping slave revolt.[70]

In many ways, colonization was a co-invention. It was the result of Western violence as well as the work of a swarm of African auxiliaries seeking profit. Where it was impractical to import a white settler population to occupy the land, colonial powers generally got blacks to colonize their own congeners (*congénères*) in the name of the metropolitan nation. More decisively, "unhealthy"

68. Gilroy, *Black Atlantic*; and Stuart Hall, "Nihilism in Black America" in *Black Popular Culture*, ed. Michele Wallace and Gina Dent (Seattle: Bay Press, 1992).

69. See Howard H. Harriott, "The Evils of Chattel Slavery and the Holocaust: An Examination of Laurence Thomas's Vessels of Evil," *International Philosophical Quarterly* 37 (1997): 329–47.

70. John Lonsdale, "The European Scramble and Conquest in African History," in *The Cambridge History of Africa,* vol. 6 (Cambridge: Cambridge University Press, 1981).

though it may appear to a critic, it must be recognized that colonialism exercised a strong seductive power over Africans on a mental and moral no less than material level. Manifold possibilities of upward mobility were promised by the colonial system. Whether such promises were actually fulfilled is beside the point. As a refracted and endlessly reconstituted fabric of fictions, colonialism generated mutual utopias—hallucinations shared by the colonizers and the colonized.[71]

The above examples suffice to show that by resorting to expedients and failing to address these central questions about life—its forms, its possibilities, and what denies it—African criticism, dominated by political economy and by the nativist impulse, has from the outset inscribed the quest for political identity within a purely instrumental and short-term temporality. When the question was asked, during the heyday of colonialism, whether self-government was possible, it was never to engage the general question of *being* and *time*—in other words, of life—but rather to facilitate native people's struggle to take over the apparatus of the state. The power to risk one's life—that is, in Hegel's terms, the ability to put an end to the servile condition and be reborn as the subject of the world—peters out in the prose of autochthony. And in the end, it can be said that everything here comes down to that one, perverse structure: autochthony.

Self, Polis, and Cosmopolis

So where are we today? What ways of imagining identity are at work and what social practices do they produce? What has happened to the tropes of victimization, race, and tradition?

First, I must note that the thematics of anti-imperialism is exhausted. This does not mean, however, that the pathos of victimization has been transcended. The anti-imperialist debate was in fact revived during the 1980s and 1990s in the form of a critique of structural adjustment programs and neoliberal conceptions of the state's relation to the market.[72] In the interim, however, the ideology of Pan-Africanism was confronted by the reality of national states that, contrary to received wisdom, turned out to be less artificial than had been thought. A more significant development has been an emerging junction between the old anti-imperialist thematics—"revolution," "anticolonialism"—and the nativist theses. Fragments of these imaginaires are now combining to oppose globalization, to

71. Cf. Françoise Vergès's reading of Fanon in "Creole Skin, Black Mask: Fanon and Disavowal," *Critical Inquiry* 23 (1997): 578–95.

72. See, e.g., Mkandawire and Soludo, *Our Continent, Our Future*.

relaunch the metaphysics of difference, to reenchant tradition, and to revive the utopian vision of an Africanity that is coterminous with blackness.

The thematic of race has also undergone major shifts. The extreme case of South Africa (and other settler colonies) has long led people, both in the West and Africa, to think that the polar opposition between blacks and whites summed up by itself the whole racial question in Africa. However, the repertoires on the basis of which the imaginaires of race and the symbolism of blood are constituted have always been characterized by their extreme variety. At a level beyond that of the simple black/white opposition, other racial cleavages have always set Africans against each other. And here may be enumerated not only the most visible—black Africans versus Africans of Arab, South Asian, Jewish, or Chinese ancestry—but also a range of others that can attest to the panoply of colors and their annexation to projects of domination: black Africans versus Creoles, Lebanese-Syrians, métis, Berbers, Tuaregs, Afro-Brazilians, and Fulanis; Amharas versus Oromos; and Tutsis versus Hutus, to give some representative examples.

In fact—no matter what definition one gives of the notion—the racial unity of Africa has always been a myth. But this myth is currently imploding under the impact of internal (as well as external) factors connected with African societies' linkages to global cultural flows. For even if inequalities of power and access to property remain (not to mention racist stereotypes and violence), the category of *whiteness* no longer has the same meanings as it did under colonialism or apartheid. Although the "white condition" has not reached a point of absolute fluidity that would detach it once and for all from any citation of power, privilege, and oppression, it is clear that the experience of Africans of European origin has taken on ever more diverse aspects throughout the continent. The forms in which this experience is imagined—not only by whites themselves, but also by others—are no longer the same. This diversity now makes the identity of Africans of European origin a contingent and situated identity.[73]

The same might be said of Luso-Africans and Africans of South Asian or Lebanese-Syrian origin, even if the historical conditions of their becoming citizens and their positions on the social map differ from those of whites and blacks.[74] The case of North Africans of Arab origin suggests transformations of

73. Cf., e.g., Ian Smith, *The Great Betrayal: The Memoirs of Ian Douglas Smith* (London: Blake, 1997); Eugene De Kock and Jeremy Gordin, *A Long Night's Damage: Working for the Apartheid State* (Saxonwold, South Africa: Contra, 1998); and Antjie Krog, *Country of My Skull* (Johannesburg: Random House, 1998). More generally, see Sarah Nuttall, "Subjectivities of Whiteness," *African Studies Review* 44 (2001): 115–40.

74. See R. G. Gregory, *South Asians in East Asia: An Economic and Social History, 1890–1980*

another kind. On the one hand, the historical relations and influences between the Mediterranean Maghreb and sub-Saharan Africa are continually both repressed and narrativized in folklore. Officially, as a matter of state policy, Maghrebi identity is Arabo-Islamic. Given a historical scope, however, it can be seen to proceed from a syncretic mixture of Saharan, Berber, Peninsular Arabian, and even Jewish and Turkish contributions.[75] On the other hand, Islam has served as the idiom of a sociocultural matrix within which adherence to the same faith and belonging to a single religious community do not do away with a master-slave relation, as we see in Mauretania or, farther to the east, in the Arabo-Nilotic region (Sudan in particular).

What can be seen here is that the symbolism of blood and colors proceeds by degrees. And as in other parts of the world, race, class, ethnicity, and gender in Africa intersect and produce, despite the ambivalence inherent in such operations, effects of violence. In general, it can be said that the forms of racial consciousness are changing all over the continent. The production of racial identities beyond the binary black/white opposition increasingly operates in accord with distinct, contingent logics as old demarcations lose their mechanical aspect and opportunities for transgression multiply. In many ways, the instability of racial categories is demonstrating that there are several kinds of whiteness as well as of blackness.[76]

Let me focus here on the trope of tradition. The project of reenchanting tradition is based on a set of fragmentary ideas and social practices—on an imaginaire that draws its referents from both local and global sources. The most powerful vectors of this imaginaire are the communitarian movements. By contrast with a universalist, cosmopolitan view, which would tend to emphasize the ability to detach itself from any kind of essence, these movements draw their power from the rehabilitation of origins and membership. The idea is that there is no identity that does not in some way lead to questions about origins and attachment

---

(Boulder, Colo.: Westview Press, 1993); also Melanie Yap and Dianne Leong Man, *Colour, Confusion, and Concessions: The History of the Chinese in South Africa* (Hong Kong: Hong Kong University Press, 1996); and Peter Mark, "The Evolution of 'Portuguese' Identity: Luso-Africans on the Upper Guinea Coast from the Sixteenth to the Early Nineteenth Century," *Journal of African History* 40 (1999): 173–91.

75. Cf. *Africanité du Maghreb,* special issue of *Africultures* 13 (1998); and *Afrique noire et monde arabe: Continuités et ruptures,* special issue of *Cahiers des sciences humaines* 16 (2000).

76. Cf., in another context, Livio Sansone, "The New Blacks from Bahia: Local and Global in Afro-Bahia," *Identities* 3 (1997): 457–93.

to them—no matter what definition of them is given or how much fiction may be inherent in that definition.

The *différend* concerning origins is supposed to be the starting point for becoming conscious of identity. At the same time, however, every such identity is expected to be translated into territorial terms. Indeed, to this way of thinking, there is no identity without territoriality—the vivid consciousness of *place* and mastery of it, whether by birth, by conquest, or by settlement. Territoriality in its clearest manifestation is to be found in the cult of locality—or, in other words, home, the small space and inherited estate where direct, proximate relationships are reinforced by membership in a common genealogy. This is the same matrix, real or supposed, that serves as the foundation for the civic space; in fact, funerals and burials are one of the chief ways of ritualizing membership in the civic space, as enacted within the boundaries of home.[77] It can thus be seen that from a combination of ideological categories (membership and origins) and spatial categories (territory and locality) emerges citizenship, which might be defined as the ability to enjoy a home, the ability to exclude foreigners from this enjoyment, the right to protection and to access to a range of collective goods and resources situated in the space thus delimited.

It can further be stated that, under contemporary processes of globalization, the idioms of kinship deployed in this process of claiming citizenship—relations such as filiation, genealogy, and heritage—can be converted into recyclable resources. One of the vehicles of this conversion is the international lexicon of rights. Whether the right being invoked in a given argument cites the protection of the environment or the claims of minorities or indigenous peoples, in each case the strategy is to assert a wounded identity. The wound is configured in the deprivation of specific rights that a discrete community then attempts to recover through this recourse to the international lexicon. Another vehicle for reenchanting tradition and recycling local identities that is coming to the fore is the market. The market's role in the process is particularly apparent in the contexts of tourism and the politics of heritage.

States of War and Regimes of Divine Sovereignty   But if global processes of symbolic exchange enter African subjectivities at (among other levels) the commodification of identities under the sign of tradition, one of the chief sites of

---

77. See Kwame Arhin, "The Economic Implications of Transformations in Akan Funeral Rites," *Africa* 64 (1994): 307–21; and Sjaak van der Geest, "Funerals for the Living: Conversations with Elderly People in Kwahu, Ghana," *African Studies Review* 43 (2000): 103–29.

mediation between global flows and local practices of reenchanting tradition turns out to be war—or, more precisely, *the state of war*. Getting beyond a consideration of its empirical aspects (e.g., the formation of militias, the privatization of violence, arms trading, and smuggling), the state of war in contemporary Africa should in fact be conceived of as a general cultural experience that shapes identities, just as the family, the school, and other social institutions do. And in a still more determinative manner, the state of war invokes regimes of subjectivity that must be explored briefly.

First among the state of war's effects can be identified as an entry into a *zone of indistinction*. This is a space set outside human jurisdiction, where the frontiers between the rule of law and chaos disappear, decisions about life and death become entirely arbitrary, and everything becomes possible.[78] In most contemporary war zones in Africa, the descent into indistinction is marked by an unprecedented degree of torture, mutilation, and mass killing.[79] Progressively, the spread of terror fragments inhabited spaces, blows apart temporal frames of reference, and diminishes the possibilities available to individuals to fulfill themselves as continuous subjects.[80] The ensuing spectacularization of suffering only serves to reinforce this process through the bequest of traumatic memories. The horror of bodily injury is everywhere to be seen. Trauma has become something quasi-permanent. Memory is physically embedded in bodies marked with the signs of their own destruction, moving through a general landscape of fragmentation and economic decay. In many places, life has taken the form of a continuous journey. One leaves one space and establishes oneself in another only to be dislodged by terror, confronted by unpredictable circumstances, and forced to settle once again where one can.[81]

The second effect that should be remarked upon is the *sacrificial dimension of war*.[82] As shown elsewhere, in several regions of the continent, the material

78. On these discussions, see Jenny Edkins, "Sovereign Power, Zones of Indistinction, and the Camp," *Alternatives* 25 (2000): 3–25.

79. Cf. Inge Brinkman, "Ways of Death: Accounts of Terror from Angolan Refugees in Namibia," *Africa* 70 (2000): 1–24.

80. See Boubacar Boris Diop, *Murambi: Le livre des ossements* (Paris: Stock, 2000); Thierno Monenembo, *L'aîné des orphelins* (Paris: Seuil, 2000).

81. Here, I draw my inspiration from Daniel Pécaut, "Configurations of Space, Time, and Subjectivity in a Context of Terror: The Colombian Example," *International Journal of Politics, Culture, and Society* 14 (2000): 129–50.

82. A dimension that we also encounter in autochthonous practices and that monotheistic religions have only accentuated. See Robin Law, "Human Sacrifice in Pre-Colonial West Africa," *African Affairs* 34 (1985): 53–87; and, more generally, J. Milbank, "Stories of Sacrifice: From Wellhausen to Girard," *Theory, Culture, and Society* 12 (1995): 15–46.

deconstruction of existing territorial frameworks goes hand in hand with the emergence of war economies (and of war as a general economy) in which violent conflicts no longer necessarily imply that those who have weapons oppose each other. Many conflicts are likely to oppose those who have weapons and those who have none. In those contexts, a marked disconnection between people and things ensues, the value of things surpassing that of people. The resulting forms of violence have as their chief goals the physical destruction of people (massacres of civilians, genocides, various kinds of maiming) and the primary exploitation of mineral resources.[83] Most of these events stem from the idea of history as a sacrificial process.

Here, the word *sacrifice* has two senses: self-sacrifice (putting one's life at someone else's disposal, getting killed for a cause) and mass murder (the physical annihilation of countless human lives). On the one hand, self-sacrifice implies that one will put to death other human beings who are identified with the "enemy." One accepts that one may be killed during this process; indeed, one believes that in such a death is found the essence of life. On the other hand, massacre constitutes the most grandiose sign of both sovereignty and what Georges Bataille called *expenditure*.[84] More than anything else, it marks the limit of the principle of utility—and thus of the idea of the preservation—of human lives. Massacre inaugurates a sovereignty of loss through the spectacular destruction and bloody waste of human beings.

It is a characteristic of actual corpses, dead things, that they all seem frozen in pastness. Doubts emerge as to whether those apparently animate beings who seem to be alive are really alive, or whether they are only the figurative corpses of what had once been alive and are now but shattered mirrors at the frontier of madness and abjection.[85] The function of this Dionysian violence is not to stun or even to dazzle.[86] Nor is it part of a consumptive process of manduction and dejection. This process is no longer a matter of appropriating the Other or turning him or her into chattel or merchandise, as happened during the period of the

83. Cf. Achille Mbembe, "At the Edge of the World: Boundaries, Territoriality, and Sovereignty in Africa," *Public Culture* 12 (2000): 259–84.

84. Georges Bataille, *La part maudite, précédé de La notion de dépense* (Paris: Editions de Minuit, 1967).

85. On "corpses" and "abjection," see Julia Kristeva, *Powers of Horror: An Essay on Abjection*, trans. Leon S. Roudiez (New York: Columbia University Press, 1982).

86. On the Dionysian character of the process, see Harris Memel-Fotê, "La fête de l'homme riche dans le Golfe de Guinée au temps de l'esclavage, XVIIe-XIXe siècles," *Cahiers d'études africaines* 131 (1993): 363–79.

Atlantic slave trade and its aftermath. Rather, it is a question of abolishing, once and for all, the very idea of a *debt owed to life*.[87]

But in the act that consists of putting to death innumerable sacrificial victims, the agent of the massacre also seeks to transcend and reinvent the self. Trembling with drunkenness, he or she becomes a sort of work of art shaped and sculpted by cruelty. It is in this sense that the state of war becomes part of the new African practices of the self. Through sacrifice, the African subject transforms his or her own subjectivity and produces something new—something that does not belong to the domain of a lost identity that must at all costs be found again, but rather something radically different, something open to change and whose theory and vocabulary remain to be invented.[88]

The third feature of the state of war to be discussed here is its relation to two central determinants already identified in the experiences of slavery and apartheid: life and property. Life is a factor here to the extent that the state of war authorizes power, even naked force, to be exercised in the extreme, in an absolute manner. As a result, the calculus governing cultural and political practices no longer has as its goal the subjection of individuals so much as the seizure of power over life itself. Its function is to abolish any idea of ancestry and thus any debt with regard to a past. There emerges an original imaginaire of sovereignty whose field of exercise is nothing less than life in its generality. The latter may be subject to an empirical, that is, biological death. But it can also be seen to be mortgaged, in the same way that objects are, in a general economy whose terms are furnished by massacres and carnage, in the manner of capital, labor, and surplus value as disposed in the classical Marxist model.

Alongside the state of war, the other form of instituting imagination through which the junction between the cosmopolitan and the local is effected is the state of religion (*l'état de religion*). On this front, the most significant development of the last quarter of the twentieth century has been the unprecedented growth of Pentecostal Christianity among popular and elite urban sectors in Africa. Crucial to this expansion have been four structures of meaning, each of which provides a means of psychic negotiation, self-styling, and engagement with the world at large. These are: the gift of tongues (the ability to speak in both heavenly and human languages), the gift of divine healing and prophecy, the ethics of sainthood, and the ethos of prosperity.[89]

87. Cf. Achille Mbembe, "Political Imagination in Times of War" (forthcoming).
88. See Ahmadou Kourouma, *Allah n'est pas obligé* (Paris: Seuil, 2000).
89. On the ethics of sainthood and the ethos of prosperity, see Ruth Marshall-Fratani, "Prospérité

In contemporary Africa, it is the subject's relation to divine sovereignty that serves as the main provider of meanings for most people. This can be said even though the various discursive formations whose symbolism is established in religious authority are far from being homogeneous. Almost everywhere, contemporary practices in the course of which divine power is mimed or staged are linked with the process of reinventing the self and the polis, in its twofold sense — earthly polis and heavenly polis (the Kingdom). Such a categorization does not reflect solely a division between this world and the beyond. It also indicates how the self arises from the interaction between the world of the empirical and what cannot be reduced to it. Through specific rituals and celebrations of various kinds, religious practice is becoming the site where the networks of a new, nonbiological relationship among members of a family or even an ecumene are formed, at the same time as notions of divine sovereignty and patronage are transformed and new dogmas emerge.

More fundamentally, the development of a new religious imaginaire is based on the mobilization of three ideosymbolic formations whose hold on contemporary conceptions of the self is evident: the exercise of charisma (which authorizes the practice of oracular pronouncement and prophecy, of possession and healing); the logic of sacrifice (mourning and funerals); and, finally, the domain of the miraculous (that is, the belief that anything is possible). Charisma is particularly interesting in that it encompasses two apparently contradictory tendencies. On the one hand, it represents the zenith of individuality as well as of shared experience. Although not every member of the congregation is supposed to be endowed with prophetic gifts per se, each one nevertheless is granted unobstructed access to the same source of power — divine grace.[90] On the other hand, charisma marks investiture with a distinct, autonomous power and authority that is benevolently exercised in the service of a community. The exercise of this authority places the thaumaturge in a hierarchical relationship with those who are not endowed with the same magic, the same know-how. An attempt is made to manage the "real world" on the basis of the conviction that all symbolization refers primarily to a system of the invisible, of a magical universe, the present belonging above all to a sequence that opens onto something different.

Finally, let me gesture to the problem of the object of desire in an economy of

---

miraculeuse: Pasteurs pentecôtistes et argent de Dieu au Nigéria," *Politique africaine*, no. 82 (June 2001): 24–44.

90. Cf. Raphael Falco, "Charisma and Tragedy: An Introduction," *Theory, Culture, and Society* 16 (1999): 71–99.

scarcity as one more transformative force in contemporary African practices of self formation.[91] It may be said that the sites and the vectors of this imaginaire of consumption are to a large extent the same as those found elsewhere in the world. But one development in particular deserves special recognition here. This is the phenomenon, in all its manifold aspects, of an economy of desired goods that are known, that may sometimes be seen, that one wants to enjoy, but to which one will never have material access. There is an element of fictiveness to these coveted goods. For in the situation of chronic scarcity, what is decisive in the formation of subjectivities is not the actual consummation of exchange relations on the material level. Where the capture and consumption of desired but inaccessible goods becomes problematic, other regimes of subjectivity come into the making.

Where shortage and scarcity prevail, the appropriation of desired goods may take place through pillage and violent seizure. If not, it can be realized only through shadow interventions in the phantasmatic realm.[92] Fantasies are thus focused on purely imaginary objects. The powers of imagination are stimulated, intensified by the very unavailability of the objects of desire. The practices of plundering, the various forms of mercenary activity, and the differing registers of falsification are based on an economy that mobilizes passions such as greed, envy, jealousy, and the thirst for conquest. Here, the course of life is assimilated to a game of chance, a lottery, in which the existential temporal horizon is colonized by the immediate present and by prosaic short-term calculations. In the popular practices of capturing the flows of global exchange, rituals of extraversion are developed—rituals that consist of miming the major signifiers of global consumerism.

Conclusion

Attempts to define African identity in a neat and tidy way have so far failed. Further attempts are likely to meet the same fate as long as criticisms of African imaginations of the self and the world remain trapped within a conception of identity as geography—in other words, of time as space. From that conflation has resulted a massive indictment of the twin notions of universalism and cosmopolitanism, and in their place a celebration of autochthony—that is, a construction of

91. Cf. Serguei Alex. Oushakine, "The Quantity of Style: Imaginary Consumption in the New Russia," *Theory, Culture, and Society* 7 (2000): 97–121.
92. See Jean Comaroff and John Comaroff, "Occult Economies and the Violence of Abstraction: Notes from the South African Postcolony," *American Ethnologist* 26 (1999): 279–303.

the self understood in terms of both victimhood and mutilation. One of the major implications of such an understanding of time and subjectivity is that African thought has come to conceive politics either along the lines of a recovery of an essential but lost nature—the liberation of an essence—or as a sacrificial process.

To be sure, there is no African identity that could be designated by a single term or that could be named by a single word or subsumed under a single category. African identity does not exist as a substance. It is constituted, in varying forms, through a series of practices, notably *practices of the self*.[93] Neither the forms of this identity nor its idioms are always self-identical. Rather, these forms and idioms are mobile, reversible, and unstable. Given this element of play, they cannot be reduced to a purely biological order based on blood, race, or geography. Nor can they be reduced to custom, to the extent that the latter's meaning is itself constantly shifting.[94]

But by now, the all-too-familiar and clichéd rhetoric of nonsubstantiality, instability, and indetermination is just one more inadequate way to come to grips with African imaginations of the self and the world.[95] It is no longer enough to assert that only an African self endowed with a capacity for narrative synthesis—that is, a capacity to generate as many stories as possible in as many voices as possible—can sustain the discrepancy and interlacing multiplicity of norms and rules characteristic of our epoch.

Perhaps one step out of this quandary would be to reconceptualize the notion of time in its relation to memory and subjectivity.[96] Because the time we live in is fundamentally fractured, the very project of an essentialist or sacrificial recovery of the self is, by definition, doomed. Only the disparate, and often intersect-

93. See T. K. Biaya, "Crushing the Pistachio: Eroticism in Senegal and the Art of Ousmane Ndiaye Dago," *Public Culture* 12 (2000): 707–20, and "Les plaisirs de la ville: Masculinité, féminité et sexualité à Dakar, 1997–2000," *African Studies Review* 44 (2001): 71–85. See also Dominique Malaquais, *Anatomie d'une arnaque: Feymen et feymania au Cameroun,* Les études du CERI, no. 77 (Paris: Centre d'Etudes et de Recherches Internationales, 2001).

94. Cf. Carolyn Hamilton, *Terrific Majesty* (Cambridge: Harvard University Press, 1998).

95. See AbdouMaliq Simone, "The Worldling of African Cities," *African Studies Review* 44 (2001): 15–41; Mamadou Diouf, "The Senegalese Murid Trade Diaspora and the Making of a Vernacular Cosmopolitanism," *Public Culture* 12 (2000): 679–702; and Janet MacGaffey and Rémy Bazenguissa-Ganga, *Congo-Paris: Transnational Traders on the Margins of the Law* (Oxford: James Currey, 2000).

96. Achille Mbembe, *On the Postcolony* (Berkeley: University of California Press, 2001); James Ferguson, *Expectation of Modernity: Myths and Meanings of Urban Life on the Zambian Copperbelt* (Berkeley: University of California Press, 1999).

ing, practices through which Africans *stylize* their conduct and life can account for the thickness of which the African present is made.

Achille Mbembe is a senior researcher at the Institute of Social and Economic Research at the University of the Witwatersrand, Johannesburg. His latest book is *On the Postcolony* (2001).

Responses to "African Modes of Self-Writing" will appear in Public Culture, *fall 2002.*

from the field

Shujen Wang

*"From Taiwan, Nationally Known Paris Bridal Salon:
France, Taipei, Kaohsiung, Beijing, Shanghai, Dalien, Shantou, National Chain"
Xi-Dan, Beijing
June 2000*

Shujen Wang teaches
media and film studies
at Emerson College.
Currently she is writing
a book on global
film distribution and
piracy.

Public Culture 14(1): 275
Copyright © 2002 by Duke University Press
Photograph © 2000 by Shujen Wang

snapshot

Islam in Public Space

Ludwig Ammann

More and more Muslims are coming out in public worldwide as Muslims, making religious difference visible through veiling and other micropractices. "Second-wave" Islamism, a social movement that has turned cultural, in this way challenges a public imagined as secular and attempts to redesign the borders between public and private. The international and interdisciplinary research project Islam and Public Space, directed by Nilüfer Göle (Ecole des Hautes Etudes en Sciences Sociales, Paris) at the Kulturwissenschaftliches Institut in Essen, studies Islamic publics in the making—how Muslim actors create new (counter)publics and transform given publics. At the same time, it seeks to understand the implications of contemporary Islamic practices for theorizing modern public spheres. The reinvention of gendered space suggests that figurations of body and space matter more than Jürgen Habermas's logocentric theory of the bourgeois public sphere indicates. For this reason, the project highlights nondiscursive, embodied practices that through habitualized performance institute publics of their own, reimagining them from below.

Hypervisible Islamist movements certainly are bids for recognition by the public at large. But they are more: highly creative and ever more self-reflexive

Public Culture 14(1): 277–279

instances of societal self-production, crossbreeding Islamogenic tradition and Eurogenic modernity. The result is ambiguity—or rather, modernity with a difference. Islamist collective imaginaries of private and public are a case in point. The importance attributed to visual privacy—the veil used as a symbolic shield in public space—is in a sense revealing of a desire to strike a new balance between public and private, to keep at bay the stranger that Western concepts of public life and address presuppose.

✦ ✦ ✦

Research was begun in spring 2000, with empirical case studies by graduate- and postgraduate-level sociologists focusing on three typologically contrasting regions: secularized Turkey, desecularized Iran, and Europe as pluralist diaspora of Muslim migrants. The case studies were presented—and engaged alongside theoretical and historiographical contributions—in a series of four workshops and conferences: Islam and Public Space (Essen), Public Space and Difference (Istanbul), New Islamic Subjectivities and Practices in Public Space (Essen), and New Islamic Imaginaries and Public Space (Istanbul). As a result, the case studies could be further developed, guided by the online and personal tuition of core-group members, and new topics, such as Islamic coffeehouses, were introduced.

The core group is made up of sociologist Nilüfer Göle, who directs the project, and two historians, Christian Geulen and Ludwig Ammann, specializing in discourse analysis and Islam respectively. Their contributions emphasize the potential of Hannah Arendt's performative concept of public space as a theoretical framework, on the one hand, and the traditional primacy of the private in Islamic urban life, on the other. Scholars ranging from anthropologists to political scientists were invited to collaborate as senior researchers. Two institutions are represented collectively: the school of sociologists established by Alain Touraine at Paris's Ecole des Hautes Etudes en Sciences Sociales, and the public sphere experts affiliated with the U.S.-based Center for Transcultural Studies. The latter group, represented here by Craig Calhoun and Charles Taylor, continue a discourse initiated by Calhoun's edited volume on *Habermas and the Public Sphere* (1992). Project collaboration aims to link this discourse on the *public sphere* with the core group's emphasis on *public space*.

The following topics have been presented so far:

- Case studies from Turkey on Islamic novels' discovery of subjectivity; Islamic coffeehouses' facilitation of religious debate and meetings between the sexes; Islamic foundations' sponsorship and education of students; the Islamic instruction of secular publics by a religious leader; and public discussion of a celebrated "religious" marriage scandal.

- Case studies from Iran on women in the public sphere; and women's periodicals.
- Case studies from France and Germany on young preachers of the Tabligh movement; types of religiosity developed by young males in different national public spheres; and German configurations of Islam, gender, and the public.
- Core-group contributions on ocular and corporal dimensions of the public; private and public in Islamic cities of the past; and the history and theory of the modern public sphere.
- Contributions from senior collaborators on cleansing Islam from the Turkish public sphere; the stranger and embodied difference in public space; public space and the struggle for visibility in Turkey; civil society between solidarity and difference; teaching Islam at German schools; counterpublics; cultures of circulation; and other topics.

From this pool of papers we plan to edit a book, which will contain most of the case studies, the core-group contributions, and selected senior contributions from Hakan Yavuz, Simonetta Tabboni, Michael Warner, and others.

Ludwig Ammann is a project assistant at the Islam and Public Space Project at the Kulturwissenschaftliches Institut in Essen. He is the author of *Die Geburt des Islam: Historische Innovation durch Offenbarung* (2001). A description in German of the Islam and Public Space Project is available on the Web at www.kulturwissenschaftliches-institut.de/projekte/p_islam_1.htm.

See inside front cover for ordering information.

COMMON KNOWLEDGE returns.

Peace process.

A decade ago, *Common Knowledge* challenged the notion of "sides" that one must "take." The journal brought together distinguished intellectuals and public figures—bridging disciplinary, geographical, and ideological rifts—to find common cause in the very issues that had divided them.

Now, after a three-year hiatus and from its new editorial offices in the Middle East, *Common Knowledge* returns with a group of essays that initiate a continuing symposium on dispute, conflict, and enmity titled "Peace and Mind."

Common Knowledge
Volume 8, 2002 (3 issues)
Vol. 8, No. 1 available January '02
Edited by Jeffrey M. Perl
Published by Duke University Press

Contributors from the 2002 volume include

Prince El Hassan bin Talal	Adam Michnik	Jean Bethke Elshtain
Susan Sontag	Caroline Walker Bynum	Adam Zagajewski
Cardinal Edward Cassidy	Fang Lizhi	Anne Carson
Clifford Geertz	Hilary Putnam	Randall Collins
General Mordechai Bar-On	Greil Marcus	Marjorie Perloff
Yves Bonnefoy	Bruno Latour	Marcel Detienne

NYU PRESS

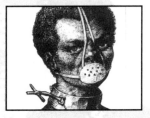

Orientations

CULTURE FROM DUKE

The Making and Unmaking of Whiteness
BIRGIT BRANDER RASMUSSEN, ERIC KLINENBERG,
IRENE J. NEXICA, & MATT WRAY, EDITORS
352 pages, paper $19.95

Georges Woke Up Laughing
Long-Distance Nationalism and the Search for Home
NINA GLICK SCHILLER & GEORGES E. FOURON
352 pages, 30 photos, paper $19.95
American Encounters/Global Interactions

Globalization
ARJUN APPADURAI, EDITOR
362 pages, 33 photos, 1 map, 2 figures, paper $22.95
A Public Culture Book

Religions/Globalizations
Theories and Cases
DWIGHT N. HOPKINS, LOIS ANN LORENTZEN,
EDUARDO MENDIETA, & DAVID BATSTONE, EDITORS
272 pages, 5 photos, paper $18.95

Blue Nippon
Authenticating Jazz in Japan
E. TAYLOR ATKINS
384 pages, 17 b&w photos, paper $21.95

Women on the Verge
Japanese Women, Western Dreams
KAREN KELSKY
312 pages, 23 b&w photos, 9 figures, paper $18.95
Asia-Pacific

Orientations

Mapping Studies
in the Asian Diaspora
**KANDICE CHUH &
KAREN SHIMAKAWA, EDITORS**
352 pages, paper $19.95

An Absent Presence

Japanese Americans in Postwar
American Culture, 1945–1960
CAROLINE CHUNG SIMPSON
248 pages, 4 b&w photos, paper $18.95
New Americanists

An Aesthetic Occupation

The Immediacy of Architecture
and the Palestine Conflict
DANIEL BERTRAND MONK
248 pages, 9 b&w photos, paper $18.95

Disrupting Savagism

Intersecting Chicana/o, Mexican
Immigrant, and Native American
Struggles for Self-Representation
ARTURO J. ALDAMA
208 pages, 1 figure, paper $18.95
Latin America Otherwise

The Exhaustion of Difference

The Politics of Latin
American Cultural Studies
ALBERTO MOREIRAS
368 pages, paper $19.95
Post-Contemporary Interventions

No Apocalypse, No Integration

Modernism and Postmodernism
in Latin America
MARTÍN HOPENHAYN
*Translated by Cynthia Margarita
Tompkins & Elizabeth Rosa Horan*
184 pages, paper $18.95
*Post-Contemporary Interventions,
Latin America in Translation/En Traducción/Em Tradução*

The Art of Transition

Latin American Culture
and Neoliberal Crisis
FRANCINE MASIELLO
352 pages, 10 b&w photos, paper $19.95
Latin America Otherwise

Reclaiming the Political
in Latin American History

Essays from the North
GILBERT M. JOSEPH, EDITOR
400 pages, 4 b&w photos, 1 map, paper $19.95
American Encounters/Global Interactions

Racial Revolutions

Antiracism and Indigenous
Resurgence in Brazil
JONATHAN W. WARREN
392 pages, 46 b&w photos, 1 map,
3 figures, paper $21.95
Latin America Otherwise

Duke University Press

Visit us at www.dukepress.edu
Or call toll-free 1-888-651-0122